CHINA'S ASCENDANCY

Western analysts, China's ranking of economic size in the world economy has suddenly jumped from a backward country to second place, and could soon overtake America. As China is seen as increasingly strong, a new breed of the old 'Yellow Peril' myth—China Threat—has emerged.

Will an economically and militarily strong China pose a threat to the U.S. and the rest of the world? For what reasons did the Western politicians, academics, and mass media spread such allegations? What is China's role in the world and what are its foreign policy objectives? This is what Dr. Sheng-Wei Wang's book is dedicated to discuss.

As far as I know, the term 'China Threat' is not new. It can be dated to as early as 1990, when Murakami Tomohide, an associate professor of Japan's Defense University, published an article, 'China—a Potential Threat,' in the Shokun August 1990 issue, in which the author depicted China as a potential enemy. It was probably the earliest version of the 'China Threat' fallacy, though it drew little attention then. Since 1992, however, along with China's economic booming, the allegation of a 'China Threat' has become prevalent in the U.S. and Japanese mass media. But Dr. Wang's book, I would say, is the first in the English literature to exclusively address this important issue.

Dr. Wang begins with the origin of Chinese history and culture in an attempt to prove that China has always been a country deeply committed to peace, harmony, and loving others as they love themselves, derived from Confucianism that still has a profound influence on today's Chinese political philosophy. Throughout thousands of years, China has never invaded foreign countries or seized their territories. Then the author refutes Japan's and America's 'China Threat' theory. From her brilliant analysis, we can come to the conclusion that the supporters of the 'China Threat' theory appear to be not only ignorant, but may have ulterior motives. First, they feel uneasy over the rise of China's economic power and international standing. By spreading this fallacy, they advocate containing China. Second, they try to sow discord between China and neighboring countries. Third, after the collapse of the Soviet Union, the U.S. needs a new potential enemy. But in the globalization age, as all nations are connected with each other, the 'China Threat' fallacy can only reflect a totally ignorant prejudice and a legacy of the Cold War mentality.

Dr. Wang outlines China's rise over the last decade with piercing perceptivity and objectivity. As she correctly points out, although China has achieved spectacular economic success and become a world power, it is still a developing country, lagging behind Japan and the U.S. in many areas. (By the way, according to a recent World Bank report, China's economy may in fact be 40 percent smaller than current estimates). Dr. Wang asks why Chinese people, who work very hard for low wages, could be seen as a threat by some Americans. With sharp insight and solid facts, the author concludes that Americans should view China's ascendancy as an opportunity rather than a threat.

After reading the whole book, I can feel that Dr. Wang's primary goal is to accentuate the importance of U.S.-China relations in this volatile world. I highly recommend this book to everyone who lives in the U.S. I'm sure that readers will better understand Chinese history and culture, as well as the strategic opportunity and potential for improved U.S.-China relations."

—Dr. Jialin Zhang, Visiting Fellow
Hoover Institution, Stanford University

"Countering the myth that China's rise is a threat to the world *China's Ascendancy* is a penetrating analysis of the logic underpinning China's globalization. Written by a friend of the U.S., Wang's advice is both timely and pertinent to all those involved in conducting relations with China. Wang will also be of interest to historians studying the shift underway in Chinese perceptions of itself, Asia and the role of the West in crafting the modern world."

—Deep K Datta-Ray, Ph.D. Candidate (University of Sussex)
Associate Fellow of the Henry Jackson Institute (Cambridge)
Commentator in Several Asian Newspapers
Foreign Service Institute, New Delhi, India

"*China's Ascendancy* deals with an important issue—whether China's rise as a world power presents a threat or an opportunity to the United States? Sheng-Wei Wang, in a well-organized and readable book, discusses the differing history and culture of China and of the United States and the resulting effects upon the development of their respective economies. She also discusses the 'China Threat Theory' concerning

iv

China's major competitors, Japan and the United States, and why China does not constitute a threat to either country. Sheng-Wei Wang recognizes that differences exist between China and the United States but believes that peaceful solutions, rather than conflict, will benefit not only China and the United States but also countries around the world."

—Judge Bruce H. Segal (Ret.)

"This book decisively refutes the China threat rhetoric from multiple perspectives with new breakthrough insights and a wealth of recent data. It is of tremendous historical significance at a juncture when Americans increasingly view China as an economic and even a military threat. The author provides a sound approach for China's and the U.S.'s policymakers to move beyond today's complex yet solvable problems and to pave the way toward a healthy, shared global economic future. *China's Ascendancy* is definitely a 'must read'! I deeply admire Dr. Wang's courage and strong sense of social responsibility in taking on a project like this!"

—Jie (Jen) Wang, JD, Chief Manager
Wang Yang Int'l Consulting Co., Ltd.

"In her book, *China's Ascendancy: Opportunity or Threat?* Dr. Wang concludes after a comprehensive analysis comparing the history, culture and strengths of the two nations, that China will not be a threat to the U.S. in areas including military, politics and economy. Instead, she offers her proof that a rising China is advantageous to the balanced development of the entire world.

Her background and interdisciplinary training have enabled her to present this in-depth viewpoint with a global characteristic. The book is not only written for the American readers, but also serves as a valuable reference for those who do research in politics, economy and business administration in China."

—Sindy Wang, Training Director
Management Consulting Committee (MCC) of
the Chinese Enterprise Confederation (CEC)

CHINA'S ASCENDANCY

Opportunity or Threat?

SHENG-WEI WANG

China's Ascendancy: Opportunity or Threat?

Copyright © 2007 by Sheng-Wei Wang
All rights reserved.

ISBN 978-0-9785095-3-8

Library of Congress Cataloging-in-Publication Data

Wang, Sheng-Wei.
China's ascendancy: opportunity or threat? / Sheng-Wei Wang.
   p. cm.
Includes bibliographical references.
ISBN-13: 978-0-9785095-3-8 (alk. paper)
   1. United States--Foreign relations--China. 2. China--Foreign relations--United States. 3. China--Foreign relations--21st century. 4. United States--Foreign relations--21st century. 5. China--Foreign public opinion, American. 6. China--Politics and government--2002- 7. China--Economic policy--2000- 8. China--Military policy--21st century. 9. Competition, International. I. Title.
E183.8.C5W36 2007
327.73051--dc22

2007037517

International Publishing House for China's Culture
2421 Pennsylvania Ave, N.W. Washington D.C. 20037-1718
U.S.A.
www.iphcc.org

Printed in the United States of America on acid-free paper
First Printing: October 2007; Second Printing: April 2008
1098765432

Conflict is not an option.
Military might may vanquish,
but not govern.

Table of Contents

Acknowledgements

This book could not have been published without the help of Mr. Hunter Huang who in early 2006 introduced to me Mr. Xiaoming Zhao, the President of the International Publishing House of China's Culture (IPHCC), a publisher of Chinese and English books in Washington D.C., Canada, Beijing, Shanghai and Singapore. Though separated by the boundless Pacific Ocean and different day-night time zones, I communicated from Hong Kong via hundreds of emails about the book with Helen Xu, IPHCC's Vice President, and Yabei Zhang, its Editor in Chief, after having briefly met them in 2006 at the Library of Congress in Washington D.C. during the new book ceremony for my English-translation book, *"One Country, Two Systems" in Taiwan* (authored by Taiwanese writer Hsing Chi). I am immensely impressed with Mary Bonaventure O'Brien (an independent consultant) who has provided the most thorough, thoughtful and stimulating content editing that complemented the writing and arguments of my book. Special thanks also go to the following people who were contracted through IPHCC's publishing service: Copy Editor Pat Adler, Publishing Service Coordinator Anne Louque of Diamond Inspiration, and typesetter and book cover designer Steve Amarillo—for their excellent work. Throughout the hard-working days and years, they have quietly become my spiritual supporters and teammates who contributed much to this work.

My heartfelt thanks also go to Dr. Gianni Hayes' Radio Show for interviewing me on February 27, 2008, and the ten world experts who wrote book reviews to strongly endorse this book. They are: Dr. R.

Mallory Starr, Director, Sequoia Presidential Yacht Group, LLC, President of U.S.-Asian Cultural Academy (UACA); Dr. Jialin Zhang, Visiting Fellow, Hoover Institution, Stanford University; Deep K Datta-Ray, Ph.D. Candidate (University of Sussex), Associate Fellow of the Henry Jackson Institute (Cambridge), Commentator in Several Asian Newspapers, Foreign Service Institute, India; Judge Bruce H. Segal (Ret.); Jie (Jen) Wang, JD, Chief Manager, Wang Yang Int'l Consulting Co., Ltd.; Sindy Wang, Training Director, Management Consulting Committee (MCC) of the Chinese Enterprise Confederation (CEC); Parag Khanna, Senior Research Fellow, New America Foundation, Author, *The Second World: Empires and Influence in the New Global Order*; Jonathan Anderson, Chief Asian Economist, UBS Investment Bank, Author, *The Five Great Myths about China and the World*; Dr. Dwan Tai, President, Award International, Inc.; and Bruce Hawker, Senior Labor Party Strategist, Managing Director, Hawker Britton, Former Chief of Staff of New South Wales Premier Bob Carr, Australia. Many of them I have never met, but they were all willing to take precious time off from their demanding schedules and have generously committed to write reviews. I am particularly indebted to Dr. Starr for many stimulating conversations and emails. He also enthusiastically introduced me to several other experts who reviewed this book.

I am grateful to Dr. Marshall M. Bouton, President of The Chicago Council on Global Affairs, for kindly allowing me to use the Council's valuable survey data in "Global Views 2006: China Topline Report" published on October 11, 2006, prior to the publication of this book. Special thanks also go to Dr. Jialin Zhang for providing me with his excellent essay on China's exchange rate, which I believe is the best introduction to the complex currency issue, and to my husband Michel A. Van Hove for his continuous encouragement and constructive suggestions. Finally, I dedicate this book to my late father Yu-Sheng Wang in recognition of his tireless and selfless devotion to my education.

Sheng-Wei Wang Hong Kong,
on Chinese Lunar New Year Day, February 7, 2008

Preface

Today China is a ubiquitous presence in the news in the United States (U.S.) as well as around the world. It is nearly impossible to miss the "Made in China" labels in stores. Smart shoppers are attracted to the well-made and reasonably-priced products imported from the mainland of China. The range of product offerings is staggering, from cellular telephones, personal computers, radios, and televisions to clothing, furniture, and toys.

Is this a "China threat," as proclaimed recently by some American journalists, scholars, and politicians? Or is such an accusation an overreaction to the astonishing rate of economic growth over the past decades in China in order for the U.S. to hold on tightly to its existing hegemony in the world? If so, then such an overreaction is likely to arouse excessive nervousness within the American government as well as among the general public, thereby inducing a more hostile attitude towards China. Currently, China has no military bases in foreign lands. Viewing China's peaceful development through a "lens of fear" would only agitate the emotions of the American people without creating any real benefit. Also, it would be unfair to the Chinese people who have made valuable contributions to world progress in spite of long suffering and tragic humiliation brought about by foreign invasions dating back to the Opium War (1839–1842).

This book aims to address with objectivity this seemingly confusing China threat theory from various perspectives. As a Chinese American, who has lived in the U.S. for over thirty years, in Taiwan for more than twenty years, in Hong Kong and in Europe for a couple of years, I bring a unique understanding of the complex issues surrounding the dynamic U.S.-China relationship. After completing a scientific education from the National Tsing Hua University in Taiwan, I earned my Ph.D. in Theoretical Chemical Physics from the University of Southern California, and later became a staff scientist at the Lawrence Berkeley National Laboratory. I was also a self-made California real estate developer for fifteen years.

I became a political activist on issues related to China, the U.S. and Taiwan in 2004 after being intrigued by Taiwan's presidential election that year. I have applied my extensive professional training and experience to thoroughly analyze the issues covered in this book. In 2006, I founded the China-U.S. Friendship Exchange, Inc.

My goal is to address the primary issues affecting U.S.-China relations today in sufficient depth to clarify and improve understanding of current conditions and problems. My hope is that after reading this book, Americans will better understand the growth of opportunity and potential for increasingly positive relations with the Chinese people. My objective is to contribute to the ongoing process of transformation and to improve U.S.-China relations in the twenty-first century.

Strictly speaking, in recent U.S. history, there have already been several waves of enthusiasm towards China. The first wave occurred during the 1950s following the establishment of the People's Republic of China (PRC) on October 1, 1949. It was at this time that the Chinese leader Mao Zedong announced the creation of a "people's democratic dictatorship." The second wave occurred during President Richard M. Nixon's first visit to China in February 1972. The reopening of diplomatic relations with China was considered a bold act by Nixon during the period known historically as the Cold War. The third wave started in the 1980s after China opened its economy to the world under the Chinese leader Deng Xiaoping. What we are experiencing now is a fourth wave surfacing worldwide.

Throughout this period of explosive growth and development, Western journalists, scholars, and politicians delineated numerous theories regarding the emergence of China as an economic and political force as well as a potential, dominant world power. Prominent growth theories include the "China opportunity" theory, the "China collapse" theory, the

"China grain threat" theory, the "China threat" theory, the "U.S.-China complex relationship" theory, and finally, the "China responsibility" theory or "China as a responsible stakeholder" theory.

This last designation was described by the U.S. Deputy Secretary of State, Robert Bruce Zoellick, to the National Committee on U.S.-China Relations. In September 2006, he remarked in his speech "Whither China: From Membership to Responsibility?" that the U.S. main expectation is to integrate China into the world community as a "responsible stakeholder." The substance and meaning of diverse theories have shifted from a discussion at the ideological level in the past to a critical examination of political, military, and economic levels that closely connect to the grassroots of American life today.

Because China is a large, populous nation of over 1.3 billion, it is not surprising that the world responds to its major initiatives in key areas such as the economy, the military, and the environment. If China were, as Napoleon once said, a "sleeping lion," it is clearly wide awake now. In fact, in many ways China's impact on the world might be compared to that of the elephant. There is a saying, "When an elephant makes love, the earth moves, and when an elephant moves, the grass shakes." Those who ride the elephant see that its massive size commands respect from other creatures and its length might be equated to the long history and rich experience of the Chinese nation.

While Americans are enjoying the fruits of rapid and successful economic development in China, some blame it for problems including the loss of jobs, or fear it as a potential competitor. But, how many Americans truly understand what is really happening in China, what it has contributed to the world, or what Chinese leaders have in their minds? Moreover, how many Americans fully understand U.S. government foreign policy related to China and whether it is correct and in the best, long-term interests of the nation?

Although China and America appear very different, both are great economic, military, and political powers. It is incumbent upon these two nations to think seriously about how to share global resources peacefully. Moreover, it is extremely important to understand the ascendancy of China objectively, based on facts not fiction, in order to answer a key question honestly: Is China an opportunity or a threat?

China has undergone dramatic changes and is evolving at a rapid pace today. Sixty years ago, the founders of the Chinese Communist Party (CPC) could not have foreseen the recent passage of a property law designed to deepen privatization and establish a market economy. Some notable developments, summarized below, provide a window towards understanding contemporary China:

- About 60 percent of China's exports come from foreign-owned producers

- In the early 1980s, China introduced market reforms. Now, only a third of the economy is directly state-controlled

On August 22, 2005, *Business Week*, a national U.S. magazine reported the following comments from the "Expert Roundtable 2: Should China Be Feared?"

> *China is more of an opportunity than threat. The best assurance of global growth and geopolitical stability is to increase globalization and interdependence.*
> —DONALD STRASZHEIM,
> CHAIRMAN & CEO, STRASZHEIM GLOBAL ADVISORS, U.S.A.

> *No, I do not think anyone should be afraid of China's growth. If one-sixth of the world population gains a better life, it is good for the planet. Gone are the days when growth, hegemony, and unilateralism were synonymous. We will increasingly live in times in which sustainability and connectedness of things will be better understood. Consequently, China will have to play the game, by the rules.*
> —SUBROTO BAGCHI,
> CHIEF OPERATING OFFICER, MINDTREE CONSULTING, U.S.A. AND INDIA

> *China's growth is certainly good for the world. There has been concern in both developed and less-developed countries over "the China price" [usually the lowest price compared with purchases elsewhere] as a threat by taking jobs from their countries. This is like seeing a glass that is half empty instead of half full . . . China's*

growth will not pose a threat because the Chinese culture is about harmony. As a superpower, China is very tolerant and does not impose its values or standards on other countries.

—Viveca Chan,
Group Chairman & CEO, Grey Global Group, Hong Kong

China's rapid rise is good for China and for the rest of the world. However, from a business perspective, China is both a threat and an opportunity. Many companies will not be able to meet "the China price" and will have to restructure or exit the market, while others will benefit from opportunities in the Chinese market and from China outsourcing. The bottom line is that companies should rethink their business model so as to develop and sustain a competitive advantage in a global environment where China is a major player.

—Oded Shenkar,
Professor of Management and Human Resources,
Fisher College of Business, Ohio State University, U.S.A.

As demonstrated by a number of cross-nation opinion polls, most countries, including most industrialized countries, view China more favorably than the U.S. In fact, most fear the U.S., not China . . . The Chinese people also have every right to enjoy greater wealth and consumption just as people in rich countries do . . . The world has to work on solutions to alternative and renewable energy, with possibly a change of [existing] paradigm[s] on our lifestyles and energy consumption patterns.

—Wenran Jiang,
Associate Professor and Associate Chair,
Department of Political Science, University of Alberta, Canada

Most of the comments by these roundtable experts were positive regarding the impact of China's economic development on the global economy.

In the book, *The Clash of Civilizations and the Remaking of the World Order*, Samuel P. Huntington, a political scientist and Harvard professor, fosters the theory of culture clashes. However, he also cites the warning in a book by Lester Pearson, *Democracy in World Politics*, written in the 1950s, that human beings were moving into "an age when different civilizations will have to learn to live side by side in peaceful exchange [coexistence], learning from each other, studying each other's history and ideals and art and culture, mutually enriching each others' lives. The alternative, in this overcrowded little world, is misunderstanding, tension, clash, and catastrophe."

Huntington concurs with Lester Pearson and writes:

> . . . *the avoidance of major inter-civilizational wars requires core states to refrain from intervening in conflicts in other civilizations. This is a truth which some states, particularly the United States, will undoubtedly find difficult to accept . . .*

> *The futures for both peace and civilization depend upon understanding and cooperation among the political, spiritual, and intellectual leaders of the world's major civilizations.*

After a visit to China in 1922, Bertrand Russell, writes the following in his essay, "China and Western Civilization Contrasted:"

> *Contacts between different civilizations have often in the past proved to be landmarks in human progress. Greece learnt from Egypt, Rome from Greece, the Arabs from the Roman empire, medieval Europe from the Arabs, and the Renaissance Europe from the Byzantines.*

His statements, made eighty-five years ago, are strongly endorsed by the 2004 Beijing Forum which found that contact among civilizations is universally regarded as an essential driving force for progress and that clashes have always been temporary, while mutual absorption, cultural, and economic convergence have been perpetual.

Nevertheless, over the centuries many conflicts and wars have erupted throughout the world. This is a phenomenon that merits deep, critical thinking. It is worth noting that during the Cold War, the U.S. and China were initially in opposite political camps. A strategic change in U.S. policy resulted in the legendary visit of President Richard M. Nixon and Secretary of State Henry A. Kissinger to Beijing in 1972. The U.S. thereby strengthened its position in its confrontation with the Soviet Union, especially after the U.S. and China established formal diplomatic relations in 1979. Meanwhile, China also benefited from this improved relationship with the U.S. and initiated a diplomatic and economic open door policy in 1978.

The lifting of the bamboo curtain enabled China's comprehensive participation in economic globalization and benefited the U.S. and the world economy significantly. Jeremy J. Siegel, the Russell E. Palmer Professor of Finance at the University of Pennsylvania, concurred by noting that "China is the only hope of the West" in driving the world economy forward.

The U.S. is striving to understand China, this immense Asian nation and its role in the world. Several issues merit attention in under-standing modern China:

First, China's development appears rapid mainly when compared to its historical low in economic, political and cultural perspectives over the past century. As a nation, China has suffered deeply throughout its modern history. China's ascendancy is not a take-off from an existing healthy and strong foundation nor is it very large in absolute terms (China's population is roughly 20 percent of the world population, but its gross domestic product (GDP) is only about 5 percent of the world total, compared with 30 percent in the prime time of the Qing Dynasty). According to a recent World Bank report, China's economy may in fact be 40 percent smaller than current estimates; it is far behind the U.S. on many levels and does not pose a threat to the U.S. There are still hundreds of millions of Chinese people living below the poverty level, and severe environmental degradation and rampant corruption are eroding the nation's progress. China has to overcome the constant struggle between its forward push and backward drag in order to move ahead. (The current winter snow and cold have devastated over one-half of the mainland, which in fact shows how fragile the country is in overstretching its capac-ity and overworking its people to create the stunning economic miracle).

More examples are: economic data show that in 2004 China's per capita income was only US$1,490 and ranked 105th of 192 world countries; the U.S. per capita income was then US$41,400 (about 28 times larger) and ranked fourth. Although China's per capita income increased to US$2,001 in 2006, the gap between its rich and poor continues to widen. In addition, the World Bank reported that the average Chinese personal asset value was only US$9,387, less than 2 percent of the average U.S. value; the average Chinese workers' wage is only about 3 percent of the American counterpart. When speaking to people in the Chinese mainland, few understand why the Chinese people who work so hard for so little money could be seen as a threat by some Americans. In addition, the U.S. currently ranks as the first most competitive economy in the world and is first in technology and innovation, technological readiness, company spending for research and technology, and quality of its research institutions. China trails the U.S. by more than 30 nations in these important areas. Among the 20 top world universities, 18 are American; the U.S. invests 3.25 percent of its GDP in higher education, compared with 0.5 percent in China; in addition, the U.S. spends 2.59 percent in research and development compared with 1.31 percent in China. China has few patents (U.S. 2.02 per 100,000 population; China 0.50). America remains by far the most attractive destination for students, admitting 30 percent of the total number of foreign students globally.

Second, the assumption that China's emerging role is like that of imperial Germany and Japan, implying that a strategic confrontation is inevitable and the U.S. had better prepare for it, lacks understanding of Chinese and world history and is as dangerous as it is wrong.

Throughout history, China's territory was mainly confined to south of the Great Wall, east of the Himalaya mountain ridges, north of the South China Sea and west of the North Pacific Ocean. China has always had the largest population among world nations, a splendid civilization, and enjoyed owning vast and fertile lands sufficient to feed its people. Except from the late thirteenth to the fourteenth century, when the military-strong Mongol Empire conquered both Asia and Europe and the Chinese Song Dynasty became extinct, the Chinese Han people had always established dynasties within their usual borders and ruled their society with traditional Confucianism, which promotes peace and harmony. Many non-Han nationalities were assimilated gradually in the racial melting pot of the Han society. The geographical peripherals became tributary kingdoms that lived in peace with China. China, in Chinese word and hearts, means the Middle Kingdom or "the center of the world." The Chinese dynasties were content with what they had been blessed. Even when the Western sea-faring nations began world-wide colonial conquests for land and resources, and imperial Germany and Japan mounted their war aggressions, China did not possess the similar urge to expand militarily. Instead, it fell prey to Western powers and Japan.

Were China not a country deeply committed to peace and harmony, there would not have been the Silk Road which spread Chinese civilization to the rest of the world. In the early fifteenth century, China had the world's largest fleet equipped with the most advanced cannon, but it did not attack other countries or seize their territories. The Chinese people have always been content with what they had, and their belief in peace, harmony, and "love of others as love of themselves" derived from Confucianism had a profound influence in the Chinese culture and political philosophy then, as is the case today. Confucianism was able to maintain a governing position in China for more than two thousand years and to cyclically renew its energy and flourish every two to three hundred years. As a basis of governance, Confucianism merits admiration. Those who support the China threat theory are encouraged to consider and understand the Chinese mentality and the true attributes of Chinese civilization.

Third, China is currently engaged in extensive domestic, economic, social, and political reform including the preparation of an adequate national defense to secure its external environment for peaceful development. China has "groped for stones to cross the river" instead of dramatic change through potentially dangerous "shock therapy." It pursued its own course to develop a rapidly growing economy. After nearly three decades of economic globalization, the Chinese nation gradually developed an awareness of its place in the world. Internationally, it has bypassed the stage of "hiding its brightness" as the guideline for its foreign policy as instructed by Deng Xiaoping. Instead, it has adopted a pragmatic approach to handle relations based on the principle of non-interference in the domestic affairs of other nations, and multilateralism for balancing the power of big countries, which is essential for global stability in the 21st century. China has emphasized stability as the foundation of its economic and political reforms and its foreign policy. The goal for the

Chinese is not conflict, but conflict avoidance. This reflects a deeply-held Chinese belief that armed conflict is a sign of failure. The whole package is termed the "Beijing Consensus" by Western scholars and politicians.

The Beijing Consensus has attracted attention and won respect from many underdeveloped and developing countries. It seems that the Chinese policy is seen favorably because China is also a Third World nation that has fought imperialism and stood with the Third World against Western pressure. The success of the Beijing Consensus lies in: 1) a strong willingness to innovate as a path to prosperity for poor countries; 2) a strong belief in sovereignty and multilateralism as a determination to find its own route; and 3) a desire to accumulate the tools of "asymmetric power projection" to balance world powers to be in charge of the Chinese national destiny. The Beijing consensus has led China not only to survival, but also along a path to success.

China is in the midst of a new revolution since 1949 and this time, it is a peaceful one. We are witnessing an unprecedented Chinese migration from rural to urban areas; this revolution is symbolized by the Yangtze River Water Dam project which has changed the course of the river and reshaped the map of China. China's ascendancy is inevitable after it was trampled down for so long in modern history. Any U.S. attempt to hinder economic modernization in China would hurt both countries. Competition is common among world powers and healthy competition between China and the U.S. should be viewed as a stimulus to progress which would benefit both nations and the rest of the world, since the competition does not have to be in terms of win-lose, as in sports.

The world should appreciate the effectiveness of China in limiting its extreme population growth and striving, for the past 59 years, to solve its own problems of unemployment, food, housing, crime, and other civic issues without seeking much help from the world. The world should also be pleased that China has successfully mediated the six-party talks concerning the Korean peninsula nuclear crisis, collaborated with the U.S. on the Iran nuclear issues and taken a positive attitude towards the request by the U.N. to send peacekeeping troops to Darfur. China is now playing a larger role in keeping world peace. Nonetheless, China still has a long way to go before becoming a developed nation. History will document the actions of the Chinese people just as history recorded the greatness of Americans with their technological breakthroughs and visions that have changed the world. Some Americans have worries and doubts about the long-range development and direction of China beyond a certain time frame. This book hopes to prove that such worries are without merit.

It is true that, in a globalized world, the fate of all nations is increasingly interdependent. We are inseparable from each other, breathing the same air, sharing common information, and consuming the same limited resources. Therefore, our choice should point unambiguously to a peaceful coexistence instead of confrontation, especially in a nuclear age. And as long as the globalization trend continues, we must learn to live with each other harmoniously to create a better, mutually beneficial world.

Over 100 years ago, the former U.S. Secretary of State John Milton Hay said that the Mediterranean Sea was the Sea of the Past, the Atlantic Ocean the Sea of the Present, and the Pacific Ocean the Sea of the Future. His propitious prophesy appears to have become reality. His prediction was supported by former Secretary of State Henry A. Kissinger who wrote in the *International Herald Tribune's* June 9, 2005, issue that "The rise of China and Asia will, over the next decades, bring about a substantial reordering of the international system. The center of gravity of world affairs is shifting from the Atlantic to the Pacific."

It is essential that the American public accept peaceful development in China as a historical trend, as suggested by Kissinger and many others. In the meantime, Americans should also take the opportunity to thoroughly understand their own strengths as the most powerful nation in the world, and their own limitations while no light can yet be seen at the end of the tunnel of the Iraq War. Military might may vanquish, but not govern. Once the soldiers and generals leave, unrest will resurface, unless the military action has achieved what the majority of the Iraqi people want. The U.S. government demands compliance with its foreign policy objectives from other nations, but fails to recognize that cooperation bought or coerced will not last. Now, it is essential to reexamine American foreign policies. The U.S. government must prudently set a new direction, so that America and China march forward together with the rest of the world.

I am not alone. Historian Niall Ferguson boldly invented on April 3, 2007, a new word, Chimerica, in his article, "Not two countries, but one: Chimerica," on www.telegraph.co.uk. The phrase has been discussed widely by the public ever since. He pointed out that "East Chimericans (Chinese) are savers; West Chimericans (Americans) are spenders. East Chimericans do manufactures; West Chimericans do services. East Chimericans export; West Chimericans import. East Chimericans pile up reserves; West Chimericans obligingly run deficits, producing the dollar-denominated bonds that the East Chimericans crave. As in all good marriages, the differences between the two halves of Chimerica are complementary." He concluded by saying "Chimerica, despite its name, is no chimera."

In conclusion, shouldn't we view China's ascendancy as an opportunity rather than a threat?

SHENG-WEI WANG HONG KONG, July 15, 2007
Updated February 7, 2008

CHAPTER I

Chinese History and Culture

Recently, I traveled to Okinawa, Japan, where I had an interesting experience watching a local, traditional geisha dance. "The Okinawan people are proud traders not unlike the legendary Venetians," exclaimed the proprietress of the popular restaurant, Tea House of the August Moon, in Naha City. A lovely young woman performed a traditional Japanese dance to a song intended to greet travelers from abroad. This stanza reflects their warm, welcoming sentiments.

Show me your face, and
I'll show you mine;
When we see each other, then
We'll not be enemies.

How true this is. The better we know and understand each other the more likely we are to become friends. The same might be said about the importance of communication, mutual exchange, and cultural understanding among nations in fostering cordial relations. Only through in-depth, open-minded understanding of another nation's history and culture can people from different countries avoid unnecessary prejudices and conflicts.

In his book, *The Clash of Civilizations and the Remaking of World Order*, Samuel P. Huntington identifies problems and warns against the potentially disastrous consequences arising from ignorance and misunderstanding. [1] The lack of communication and profound cross-cultural misunderstanding could be averted through dialogue among different civilizations. In the future, peaceful change and economic evolution that shift the balance of power can be achieved in a manner that prevents the human and social costs of a brutal war. Because so much is at stake, it is essential to conduct a reasoned discussion of the so-called China threat theory popularized in the media and numerous publications.

The first priority is to focus on a basic understanding of Chinese and American histories, cultures, and politics. The goal is to learn from the strengths and weaknesses of both cultures to better meet the unprecedented challenges of the twenty-first century.

Failure to learn and benefit from such knowledge, combined with an acceleration of China threat rhetoric, might lead to an irreversible downward spiral in relations between the U.S. and China. In short, if we do not make a concerted effort to promote strong, constructive, mutually beneficial relationships, we will face an extremely rocky ride that may lead Americans or the Chinese to another unnecessary confrontation or, worse, a counterproductive war. We must leverage economic and financial opportunities, rather than turn potential opportunity into disaster.

This chapter provides a discussion of Chinese history and culture, followed by an overview of key events in U.S. history in Chapter II.

1. China Is the Oldest Country in the World

China, located in Asia, is considered the cradle of the oriental civilization. Chinese culture is one of the most important ancient civilizations existing today. As the oldest country in the world, the early history of China dates back to sixty thousand BC and the earliest Chinese writing system was recorded almost four thousand years ago. Chinese civilization flourished independently along the Yellow River while four other major civilizations started in regions near the Nile, the Ganges, the Tigris, and the Euphrates Rivers.

The Chinese people have shared a common culture longer than any other group on Earth. Chinese feudal systems lasted for over four thousand years beginning with the legendary Xia Dynasty before 1766 BC followed by the Shang Dynasty (1766–1122 BC). Subsequent major dynasties are shown in Exhibit 1. The Chinese feudal system finally ended with the revolution in 1911 which established the Republic of China (ROC) on January 1, 1912.

Much earlier, before the Qin Empire (221–206 BC) unified China, there were unsettled periods known as Chun Qiu and Warring States. After the Qin Dynasty, there were four more partitions: the Three Kingdoms period, the Northern and Southern Dynasties (these two periods lasted from AD 220 to AD 581), the Five Dynasty period (AD 907 to AD 960), and the present separation between the PRC and the ROC that has existed since 1949. Exhibit 1 presents a more detailed chronology. During the unsettled periods, various states and kingdoms fought frequently and fiercely for territories and power, not unlike similar wars among European countries in the nineteenth and twentieth centuries, and earlier.

The long history of China is best described by a well-known Chinese proverb: "The world must separate after a long union, and must reunite after a long separation." While Chinese dynasties were changing hands, Western Imperial Rome rose and collapsed by the fifteenth century following the end of the earlier Greek period of civilization. Such shifts occurred around 44 BC until the fall of the Western Roman Empire to the Germanic invaders recorded as September 4, 476 AD; whereas the Eastern Roman Empire lasted from 395 to 1461 until they were conquered by the Ottoman Empire on May 29, 1453. Then came the era of emerging sea-faring powers in the West, which extended their influence over the next five centuries. China is a unique nation with an essentially continuous 5,000 year history (except for the rule of Mongols and Manchus) and uninterrupted self-government (except for 1895–1911, see later discussions).

Unlike the ancient Roman Empire, Mongol imperial control, European dominance, British paramountcy, and American global supremacy, China's regional and world influence was mainly due to a fervent propagation of Confucianism. In his book, *The Grand Chessboard*, Zbigniew Brzezinski stresses that the long existence of

China was primarily based on a self-contained and self-sustaining economic, cultural, and political system with a shared ethnic identity. [2] He writes further that there was "relatively limited projection of central power over ethnically alien and geographically peripheral tributaries."

Through its long history, China developed a pluralistic culture that blended many great philosophies. Among these are: Confucianism, Taoism, Legalism, Mohism, Buddhism, Islamism, and numerous folk traditions. Nonetheless, the most important Chinese cultural heritage is Confucianism taught by Confucius, and later interpreted and promulgated by his disciples for generations. It is, therefore, worthwhile understanding some of the basic tenets and teachings of Confucius since he was one of the most famous and influential individuals in ancient China. He is considered a wise philosopher and a Great Master. His teachings are not only deeply imprinted on the consciousness of the Chinese people, but also profoundly influence social order and political philosophy.

Confucius was born to a poor family in the year 551 BC in the state of Lu during the Chun Qiu period of the Zhou Dynasty. He became a teacher. He usually traveled with a small group of selected disciples. His philosophy centers around ideas concerned with human behavior and specific rules that one should follow to ensure a successful life, a harmonious society, and an effective government. Confucianism has influenced Chinese society for over two thousand years.

For example, neither the 1919 May Fourth Movement which protested the unfair and unjust Versailles Treaty and sought national dignity, nor the more recent Cultural Revolution of 1966–1976 that ended formally with the arrest of the Gang of Four, could eradicate the deep-rooted Confucian influence in Chinese culture. The former promoted the questioning and re-appraisal of millennia-old Chinese values and the latter tried to erase the impact of Confucianism on the Chinese people.

Today, the tradition that the children of Chinese families practice filial piety at home remains strong. In the PRC, existing law requires that grown children provide support for their parents. Another example is the proclamation of Chinese leader Hu Jintao in the eleventh Five-Year Plan developed to construct a harmonious society that manifests traditional Chinese characteristics. The foundation of the plan is, in essence, the basic Confucian concept that holds that social order is maintained through the practice of courtesy in human relationships.

The nature of Confucianism and how it has shaped Chinese society and government are addressed in this chapter. Following this analysis, it will become clear that Chinese culture and tradition contradict precepts held by the so-called China threat theory.

Chronology of Chinese Dynasties to Present Government

Exhibit 1

Xia Dynasty	before 1766 BC
Shang Dynasty	1766–1122 BC
Zhou Dynasty *Western (Early) Zhou* *Eastern (Later) Zhou*	1122–221 BC 1122–771 BC 771–221 BC
Qin Empire	221–206 BC
The Han Empire *Western (Early) Han* *Eastern (Later) Han*	207 BC–AD 220 202 BC–AD 9 AD 23–220
The Northern and Southern Dynasty Period of Disunity	220–581
Sui Dynasty	581–618
Tang Dynasty *Paper, printing and powder invented*	618–907
The Five Dynasty Period of Disunity	907–960
Song Dynasty *Northern (Early) Song* *Southern (Later) Song*	960–1279 960–1126 1126–1279
Yuan (Mongol) Dynasty	1279–1368
Ming Dynasty	1368–1644
Qing (Machu) Dynasty	1644–1911
The Revolution of 1911	
The Republic of China *The People's Republic of China* *The Republic of China*	1912–1949 1949–present (in the mainland) 1949–present (in Taiwan)

2. **Rule by Rites vs. Rule by Law**

In ancient times when concepts relating to "democracy" or "human rights," were in their infancy, Confucius said: "If you govern your province well and treat your people kindly, your kingdom shall not lose any war," and "If you govern your people selfishly, your kingdom will not only lose a war but your people will break away from your kingdom." [3]

In addition, Confucius said: "Rulers can be great only if they themselves lead exemplary lives and are willing to be guided by moral principles. This way, their states will inevitably become prosperous and happy."

In other words, Confucius demanded a ruler's devotion to the people and recommended striving for perfection of character to serve as a role model for society. Personal example is preferred over the imposition of laws and rules to enforce proper behavior.

Confucius criticized the social disorder and lack of moral standards during the turbulent Chun Qiu and Warring States periods. He argued that "the best government is one that rules through 'rites' and natural public morality, rather than using bribery and force." He explained, "If the people are led by laws, [. . .], they will try to avoid the punishments, but will have no sense of shame. If they are led by virtue, [. . .], they will have the sense of shame, and moreover will become good." This sense of shame is an internalization of duty, where the punishment precedes the evil action, instead of following it in the form of laws as in legalism. [4]

In this sense, his philosophy can be thought of as the teaching of ethics to the rulers and the ruled. And as long as people have a sense of shame, they would not do harmful things to others so that the society sustains order and harmony. The popularity of Confucianism over a long history proves that ancient Chinese society was guided primarily by rule by rites as opposed to rule by law.

Here we can see some of the differences that laid the foundation for the traditional Chinese and modern Western political theories: the former places emphasis on ethics by using moral guidelines and the latter is understood in terms of right and wrong—just and unjust, in the context of written laws. It is true that before the establishment of the modern Western legal system, Christianity also established guidelines for moral and social behavior. Among the Ten Commandments is the widely known "Love thy neighbor as thyself." However, despite the fact that Confucianism and Christianity share the similar values of maintaining high moral standards in personal conduct, there are clear differences. The latter assumes people are sinners to begin with and doing good will offset their sins to earn a place in Heaven after death, whereas the former works without that assumption and uses morality as a tool to keep social order.

This moralistic way of ruling taught by Confucius has not only been followed by many great emperors and feudal bureaucrats in Chinese society but has also served as a role model for many rulers of kingdoms and states throughout Southeast Asia. By the year 372, there was a Confucian University in Korea and by the eighth century, Confucianism spread to Japan and remains a strong influence through modern times.

Confucianism was spread to the U.S. by Chinese immigrants arriving in the mid-nineteenth century. They were drawn to the country by news of the California Gold Rush, jobs, and economic opportunity. They met the need for low paying jobs in mining, manufacturing, and farming and were a major force in the building of the Transcontinental Railroad

In recent years, the Chinese government has established over one hundred Confucius Institutes (similar to British Council and Alliance Française) throughout the world to spread Chinese traditional culture and language. There are thirty million Chinese language students throughout the world. It is projected that this number will increase to 100 million over the next five years. [5]

The Chinese leadership has expanded development plans for the Confucius Institutes. They intend to use Confucius Institutes as a platform for enhancing language and cultural exchanges, and for serving as centers for Chinese enterprise, businesses, and other commercial organizations.

According to many Eastern and Western experts, Confucian philosophy can be considered as a Chinese variant of humanism and "soft power." This was a term coined in the book, *Soft Power: The Means to Success in World Politics*, written by Joseph S. Nye, Jr., former Dean of the Kennedy School of Government at Harvard University. [6] He meant that the best method to achieve certain desired outcomes from other nations is to persuade and attract, not command and coerce. Such ability is characterized as a nation's soft power.

Based on Confucianism, ancient Chinese government developed a set of standards for wielding power and administering the country's day-to-day operations without heavily relying on Western concepts and practices such as legal systems, democracy, and human rights. At a time when China was almost totally isolated from the rest of the world, the Chinese dynasties were prosperous and self-sustaining both economically and politically. This led the Chinese people to think that their country was the center of the world, namely, the Middle Kingdom.

3. The Family, Social, and Religious Values of Confucianism

Confucius taught values, rules and standards for individuals to live by. A successful personal life is viewed as the product of many factors that emphasize, for example, strong family loyalty, loyalty to superiors, ancestral worship, respect of elders by children, and of husbands by wives. The moral values related to this family model are also seen as a basis for an ideal government. [7]

With respect to Confucian thought on deepening and strengthening the root of good order in a family, it is worth mentioning the Master's *The Classic of Filial Piety*. Confucius said: "Now filial piety is the root of [all] virtue, and [the stem] out of which grows [all moral] teaching."

In an orderly description of the acts of filial piety, he writes:

> The service which a filial son does to his parents is as follows: [. . .] when they are ill, he feels the greatest anxiety. In mourning for them [death], he exhibits every demonstration of grief. [. . .] He who [thus] serves his parents, in a high situation will be free from pride, in a low situation will be free from insubordination, and among his equals will not be quarrelsome. In a high situation pride leads to ruin; in a low situation insubordination leads to punishment; among equals quarrelsomeness leads to the wielding of weapons.

8

With respect to exerting resilience, and averting weakness and extremes, his *The Doctrine of the Mean states:*

> The superior man cultivates a friendly atmosphere, without being weak. He stands erect in the middle, without inclining to either side. [8]

In Confucianism, the society was made of a collection of family units and every individual in the family must play a proper role. For example, every man and every woman must get married after growing up and must have children (at least a son to continue the family name) and individuals in the society must practice benevolence, righteousness, etiquette, love others as they love themselves, and do not do to others what you would not have them do to you.

Next, to achieve a harmonious society, Confucius defined rules for social relationships in categories including people-to-people, people-to-family, people-to-government, people-to-surroundings, and finally, people-to-universe (Heaven). In Confucianism, personal freedom is not advocated. Instead, relationships take precedence over individuality, and actually define individuality. Thus, the inter-independent individuals would then make the Cosmos bigger and bigger until it reached the state known as "heaven and man as one."

However, this relationship paradigm has no counterpart in the transcendent God of Western philosophy or the individual God duality that later led to the Western concepts of individualism, human rights and democracy. In mainstream traditional Chinese culture, there was no search for a real God. It is fair to say that China does not have its own religion; the only exception may be Daoism, which was "Made in China." But even if Daoism was created some 140 years after Buddhism emerged in China, it lacks the strict characteristics of a real religion as it promulgates longevity and satisfaction through many practical means and desires in real life.

Chinese people are very tolerant about religions and there has been no serious religious war in China during its long history in contrast to the development of Western civilizations. Although Confucianism is a very pragmatic philosophy that does not address God, many Chinese people worshipped their ancestors at home and revered many local folk gods as role models—some of them were great ancient generals or scholars—to ask for compassion and good fortune. However, this is different from worshipping God or being ruled by church influence as in certain periods of the Western history. An interesting phenomenon is that within Chinese families, you may find some individuals who believe in Jesus Christ while also engaging in ceremonies worshipping their ancestors, which they consider a respect, not a religion.

During modern Chinese history, there was a proliferation of Christianity in China prior to Mao and the Cultural Revolution. Critics say that under communism, such religious practice was prohibited; foreign missionaries were expelled and churches and monasteries were destroyed. However, such brief turbulence represented only a small drop in the sea of Chinese history and took place during a very unstable period of development. There has been some encouraging lifting of restrictions accompanied by China's economic reform. Surprisingly, roughly 400 million people, or 31.4 percent of Chinese sixteen or older, think of themselves as religious today. [9] This suggests that the traditional characteristic of a pragmatic Chinese philosophy and approach to religion remains intact.

The most popular religion in China is Buddhism, imported from India. Many Asian people and most Chinese believe that the combination of the tranquility of Buddhism and the moral teachings of Confucianism help believers cope with a swiftly changing modern society, plagued by a huge wealth gap and increasing social unrest.

Confucius' rules are broad enough to cover every individual in a family as well as all members of society. Through this analysis, we can understand why modern Chinese society with a huge population, but without a Western democratic political system, functions properly, effectively, and maintains sustainable stability under authoritarian rule without serious unrest. An exception to this was the June 4, 1989, Tiananmen Square Incident triggered by angered students and the Chinese public who demanded democracy and actions against corruption. The Chinese government has remained silent about the incident. However, it was apparent that the Chinese government has accelerated its economic "openness" and allowed more personal freedom, while maintaining a fairly tight grip on political power.

Based on real life experiences, the Chinese forefathers also realized the limitation of human abilities relative to the unlimited universe of nature. They advocated the importance of being content with one's lot, and avoidance of challenging the perceived natural order of the universe.

In addition, it is apparent that after generations of gradual and edifying influence of traditional culture, Confucianism is embedded in the blood and psyche of the Chinese people. It would not be an easy task to transform the Chinese political system into a Western-style democracy that stresses individual freedom and rights without applying severe external pressure or drastic internal force.

History has shown that neither internal nor external forces have yet succeeded in establishing a Western-style democracy in the PRC. We shall discuss China's political system in the latter part of this book.

4. The Chinese Peasant Society and the Governing Force

In ancient China, most people were peasants. Due to a lack of transportation, people rarely traveled far from their agrarian communities. Most of them lived in their own villages and worked on nearby farms for their entire lives. Because farming is labor intensive, peasant families raised as many children as possible to work in the fields. They wanted to have big families. It was not uncommon for several generations to live together and divide the labor assigning individual responsibilities. This was similar to early Western family farming practices.

Confucian teaching of respect of elders by children, husbands by wives, and the use of the family as a basis for an ideal government was particularly attractive to the peasants because it helped maintain stability and harmony within families. Hence, Confucianism easily became the rudimentary social norm for Chinese agrarian society. United families supported each other, young and old, with love and care through good and bad times. They formed economically independent and socially self-sustaining units that were interconnected with other similar units to form the larger social structural unit, like a giant fishnet.

The power of governance was given solely to the one imperial family at the very top of this gigantic unit based on blood lineage generation after generation until the last day when the dynasty was forced to end. The Chinese people did not raise many questions then about the fairness of the system or equality and human rights issues. They accepted it as a pragmatic method of structuring and operating society. The emperor acted like the head of a big family and took care of all the responsibilities of ruling and defending the country with help from his obedient entourage and a large number of administrative bureaucrats. Chinese families at the bottom of the social network played an extremely important role in stabilizing the society.

Confucianism unified the Chinese Han people over China's long history using families as the cornerstone for social stability. South of the Great Wall and in the territory where they originated and developed their civilization along the Yellow River, the Han people established dynasties and ruled their society with traditional Confucianism. Many non-Han nationalities were assimilated gradually in the racial melting pot of the Han society. Partition was only temporary and unification was more often the normal condition. The Middle Kingdom was ruled by a centralized authoritarian government comparable to the structure of a Chinese family. The benevolent manner in which Han people were ruled produced a cultural soft power of tolerance. This meant acceptance and tolerance of others and included treating all nationalities equally. The Chinese deeply believed that benevolence and righteousness are the highest forms of governance of a country.

For comparison, two thousand years ago, the Western world was ruled by the Roman Empire, which succeeded the 500-year-old Roman Republic (510 BC–first century BC). From England to Africa and from Syria to Spain, one in every four people on Earth lived and died under Roman law. The Roman Empire was a vast, multicultural melting pot and its influence upon culture, law, technology, arts, language, religion, government, military, and the architecture of Western civilization continues to this day.

The Roman Empire was ruled by an autocratic form of government. The empire was an enormous achievement, but started to decline when its armies grew pampered, spoiled, and weak. The Empire was split eventually in two. The capital of the Western Empire was Rome and the Eastern Empire's capital became Constantinople, founded by

Constantine. Rulers of each part worked to help rebuild Rome, but to no avail. Barbarians, attracted by the wealthy cities and rich farmlands attacked, leaving Rome in ruins. [10] The greatest empire of that time fell.

The end of the Roman Empire is traditionally placed at AD 476. The Greek-speaking Eastern Roman Empire, known today as the Byzantine Empire, preserved Greco-Roman legal and cultural traditions along with Hellenic and orthodox Christian elements. It collapsed at the hands of the Ottoman Empire in 1453.

The Soviet Union was the last large empire in Europe. It collapsed after the Cold War, whereas the enormous British Empire gradually lost most of its colonies following World War II. More recently, the European Union (E.U.) unified currency and established many laws and rules, but it has failed so far to develop a common Constitution.

In other parts of Asia, during China's Tang Dynasty (AD 618–907), Indian Buddhism was destroyed by the Hindu religion in India. But Confucianism was able to maintain a governing position in China for more than two thousand years and cyclically renew its energy and flourish every two to three hundred years. As a basis of governance, Confucianism merits admiration. [11] Those who support China threat theory are encouraged to consider and understand the true attributes of Chinese civilization before hurling baseless accusations.

5. Chinese Indifference to Imperial Power

An old Chinese peasant saying notes: "When the sun rises, I work; when the sun sets, I rest. What does imperial power have to do with me?" Since imperial power was based on blood lineage of only one family, that family must work very hard to rule properly to protect its power. As long as the emperor was healthy and did a decent job, the ordinary Chinese people did not feel much need to express their political opinions.

This was very different from Western thinking after the French Revolution (1789–1799), which sought liberty, equality, fraternity, democracy, and republicanism as extremely important elements in human life. The revolution eventually replaced the absolute monarchy in

France with a more democratic system of government. The only way for ancient Chinese people to get involved in politics was to become scholars and take the imperial civil service exams. If successful they could become political elites working for the emperor as feudal bureaucrats in the complex central government. The government managed much of the bureaucracy including petitions and recommendations to the throne.

The influence of Confucianism on the daily political functioning of the central government was profound. Many great emperors thrived by ruling according to what the Master said, while others failed and were overthrown for their lack of wisdom and failure to lead exemplary lives. Mencius, one of Confucius' disciples, argued that:

"If the king was not acting like a king, he would lose the Mandate of Heaven and be overthrown," [. . .] "Therefore, tyrannicide is justified, because a tyrant is more a thief than a king." [12]

Indeed, several peasant revolutions took place in Chinese history; some succeeded in overthrowing the emperors and establishing new dynasties. Finally, in 1911, the revolution to overthrow the Manchurian emperor resulted in the end of Chinese dynastic history and in establishment of a republic. From this overview we may appreciate that revolution was justified and permitted by Chinese political philosophy and the wielders of power who must work hard for the people and rule properly to safeguard their power. The June fourth Tiananmen Square Incident mentioned earlier can be considered as a failed precursor of revolution.

6. The Splendid Ming Dynasty and the Fall of the Qing Dynasty

During China's long history, two dynasties were established by "foreigners" instead of the Han majority. The first instance occurred when the Mongols invaded and defeated China to establish the Yuan Dynasty (1279–1368). Soon after that defeat, adventurous Westerners such as Marco Polo traveled to China and brought the first reports of its wonders to Europe. Later the peasant revolts against the rule of the Mongols led to the establishment of the Ming Dynasty (1368–1644) and a revival of Chinese culture.

At the beginning of the fifteenth century, when the Eastern Roman Empire power had peaked, China was already an advanced economic power. Without political or commercial exploitation, Chinese merchants peacefully explored all of the Indian Ocean, reaching East Africa. Most remarkable were the voyages of Zheng He, a Chinese admiral, whose largest fleet had more than 700 ships equipped with the most advanced cannons. His fleet was manned by more than 27,800 men. At the orders of the Emperor, he traveled at least seven times across the Indian Ocean and beyond (some even said that he discovered the American continent before Columbus) to bring greetings from the Emperor and goods for trade.

Following 276 years of Ming rule, China fell into the hands of the militarily powerful Qing foreigners, the Manchus. They represented two percent of the Chinese population and adopted Chinese institutions, traditional Confucian virtues, and advocated the "eight-part essay" (i.e. stereotyped essay in literary writing) as the format for imperial civil service exams.

Such a set of examination rules put strict limits on the design of the test content and severely constrained vigorous development of new thought. Also, the Qing Court became complacent after the earlier achievements of its first few competent emperors, increasingly choosing isolation.

The Qing Dynasty ruled from 1644 to 1911. Its GDP was almost equal to the total GDP of the entire European continent at that time, and its economy reached a peak for that time in ancient China. The Qing population also increased tremendously from 100 million in 1644 to 430 million in 1850 during this peaceful period. This was many times greater than the total of all the previous dynasties of China and was almost 200 times the U.S. population in 1850. It was even larger than the U.S. population of about 300 million in 2007.

During the Qing governance from the period of 1770 to 1820s, China had a big balance of trade surplus. China accumulated gold, silver, and credits from the West to pay for its silk, porcelain, and other luxury goods. China had the largest population and GDP in the world at that time. The West, and Britain in particular, were only able to alter this by exporting opium, according to Jonathan Apence, a well known historian and China trade authority. [13]

However, a nation's strength cannot be judged only by its GDP; the more important aspect is the GDP components. For example, the larger Chinese GDP was due to production of tea, porcelain, and textiles; whereas Japan's GDP was only one-quarter of China's at the time, its components being cannons, guns, and boats. In addition, the lack of modern agricultural technologies put huge pressure on the limited cultivatable acreage and gradually weakened the Qing Dynasty. Domestically, the late Qing period suffered from massive economic stagnation accompanied by social instability. Externally, it faced Western penetration and attacks. Finally in 1839 the Sino-Britain Opium War broke out. The Western "gun and boat" GDP defeated the "tea and textile" GDP and China lost the war. [14]

China's defeat marked both the onset of an economic decline and the initial success of Western initiatives that included economic globalization, expansionism, and colonialism in China. In the Second Opium War (1856–1860), the United Kingdom and France fought jointly against and defeated the Qing Dynasty of China. With more wars to come, China was subsequently forced to sign a series of unfair treaties such as the Treaty of Nanjing and the Treaty of Beijing, which were the basis of an unequal treaty system that strangled the development of China for the next 100 years. This treaty system caused China to gradually sink from an independent and self-sustaining feudal society into a semi-colonial/semi-feudal society. China signed many more unequal treaties afterwards, ceding land and paying reparations.

In 1894, Japan defeated China in a brief and humiliating war, the first China-Japan War. China was forced to sign the Treaty of Shimonoseki in 1895 and ceded Taiwan to Japan. After this Treaty, the Western powers started a mad dash to partition China and China was like a deer falling prey to a lion. In 1900, the United Armies of eight nations, composed of American, Austro-Hungarian, British, French, German, Italian, Japanese, and Russian forces, jointly invaded China. This was the only time in world history that a single nation had to fight against all the powerful nations on Earth at the same time. A bitter defeat forced China to sign the humiliating 1901 Treaty and forfeit its sovereignty. The 1895 and 1901 treaties completed China's transformation into a semi-colonial society under foreign powers. [15]

Although the revolution led by Dr. Sun Yat-sen, China's "Father of Revolution," overthrew the Qing Dynasty in 1911 and established the ROC in 1912, the Japanese invaded China again from 1931 to 1945, and the situation could not have been worse. Thirty-five million Chinese lost their lives or were injured, and China incurred US$500 billion in damages and US$100 billion in property loss in the bitter war against the Japanese invasion. Many Chinese have difficulty erasing memories of the brutality of the invasions, rapes, and massacres throughout this traumatic period. [16]

In contrast, America emerged as a world power in the early twentieth century after years of peaceful development despite the very hard lives of early settlers and pioneers and the bitter Civil War which ended in 1865. Americans enjoyed lives of abundance bestowed by the nation's industrial development. Even though subsequently America also suffered the depression, the dustbowl and widespread crop failures along with the stock market crash of 1929, and record rates of unemployment and poverty, these were hardly comparable to the prolonged wars, brutality, and humiliations suffered by the Chinese that nearly destroyed their national pride and confidence. It was so tragic that some poverty-stricken Chinese parents were forced to sell their children in order to survive. As stated, thirty-five million or more Chinese lost their lives or were injured in the War against the Japanese invasion alone, compared with a total of 62 million who died during World War II.

Beginning with its defeat in the Sino-Britain Opium War in 1839, China lost every war against the foreign aggressors and was forced to sign unfair treaties to open ports, cede Hong Kong to Great Britain and Taiwan to Japan, make concessions, and pay reparations.

All Chinese genius seemed to perish with these conflicts. Yet, the Chinese governments (both the PRC and the ROC) did not demand reparation from the defeated Japanese government. No other victors of World War II responded as China did.

It is possible to attribute this lack of vengeance and lenient response to foreign aggressors to the deep influence of Confucian humanism that includes "benevolence" within traditional Chinese culture. Nevertheless, when Chinese people read the history of this dark period, some still smell blood and weep. To most, it is emotionally confusing to perceive a shift in China's international image from war victim to a sudden "threat" to the world community.

7. The Emergence of the People's Republic of China

Throughout Chinese history, whenever imperial rule was weak, civil unrest followed. Dr. Sun Yat-sen based his idea of revolution, in contrast to the Qing Court, on three principles: nationalism, democracy, and equalization. Among these, democracy was important to the new government but was also a foreign concept to the Chinese. After being ruled under an imperial system for so long, the Chinese people were facing the challenge of governing their country with entirely new concepts. It was not surprising that Dr. Sun Yat-sen was unable to form a strong new government to carry out his mission, and that the ROC was weakened by many powerful local warlords.

Dissatisfied with the country's plight, the New Culture Movement began in 1915 and was followed by the May Fourth Movement which started on May 4, 1919. The May Fourth movement was a nation-wide protest against the perceived unfair and disrespectful Versailles treaty that hurt Chinese national interests and dignity. Both movements, initiated by intellectuals and students, promoted a reappraisal of traditional Chinese values and advocated reforms. The adoption of more radical lines of thought later planted the seeds for the irreconcilable conflict between the CPC and the Kuomintang (KMT or Nationalist Party).

Dr. Sun's national goals were unmet at the time of his death in 1925, leaving a power vacuum in China that fueled the era of the "warlords." Finally, Chiang Kai-shek seized control of the KMT and completed the Northern Expedition by defeating the warlords using military force. China, for the first time in history, had two political parties. They were constantly struggling for power and ideological leadership. Finally, in 1927, Chiang started his relentless military pursuit of the CPC armies. The CPC, left with only a few thousand members, retreated to the desolate northwest of China and established a guerrilla base under the leadership of Mao Zedong.

The Civil War between the CPC and the KMT lasted until 1949, four years after the Japanese defeat. By then the CPC occupied most of the mainland of China and established the PRC, whereas Chiang Kai-shek fled with the KMT members taking remnants of his government and military forces to Taiwan. For more than fifty-eight years, the two parties ruled the mainland of China and Taiwan independently of each other. Currently, 169 countries in the world recognize the PRC (the mainland of China), whereas only twenty-four pocket-sized nations recognize the ROC (Taiwan). The U.S. is the strongest ally of the ROC.

8. Three Cultural Movements Condemned Confucianism

The decline of Qing rule and institutional decay was caused in part by government corruption, inefficiency, and isolation combined with the Court's complacency towards widespread famine, opium addiction, and a general sense of hopelessness. Harsh exploitation of peasants by landlords and exorbitant levies and taxes by the ruling government exacerbated these problems. The society was in chaos and Confucius' teachings on ethics had nearly disappeared. Confrontation of these internal problems as well as the threat of Western dominance led scholars to blame Confucianism and traditionalism as their source. Consequently, an intellectual revolution and sociopolitical reform movements began.

Lu Xun (1881–1936), was a leading proponent of change. As a writer, essayist, critic, and literary theorist, he is considered one of the most important figures in twentieth century Chinese literature that exerted a great influence during this critical time. He was a contemporary of PRC founder Mao Zedong (1893–1976). Lu Xun criticized the dark side of Chinese traditional culture and condemned what he viewed as the oppressive nature of Confucianism. He described it as a "man-eating" society.

His novel, *True Story of Ah Q*, highlighted what he believed was a twisted Chinese habit of naming defeat a "spiritual victory," and by revealing Ah Q's weakness, he showed how the Chinese were unprepared to deal with the impact of Western culture and technology. Lu Xun's worry was well-justified in view of the momentous changes in Europe, the U.S., and Japan at the time.

The Western Industrial Revolution began in the mid-1700s (approximately one hundred years after Qing ruled China) in Britain and later swept across Western Europe and much of North America. It consisted of a series of breathtaking technological breakthroughs such as Watts' radical improvement of the Newcomen steam engine which replaced manpower with mechanical power. There were transformative changes in agricultural methods that included crop rotation and improvements combining and forging metals and in the production of textiles from new imported raw materials such as silk from China.

The Industrial Revolution altered daily life, lifted the standard of living, and spurred colonialism, to which China became prey. In 1776, the U.S. declared its Independence from Britain. Between 1789 and 1799, the French Revolution replaced the absolute monarchy. And in 1848, the European Revolution took place, which involved both political reform as well as sociotechnological change to promote liberalism, nationalism, and socialism. Revolution erupted in Sicily, Italy and was triggered by the revolutions in France, which spread to the rest of Europe and as far abroad as Brazil. The few nations that escaped the tumult were the United Kingdom, Russia, and Ottoman Empire.

In 1861, the Soviet Union began its reform and in 1868, Japan initiated the Meiji Restoration. By 1871, Germany achieved unification. Unlike China, Japan made a very quick and decisive change to emulate Western technological advances, followed by political reforms, and became a powerful industrialized nation at the turn of the twentieth century.

By the mid-1920s, a few years after Lu Xun wrote *The True Story of Ah Q*, Werner Heisenberg and Erwin Schrödinger, working essentially independently, created a full formulation of quantum mechanics that established the foundation for modern science and technology. But the Middle Kingdom seemed intoxicated by past glory and was slow to react, like a sleeping lion unaware of the dangers approaching.

There were three major cultural movements in recent Chinese history. All were aimed at eradicating the deep-rooted Confucian influence upon Chinese culture. Earlier we described the New Culture

Movement that began in 1915 and the May Fourth Movement which occurred in 1919. These two movements were peaceful and were initiated by Chinese intellectuals and students calling for liberal democracy, national independence, social equality, and the rebuilding of society and culture. The third movement was the Cultural Revolution which lasted from 1966 to 1976. It took place amid a fierce political struggle that was initially confined within the CPC in the mainland of China.

9. The Cultural Revolution

The third cultural movement, also known as the Great Proletarian Cultural Revolution or Cultural Revolution, merits special attention. It took place in the midst of a CPC intra-party power struggle between the leftists (communists and revolutionists, represented by Mao Zedong and Lin Biao) and the rightists (capitalists and reformists, represented by Liu Shaoqi and Deng Xiaoping). It was launched by the CPC Chairman Mao Zedong in October 1966 to secure Maoism in China as the state's dominant ideology and eliminate political opposition. Later the leftist Maoists turned to middle-school students, known as the Red Guards, to rekindle Chinese revolutionary enthusiasm and destroy outdated, counterrevolutionary symbols and values, including Confucianism. [17]

Mao Zedong was born to a peasant family and was fond of reading Chinese history and political philosophy. He was a devoted Chinese Marxist theorist, revolutionist, and statesman who emerged during China's communist revolution. Mao knew well that the majority of the Chinese were peasants and that their livelihood depended on farming. Generation after generation, Chinese peasants developed a deep passion for their land and were willing to fight to protect their livelihood. Mao lived at a time when many Chinese peasants were severely exploited by landlords. He believed deeply in Karl Marx's theory of class struggle and communism to redistribute and equalize wealth for the working class. His empathy and understanding of peasant exploitation and their needs enabled him to launch a successful revolution that gained their support. Mao's "Peasant Revolution," though lacking supplies, materials, and equipment successfully liberated the Chinese mainland. The success of the Peasant Revolution with its promise that peasants could farm on their own land was key to the defeat of the Nationalists led by Chiang Kai-shek who were equipped with far superior American military weapons and supplies. Mao greatly admired the writings of Lu Xun and thought similarly that China's weakness due to corruption, obstinacy, and backwardness, was derived from Confucianism. He therefore condemned Confucianism.

During the Cultural Revolution, the government supported purging intellectuals and imperialists. Millions of Red Guards were encouraged to criticize and shout slogans like "Destroy the Confucius Shops." They also fought and attacked the "four olds," namely: old ideas, old culture, old customs, and old habits. They wanted to replace them with the "four news:" new ideas, new culture, new customs, and new traditions. All connections to the West or upper class culture were vigorously condemned and eradicated. This was the most significant and severe cultural cleansing in recent Chinese history. It lasted for ten years until Mao's death and the arrest of the leftist Gang of Four. Many schools and factories were shut down and massive civil disorder resulted from social clashes among rival Red Guard gangs and between the gangs and local security authorities.

The Red Guards engaged in numerous acts of violence. Almost all Chinese suffered during the Cultural Revolution. Persecution of high-placed leaders and intellectuals was especially harsh. During the Cultural Revolution, much economic activity was halted. The Chinese educational system reached a virtual standstill. Nearly an entire generation forfeited adequate education. Today, the Cultural Revolution is seen by most people in and out of China as an unmitigated disaster to be avoided in the future. [18]

From the previous analysis it is possible to conclude that many of the cultural movements designed to eliminate the influence of Confucianism in Chinese society failed. Confucianism is deeply ingrained in the consciousness of the Chinese people whereas Western culture, philosophy, political thought, science, technology, and other intellectual imports are integrated into Chinese culture with a unique Confucian approach, influence, and Chinese characteristics.

10. Did Confucianism Hinder Chinese Innovations?

When the Qing Dynasty was weak and China was invaded, many Chinese intellectuals searched for the causes of weakness and failure to resist Western imperialism. Was it true that Chinese traditional culture and the bureaucratic government built on Confucian principles had hindered development of science and technology as claimed by the culture movements discussed previously? Was it also true that Confucianism should be singled out for the late Qing's backwardness and technological gaps as proffered by Lu Xun and others?

The answer is certainly "No."

In the book, *The Genius of China*, Robert Temple states that Isaac Newton's First Law of Motion in the eighteenth century had been discovered in China in the third or fourth century BC. [19] In the Mo Ching, this law was stated as: "The cessation of motion is due to the opposing force . . . If there is no opposing force . . . the motion will never stop . . ."

In Temple's chapter, "The West's Debt to China," he writes:

> One of the greatest untold secrets of history is that the "modern world" in which we live is a unique synthesis of Chinese and Western ingredients. Possibly more than half of the basic inventions and discoveries upon which the "modern world" rests come from China. And yet few people know this.

Temple cites respected China expert Joseph Needham who states that modern research shows that the bureaucratic organization of China, in its earlier stages, strongly championed advances in science; only later was progress forcibly inhibited, thereby preventing major breakthroughs which occurred in Europe.

His observation is in agreement with the views in this book and can be elaborated as follows:

China had been a leading civilization in innovation and emerging technology development in the tenth to the thirteenth century. Innovations included the production of paper, silk, gun powder, and development of the compass, navigation systems, book-printing, and porcelain. [20] By contrast, in the late Ming Dynasty, scholars seemed to excessively exalt and promote only guidelines and a framework for governing society. As a result, scientific activities and innovation were discouraged during the last 100 years of the Ming Dynasty. This was one of the causes that gradually weakened Ming dynasty strength and finally led to its conquest by the militarily powerful Manchurians in 1644. They started the repression of Chinese intellectuals. Chinese innovation appeared to stop entirely during the Qing (Manchu) Dynasty which followed.

The Manchu emperors killed an estimated 50 percent of the Han people. Western priests were prohibited from having any contact with the Han people. [21] In addition, the Manchu emperors resorted to what might be characterized as a literary inquisition, persecuting and imprisoning writers and intellectuals who were out of favor. In this way, the Manchu leadership sought to control the minds and the thoughts of the Chinese people.

Entry into the Civil Service required passing a new eight-part essay. As discussed, its strict format was of limited scope and severely constrained vigorous testing of skills. It discouraged development of rigorous analysis and new ideas. In spite of earlier achievements, the Qing Court became complacent and increasingly chose isolation. The Court adhered to policies which forcibly inhibited innovation, modernization, and further development of inventions. Complicating this period of repression and stagnation was the extensive use of opium resulting in widespread addiction.

This epoch differed vastly from that of the Yuan Dynasty (1279–1368), when China was first ruled by foreigners, the Mongols. Despite attempts to rule in a Chinese manner, the Mongols were culturally very different from the Chinese. The government of the Yuan Dynasty had virtually no Chinese. Nonetheless, the Mongol rulers allowed the Chinese intellectual freedom to do whatever they wanted. Thus, Chinese innovation and new inventions flourished during the thirteenth and fourteenth centuries. The militarily strong Mongol Empire conquered both Asia and Europe. Following a relatively brief ninety-year rule, Han uprisings ended the Yuan Dynasty's Mongol rule. This was attributed to overextension in the acquisition of territories and a lack of governing skills.

In summary, the cultural movements that called for condemnation of Confucianism appear to sow seeds for drawing on the strengths of Western culture and practices to offset weaknesses in traditional Chinese culture. Advocates of this approach want China to modernize in order to catch up with Western technological advances. However, this book concurs with Joseph Needham and does not believe that it was Confucianism that hindered modern scientific developments in China. Judging from China's recent rapid economic development and modernization as well as pervasive high-tech developments in Japan, South Korea, Taiwan, and Singapore where Confucianism prevails, it is evident that its precepts do not negatively impact a nation's ability to innovate.

11. Conclusions

Chinese history is replete with periods of growth, invention, and decline. Traditional Chinese culture has always centered on Confucianism. Chinese civilization is not a religious culture, it is not aggressive by nature and it advocates tolerance and benevolence.

The latest three cultural movements that aimed at eradicating the deep influence of Confucianism in Chinese society shook the culture in different ways, but none shattered its influence completely. However, these initiatives laid the groundwork for drawing on the strengths of Western civilization needed to offset some weaknesses in traditional Chinese culture.

Confucius, the Great Master, taught ethics, and advised that society must practice benevolence, righteousness and etiquette, which are particularly needed in our bewildered world where crime, disrespect, corruption, and disorder are prevalent. Although some of his teachings require adaptation to modern society and conditions, the basic spirit and principles remain truly valuable. Recently, I learned that in addition to expanding Confucianism through cultural exchanges and trade at one hundred Confucius Institutes worldwide, the Chinese government is also restoring civil education in Chinese schools. The goal is to teach students morality and social values.

It is evident that traditional Chinese culture is peaceful and China is on the right track in its quest to restore a valuable cultural asset which advocates morality, responsibility, and harmony. Confucianism contains no elements that encroach, invade, harass, threaten, or infringe upon the American way of life or culture. As a strong, rising power, China is very tolerant and does not want to impose its values or standards on other countries. Cultural clashes will not occur with others if people remain open-minded and engage in frequent dialogue on culture and civilization.

CHAPTER II

American History and Culture

Compared with China, the United States of America is a very young country. The Declaration of Independence was signed on July 4th, 1776, the Constitution was adopted in 1787, and the inauguration of its first President George Washington took place in 1789. Currently, George W. Bush is the forty-third President of the U.S. and is in the third year of his second term. America celebrated its 231st birthday on July 4, 2007.

The U.S. has a democratic, representative political system and is militarily the strongest and economically the wealthiest nation in the world today. If some factions in the U.S. perceive China as a threat, it is helpful to review aspects of American history that might illuminate aspects of the culture and other factors that might lead to such thinking.

1. The Making of the United States of America

It is well known that Christopher Columbus reached America from Europe in 1492. Native Americans in search of game crossed the Bering land bridge from Northeast Asia to Alaska much earlier. Reliable dating of this crossing is identified as occurring around 12,000 BC, according to U.S. government sources. [1]

By the early seventeenth century, America was dominated by European settlers, explorers, and adventurers seeking fame, fortune, and freedom. This was shortly before the Western Industrial Revolution in Europe and the corresponding late Ming Dynasty era of China. There were ongoing battles for territory among colonials from Great Britain, Spain, France, and the Native Americans. Other early settlers arrived from Holland, Germany, Ireland, Scotland, and Sweden. There is reliable evidence, however, that the earliest European explorers were Norse traveling west from Greenland around 985.

The thirteen original states in North America were separately chartered and governed. The Declaration of Independence asserted the independence of the colonies from Great Britain, and formally broke with the Kingdom of Great Britain. Independence was won from Great Britain following the American Revolutionary War (1775–1783) which established the United States of America. The U.S. now has fifty states. Of these, forty-eight states are contiguous including Alaska in the northwest North America. Hawaii, composed of eighteen islands in the Pacific Ocean, became the fiftieth state in 1959.

The American nation was built on colonized parcels seized from the Native American Indians, purchased from other colonial powers, and gained in various wars. Apart from the earlier settlers, the American population grew from an unprecedented wave of immigration: 37 million people arrived between 1820 and 1920 from Europe primarily and an additional 29 million came between 1920 and 2000 from Latin America and Asia. The earlier immigrants brought the European culture, skills, and experience needed for industrial growth to their new homeland. They ushered in the Second Industrial Revolution in America—the first took place in Great Britain in the eighteenth century.

Eighty-five years after the U.S. Declaration of Independence, the Civil War occurred from 1861 to 1865. This was a very serious internal conflict between the North and South of the country and, in fact, among the bloodiest wars the U.S. had ever entered. There were 524,509 total known deaths in the Civil War: 359,528 Union and 164,981 Confederate. [2]

Twice as many soldiers died of disease as were killed in action, but nothing, in the minds of the soldiers, matched the experience of a full-blown battle, for sheer terror as this one. [3] U.S. Army Colonel Ernest Dupuy describes the military tactics of the day as mobile warfare and "the spirit of the offensive; a blitzkrieg geared, of course, to the horse-and-buggy age . . ." He also writes that the Civil War "became the prototype of a blitzkrieg and total war of a later day; why its operations became required study for military men throughout Europe." [4]

The war was caused by a myriad of conflicting pressures, principles, and prejudices, fueled by sectional differences and pride. At the root of all the problems was the institution of slavery, which had been introduced into North America in early colonial times. The agricultural Southern states wanted to preserve slavery and extend it into the new territories whereas the industrialized Northerners, largely not dependent upon slavery for their economic survival were opposed to the extension of slavery into the new territories. The North wanted to eradicate slavery eventually everywhere. As the war broke out, the sixteenth U.S. President Abraham Lincoln led the Northern states to fight against the Southern states, united as a "Confederacy," in order to free the African American slaves in the Southern states.

At the end, the Northern states won and slavery was abolished. America gradually reconstructed itself to become a leading industrial power in the world by the late nineteenth century.

2. The American Ethnicity: A Nation of Immigrants

It is not an overstatement that America is a nation built by immigrants and continues to evolve in this way today. In 2000, white Caucasians comprised the majority 69 percent of the total population, according to the U.S. Census Bureau. African Americans, Latinos, American Indians, Alaskan Natives, and Asians make up nearly 31 percent of the population. Of these, approximately 12 percent are Hispanic, 12 percent Black, 4 percent Asian and Pacific Islanders. An estimated 3 percent are derived from other ethnic and racial groups. In this census, U.S. federal laws defined Hispanic to indicate any person with ancestry from a Latin American country or Spain. In 2005, the Census Bureau delineated the U.S. population using different categories: 1) White American 74.7 percent (here the definition of White includes European Americans, Middle Eastern Americans, i.e., Arab Americans, Central Asian Americans, and Hispanic Americans who reported as White in the 2000 Census); 2) Black or African American 12.1 percent; 3) Asian American 4.3 percent; 4) American Indian 0.8 percent; Native Hawaiian or other Pacific Islander 0.1 percent; other races 6 percent, and two or more races 1.9 percent. Each of these five categories included people who identified themselves as Hispanic. Based on the 2005 Census, there were 14.5 percent of Hispanics of any race in the above categories and it is not clear what the percentage of the Hispanic population in 2005 was in the first category as compared with the 69 percent in 2000.

However, the U.S. census in 2000 projected that the non-Caucasian population would increase to 47.2 percent of the total population by the end of 2050. The Hispanics already constituted 13.7 percent of the nation's total population on July 1, 2003 (39.9 million, which did not include the 3.9 million Hispanic residents of Puerto Rico), and 14.5 percent in 2005. The projected Hispanic population by July 1, 2050, is 24 percent of the total national population or 102.6 million. This would be an increase of 188 percent, a near tripling from 2004. It is now the nation's largest race or ethnic minority. [5]

In 2005, the Pew Hispanic Center published a research report stating that America has 12 million illegal immigrants. Of these, 46 percent are Mexicans. [6] The issue of controlling illegal immigration is considered a serious problem by many Americans. [7] Illegal immigrants often work in low-paying jobs that many Americans are unwilling to take since the income is inadequate and few if any benefits such as health care are provided by the employers. It is worth noting that there were over 46 million uninsured Americans lacking health care in 2005; many are working class in small businesses that cannot afford coverage. It appears that many legitimate citizens face difficult socioeconomic problems similar to those of illegal immigrants. Illegal immigration has caused a myriad of social and economic problems such as overburdening of community emergency room services, hospitals and health care clinics as well as public schools and welfare systems. Issues related to resolution of illegal immigration from Central and Latin America, in particular, are a high priority for U.S. political leaders.

Recently, a wave of protests erupted against the U.S. anti-immigration Bill, HR4437, in many states including California, Texas, and Nevada, where there is a high concentration of illegal immigrants. High school students walked out of their classrooms and took to the street to demand fair treatment and legal status. For over twenty years, the U.S. government failed to provide immigration asylum to illegal immigrants. These protests and demonstrations can easily develop into a new civil rights movement. [8] Illegal immigrants have lived in the U.S. for over two hundred years and the fences built along the U.S.-Mexico border do not seem to fend off the influx of these willing workers seeking the American dream in spite of the risk of being captured, injured, or killed. [9] The conflict between the legal Americans and the illegal immigrants has historic roots dependent on U.S. economic conditions. Americans seem to have mixed emotions towards illegal immigrants. But as long as the U.S. needs additional manpower, legal and illegal immigrants will continue to arrive seeking economic prosperity and freedom.

Some experts estimate that it is only a matter of time before the Hispanics, as a group, achieve dominant representation in the American population and the U.S. will become a primarily Hispanic nation. [10] Many people are beginning to wonder how the American culture will evolve as it becomes more Hispanic in the future.

The African American struggle for equality continued for nearly a century following the Civil War up to the American Civil Rights movement in the 50's and 60's. A breakthrough came on May 17, 1954, when Chief Justice Earl Warren read the landmark decision of a unanimous Supreme Court on school desegregation:

> We come then to the question presented: Does segregation of children in public schools solely on the basis of race, even though the physical facilities and other 'tangible' factors may be equal, deprive the children of the minority group of equal educational opportunities? We believe that it does . . . We conclude that in the field of public education the doctrine of

'separate but equal' has no place. Separate educational facilities are inherently unequal. Therefore, we hold that the plaintiffs and others similarly situated for whom the actions have been brought are, by reason of the segregation complained of, deprived of the equal protection of the laws guaranteed by the Fourteenth Amendment.

The turmoil of the Civil Rights struggle left deep marks on America and laid the groundwork for expansion and protection of basic human rights for women and all ethnic and racial minorities. More than forty years later, civil rights leader Dr. Martin Luther King's words "I have a dream!" continue to resonate in the hearts of Americans. While much progress has been made, true equality for all races and elimination of social ills including poverty and unemployment remain challenging.

Chinese Americans are now the third largest ethnic group in the U.S. following the African American minority. There were 1.8 million Chinese Americans in the U.S. as of July 2004, and 3.3 million as of July 2007. [11] Early Chinese immigrants endured a long and difficult struggle working as coolies building railways. More recent twentieth century Chinese immigrants, however, made tremendous progress towards improving their social status and professional achievement by adhering to Chinese cultural tradition emphasizing education and persistent hard work.

Although still small in number, Chinese Americans represent about 1 percent of the total U.S. population and have made admirable progress. A few prominent Chinese Americans include Jerry Yang, co-founder of Yahoo, C.N. Yang, T.D. Lee, Samuel C.C. Ting, and Steve Chu—four Nobel Laureates in Physics, Yuan-Tseh Lee, a Nobel Laureate in Chemistry, and Michelle Kwan, the World Figure Skating Champion.

Other notable Chinese Americans include Michael Chang, a World Champion at the French Open Tennis Competition in 1989, Yao Ming, center for the Houston Rockets, and Elaine Chao, U.S. Labor Secretary from 2000 to the present. They are either first or second generation immigrants. These Chinese Americans have made great contributions to America and to the world. They serve as role models for other immigrants who seek the American dream.

The mainland of China is a far more homogeneous society united through thousands of years of history, assimilation of outside conquerors, and the powerful influence of Confucian culture. Other than the majority of Han people, there are fifty-five other officially recognized minority nationalities. The Tibetans and Uigur are still in the process of being assimilated despite the fact that some Tibetans have resisted assimilation and the Dali Lama is in exile. But the Dali Lama's recent political stance is described as leaning towards establishing Tibet as an autonomous region of China.

The American racial situation is very different from that of the Chinese because of the continuous influx of immigrants from around the world. Assimilation in the U.S. is a continuous process and the center of gravity of its population is shifting.

Such an interesting contrast prompts us to ask: How will American culture change as time goes on? What will the American national identity be? And what will Americans share in common? Will racial divisions continue to foster a culture and dominance that existed in the past? Some think that this last question is irrelevant and outdated. They argue that, in relative terms, improvements in race relations are recent, but the country now has an African American running for President and there are numerous Hispanic leaders holding high government positions.

This does not mean that prejudice is nonexistent. However, White Supremacists are a marginal, tiny part of the U.S. population today. It remains a real challenge to see whether an African American candidate indeed can break the glass ceiling to become the next U.S. President in 2009. If he succeeds, America can truly celebrate the accomplishment of a great milestone.

3. The American Culture

Perhaps it is easier to identify American character by ideology than by race, ethnicity, and culture, although ideology is a weaker bond between people than blood lineage. Despite the fact that some of his work is controversial and considered negative by experts, Samuel P. Huntington has a good description of American culture and identity in his book *Who Are We? America's Great Debate.* [12]

The American Creed, as initially formulated by Thomas Jefferson and elaborated upon by many others, is widely viewed as the crucial defining element of American identity. The Creed, however, was the product of the distinct Anglo-Protestant culture of the founding settlers of America in the seventeenth and eighteenth centuries. Key elements of that culture include: the language; Christianity; religious commit-ment; concept of the rule of law, the responsibility of the rulers, and the rights of individuals; and dissenting protestant values of individualism, the work ethic, and the belief that humans have the ability and the duty to try to create a heaven on Earth, or a "city on a hill" from a Chinese perspective.

This statement clearly delineates the founding principles of the U.S. as primarily defined by its European cultural heritage. It is a Western country with an Anglo-Christian core culture and a political creed of liberty and democracy. Preeminent among beliefs and core values shared by the vast majority of Americans is the Bill of Rights contained in the First Amendment of the U.S. Constitution. It states:

Congress shall make no law respecting an establishment of religion, or prohibiting the free exercise thereof; or abridging the freedom of speech, or of the press; or the right of the people peacefully to assemble, and to petition the government for a redress of grievance.

In short, there are five freedoms guaranteed by the first Amendment. These freedoms are the right to worship, speak, publish, assemble, and raise grievances with the government. Here the concept of the rule of law, the responsibility of the rulers, and the rights of individuals are writ-ten clearly as crucial defining elements of the American Creed, or American identity shared by immigrants from all over the world.

Other elements in the American Creed, such as "dissenting protes-tant values of individualism, the work ethic, and the belief that humans have the ability and the duty to pursue happiness and prosperity," require an understanding of the religious nature of the American culture.

American culture strongly supports religious beliefs and practice. As of 2001, a survey showed that 77 percent of the American population were Christians. [13] In the beginning, mainstream American culture was based on Anglo-Saxon Protestant culture inherited from England in which a central belief is the fundamental opposition of good and evil, right and wrong, God and the Devil. The individual must bear the responsibility to do good in this world and work hard in order to become successful. The work ethic is a central feature of Protestant culture, and from the beginning America's religion has been the religion of work.

In short, if each individual succeeds by working hard and utilizing his or her talents, then collectively Americans can make their society into a promised land, a heaven on Earth or a "city on a hill." The spirit of religion and the spirit of liberty are the two most important principles in American life. When asked in 2003, ninety-two percent of Americans said they believe in God. De Tocqueville in *Democracy in America* writes, "In the United States, religion . . . is mingled with all the habits of the nation and all the feelings of patriotism, whence it derives a peculiar force."

Americans bring together their secular politics and their religious doctrine to marry God and country, and thus, merge what could be conflicting loyalties into honor and fealty to a country protected by God.

The preceding analysis indicates that American society is built on individualism and the individual-God dual relationship. Each individual serves both God and country through the fulfillment of potential and is encouraged to excel through work and productivity in life. When a culture highly prizes individualism, its aim is to increase each person's ability to achieve in order to fulfill individual desires and ambitions. However, if this culture does not strongly promote social harmony and world peace at the same time, it inevitably encourages individual competition at home along with a passion for military conquest and dissemination abroad of its own moral values and principles.

The latter was evidenced by the activities of American priests and missionaries in China in the nineteenth and twentieth centuries as well as a U.S. foreign policy which promoted democracy and more liberal concepts throughout the world both peacefully and forcibly. Unless the people of other countries are willing to accept American values, conflicts may arise. The most recent example of this tendency is the U.S. invasion of Iraq to "build a new Middle East" with democracy and freedom. Due to the resistance of the Iraqis, the extended war has unfortunately sunk the U.S. into a mud trap and substantially damaged its world image.

In Chinese culture, the building blocks of the society are family units and harmonious interrelationships, which are extended farther and farther until they finally reach the state defined as "heaven and man as one." In American culture, it is the individual, the direct individual-God dual relationship, and the concept of individualism, that lead to freedoms such as the right to worship, speak, publish, assemble, and raise grievances with the government. These rights and the democratic system of representative government empower individuals to elect their leadership that includes members of Congress, governors, and the President. The same individualism also encourages at times fierce competition among individuals in sports, academics and business. Although in Matthew 22, Jesus' command, "Love thy neighbor as thyself," is central to Christian beliefs and absolutely and explicitly requires harmony in relationships; the fierce competition among individuals for personal success often conflicts with the Bible teaching of keeping social harmony.

Throughout Western history, religion has been the source of many conflicts. The competition for power and influence among the different religious schools was so severe that many religious wars took place and shattered social harmony. In Europe, the last major war of religion was the Thirty Years' War (1618–1648) between the German Protestant community and Catholics. Initially, it was primarily a conflict between the German Habsburg dynasty and France. Later it engaged many other European powers. When the Thirty Years' War ended with the Treaty of Westphalia several million Europeans had died, the European territories were redefined and the seeds were sown for Prussian-German militarism.

In America, while there has been no religious war between the Protestants and Catholics, the 9/11 (September 11, 2001) attack by Islamic terrorists on the Twin Towers in New York City appears to mark a serious and bitter new religious and ideological conflict. In America's new war against terrorism, the enemies are not all nation-bound and they possess a different religion, Islam. Some people call this confrontation a religious war despite the fact that the terrorists' motives were not simply to bring down the so-called infidels who, by definition, are any non-Islamic religious group. Rather their goal was to destroy the financial center, a symbol of world power and a value system of personal freedom and private enterprise, which they perceive as evil and a source of economic domination.

4. The American Industrial Development

As mentioned, early American immigrants brought European culture and the "know how" for industrial growth to their new homeland and ushered in the Second Industrial Revolution in America. The period from the late seventeenth century to the 1870s witnessed American industrial advances in many areas including: mills, master-apprentice systems, arms manufacture, printing, textile production, transportation systems, photography, and agriculture. It was also during this period that America's industrial infrastructure was developed such as roads, highways, building construction, rail transportation, manufacturing plants, and factories. After the four-year interruption of the Civil War from 1861 to 1865, America's industrial development gradually regained strength and technical innovations fueled the creation of jobs. From the 1870s to the 1920s, America's technical developments not only changed lifestyles and raised standards of living, but also transformed production systems to include assembly-line techniques in factories.

America, by the turn of the twentieth century, operating within a capitalistic, free market economy, and supported by public policies which favored innovation, became one of the most important industrialized nations in the world. American productivity and living standards reached a historic high point. Social changes were also reflected in the complex interrelationships between government and society, and progress was made in the revitalization of rural America, new production techniques, and military advances. There is little doubt that the Americans created a heaven on Earth and a "city on a hill," guided by their religious beliefs, patriotism, cutting-edge technological innovations, improved financial policies, and a democratic political system.

America's period of industrial development overlapped with China's Qing Dynasty (1644–1911) when it gradually regressed into the black whirlpool of ceaseless terrors and the wreckage of war. Today, in the first decade of the twenty-first century, the relatively young America is the strongest and wealthiest country in the world with unchallengeable military supremacy. At the same time, the ancient Middle Kingdom emerged from the ashes and ruins of numerous wars and turbulence and is striving to restore its vigorous spirit and reclaim its past glory.

5. Will the American Creed
Face Challenges?

The American Creed has not yet faced serious challenges in the relatively brief history of the U.S. The Civil Rights movement of the 50s and 60s served to extend basic freedoms guaranteed under the Constitution to people of all colors and genders, in particular women and African Americans. Naturally, the U.S. will continue to change and evolve, and this will be a constant process. However, when the U.S. demographics change and white Caucasians are no longer the majority, as projected for 2050, new problems and challenges may develop. Can the core value of the American Creed derived from the dominant European culture continue to dominate? Samuel P. Huntington has raised this serious question and calls it "America's Great Debate."

It is undeniable that many Hispanic people and other immigrants from around the world come to the U.S. because they are attracted to the American core culture, which embodies religious values, personal freedom, economic opportunity, and democracy. They are expected to embrace this core culture, not to destroy it. However, among them are many who come primarily for economic reasons or to seek a better future because America is the wealthiest country in the world that offers jobs, education, housing, and other opportunities. It is also understandable that not all of them will be willing or able to shrug off immediately their motherland culture simply because they move to a new land.

The U.S. population growth rate has been about 1.3 percent or approximately 3.3 million annually according to the Census Bureau's decennial census. Since the growth rate includes a natural increase of about 1.6 million per year (total birth about 4 million minus deaths), the U.S. has therefore admitted about 1.7 million immigrants annually. Thus, the total population could be more than tripled during the twenty-first century. The next few decades will reveal whether the large numbers of Hispanic immigrants will assimilate as other groups have in the past and whether a "dominant European culture" will prevail as a major influence.

The religious profile of the American population is also changing. The American Religious Identification Survey, indicates that 1) the proportion of the population that can be classified as Christian has declined from 86 percent in 1990 to 77 percent in 2001; 2) The proportion of non-Christians has increased only by a small amount from 3.3 percent to about 3.7 percent; 3) The non-religious, atheist, or agnostic population showed the greatest increase in absolute as well as in percentage terms, more than doubled from 14.3 million in 1990 to 29.4 million in 2001, or from 8 percent of the total in 1990 to over 14 percent in 2001; and 4) The adults who refused to reply to questions about their religious preference jumped from about 4 million or 2 percent in 1990 to more than 11 million or over 5 percent in 2001. [13]

Has the decline of American religious identification impacted the content of the American Creed in any way? Why were there big increases in the non-religious population and a jump in adults who refused to reveal their religious preference? Are the American people beginning to show less faith in God nowadays? This survey was performed prior to the 9/11 terrorist attack in 2001. It would be worthwhile to gather new data in the 2010 census to see whether this trend continues and whether they have impacted one of the major building blocks in the American Creed—the Christian faith and American society—in any way.

While the influence of religion in the U.S. may be waning somewhat, its importance in China is growing rapidly and dramatically. It may not be easy to identify the reasons for the decline of the religious population in the U.S., but there are more obvious reasons for agnostic communists to discover religious values after suppression of religious freedom by the PRC government. This will be discussed further in Chapter IV.

6. Conclusions

America is an immigrant nation and a melting pot for people who come from all over the world seeking fulfillment of the American dream. The American Creed joined people together to form the strongest country in the world. America will retain its leadership position for the foreseeable future in many areas including economic, political, cultural, scientific, technological, and military.

Religion is a foundation for many Americans, but not for all American values. Freedom and democracy, for example, are concepts that extend well beyond religion. It is our hope and belief that even if the religious influence declines substantially over a long period of time in the future, Americans will be able to thrive on the nation's building blocks of freedom, democracy, and rule of law. Unfortunately, America's unchallenged strength led the U.S. Bush administration into a dangerous violation of the spirit of the American Creed through an ill-conceived war in Iraq.

In a world of increasing multinational corporations, economic globalization, and cultural co-mingling, are Americans led by the current administration to swim against the tide? Will America's foreign policy create an environment in the U.S. which evolves to become what Zbigniew Brzezinski calls, "the first, only, and the last true superpower?" [14]

CHAPTER III

Where Does China Stand Now?

This chapter provides an overview of China's political and economic development, and its foreign policy.

1. The PRC's Political and Economic Development Prior to 1978

The PRC was established in 1949 with its capital at Beijing. The national anthem was written in 1935 at the height of the War against the Japanese invaders in northern China when the fate of the nation was about to crumble. The lyrics are as follows:

Arise, ye who refuse to be slaves;
With our very flesh and blood
Let us build our new Great Wall!
The Peoples of China are in the most critical time,
Everybody must roar his defiance.
Arise! Arise! Arise!
Millions of hearts with one mind,

Brave the enemy's gunfire,
March on!
Brave the enemy's gunfire,
March on! March on! March on, on

Moving and powerful, the song signified China's admirable tradition of courage, resolution, and unity in fighting foreign aggression. [1] Its painful history over the past 150 years has left deep wounds and scars on many Chinese hearts and minds. It is difficult to imagine that China would become a military aggressor as the China threat theorists propose while the Chinese people remain in the midst of a recovery from tragic historical events.

The political system in China also had a fresh start. The PRC is based on a constitutional system which was adopted by the National People's Congress (NPC) in 1982. The Constitution states that the CPC is the country's sole political party in power, which governs a population of 1.3 billion, more than thirty provinces, several autonomous regions, and fifty-six nationalities. The CPC currently has 70.8 million party members selected from leaders in all professions.

The membership receives continuous party education and training. The strength of the CPC derives from party organizations at all levels from the grassroots to the top. In recent years, the CPC has trained a large number of young members by improving their educational background and by sending them abroad to learn advanced administrative skills. Their aim is to help China develop socialism with Chinese characteristics by establishing a market economy, expanding democracy, and improving the rule of law.

China's organizational principle for its state organs is democratic centralism. The country is now headed by the President and Vice President elected by the NPC. The NPC and the local people's congresses at various levels are the mechanisms through which the populace exercises state power. The NPC deputies are elected from the provinces, autonomous regions, and municipalities under the central government or they are elected by the armed forces. The local people's congresses are established in provinces, autonomous regions, and municipalities directly under the central government, autonomous prefectures, counties, autonomous counties, cities, municipal districts, townships, ethnic townships, and towns. [2] In addition, the Chinese People's Political Consultative Conference (CPPCC) was established in 1949, which consists of elite members of Chinese society who are willing to serve as a think tank for the country's legislative and judicial organs.

During the period of Mao's rule from 1949 to 1976, the Chinese government instigated new major political structures and systems including the centralization of party and government administration. In the midst of these major political changes, there was also an agricultural drive accompanied by land reform and a militant approach towards faster and greater economic development launched in 1958 as the Great Leap Forward. This effort was undertaken to speed up the pace of socioeconomic and technical development. The Great Leap Forward created the people's communes as self-supporting communities for agriculture, small-scale local industry, schooling, marketing, administration, and local security. The system constituted a fundamental attack on the institution of family, the most basic unit in Confucianism and the backbone of the Chinese society. It was a major economic failure and Mao Zedong had to step down from his position as president of the PRC as he was chiefly responsible for the Great Leap Forward fiasco.

Between 1949 and 1978, Chinese society was basically orchestrated by Mao's version of Marxism and a planned economy in which the Chinese government provided food, housing, health care, schooling, etc. to its entire population. Although the Chinese people were often short of material comfort, the crime rate was low and corruption was not tolerated.

Mao Zedong started the Cultural Revolution amid an internal struggle for party power from 1966 to 1976. The Cultural Revolution devastated the country. The radical tide of the Cultural Revolution receded in 1968 after Mao Zedong realized the uselessness of further revolutionary violence.

U.S. President Richard M. Nixon met with the Chinese leadership in 1972, during the Cold War, as a means of counterbalancing Soviet power. Although the U.S. had a formal diplomatic relationship with Taiwan, this historic renewal of relations was a reversal of decades of antagonistic American policy towards the leadership of the Chinese mainland. China, in turn, raised the "Bamboo Curtain" and stepped onto the world stage through diplomacy. History always ran its own course and the U.S.-China courtship reinforced a saying in international diplomacy: There is no "forever friend" or "forever enemy," only the "forever interest."

2. The Open Door Policy and China's Embrace of a Market Economy

When the Cultural Revolution entered its ninth year in 1975, the Chinese economy had nearly collapsed. Chinese Premier Zhou Enlai articulated what he named the Four Modernizations: Agriculture, Industry, Science and Technology, and National Defense. His goal was to revive the Chinese economy and mitigate the damage caused by the Cultural Revolution. The Chinese viewed Mao Zedong as a revolutionary, and Zhou Enlai was the only one who could put out Mao's continuously burning fire. Sadly, Zhou had cancer and was too weak to fight the notorious Gang of Four. He died in January of 1976, followed by Mao Zedong's death nine months later.

Following the death of Mao, the reformist Deng Xiaoping regained full power and leadership. In order to maintain the momentum of the Four Modernizations and expand China's economy, the government invested heavily in the four areas designated for modernization. Deng Xiaoping visited the U.S. in 1978 and began the Chinese open door policy the same year. He wanted to bring China into the global community of advanced industrial nations by the start of the new millennium and promote participation in the world market economy. The policy was dressed up in the words of Deng Xiaoping as "socialism with Chinese characteristics."

Deng was the last of China's original Communist revolutionaries. He was a great statesman, military strategist, and diplomat. He was also veteran communist advocate, founder of the Deng Xiaoping Theory, which encapsulated the various policy pronouncements that guided the reform process. As the chief architect of China's socialist reform which included modernization, two of his famous dictums were: "It always stands to reason to develop the economy faster," and "The economy must cross a new threshold every few years."

He was a brilliant interpreter of pragmatic Marxist thinking and demonstrated great political foresight. He was intensely faithful to the CPC and possessed an unswerving commitment and a deep love of the Chinese people. Throughout the 1980s, Deng revealed his philosophy through slogans including:

"Seek truth from facts, and correct mistakes whenever they are discovered,"

"Groping for stones to cross the river,"

"Black cat, white cat, all that matters is that it catches mice," and

"To get rich is glorious."

Deng's motivational slogans inspired and encouraged the Chinese people, gradually transmuting the more recent grim past. Now, China has become one of the fastest growing economies in the world. Deng clearly had a hand in this dramatic economic evolution and in the redirection of political thought. As a result of Deng's efforts and transformed priorities, significant economic progress occurred.

Deng Xiaoping died on February 19, 1997, just months before Great Britain returned Hong Kong to China's sovereignty. When he died, many Chinese were genuinely saddened. A Western observer wrote, "Deng changed the face of China's economy to what we see today which is a growing economy with increasing links to the outside world." [3]

After the demise of Deng, a third generation leader, Jiang Zemin, emerged to continue Chinese economic reform. The current President, Hu Jintao, and Premier Wen Jiabao are fourth generation leaders following Mao Zedong, Deng Xiaoping and Jiang Zemin. The present leadership holds office for two terms of ten years that began in 2003.

3. An Explosive Chinese Economy Startles the World

Americans are impressed with the size of China and it is no wonder that *Newsweek* journalist, Fareed Zakaria, has the following in his article "China's Century:" [4]

He bluntly writes: "Americans admire beauty, but they are truly dazzled by bigness. [. . .]That is why China hits the American imagination so hard. It is a country whose scale dwarfs the United States—1.3 billion people, four times America's population. [. . .]China was very big, but very poor."

China is in the midst of a historic transformation and is turning the corner economically. During the twenty-eight years from 1978 to 2006, China's real GDP grew at an average rate of over 9.4 percent a year, more than three times the U.S. growth rate. At its current rate, China is doubling output and incomes every ten years. Suddenly, China is growing as an economic powerhouse. The World Bank predicted Chinese economic growth in 2006 would exceed 9 percent. [5]

In fact, China reported a startling annual 10.9 percent GDP growth in the first half of 2006 (the second quarter GDP growth alone was 11.3 percent annually). This growth has enhanced stability in broad production sectors, and increased imports and domestic consumption growth by 12.4 percent. [6]

In 2005, China's GDP, US$2.29 trillion (about 5 percent of the world's GDP), grew 10.2 percent over the previous year and ranked fourth in the world, after the U.S., Japan, and Germany. [7] This was about one-sixth of the U.S. GDP; whereas in 1978, China's GDP was only US$147.3 billion. In 2005, China's total trade volume ranked third after the U.S. and Japan, foreign direct investment (FDI) of US$60.3 billion ranked third after Britain and the U.S., and export trade surplus reached US$101.9 billion. This was double that of 2004.

In an international survey of more than 10,000 people in nine countries, 50 percent thought that by 2020 China would reach economic status equal with the U.S. and that both nations would lead the world together. [8] Most economists acknowledge that the Chinese contribution to world economic growth surpasses that of Japan and is only second to the U.S. Since 2003, China has eclipsed Japan to become the third largest trade partner of the U.S.

On the financial side, China's foreign currency reserves reached US$853.7 billion surpassing Japan as the world's largest at the end of February, 2006. [9] China's current foreign exchange reserves are over US$1.3 trillion, about 70 percent of it is U.S. dollar asset. The U.S. is both importing heavily and borrowing heavily from China to finance purchases, thus continuously depressing the value of the dollar.

The Chinese government now holds a large share of its reserves in U.S. government treasuries. [10] The largest area of economic growth was in agriculture, the second in industrial production, and the third in service industries. Most Asian countries had a trade surplus in their bilateral trade relationships with China. For example, Taiwan's trade surplus is almost completely derived from trade with China. Many economists speculate that China could become the world's largest economy within two decades. Chinese leader Hu Jintao said in his speech at the Vietnamese Congress on November 1, 2005, that "We have found that constructing socialism with Chinese characteristics is a development path that suits our nation's condition." [11]

Fareed Zakaria observed China's dramatic economic progress and addressed a new American concern: After commenting on China's poverty in the past, he writes, "All that is changing. But now the very size and scale that seemed so alluring is beginning to look ominous. And Americans are wondering whether the 'China threat' is nightmarishly real."

Is this worry justified? Economic data shows that in 2004, China's per capita income was only US$1,490. This number ranked 105 of 192 world countries, whereas the U.S. per capita income was US$41,400 (about twenty-eight times higher) ranked the fourth. Although China's per capita income increased to about US$2,000 in 2006, its urban and rural income gap continues to widen. In addition, the World Bank reported that the average Chinese personal asset value was only US$9,387, less than 2 percent of the average U.S. value.

These data indicate uneven economic development in China concentrated mostly along the coastal areas while the majority of the inland areas have not been developed. The population in the rural areas remains economically backward. Recent rapid growth does not compare with Japanese economic growth after World War II: from 1945 to 1955, the Japanese economy recovered rapidly to reach its prewar level. After 1955, Japan's GDP grew 10 percent annually for eighteen years. By 1968, Japan's GDP reached US$159.7 billion, exceeding West Germany, Britain, and France. After 1973, it entered into a steady 5 percent annual growth period and in the 1980s it became the second largest economic entity in the world. Other than the national GDP, Japan's per capita income was only one-fourteenth of U.S. value (US$131 vs. US$1,897) in 1950, but by 1987, Japan's per capita income surpassed the U.S. In other words, Japan's per capita income multiplied 151 times in forty years.

In 2005, the U.S. international trade imbalance reached US$726 billion (about 5.8 percent of the U.S. GDP), of which about 28 percent, was attributed to China's contribution. [12] But in the same year, U.S. exports to Japan alone were more than twice the combined China and India exports to the U.S. Moreover, commercial sales by American companies to Japan and Germany were more than six times that of combined China and India sales to the U.S. [13] Although Chinese trade surplus had a higher percentage share of the U.S. trade deficit, the absolute trade volume was relatively smaller than that of Japan and Germany.

4. China Faces Uphill Task in Job Creation

In contrast to the rosy trade numbers, *Xinhuanet* (Beijing) reported on March 6, 2005, that China expected a higher urban unemployment rate by the end of 2005 than in the previous year. There were "11 million urban residents, including those entering the workplace for the first time, ex-servicemen and college graduates who need to find employment. There are now 13 million unemployed and laid-off urban workers, and large numbers of surplus rural laborers need to find jobs in urban areas." Although the government figures normally showed an unemployment rate between 4-5 percent, unofficial records indicated that in certain rural areas the unemployment rate was as high as 20 percent.

Employment pressure was very intense in 2006. China faces an unemployment crisis of unprecedented proportions. Imagine, twenty-five million men and women—the combined population of Australia and New Zealand—are pressing for new jobs. "New figures from China's National Development and Reform Commission indicate a shortfall of fourteen million jobs, a pattern that they predict will continue for at least five years and one likely to exacerbate concerns over rising crime rates and social unrest." [14]

Prior to his visit to China in late 2005, President George W. Bush said that he created a few million jobs over his five years in office. The number of American poor also increased by about five million during this period. Hu Jintao is challenged to create twenty-five million jobs every year for China.

Despite the near double-digit average GDP growth in China for the past twenty-eight years and a red-hot economy, the nation is simply not growing fast enough in key sectors to create enough jobs to fill the gap. The Chinese government is struggling to create jobs while starting salary expectations among graduates have dropped from US$300 a month to just US$100 a month. Massive lay-offs resulting from closure of thousands of inefficient factories and companies took place in the process of the nation's move to a market economy. This left millions of workers to fend for themselves.

The majority of Chinese have no social security protection. Forty million peasants lost their land; 16 million factory workers were laid off; the Genii index that reflects the rich-poor gap reached a dangerous 0.5 (above 0.4 indicates a severe rich-poor gap). [15] About 65.7 percent of Chinese have no medical insurance. [16] Up to 90 percent of the 800 million people in China's countryside lack affordable medical care and children go unvaccinated. AIDS patients can get free anti-retroviral drugs, but cannot afford the monitoring or additional drugs they need. These conditions are extremely unbalanced.

Chinese farmers pay most or all of their own medical expenses, while city dwellers who earn nearly three times as much pay for only a portion of their medical cost. [17] Deng Xiaoping's push to "get a portion of people rich first" has created a huge rich-poor gap and deepened social problems. Only a small percent of the population will receive retirement income, most of them are government employees. The PRC announced a deficit of more than US$9 billion in individual social security fund accounts in 2005. The money, deposited by employees in these accounts to fund part of their future pensions, is used by the government to pay people who have retired. [18]

But thanks to the fast growth of the economy, in one recent survey of 2,600 companies in twenty-five provinces, 80 percent of the employers planned to recruit more workers. [19] China has already moved about

300 million people out of poverty according to World Bank records, but there are still about 800 million people living in rural areas that need to be trained, educated, and integrated into urban life. This prompted Chinese leader Hu Jintao to say that Chinese leaders are vigilantly aware that China has a huge population and limited resources for funding new employment and balancing wealth distribution. China confronts a mix of contradictions and problems as it strives to achieve relative affluence. The Chinese people must continue to make arduous efforts to succeed. [20]

In China's five thousand year history, the peasant issue has always been a major concern of the Chinese government. If China's government policies are not supported by the peasants, they will have no chance of success. Hu Jintao clearly understands this point. [21]

The American media and politicians have painted a very rosy picture of Chinese economic development, and the China threat theory intensifies this perspective. But to most Chinese, twenty-eight years of economic development is only a drop in the vast ocean of history and many of them are still facing economic hardship.

A huge urban shift in China is projected to move another 200 to 300 million people into cities over the next twenty years which will fuel strong growth, At the same time, China has to solve wide ranging resource problems to provide food, housing, employment, and health care to the swelling urban populace. In addition, managing the police force, maintaining social order, and providing important civil services will present new challenges. China has no alternative but to continue to reduce social divisions and the pronounced gap between the wealthy and the poor. Growth in the labor market would keep Chinese salaries and wages low relative to the West and would fuel continued robust exports to other nations.

5. Prosperous Foreign Companies and Economic Cooperation

American companies are prospering as they gain greater access to the Chinese domestic market, according to a seven-year annual survey conducted by the American Chamber of Commerce. About 38 percent of respondents in the year 2000 cited market access restrictions as a top barrier to profitability, while 66 percent reported negative effects from business scope restrictions. However, substantial progress has been made since 2000. From 2002 to 2005, two-thirds of the respondents were successful in expanding products and services offered in China. [22]

In addition, private foreign enterprise increased 60 percent in 2005, versus a 33 percent rise in 1999. In recent years, foreign firms have introduced more products and services to the Chinese market. Twenty-seven of the forty-six insurance companies included in the Fortune 500 list of leading companies have opened business branches in China.

And by late 2005, there were eighty-two insurance companies across China, out of which forty were financed by overseas investors. The report also indicated that China was working aggressively to fulfill promises made to enter the World Trade Organization (WTO) in 2001.

Two-thirds of American companies surveyed made appreciable profits in China and 42 percent reported that profits made in China were higher than world-wide averages for other countries. A typical example is General Motors. It reported a 28 percent rise in China sales in first three quarters of 2005. [23]

Wal-Mart also makes greater profits through selling products made in China because of lower labor costs. Bank of America and HSBC Holdings PLC doubled their investment by purchasing stock option shares of China Construction Bank Corp. and Bank of Communications Co., Ltd., respectively. [24]

Further, China is increasing imports from the U.S. The day before President Hu Jintao visited the U.S. on April 18, 2006, China's biggest computer manufacturer Lenovo agreed to buy US$1.2 billion worth of Microsoft software for installation on its computers. [25] Hu Jintao's first stop on his four-day trip to the U.S. was in Seattle where he met with Microsoft Chairman Bill Gates. Mr. Hu said, "Bill Gates is a friend of China and I am a friend of Microsoft." Mr. Gates responded, "Thank you, it's a fantastic relationship."

According to the recent data given by the Shanghai Foreign Investment Commission, China's rapid economic development and revised business laws are attracting many foreign retailers to invest in

China. For example, the Golden Resources Mall in Beijing is bigger than the Mall of America in Minnesota. Best Buy used US$180 million to purchase shares in Jiangsu Five Star, a home electronics company, and Home Depot is considering the purchase of shares of Chinese companies like Orient Home and Homeway, a building materials retailer. [26]

On April 11, 2006, Vice Premier Wu Yi led a delegation to the seventeenth meeting of Sino-U.S. Joint Commission on Commerce and Trade in the U.S. where she signed more than 100 lucrative business contracts with U.S. companies valued at US$16.2 billion. These included eighty Boeing 737 jets and Motorola communications equipment. [27]

Airbus SAS, the world's largest manufacturer of commercial aircraft said, it will make its first A320 aircraft in China by the end of 2008. This would be its first assembly plant outside Europe. [28] Following development of China's manufacturing industry its air cargo transportation will become the fastest growing market in the world and is expected to soon surpass the air passenger market. China's demand for cargo transportation over the next twenty years will most likely grow at a pace of 10 percent per year and China's domestic cargo demand will grow very fast. [29]

In 2005, more than 44,000 foreign enterprises were located in China with total investments of an estimated US$60 billion. American technology investors view China as the fastest growing technical market. According to one estimate, there are 110 million Internet users in China today. By 2010 the number could reach 250 million. [30]

The American Chamber of Commerce Chairman Charlie Martin said that some American companies failed to enter the Chinese market because of a lack of experience, contacts, and reliable distribution networks. If the American consulate in China increased its in-house business services to encourage trade and investment, more companies would succeed.

The Chamber report suggested a much friendlier tone on the trade with China in contrast with the official stance of the U.S. government, which was influenced by the large Chinese trade surplus of US$201.62 billion with the U.S. in 2005.

The Beijing Technology and Business University issued a report entitled the "International Trade Investment Risks Index." It states that

China is among the ten regions worldwide with the lowest investment risk. The report compares world development, global competition capability, and related statistics in four categories or indexes. They are political risks, economic risks, policy risks, and payment risks. The ten countries are China, China's Hong Kong Special Administration Region, Denmark, Finland, Ireland, the Netherlands, Norway, Singapore, Sweden, and Switzerland. According to the report, with the exception of China, the nine others with the lowest investment risk are high-income nations. The report reviewed risk levels in seventy-five countries and regions in Africa, Asia, Europe, Latin America, North America, and Oceania. They account for 94 percent of the world's total GDP, 91 percent of the world's total export and 89 percent of the world's direct investment. China now ranks the second in its research and development investment next to the U.S. [31]

It was no surprise that recently Intel made an announcement of its plan to build a plant in Dalian, a city in northeastern China that will produce semiconductors, including microprocessors, on 300-millimeter wafers using a 90-nanometer manufacturing process. The most advanced manufacturing technology currently used by Intel is a 65-nanometer process. The planned plant will cost US$2.5 billion and will be the first constructed by Intel in China. The plant will have a monthly production capacity of 52,000 chips. [32]

6. Rapid Infrastructure Development

The titanic socioeconomic transformation in China combined with a new atmosphere and positive attitude towards foreign enterprises are signs of China's economic progress.

Another example of China's commitment to growth on a gigantic scale is the controversial engineering project on the Yangtze River Water Dam or Three Gorges Dam. This is an enormous project, begun in 1993, designed to alter the flow of the river to avoid potential flooding and drought in the future. It will also assist irrigation, generate electric power, and facilitate transportation to rural areas. The environmental impact of the Three Gorges Dam project and prospects for achieving the intended power generation remain unclear and are hotly debated. The project is scheduled for completion in 2009.

We are witnessing a peaceful economic revolution that is reshaping Chinese society and the map of China. The construction of nation-wide infrastructure sprang up like mushrooms one after another in the last decade. They include:

- Water dams and highways

- Government and commercial buildings

- Bridges, airports, harbors, and ports

- Residential communities, parks, and recreational centers

- Cars, trucks, ships, trains, and railways

- Factories, power plants, military bases, spaceports, spacecraft, shuttles, and payload processing facilities

For example, the Chinese government spent US$703 million on highway construction across the plateau region in Tibet in 2006. This includes upgrading the highway connecting China to Nepal. Tibet is known as the "roof of the world," and has had poor roadways for many years. [33]

In 2005, Chinese automobile sales reached 5.92 million vehicles, ranking number two in the world, unexpectedly exceeding production numbers in Germany and Japan, second only to the U.S. in volume of vehicles manufactured. Sales for 2006 were estimated at a growth rate 10 to 15 percent or 6.4 to 6.6 million cars. [34]

China now ranks as the third largest shipbuilder in the world. However, its average productivity is only about one-sixth of the world's top two—South Korea and Japan. China's original design for a feeder passenger jet with seventy to ninety seats is considered among the most advanced regional jets of the twenty-first century. The ARJ21 is expected to make its first flight in 2008. [35] The plane's engine will be made by the General Electric Company.

A project to build a high-speed railway linking Beijing and Shanghai has been approved by the Chinese Central Government. [36] The construction of a new railway line linking China's poor western and prosperous eastern regions began in February 2006. The total length of the rail line will be about 566 miles. It will be known as Taiyuan-Zhongwei (Yinchuan) line and operate forty passenger trains each day transporting sixty million tons of cargo annually. Currently, only one major railway, the Longhai railway, links China's west to its east. [37] In October of 2005, the Qinghai-Tibet rail began operations. It travels at the world's highest altitude, moving from Golmud in Qinghai to Lhasa in Tibet. The line extends a total length of approximately 1,956 km or 714 miles across a 5,000 meter high mountain range.

The railway construction work was performed at a high altitude where the oxygen content was only about half that at sea level and at temperatures as low as Celsius 5 degrees. It was more difficult and complicated than the development of the American Transcontinental Railway. The construction team consisted of one hundred thousand workers who labored for four years. The project cost US$4.1 billion and finished one year ahead of schedule. The completion of this project is viewed as a national triumph for making the seemingly impossible possible. China opened the highest topographical railway worldwide on July 1, 2006. [38] This improved transportation system will facilitate cultural and economic exchange and development between landlocked Tibet and the outside world. The rail will also support economic and cultural relations among Bangladesh, Bhutan, China, India, and Nepal. The overriding goal is the positive effect of a harmonious region in South Asia.

Interesting anecdotal information was provided by seven senior reporters from India who traveled by the Qinghai-Tibet rail to visit the famous Qinghai-Tibet plateau, also known as the "ridge of the world." They described their journey as "full of surprises." For example, when the Chinese officials told them that Gansu was one of the poorer provinces in the economically lagging western region, they found the Lanzhou Airport remarkably modern, clean, and better than the airport in New Delhi, India's capital.

After visiting Lhassa, one of the reporters remarked that she read Western reports attacking the way the Chinese government oppressed Tibetans economically and in their practice of the Buddhist religion. Today it appears the reality is much different. She commented that in Lhassa streets, many Tibetans wear attractive traditional garbs and numerous stores are owned and operated by Tibetans. Also, temples are crowded with worshippers. [39]

China's ports are projected to handle 25 percent more cargo by 2010 than their current capacity. [40] China is steaming ahead with its plans for the first expressway network to connect all towns and cities with populations exceeding 200,000. The network will consist of seven key expressways radiating from Beijing, nine running from north to south, and eighteen crossing from the east to west. The network is also known as the "7–9–18." Chinese expressway systems are ranked as second largest in the world after the U.S. There is a new plan to expand the expressway network to 5,100 miles—which is 6,000 miles longer than its current interstate network. This will reduce annual transportation and logistics costs which account for 18 to 22 percent of total GDP, compared with 9 percent in the U.S. and 5 percent in Europe. [41]

Beijing also plans to spend at least US$37.5 billion to divert water from the highest plateau in the world to the north despite concerns about technical feasibility and environmental costs. The south-north diversion of the project that started in 2002 is designed to bring water from the Yangtze northwards along three routes in western, central and eastern China to Beijing and the north. It is expected to take more than fifty years to complete. The central route will divert about one-third of the annual flow of the Han River, a major tributary of the Yangtze to reach Beijing before the 2008 Olympics. The western route would draw water from the Yalong, Dadu, and Jinsha Rivers in the west and divert water to the drought-plagued northwestern regions that include Ningxia and Gansu. The construction of the western route could be more difficult than the Qinghai-Tibet railway. [42] Because of unresolved conflicts, the western route will not begin in the near future. In addition, the upper stream of the Yangtze River is badly polluted, therefore, serious controversy and opposition have surrounded continuation of the project.

Over the past twenty-eight years, Shanghai has built over 3,000 skyscrapers, literally one every three days! Architects from all over the world flock to China. One New York architect said that in China, the number of buildings he designed in two short years could not possibly compare with the number he would have the opportunity to develop in the U.S. Skyscrapers in China are like weeds cropping up all over the place.

Terminal Three of Beijing Capital International Airport is rising in the arid eastern part of the city. The construction started in April 2004 and will be completed by December 2007 for the 2008 Beijing Olympics. "It is the largest covered structure ever built," according to the well known architect Norman Foster. [43] There are forty thousand workers on site, working eight-hour shifts around the clock, seven days a week, and each earns about US$7 per day. Five thousand more workers arrived before the end of 2005. Most of them come from remote and undeveloped areas of China. Nothing will stop the cranes, the cement mixers, and the welding machines. A British reporter of the *Observer* remarked admiringly:

Although in Foster's computer drawing, the airport looks like a fashionable and elegant glass and steel architecture, in reality now, it looks more like a medieval battleground in an ancient Japanese epic with large numbers of laborers working feverishly next to a giant crane.

At the construction site, colorful flags wave everywhere, each imprinted with a construction team's name. Individual teams have their assigned work site where workers move like disciplined ant armies. You can distinguish identities by helmet colors.

In the daytime, the workers are exposed to blowing sand and dust, and searing heat under the sun. At night, they continue their work under flood lights. The construction site is surrounded by green military tents and tottering sheds where workers sleep. Roofs are covered with flimsy plastic sheets. These people live in the twenty-first century, but their lives are no different from laborers who built railways and canals for Great Britain in the 1800s. [44]

Another British reporter observed that young Chinese men and women flock to the cities where they plan to work very hard under harsh conditions for a few years. Their hope is to save enough money so they may return to their villages and settle down to live like traditional Chinese families.

An interesting question is whether the rural-urban transformation will eventually alter the peasant lifestyle? Or whether Confucian traditions will be modified by the increasingly industrialized and urbanized society? No one can tell. But it would not be surprising if most Chinese live and work in urban areas at some future date.

Basic Confucian concepts of benevolence, righteousness, etiquette, "love others they as love themselves" and do not impose on others what you do not want imposed on you, would still remain the cornerstones of Chinese social mores to maintain social harmony.

7. China Tackles Energy and Pollution Problems

In 1993, China began to import energy on a significant scale. China is now the second largest consumer of energy in the world next to the U.S. and the third largest oil importer after the U.S. and Japan. It accounts for about 7 percent of the world's total annual oil consumption. Presently, 40 percent of Chinese oil needs are met by imports. By 2010, that number will increase to 50 percent. [45] By 2030, China may have to import more than 80 percent of the oil it consumes annually. The Chinese government predicted that by 2020, its oil imports will reach 300 million tons (about 1.103 billion barrels, one metric ton is about 7.676 barrels)) in comparison with the 130 million tons (about 478 million barrels) of 2005.

Chinese natural gas imports are expected to increase to more than 60 billion cubic meters (about 2,120 Bcp, 1 Bcp = 1 billion cubic feet) in 2020 compared with a little over 20 billion cubic meters (about 707 Bcp) today. [46] China is concerned about energy resource policies. At present, coal is used to generate more than two-thirds of China's electricity. But to curb accidents and pollution, China's biggest coal producer, the northern province of Shanxi, plans to slow expansion of the mining industry. [47] Chinese authorities are encouraging installation of emission controls and a shift to cleaner fuel sources such as natural gas and nuclear energy.

Beginning in 2005, China approved the construction of 168 electrical power plants and Chinese oil companies worked to identify new energy sources in countries like Russia and Kazakhstan.

In 2003, Russia confirmed plans to build the Angarsk pipeline that would reach the Chinese Daqing region. In time, Japan entered the competition. Following negotiations between China, Russia, and Japan, it was determined that the final pipeline would lead to Nakhodka, which is close to the China-Russia border. This would locate a branch pipe at

Daqing in China. The pipeline is expected to be completed in 2008. Russian oil exports to China face many uncertainties. Presently, China is focusing on Central Asia and the Persian Bay to establish a multilateral framework to ensure a sustainable energy supply.

As mentioned, China collaborated with Russia and Kazakhstan on the export of additional oil to meet its burgeoning energy needs. The China National Petroleum Corporation (CNPC) and Russia's oil transportation company agreed on the financing for construction of oil pipes in Russia. A new oil pipeline between China and Kazakhstan was completed in November 2005, and Kazakhstan is exporting oil to China along this pipeline which passes through the Xinjiang Uigur region. [48] The vast Central Asian state's oil output is expected to nearly triple to 3.5 million barrels per day by 2015, making Kazakhstan an important world oil producer. [49]

In January and February of 2006, China and India signed an agreement to completely change their vicious competition for overseas oil resources. Further, China developed agreements with Central Asian countries and Pakistan on energy resource distribution issues. Professor Stephen Blank of the U.S. Army War College noted that China usually avoids the market and invests directly in the oil fields through bilateral negotiations where it purchases stock in foreign oil companies, or signs long term contracts to obtain rights for oil exploration. In this way, China hopes to guarantee a stable supply of oil without suffering the impact of market price fluctuations. Professor Blank states further that ". . . there is also a defect in this kind of approach. It is costly to buy stock shares from foreign oil companies, besides, the oil output is generally uncertain." [50]

Along with the critical nature of oil supply as an energy resource and creation of an adequate energy infrastructure, the Three Gorges Dam project deserves special attention. The enormous infrastructure project has been a source of controversy for many years. Economic conditions delayed progress as did political conflict and corruption. Despite these hurdles, once the dam begins operation in 2009, the power generated is expected to supply an estimated 10 percent of China's electricity needs.

On February 24, 2006, China began construction of the first coal-based synthetic oil facility in the northern Shanxi Province. Plant operations are designed to transform low-quality coal with high sulfur content into clean, liquefied fuel that can be used in cars. This fuel technology is highly efficient permitting a consumption rate of 4.5 to 5 liters per hundred kilometers (about 2 to 2.2 gallons per 100 miles). [51]

The largest Asian coal gas project was built in Henan Province in central China. It began operation in September 2006. The project is intended to bring daily gas output to three million cubic meters (about 0.106 Bcp), be environmentally friendly, and reduce annual sulfur dioxide emissions by 76.25 tons and carbon dioxide by 11.50 tons. [52]

China has announced plans to step up efforts to develop innovative nuclear power technologies. Currently, China has nine nuclear generators in operation. The combined electricity generated by nuclear power accounts for 2.3 percent of the country's total. With respect to the limited hydropower resources and the less environmentally friendly oil and gas power, nuclear power technologies provide a better solution to the energy shortage problem. China is actively involved in efforts to promote international cooperation, especially with the E.U. [53]

China plans to build thirty-two nuclear plants over the next fifteen years. With the new plants, the country's nuclear generating capacity will reach 40 gigawatts, or 4 percent of the national total. [54] Also, China mandated energy efficiency standards for the first time in urban construction. If effective, by 2020, the resource savings in the construction sector will approach the level of a moderately developed nation. It was reported that energy efficiency in building construction has been written into China's eleventh Five-Year Plan (2006–2010), which could save 50 percent or more in energy usage compared to the current level in many cities. [55]

The Chinese National Development and Reform Commission developed a plan to build thirty wind power projects of at least 100 megawatts of generating capacity each over the next five years, and wind farms of 1,000MW each will be established in Gansu, Hebei, Inner Mongolia, and Jiangsu. The plan aims to reduce energy consumption by 4 percent, cut emissions of major pollutants by 2 percent in 2006 and make the Yellow River Delta and the Three Gorges Dam region experimental sites for developing renewable energy industries. Meanwhile, the plan also addresses needs for continuing initiatives to control China's population at a level below 1.36 billion to limit energy demand. [56]

In addition, the southern provinces and regions of China recently established plans to import five million tons of coal from Vietnam over the next three to five years to ease energy shortages in the area. [57] All of these efforts demonstrate the national determination to meet its energy needs and solve pressing energy problems.

8. China's High-Tech Development

During the Fourth Plenum of the Tenth National People's Congress, Chinese Premier Wen Jiabao reported that the Chinese Central Government will invest US$71.6 billion in science and technology development, a 19.2 percent increase over 2005. This is the largest level of investment since establishment of the open door policy. He said: "China has already entered a phase that requires greater technological advancement and innovation to expand social and economic development."

By 2010, research and development investment will increase to 2 percent of GDP; and by 2020, the ratio will be increased to 2.5 percent or over US$900 billion. [58] In 2006, China began development of a Maglev train with a new advanced technology design. The Maglev train is a high-speed train that uses electromagnetic force. It is the world's first commercial application of a high-speed maglev line. The present Shanghai-Pudong line uses a German design. It can reach a top speed of 431 km/h or 268 mph and maintains an average speed of 250 km/h or 150 mph. Other maglev projects worldwide are being studied for feasibility. Scientific, economic, and political barriers and limitations have hindered the widespread adoption of this technology. [59] However, the first fast conventional line applying Chinese technology, known as the China Railway High-Speed, or CRH bullet train, which connects Shanghai and Hangzhou, began operations on January 28, 2007. It travels a distance of over a hundred miles with a speed of 120 miles an hour. It is now ready for the 2010 Shanghai World Expo. [60]

Other achievements in economic development in China include creation of a Silicon Valley at an enormous high-tech business park known as Zhongguancun. Brilliant young men and women flock to this

Beijing technology epicenter with ambitions not unlike those of American inventors Steve Jobs and Steve Wozniak who started the Apple computer in their garage decades ago.

There are now 17,000 high-tech companies in Zhongguancun registering a combined sales income of about US$60 billion in 2005. This constitutes one-seventh of the total income of all Chinese high-tech development zones. Sales include many hardware and software products. At the end of 2005, there were 620,000 people working in this Beijing Silicon Valley; seven thousand of them were Chinese students who returned after finishing their studies overseas. Zhongguancun expects to double its sales income to US$125 billion by 2010. [61]

Other significant advanced technology industries are located in Dongguang, Shenzhen in Guangdong Province, and Kunshan in Jiangsu Province along the coast.

Sixteen years ago, Kunshan was in decline as a small farming community. It lacked paved roads and industry. It was considered unimportant as an economic force by nearby Shanghai or Suzhou. Today, Kunshan is the strongest economic county in the PRC with an annual technical production over US$15 billion. This represents twice the output of the entire assembly production of Taiwan. Kunshan has an impressive growth rate of 30 percent per year because of the diligence and foresight of county officials over the past sixteen years. They worked ceaselessly without a single day off during the development period. The business card of the county mayor included his cell number so that he could be reached twenty-four hours a day.

Their working principles were:

- Treat merchants well, make them comfortable, and help them make money

- Provide effective, efficient and fair contracts, and services

- Provide quality health care and hospital services

This approach and tireless effort strengthened their competitiveness and efficiency. In the past, Taiwan controlled 85 percent of worldwide notebook PC production. In September 2005, Taiwan shut down its last production line and moved the notebook PC business to the Yangtze

River Delta region. Now the Yangtze River Delta region is the key manufacturing base for notebook PCs and cell phones.

Now Kunshan replaces Taiwan as a world leader in the manufacture of these electronic products. One of every three notebook PCs are produced at Kunshan. [62] Kunshan's success demonstrates that "As long as there is good leadership, there is opportunity for success."

Moreover, Internet users in China increased from a mere 1 million in 1998 to 110 million users in 2005, a hundred-fold increase in just seven years. In the near future, China will surpass the U.S. to become the largest market of Internet users. China is also expected to become the largest global producer and consumer of digital televisions, DTVs, and receivers by 2010. [63]

9. China's Foreign Policy

When the PRC was established in 1949, only eleven countries in the world recognized China and they were all communist countries. In 1971, the PRC replaced the ROC as a United Nations Security Council Member and the sole representative of China worldwide.

Along with the United Nations (U.N.), 169 countries of the 196 countries worldwide recognize the PRC as official China which also includes Taiwan. There are, however, only twenty-four countries with diplomatic relations with the ROC. These are primarily impoverished nations in need of aid. The Caribbean nation Grenada and Senegal in Africa resumed diplomatic ties with the PRC in 2005. [64]

Modern China is making every effort to improve relations with world nations and economies. In many ways, China views Singapore as a role model. Singapore successfully eliminated poverty within a short span of thirty years and developed a free economy while preserving traditional Chinese cultural values. The reason for using this model is a strong motivation to globalize and the desire to establish a government based on the rule of law.

Chinese leaders have become more proactive to change China's role and image in the international world community. They seek to expand the country's economic interests while minimizing rising international concerns about its growing power. Economic diplomacy, with energy and trade high on the agenda, has become a major diplomatic priority. China has reached out to the international community and is making substantial contributions. Even the Roman Catholic Holy See is considering reestablishing diplomatic relations with China, according to a top Vatican official. [65] The 2008 Olympic Games will he held in Beijing and the 2010 World Expo, also known as the "Economic Olympics," will be held in Shanghai. [66]

China intends to provide Asia and the world with international public goods which benefit most people. "Public goods" is an economic concept that is also used in international relations. The concept refers to universally understood intangible mechanisms, rules, systems, or ideas that can benefit all members of the international community. In the twenty-first century, China wants to further broaden its horizons and explore a new diplomacy that would enhance friendly cooperation with developing and developed nations, promote the construction of a regional cooperation mechanism, and establish a fair and harmonious world. This demonstrates that China is a responsible nation. [67] Chinese diplomatic relations with Japan and the U.S. are discussed separately in Chapter V.

China's current foreign policy initiatives in Asian countries concentrate mainly on increasing trade. China has fourteen neighboring countries: Afghanistan, Bhutan, Burma, India, Kazakhstan, Kyrgyzstan, Laos, Mongolia, Nepal, North Korea, Pakistan, Russia, Tajikistan, and Vietnam. China works closely with these border countries and other countries in Southeast Asia to promote regional cooperation. China wants to enhance stability, neighborliness, and mutual trust to ensure peace and prosperity for all these nations. The idea of building a harmonious world is actually an extension of the concept of a harmonious society at home that originated with Confucianism.

Chinese President Hu Jintao called for the building of a harmonious Asia of enduring peace and common prosperity at the second summit of the Conference on Interaction and Confidence Building Measures in Asia in June 2006 at Almaty, Kazakhstan. The organization now comprises seventeen members and has many nations as observers. Its first summit was held in Almaty in June, 2002. "Asia is crucial for China's development," Hu said. He also stressed that the Forum has become a platform where different nations and cultures can have a dialogue and seek mutual understanding. [68]

In the following, China's historic ties to other nations are presented starting in the north:

i) China-Mongolia Relationship: In the thirteenth century, China was conquered by the Mongolian hero Gengiskhan from the north. The Chinese Great Wall was originally constructed as a defense barrier in the seventh century B.C. by the vassal states under the Zhou Dynasty in the northern parts of the country. After the Qin Dynasty unified China in 221 B.C., it joined the gaps in the walls to hold off the invaders from the Xiongnu (Mongol) tribes from the north. The Wall was renovated from time to time. A major renovation started with the founding of the Ming Dynasty in the fourteenth century and took 200 years to complete. The Wall we see today is almost exactly the result of this effort. In the past, Mongolia was part of China. It is located between Russia and China and became independent in 1921 amid internal power struggles. In 1991 the Mongols prevailed, winning freedom after decades of Soviet dominance.

Today, the Mongolian government favors democratic rule. Nearly half of the 2.5 million population are nomadic herders. Mongolia has deep economic ties with China. Forty-eight percent of its foreign trade is with China. China buys 99.9 percent of its copper mineral imports from Mongolia. In addition, Mongolia exports other raw materials to China and bilateral trading has benefited both nations greatly. [69] The Mongolian leaders know they need Beijing and that Chinese growth supports Mongolia financially.

ii) China-Russia Relationship: China and Russia experienced border tensions for more than forty years, including a brief border war in 1969. The two countries share a 2,580 mile (4,300-kilometer) long boundary. They signed two border agreements in 1991 and 1994 respectively. The agreements delimit the eastern and western sections of the boundary line, leaving only two disputed areas of land in the eastern section requiring further resolution.

By October 4, 2004, the two nations signed a complete boundary delimitation agreement and put an end to forty years of negotiations. The terms specify that the disputed land is to be shared on a fifty-fifty basis.

The disputed land includes a group of islands totaling 375 square kilometers. The China-Russia partnership has recently entered a very important stage of development. Since the two countries set up a strategic partnership for cooperation in 1996, much progress has been made in strengthening political ties and cooperation in energy and security matters.

Russia is impressed with economic development in China and believes that China has shown that a nation can establish a viable market economy without a political plurality. Both nations want to leave the problems of the past behind and continue to engage in constructive and pragmatic dialogue to increase closer ties. On July 1, 2005, China and Russia issued a joint statement on a new world order in the twenty-first century. In it they set forth their common position on major international issues such as U.N. reforms, globalization, North-South cooperation, the world economy, and trade. Both Beijing and Moscow have repeatedly pledged commitment to a "multi-polar world" and warn other nations about attempts to dominate global affairs and interfere in the internal affairs of sovereign nations. The two countries conducted a successful first joint military drill in the Yellow Sea in August 2005.

A second round of the Sino-Russia Strategic Security Talks involved negotiations on issues related to anti-terrorism and anti-proliferation of nuclear weapons, as part of the Shanghai Cooperation Organization (SCO). [70] Both sides issued a joint communiqué in November 2005 pledging to deepen cooperation for mutual benefit in diverse fields. [71–72]

Russia surpassed Saudi Arabia as the world largest oil exporter in 2006. It was the main supplier of oil to China that year providing a total of fifteen million tons (about 55 million barrels) of crude oil via rail links. [73]

Russia President Vladimir Putin and Chinese President Hu Jintao met in Beijing in 2006 for the fifth time in a year to sign fifteen agreements. Both sides pledged to boost energy links as follows: Russian gas giant Gazprom and China's biggest energy firm, CNPC, signed a memorandum to build two gas pipelines to western and eastern China, which would start deliveries in approximately five years. [74]

By 2030, one-third of Chinese energy imports will come from Russia. China-Russia trade volume in 2005 increased by 37.1 percent over 2004, and in 2006 increased by 14.77 percent over 2005 to reach US$33.4 billion. Russia is now the eighth largest trading partner of China. [75] In 2006, China and Russia forged strong cooperative agreements marking new milestones in the fields of investment, energy, and strategic partnership. [76] In 2007, Chinese leader Hu Jintao visited Russia on March 26–28, and signed a US$4 billion trade agreement. Both nations signed a joint statement to further deepen their cooperation. [77] The relationship between the two nations has reached a historic high point. Russia plans to export thirty billion cubic meters (about 1,060 Bcf) of natural gas annually and complete construction of a gas pipeline that will go through Xinjiang Province of China. This oil pipeline will reach the north-eastern region of China. [78]

iii) China-Kyrgyzstan and China-Kazakhstan Relationships: For many years China neglected its relationship with Central Asia. Today, in order to secure energy resources, great attention is focused on this region. China and Central Asia are building a stable market to jointly explore energy resources.

From China to Central Asia, a new Silk Road is gradually developing; the extensive oil pipelines, highways, and railways are replacing the ancient camel caravans in enhancing trade—the Silk Road is becoming the Energy Road. China established a territorial boundary agreement in 1999 with Kyrgyzstan and Kazakhstan based on earlier agreements signed with these two countries in 1996 and 1994, respectively.

In the meantime, China and Kyrgyzstan will adhere to the existing Sino-Kyrgyz agreement known as the Good-Neighborly Treaty of Friendship and Cooperation and other bilateral documents to boost bilateral cooperation politics, trade and economy, and culture. [79] Both sides reached broad consensus on economic and trade cooperation, mutual trust, security, energy resources, education, and cultural exchanges within the multilateral framework of the U.N. and the SCO.

The China-Kazakhstan partnership completed a land oil pipeline that connects to another that runs from Kazakhstan to China's Urumqi City in Xinjiang Province. Later, it will be extended through the Gansu Corridor to Lanzhou City in Gansu Province. When this west to east oil pipeline is completed in China, it will eliminate previous railway transportation and provide crude and refined oil not only within Xinjiang, but also Gansu Province and through other pipelines to eastern and south-western regions in China. [80]

Crude oil from Kazakhstan poured into China in May 2006. The pipeline, extending 578 miles from Atasu in Kazakhstan to the Alataw Pass of Xinjiang, was completed in November 2005. It is designed to transmit twenty million tons of oil annually. In 2005, China imported 4.78 million barrels of crude oil from Kazakhstan via Alataw Pass. It is predicted that the figure will climb to 17.46 million barrels in 2006 and around 29.41 million barrels in 2008. [81]

iv) China-Pakistan and China-India Relationships: Prior to independence from British colonization in 1947, Pakistan was part of the Muslim League of India. Since then China and Pakistan have established a very close strategic military relationship in addition to economic cooperation. Pakistan reported that the two countries are engaging in a broad energy resource cooperation agreement which includes nuclear power plants to generate electricity. China and Pakistan will establish a more detailed five-year plan on collaboration for a nuclear electrical power plant.

In addition, China and Pakistan will build oil pipelines from Pakistan to ship oil via India or directly from Pakistan into China. This pipeline is a long-term project and completion of the Qinghai-Tibet Rail has created the necessary conditions for shipping oil from ground pipes in Pakistan into areas of need in China.

Following the severe 2005 earthquake in Pakistan, China announced a loan of US$300 million to fund reconstruction and rehabilitation plans in devastated areas. Both countries also celebrated the fifty-fifth anniversary of the establishment of diplomatic ties and were ready to promote further mutually beneficial cooperative agreements, and exchange views on international and regional issues of common concern. [82]

Economic progress in China and India is viewed worldwide as a sign of the rising importance of Asia. India is the second largest country in the world with a population of 1 billion, second only to China. China and India represent the largest communist and democratic countries in the world, respectively. Both are developing countries that face similar economic, social, and development challenges.

India was a British colony until 1947 and its border with China was unclear due to arbitrary demarcation of the McMahon Line laid down in

1914 by Sir Arthur Henry McMahon, the colonial British plenipotentiary. The two countries fought a brief border war in this region in 1962 and there were several border clashes in 1967, 1986, and 1987. [83] Talks held in 1993 and 1995 eased tensions along the China-India border through mutual agreement to honor the existing demarcation until formal talks are held to resolve existing differences.

Border troops on both sides have been reduced by nearly 80 percent to improve relations. New Delhi disputes Beijing's rule over a vast area of uninhabited land on the Tibetan plateau, which China seized during the war, whereas China claims 32,400 square miles of territory located primarily in the Indian northeastern province of Arunachal Pradesh, which borders Tibet. [84] China and India have scheduled a new round of talks and a deadline to resolve border disputes. [85] China and India agreed on June 18, 2006, to reopen border trade at Nathu La Pass— which was closed for forty-four years—on July 6, 2006. [86] The resumption of border trade was a historic event, which not only enlarged trade, but also enhanced improved relations between two great countries.

The two countries signed a memorandum of agreement for energy resource cooperation that includes oil exploitation, building oil refineries, and the improvement of production efficiency. [87] Both sides are eager to revive the centuries-old Himalayan trade route by setting up infrastructure on both sides of the border. [88] The two economies are complimentary and are drawn to each others' huge markets. Their trade volume is rising fast, reaching US$18 billion in 2005, up from US$13.6 billion in 2004 and US$3 billion in 2001. [89]

China is the second largest trade partner of India, followed by the U.S. Bilateral trade volume is predicted to reach US$20 billion in 2007. [90] For the most part, China imports agricultural products from India, and India imports electronic products from China. The India-U.S. trade volume of US$22 billion in 2004 was much smaller than the China-U.S. trade volume of US$231 billion in the same year.

India is strong in the computer software and information technology industries. India aims to hire over two thousand Chinese computer engineers over the next two years to make China a global research and development center for Indian companies. Recently, Chinese telecom equipment companies, like Hua Wei Technology Co., Ltd. in Shenzhen, hired 700 Indian software engineers for its staff of 8,000 people to enter the Indian market. Now Chinese products are everywhere in India. [91]

With rapid economic development in China and India and increasing demand for energy resources, effective interdependent relationships become more important, since most of China's oil imports are shipped through the Indian Ocean over a distance of 3,000 miles. India would like to get oil from Russia by building oil pipelines through western China, in order to protect and secure their oil imports.

President George W. Bush advocates a civilian nuclear accord with India, and the U.S. House of Representatives provided overwhelming support of this nuclear cooperation agreement. [92] It permits India to continue development of nuclear weapons, despite critics who regard the pact as representative of a double standard vis à vis U.S. nuclear policy towards other nations, which could also undermine the Nuclear non-Proliferation Treaty (NPT). [93] Although President Bush refutes this position, other experts believe the agreement was made with the intention of containing China. In response to U.S-India nuclear cooperation, Chinese Foreign Ministry spokesman Liu Jianchao said, "Relevant cooperation should abide by international regulations, and contribute to the international efforts of non-proliferation." [94]

On July 9, 2006, India tested its first long-range missile, the Agni III, designed to carry nuclear warheads capable of crossing the entire landmass of the mainland of China, much of Asia and the Middle East. This occurred five days after the Pyongyang missile test. [95] Nonetheless, the Agni III test was unsuccessful.

The Indian media stated bluntly that the intended target of the missile launch was Pakistan and China. [96] This allegation was vigorously denied by the Indian government. It was reported further by the media that top U.S. general, Peter Pace, approved the test during his visit to India in June 2006. These events illustrate a U.S. double standard regarding nuclear testing reflected in its opposition to North Korean and Iranian nuclear development activities. North Korea and the Iranian governments are considered threats to U.S. national security whereas India is viewed as an ally.

Experts believe that completion of the Qinghai-Tibet railway will produce dramatic positive changes in the current China-India relationship. In addition, the effectiveness of Indian diplomacy in South Asia is dependent, to a large degree, on its relationship with China. China, for example, has become the largest trading partner with Bangladesh and also has deep political and military relationships with both Pakistan and Burma.

v) China-Vietnam Relationship: During the Vietnam War (1965–1973), China supported Communist North Vietnam in its fight against the U.S. which backed South Vietnam. After the war, North Vietnam unified the whole country and the China-Vietnam relationship deteriorated when Vietnam invaded Cambodia. Further, the two nations had a brief border clash in 1979. By 1991, diplomatic relations were reestablished. Vietnam and Cambodia adopted communist political systems, but implemented free market economic reforms.

Vietnam used China as a model in formulating plans for economic development. In Ho Chi Minh City, the Chinese imprint is everywhere from the Chinese-style temple to promotional signs in stores and TV soap operas. Vietnam benefited from China's experience as it prepared to join the WTO. Historically, Chinese influence is deep in Vietnam and includes a profound mutual understanding of cultures and values.

In November 2005, China and Vietnam agreed to speed up the process of land border demarcation and work closely to ensure completion of a new border administration document by 2008. Both countries value the agreement signed with major oil companies from China, Vietnam, and the Philippines to jointly exploit the oil and gas resources in the South China Sea. China and Vietnam pledged to abide by the principles contained in the Declaration on the Conduct of Parties in the South China Sea to safeguard stability in the area. The document between China and the Association of Southeast Asian Nations (ASEAN) was signed on November 4, 2002, in Phnom Penh of Cambodia. [97] The two countries plan to increase high-level exchanges—military, economic, and trade cooperation—so that by 2010 its bilateral trade volume will reach US$10 billion. [98]

The Vietnamese media reported that the Beijing government is now providing Vietnam with a loan of US$1 billion to support economic development. China and Vietnam also agreed to speed up a joint oil gas exploration project. China is now the biggest trading partner of Vietnam and was its number one import market and third biggest export market in 2005. Vietnam does not view China as a threat. Rather, it regards China as a rare market opportunity and wishes to ride this "Orient Express" to develop its own economy.

vi) China-South Korea Relationship: South Korea was a Japanese colony from 1910–1945. But at the end of World War II, Korea was split into the Democratic People's Republic of Korea (DPRK) in the north and the Republic of Korea (ROK) in the south. The thirty-eighth parallel was established as the general demarcation line. South Korea is governed under a democratic political system while North Korea is governed by a communist political system and dictatorship. China established diplomatic relations with North and South Korea in 1949 and 1992, respectively. North and South Korea remain officially at war because the 1950–53 Korean War ended in a cease-fire, not a peace treaty.

Although territorial issues in the areas around the Yellow Sea remain unsettled, China and South Korea have determined not to address these at present. For a number of decades, South Korea defined itself primarily as a U.S. ally, with its principal enemy to the north. Presently, South Korea is indicating interest in more cooperation with North Korea and is seeking to enhance its position in Asia through stronger economic ties with China. For over a decade, the relationship between China and South Korea has undergone a transformation. Today, South Koreans are truly fascinated by Chinese economic progress and evolution.

In 2004, China surpassed the U.S. to become the number one trading partner of South Korea. This relationship has been a critical element in its economic recovery since the late 1990s. The two countries now are close partners in many key areas including education, trade, and investment. Bilateral trade between Seoul and Beijing reached US$90 billion in 2004, a 42 percent increase from 2003. [99] South Korea's trade surplus with China, including Taiwan and Hong Kong, has been soaring in recent years. Both countries decided to promote close economic and cultural ties to develop a comprehensive partnership. China and South Korea share many common interests and concerns. Currently, there is a serious shared concern regarding nuclear proliferation on the Korean Peninsula.

Chinese Premier Wen Jiabao met with South Korea President Roh Moo-Hyun in Helsinki, Finland, at the sixth biennial summit of the Asia-Europe Meeting, where he advocated the development of a deeper relationship between the two nations. Wen Jiabao stated that the reason for the sensitivities on the Korea Peninsula nuclear issue is the residual effect of the Cold War. Long-term antagonism has led to profound distrust. In order to resolve the problem, patience is required and dialogue is critical to the resolution of differences. [100]

vii) China-North Korea Relationship: This relationship is complicated by the Korean Peninsula nuclear crisis. China is rapidly increasing its investment in North Korea and helping the communist DPRK to find a "Chinese way" to develop: namely, increasing economic openness without sacrificing political control. In 2003, China invested only US$1.1 million in North Korea. In 2004, investment jumped to US$50 million; and in 2005, it reached US$85-90 million. China is now its largest foreign trading partner.

North Korea has the fourth-largest army in the world. It has an estimated 1.2 million armed personnel for a total population of 22.7 million. After the Korean War, North Korea deployed the bulk of its forces along the demilitarized zone (DMZ), which is approximately twenty-five miles from Seoul, the South Korean capital. During the Cold War era, South Korea and the U.S. fought North Korea, which was allied with Russia and China in the Korean War. The U.S. imposed a total embargo on trade with North Korea in June 1950 when the war started. Both camps suffered severe casualties. The war ended in 1953 with a cease-fire agreement. Since 1989, the U.S. eased sanctions against North Korea. China has been a strong ally of North Korea and provided vital economic support to its government.

North Korea operates under a centrally-planned economy. Its infrastructure is generally poor and outdated. Both the U.S. and the Korean Peninsula Energy Development Organization placed an embargo against North Korea because of its nuclear weapons program. China, South Korea, and international non-governmental organizations have helped North Korea with food, fertilizer, and investments. China also provides energy resource assistance to North Korea.

North Korea joined the NPT as a non-nuclear weapons state in

1985, but has violated the NPT by declaring that it has manufactured nuclear weapons. Pyongyang shocked Tokyo and other nations in 1998 when it test-fired a ballistic missile over Northern Japan. It has since test-fired short-range missiles many times. In President George W. Bush's famous "axis of evil" speech in 2002, he identified a triad of threats from Iraq, Iran, and North Korea as the three most pressing post–9/11 challenges facing the U.S. [101, 102]

North Korea withdrew from the NPT and threw out inspectors from the International Atomic Energy Agent (IAEA) in 2003. This occurred as American forces were flowing towards the Middle East in January of that year. It is likely North Korea produced enough fuel for six or more nuclear weapons since then.

During the administration of President William J. Clinton, U.S. government negotiations with North Korea led to a moratorium on nuclear weapons development. Namely, the North Koreans agreed not to fire any more missiles while the talks continued. North Korea made it clear then that they were willing to stop, if the U.S. would compensate them financially because such support was a principal source of foreign income. However, the U.S. has been unwilling to do this. Still, the Clinton administration provided foreign aid including food and oil to North Korea. [103]

After President George W. Bush took office, the U.S. government took a hard line approach on the North Korean weapons program. In response, North Korea resumed missile tests. DPRK broke the agreed upon the Framework Accord signed in 1994 under President Clinton, with the explanation that President George W. Bush abandoned Clinton's promise, voiding the basic tenets of the agreement. Another short-range missile was test fired on March 8, 2006. [104]

The U.S. refused to engage in bilateral talks with North Korea on the grounds that the U.S. was already committed to multilateral talks that would include South Korea and China. [105] China has played the role of mediator in the six-party talks in pushing for a peaceful resolution of the nuclear proliferation issue as follows:

Although the Chinese army fought together with North Korean soldiers during the Korean War, the DPRK leaders gradually turned to Russia after the war and were distant in relations with China. North

Korean dictator, Kim Jong II implemented a strange diplomacy that kept Beijing at a distance. Kim Jong II was involved in the kidnapping, murder, and starvation of his own people. Many of his actions have been called war crimes by legal experts. Beijing was not aware of the nuclear issue initially and was not involved in it either. In time, Kim Jong II restarted the nuclear program and the U.S. asked China to help by exerting its influence on North Korea to desist.

The hosting of the six-party talks by China forces the U.S. and the DPRK to sit at the negotiating table to work towards a peaceful solution of the Korean Peninsula nuclear dispute. North Korea agreed to three-party talks with the U.S. and China in Beijing in April 2003. The first round of six-party talks was with the U.S., China, South Korea, Japan, and Russia in August 2003 in Beijing. North Korea agreed to the eventual elimination of its nuclear programs if the U.S. were first willing to sign a bilateral non-aggression treaty and meet various other conditions.

China hosted a second round of six-party talks in Beijing in February 2004. The U.S. saw the results as positive. Later, in the third round of the talks, the U.S. tabled a comprehensive, substantive proposal aimed at resolving the nuclear issue. All parties agreed to hold a fourth round of talks by the end of September 2004. However, the DPRK refused to return to the table and later declared it had manufactured nuclear weapons and was indefinitely suspending its participation in the six-party talks. Following intense diplomatic efforts, the fourth round of six-party talks was held in Beijing over a period of twenty days from July to September 2005. China opposed economic sanctions proposed by the U.S. fearing arousal of unnecessary tensions among the parties and made extensive efforts in negotiations to resolve disagreements in the talks. Ramon Myers, a Senior Research Fellow with the Hoover Institution, a think tank on the campus of Stanford University, commented that China not only played an important role in the six-party talks, but also accomplished a major diplomatic victory by pushing North Korea to guarantee the surrender of its nuclear program. [106]

In the end, all parties agreed to a Joint Statement of Principles to unanimously reaffirm the goal of verifiable denuclearization of the

Korean Peninsula in a peaceful manner. The DPRK agreed, for the first time, to abandon all nuclear weapons and existing nuclear programs and to return, at an early date, to the NPT and IAEA safeguards in exchange for energy aid and security guarantees. The fifth round of six-party talks was scheduled to be held again in Beijing on November 9–11, 2005, to outline details, means, and procedures for the implementation of the joint statement adopted in September 2005.

However, the six-party talks were suspended after the fourth round meeting, because North Korea and the U.S. lost confidence in each other. Chinese leader Hu Jintao invited Kim Jong II for an eight-day visit to China in early 2006, and tried to tell Kim that "nuclear extortion" will not help eliminate poverty. Both China and South Korea are worried about a potential collapse of North Korea, and each continues to supply the country with food, energy, and other resources. North Korea declared that as a sovereign nation, it has the right to launch missiles.

North Korea criticized Japan for having gradually violated the Japan-DPRK Pyongyang Declaration which was signed to confirm shared recognition of the importance of a fruitful political, economic, and cultural relationship between Japan and the DPRK. For example, Japan launched surveillance satellites, changed the exchange rate which adversely affected North Korea and prohibited specific ships from entering their harbors. North Korea also accused the U.S. of exerting military pressure on North Korea and criticized Pyongyang's human rights record.

Despite strong warnings coming from Washington, North Korea test-launched its long-range ballistic missile Taepodong-2 on July 4, 2006. It failed some forty seconds after lift-off. This test was followed by the launch of short-range and medium-range Nodong missiles that fell in the Sea of Japan. [107] Subsequently, North Korea launched four more missiles for a total of seven missiles that night. The Taepodong-2 has a possible range of 3,500 to 4,300 km, which has the potential to strike areas of the U.S. The Nodong missiles with a 1,300 kilometer range are capable of striking any target in the Korean Peninsula as well as nearly all of Japan. [108] North Korea threatened an annihilating strike, if the U.S. military attacked its nuclear facilities preemptively. In addition, North Korea warned Japan that any economic sanctions would be considered a declaration of war. North Korea threatened to continue to launch missiles aimed at pressuring Washington to make concessions.

It would be embarrassing for the U.S., if North Korea's long-range ballistic missile test succeeded without interception by the U.S. national missile defense (NMD) system. The NMD system costs about US$9 billion annually and is in early stages of development. Weakness in the U.S. defense system would be exposed. Japan is collaborating with the U.S. on similar systems designed to shoot down missiles after launch.

How should the U.S. and international community handle North Korea? Pyongyang was unhappy that China and Russia supported the U.N. resolution. However, given its economic and diplomatic relationship, Pyongyang understands that it needs Chinese and Russian support and mediation, and eventually must conform to the rules of international diplomacy.

North Korean missile tests have created new challenges for the resolution of nuclear issues on the Korean Peninsula and complicated regional and other international relationships. China has played an important role in negotiation with the U.S., North Korea, Japan and other nations to mediate the North Korean issue. Its biggest concern is that DPRK nuclear proliferation may induce other countries like Japan and Taiwan to develop nuclear weapons and destabilize the Asia-Pacific region.

Finally, North Korea conducted its first nuclear test on October 9, 2006. This event alarmed the international community as it represented a potential threat to stability in the Asia-Pacific region. Pyongyang's nuclear test has challenged the diplomatic skills of all the parties involved in the six-party talks, including China. The world must recognize that sanctions will not succeed in North Korea, since it is already the most isolated country in the world; a positive incentive rather than a punishment may be what the U.S. must use to entice Kim Jong II to return to the negotiating table. [109]

After painstaking mediations, and bilateral discussions between North Korea and the U.S. representatives in Berlin and New York, the long-delayed fifth-round of the six-party talks were held in Beijing starting from February 8, 2007. On February 13, 2007, North Korea agreed to shut down its main nuclear reactor and eventually dismantle its atomic weapons program. The draft accord basically followed the Clinton-era deal of the "Agreed Framework." Key points are summarized as follows:

[110]

Within sixty days North Korea will:

- Shut down and seal its nuclear facilities at Yongbyon and invite U.N. nuclear agency staff to monitor and verify procedures and processes

- Start bilateral talks with the U.S. and with Japan on moving to full diplomatic ties

Within sixty days the U.S. will:

- Release US$25 million of North Korean's funds held in Banco Delta Asia Bank in Macau

- Begin steps to remove North Korea from the list of state sponsors of terrorism

- Start providing energy aid, with China, Russia, and South Korea, equal to 50,000 tons (about 183,800 barrels) of fuel oil

Under the second phase:

- The four nations and Japan will supply aid equal to a further 950,000 tons (about 3.49 million barrels) in return for North Korea declaring all nuclear programs ended and facilities disabled.

viii) China and the Middle East: China is attentive to activities in the Middle East and is concerned about peace and stability in the region. Nations in the Middle East have unique historical traditions, religious beliefs, and cultures. China believes that any action taken by a foreign nation in the region should promote peace and help resolve the difficult issues to facilitate peace, stability, and development. China respects the wishes of the people and nations in the region and wishes to provide effective support that could help mitigate clashes such as longstanding tensions between Israel and Palestine. China has proposed peaceful methods and political negotiations, and hopes Israel and Palestine will continue to abide by U.N. resolutions which include the principle of using land in exchange for peace. China is Israel's largest trade partner in Asia and Israel is China's third largest export market in the Middle East.

China has pleaded for mutual respect towards different cultures in the Middle East. On the Iraq issue, China strongly supports the unity, sovereignty, and independence of this nation. China encourages dialogue among different ethnic groups and advocates reconstruction to stabilize the nation.

China and Iran are on the verge of signing agreements to collaborate on energy resources valued at an estimated US$100 billion. The total trade volume of the two countries increased from US$1.2 billion in 1998 to US$10 billion in 2005. In the near future, China will become Iran's number one trading partner. In January 2006, Iran moved ahead of Saudi Arabia to become the largest oil exporter to China. As a result of joint exploitation of resources in the Yadavaran natural gas field, Iran is projected to export 404 million barrels of liquefied natural gas, worth US$20 billion to China over the next twenty-five years. [111]

China intends to work with the international community including the U.N. to resolve the Iranian nuclear issue. Iran is an observer of the SCO. Iran began its nuclear program in the 1950s with U.S. assistance. After the 1979 Islamic revolution, the U.S. halted support for the Iran nuclear program. An eight-year war between Iraq and Iran followed suppressing nuclear development ambitions. In 1993, Russia helped revive Iran's nuclear program. With mediation from Germany, Britain and France, Iran joined the NPT in 2003. [112]

When Iran announced that it was ready to restart nuclear research in January 2006, there was a strong negative response worldwide. Iran's violation of the NPT regulations which conflicts with the U.S. Middle Eastern plans was objected to strenuously by Israel, Arab nations, and Sunni-dominated Islamic countries. However, the Iranian leadership believes they are being held to a different standard than India and Pakistan since these two countries succeeded in conducting nuclear tests in May 1998. However, neither India nor Pakistan has called for the destruction of Israel as Iran did. The Iranian government argued that they should have an equal right to develop nuclear weapons for the purpose of self-defense. It is apparent that the U.S. imposes a double standard in this matter which has strengthened President Mahmoud Ahmadinejad's determination to go forward with his own nuclear plan. Iran stated that its fear of attack from the U.S. and Israel prompted its decision to with-hold nuclear information from the IAEA. [113]

Representatives of six nations, Britain, China, France, Germany, Russia, and the U.S., met in London on January 16, 2006, for seven hours to express serious concern regarding nuclear proliferation. In order to win international support and avoid censure by the U.N. Security Council, Iran proposed a resumption of nuclear talks with the Europeans and proposed continued cooperation with the IAEA. To defuse the crisis, the next day, a Chinese Foreign Ministry spokesman said that Beijing favored diplomacy and urged all sides to remain patient and make every effort to resume negotiations among the Europeans and Iran.

Previously, Russia offered Iran the option of allowing it to enrich Iranian uranium on Russian soil under strict controls to prevent any feared diversion to a weapons program. [114]. But, this proposal was rejected. "As long as you make one exception you open the way for logi-cal arguments of why him and not me," Foreign Minister Prince Saud Al Faisal of Saudi Arabia said, and "The West in allowing Israel to establish its nuclear capability has done the damage." [115] In February, the IAEA's thirty-five-nation board put the U.N. Security Council on alert about Iran's nuclear program. On March 3, 2006, Iran and the E.U. began talks. Efforts were made to reach a compromise that would allow Iran to run a small scale uranium enrichment program after re-imposing a freeze of Iran's nuclear activities indefinitely to rebuild international trust.

Russia and China persuaded the U.S. to soften its position. [116–117] Western powers offered a six-nation (as listed above) package of economic and energy incentives in exchange for halting enrichment of uranium in June and July of 2006. [118] China called on world powers to exercise restraint in the dispute to avoid a further escalation of tensions. [119] Nonetheless, Iran ruled out responding to international incentives to suspend its nuclear program, replying that the offer contained too many ambiguities that must be removed first in order to have serious talks. [120] The six nations pressed for an agreement before the July Group of Eight Summit in Russia. After Iran's refusal, Russia and China agreed to join the U.S. and Europe in seeking a U.N. Security Council resolution ordering a freeze of its nuclear activities or face sanctions. [121]

On August 2, Iran's President Ahmadinejad said that Iran was still considering the package offered by the six nations in early June that includes economic incentives. [122–123] But on August 6, 2006, Iran's security chief and top nuclear negotiator Ali Larijani condemned the West and said that it had engaged in double-dealing, by first offering a package of incentives in exchange of suspension of Iran's nuclear-enrichment program, and then by issuing a threat; hence, Iran would ignore the U.N. deadline on the uranium program. [124] Iran warned on August 13, 2006, that it would withdraw from the IAEA, if it is deprived of its "inalienable rights." [125]

As expected, on August 22, 2006, Tehran rejected suspension of its nuclear activities as demanded by the U.N. Security Council, proposed a "new formula for resolving the issue through talks, but the details of the new formula were not yet known." [126] Although the U.N. Security Council 1696 Resolution calls for sanctions if Iran does not stop its uranium enrichment activities, most countries in the world prefer to resolve the Iranian nuclear issue politically. [127] China continues to insist on diplomatic resolutions of the current Iran nuclear crisis for two reasons: first, sanctions are political tactics used by hegemonies; second, China has made a significant investment and naturally has strong energy interests in Iran. At the same time, China does not wish to destroy its relationship with the U.S. or risk diplomatic isolation. In short, China is working vigorously to become an important and respected member of the international community despite its self-interest in energy resources. China is caught between Iran's rigid position and increased Western pressure on Tehran.

On March 24, 2007, the U.N. Security Council voted unanimously to adopt Resolution 1747 that bans all Iranian arms exports and freezes some of the financial assets linked to Iran's military and nuclear agencies. [128] Following Iran's immediate rejection of the resolution, Russia brought its nuclear experts in Iran home. U.S. soldiers deployed to the Gulf reached 170,000, almost the same number as at the beginning of the Iraq War, and a French navy aircraft carrier joined three of the U.S. aircraft carriers near the waters of Iran. [129] All signs were pointing in the direction that a peaceful resolution of this nuclear issue will not be in sight soon.

ix) China-Africa Relationship: The year 2006 marks the fiftieth anniversary of ties between China and Africa. China's renewed interest in African countries revives their close historic relationship. Egypt was the first African nation to establish diplomatic relations with China at the ambassadorial level fifty years ago. Since then, China has established diplomatic relations with forty-seven African countries. [130] Following much time and international turbulence, China and most African nations have become closely collaborated nations.

China's African policy has three characteristics: 1) political friendship and equality; 2) economic cooperation; and 3) mutual understanding and support on world issues. "China will establish a new type of strategic partnership characterized by political equality and mutual trust, economic win-win cooperation, and frequent cultural exchange," said Lu Guozeng, Chinese Assistant Foreign Minister. [131] Lu said in a press briefing of Beijing's African policy paper that "Chinese enterprise investment and development in Africa has strong potential because Africa is abundant in natural resources which are urgently needed for Chinese economic development, " and further, "The two sides are highly complementary to each other." [132]

China and Africa will step up cooperative agreements in four areas: politics, economics, trade, education, and international affairs. [133] China is developing a new strategic partnership with African countries to share energy and material resources; to become mutually complementary and beneficial.

Egypt hopes that China will become its biggest trade partner in 2010. In addition, China deepened cooperation in energy and trade with Sudan, Namibia, South Africa, and Tanzania. [134] China and Zambia signed cooperative agreements on the economy and technology in December 2005. Their diplomatic relationship dates back to 1964. [135] The Tunisian Ambassador to China, Mohamed Sahbi Basly, highly praised its Sino-African friendship and cooperation in politics, economy, culture, and social development. [136]

When interviewed by the press, the Angolan Ambassador to China, Joao Bernardo, stated that China's African Policy Paper, which highlights Chinese aid to Africa "without any political conditions," is a reliable document giving strength and courage to the African people. [137] Cooperation with Angola is mutually beneficial and "China's development does not represent any special threat to the world, but rather serves as a model for African development and prosperity," added Ambassador Bernardo. Many Africans can now afford to buy bicycles and motorcycles made in China to improve their daily living standard.

China benefits from raw materials available in Africa, and the many nations on the continent need cheaper products made available by China. However, there are deeper political objectives: China wishes to strengthen its relationship with African nations since their political support of another developing country is very important, especially in the U.N. African people view China as a role model since China was poor, but is now rapidly developing. African nations want to collaborate with China and learn how China is developing so quickly.

By November 2006, while the two-way trade volume between Africa and China rocketed from US$4 billion in 1995 to some US$40 billion in 2005, the investment volume was relatively low. Leaders discussed how to raise mutual investments. According to statistics from the Ministry of Commerce, total Chinese investment in Africa has reached US$6.27 billion. Over 800 projects were launched in forty-nine African countries which include trade, manufacturing and processing, resource development, communications, and agriculture. [138]

China is now the third largest trade partner of the African nations behind the U.S. and France. The current trade volume of about US$40 billion is increasing continuously and is not limited to oil and minerals. China is investing capital technology and manpower in Africa. In addition, China is building hospitals and railways in Angola, highways and bridges in Sudan and Kenya, water dams in Libya and Ethiopia, and telecommunication infrastructure in Zimbabwe and Ghana. [139] China has consolidated its relationship with African countries whether or not these countries possess oil or other strategic mineral resources. African leaders welcome their booming trade links with China, but critics accuse Beijing of dealing with repressive regimes. Beijing's response is that it is just doing business and has no political agenda.

In the past, Western nations including the Belgians, British, French, Germans, Italians, Portuguese, and Spanish colonized Africa to exploit resources. They imposed their own systems of government and enslaved Africans. Later when the colonizers left, many African nations were in a dilapidated state with corrupt governments and destabilized social structures.

China has lifted 300 million Chinese people out of poverty in the past twenty to thirty years according to World Bank data and its approach can be adopted by the African nations.

In 2006, China provided US$8 billion in loans to African nations, which was twice the amount provided by the U.S. Total U.S. aid to Africa was US$4.2 billion in 2005. [140] China will train 15,000 African experts and provides scholarships to 4,000 African students for studying in China. [141] China has made substantial contributions to the economies of African nations.

x) China-Arab Relationship: The year 2006 marks the fiftieth anniversary of China-Arab friendship. Some sixty Chinese journalists and scholars traveled on a cultural expedition to twenty Arab countries to promote the China-Arabian non-government exchange activities. [142]

Chinese President Hu Jintao promoted a three-point proposal to cement ties between China and Jordan. "We are willing to work closely with China to build consensus and facilitate exchange and cooperation in the spheres of politics, economy, culture, education, and energy," according to Jordanian King Abdullah II Bin Al-Hussein while visiting Beijing. [143] China plans to increase dialogue with the Organization of the Petroleum Exporting Countries, in order to contribute to the stability of the world oil market. Cooperation with oil-rich Kuwait on oil exploitation could deepen energy cooperation to achieve a mutually beneficial result. [144]

On January 23, 2006, Chinese leader Hu Jintao made a four-point proposal to Saudi Arabian King Abdullah bin Abdul-Aziz al-Saud in Beijing on furthering bilateral relations. A protocol on bilateral cooperation in petroleum, natural gas, and minerals was signed as well as several other cooperative documents concerning the economy and the training of professionals. [145]

Saudi Arabia is now China's biggest trade partner in West Asia and North Africa, and has become its second largest oil provider. The oil giant and China established early diplomatic relations in 1990 and both countries expected to further enhance their growing relationship. Saudi Arabia is the world's second biggest oil producer after Russia and accounts for about 17 percent of China's imported oil. In 2005 it exported 163 million barrels of oil to China, or a little less than half a million barrels a day. [146] Saudi Arabia is China's eighth largest trading partner.

In 2005, China imported petrochemical products worth US$5.37 billion from Arab countries or nineteen percent of China's total. The liquefied natural gas China imported from Arab countries is 55 percent of China's total imports. Karim Ebrahim Al-Shakar, Ambassador of Bahrain to China, said that China is a strategic market for Arab nations. Government officials and entrepreneurs from ten Arabian countries including Algeria, Bahrain, Jordan, Libya, Oman, Saudi Arabia, Sudan, Syria, Tunis, and Yemen attended a seminar held as part of the Tenth China International Fair for Investment and Trade in Xiamen City to discuss bilateral petrochemical cooperation. [147]

xi) China-E.U. Relationship: In 2005 China and the E.U. developed a new comprehensive strategic partnership marking the thirtieth anniversary of official ties. The bilateral trade volume between China and the E.U. amounted to US$157.79 billion in the first three quarters of 2005, up 23.3 percent over the same period in 2004. [148] The E.U. remains China's largest trade partner, the U.S. ranks the second and Japan the third.

While the China threat rhetoric is pronounced in the U.S., the China-E.U. relations may be characterized as strong and flourishing, according to Poul Nyrup Rasmussen, President of European Socialists and former Prime Minister of Denmark. He remarked that Chinese economic development is a very important achievement rather than a threat to the development of Europe and the world as a whole. "As an economist and President of the European Socialists, I can tell you that a fast and strong Chinese economy is a sign of a good social progress and a good regional development." [149] The following China-E.U. exchange reinforces this perspective:

China and the E.U. discussed global energy and Mr. Martin Schulz, Chairman of the Socialist Group in the European Parliament told the press during his visit to Beijing on February 28, 2006, that "In the dangerous time we live in, both Europe and China should contribute to world peace. China plays a large, constructive role in peaceful solutions to international conflicts," and "We will be prepared to cooperate with China not only on the economic level, but especially on the political level to increase multilateralism in the world." [150]

China and France reached a breakthrough in economic and trade cooperation with the two-way trade volume valued at US$17.58 billion, up 31.3 percent over the same period in 2004. China signed a series of significant cooperative agreements with European aviation and space companies. A Chinese official remarked, "We are satisfied with the comprehensive growth of Sino-French relations." [151] The French Suez Company, the largest French environmental industry group, said it would double its investment in China over the next two years. Up to 2006, the Suez organization invested US$641 million in China. It plans to move its Asian Pacific regional headquarters to Shanghai in 2006. [152]

Chinese President Hu Jintao and Britain's Prime Minister Tony Blair signed commercial aviation contracts worth US$1.3 billion: US$800 million to buy a fleet of Airbus wide-body jets with Trent 700 engines, and US$500 million for China Aviation Industry Corporation to build wing boxes for the Airbus. [153] China also agreed to open its markets to Lloyds of London, the world's leading insurance underwriter. [154] The commercial deals would give a further boost to the rapidly growing business between China and Britain. The successful resolution of the Hong Kong question between the two nations through peaceful negotiations has laid a sound foundation for the growth of bilateral relations, but China still has a long way to go before reaching the average economic level of developed countries. [155] China, at present, has 26 million peasants living in abject poverty and 21 million urban residents earning very low incomes. China must develop in a peaceful, open, and cooperative direction. and need a provision for Washington to offer Iran some nuclear technology, lift some sanctions, and join direct talks.

China-Germany's smooth bilateral relations stem from two sources: first, the Sino-German relationship has a solid political foundation. The two countries have no direct conflicts of interest. China supported German reunification and Germany has adhered to the one-China policy opposing Taiwan independence. Secondly, both countries have attached great importance to improving their relationship. In May 2004, both countries issued a joint statement establishing a partnership with global responsibility within the framework of a comprehensive strategic partnership between China and the E.U. China's rapid development and efforts in poverty alleviation over the past two decades have drawn worldwide attention and its influence and role in international affairs is also growing. [156] Apart from increasing bilateral trade, the Germans recognize that Western nations can no longer solve world problems alone.

Germany is China's largest trading partner in Europe and China is Germany's largest in Asia. Germany has more than 1,800 companies operating in China and German exports to China are more than US$165 billion in 2005 (up from US$247 million in 1972). [157] Siemens was awarded China's contract in late 2005 for a high-speed train (ICE 3) worth US$1 billion. The train will travel at 180 miles per hour and will be manufactured in China with core technology from Germany.

Dresdner Bank and Sal. Oppenheim Bank are going to own 14 percent of China Huaxia Bank. [158] Germany is also the first developed country to have signed legal exchange and cooperation agreements with China and has jointly built science-promotion centers in China. [159]

China also signed numerous contracts and formal cooperative agreements with other E. U. countries like Spain, Greece, Slovakia, the Czech Republic, Portugal, and Iceland. [160–164] There is hope that Chinese business and government support will inject new vigor into the depressed European economy. Today the Europeans are positioned in the middle of giants like China, India, Russia, and the U.S. The Europeans need China no less than they need Russia, for example, on the nuclear issue.

xii) China-Latin America and China-South Pacific Relationships: Development of close relations with Latin America seems a longer term prospect. China-Latin American ties began with the Ming Dynasty according to some records. Towards the second half of the nineteenth century, large numbers of Chinese laborers traveled to Latin America. There they built railways near North Mexico and grew rice in Peru. With recent globalization, the China-Latin America trade volume has reached

US$40 billion. By 2005, Latin America replaced Asia as China's largest FDI region. Brief summaries of these relationships follow:

China-Argentina Relations

Chinese language and culture are now a fascination for Argentineans who understand that there is more to China than eating Peking duck and purchasing Chinese herbs. After the visits by the countries' leaders, many Argentineans recognize the business potential of the PRC. Now China is Argentina's fourth export nation and the third largest import partner. In Buenos Aires, the capital of Argentina, many Chinese stores flourish as their businesses become increasingly prosperous.

China-Bolivia Relations

Bolivian President Evo Morales visited Beijing in early January 2006. Morales said that Bolivia would like to form an ideological and political alliance with China that would support development of needed infra-structure in his country. [165] Bolivia is the poorest country in South America. Morales pressed Chinese business leaders to help develop Bolivia's rich natural gas resources to gradually alleviate his country's poverty. Morales called Cuba's Fidel Castro and Venezuela's Hugo Chavez "an axis of good."

China-Venezuela Relations

During his six-day state visit to China, Hugo Chavez remarked to reporters that the world might think the most important event in the twentieth century was America's landing on the Moon, but he thinks China's economic revolution is an even more important event. [166] Critics might think differently about Hugo Chavez's comments, since he is no longer a friend of America. We will cover discussions on American foreign policy in Latin America in later chapters. The U.S. Federal Reserve Bank Chairman Ben Bernanke also said that China's speedy economic recovery and development in less than thirty years is unprece-dented in history.

Venezuela is the fifth largest oil exporter in the world. It produces about 3 million barrels of crude oil per day and exports 150 thousand barrels of crude oil daily to China. This represents 2.3 percent of China's total crude oil import. This is far less than Angola's 18 percent, Saudi Arabia's 16 percent and Iran's 12 percent. [167] The volume is expected to increase to 200,000 at the end of 2006; 300,000 in 2007, with a steady increase to 500,000 barrels per day by 2010. If its oil production can reach 5,800 thousand barrels per day before 2012, then it will likely export 500 to 1,000 thousand barrels per day to China. [168] Venezuela is willing to meet 20 percent of China's oil import needs, according to President Chavez. America is Venezuela's largest oil importer; it imports 1.5 million barrels of oil from Venzuela daily. China National Petroleum Corporation and Petroleos de Venezuela S. A. signed an agreement to develop the Junin area of Venezuela's oil belt. [169] However, there are some technical issues to be resolved concerning China's ability to refine Venezuelan oil. It may take China five years to overcome these technical issues.

On November 1, 2005, the Venezuela President signed a contract for a tele-communications satellite with China. China will design, manufacture, assemble, test, and launch the satellite scheduled for delivery in 2008. This will be the first satellite produced and launched for the Latin-America countries. [170] It will provide telecommunications services to all parts of Venezuela.

Venezuela hopes that China will support its bid to become an elected member of the U.N. Security Council (China is a permanent member) and use its growing authority to influence U.S. policies. China knows the importance of Latin America to the U.S. and it has no interest in causing tensions in America's backyard.

In summary, China has demonstrated special interest in Chilean copper, Brazilian and Argentinean agricultural products such as beans, and Venezuelan oil. Cuba purchased Chinese manufactured trains which were later exported to Latin America and the Caribbean in January 2006.

China is now an observer member of the Organization of American States. China is expanding economic and trade relationships with Latin America and the Caribbean, since the region contains twelve of the twenty-four countries that still maintain official diplomatic relations with Taiwan. These nations are the six Central American countries – Belize, El Salvador, Guatemala, Honduras, Nicaragua, and Panama; three

Caribbean countries – Haiti, St. Kitts and Nevis, and St. Vincent and the Grenadines; and one South American country – Paraguay. [171] China wishes that these nations clearly recognize the world situation, and develop cooperation with China based on the One-China Principle. [172]

xiii) China-South Pacific Relationships: The relationships can be categorized into the following groups:

China-Pacific Island Relations
China is working to develop economic ties with South Pacific nations. Out of fourteen member states of the Pacific Islands Forum, eight have already recognized the PRC. Chinese Premier Wen Jiabao was invited by leaders of Australia, Fiji, New Zealand, and Cambodia to attend the First China-Pacific Island Countries Economic Development and Cooperation Forum held in Fiji. This included a four-nation tour from April 1 to 8, 2006. [173] The purpose of the trip was to enhance cooperation with the South Pacific nations without any political strings attached to it other than supporting the One-China Principle. China promised to provide US$375 million over the next three years in the form of a low interest loan to Pacific Island nations to strengthen mutual development in areas including resource development, agriculture, forestry, fishery, and tourism. China also intends to eliminate tariffs for some of the less developed countries that have diplomatic ties to China. Wen Jiabao said that this is a strategic policy. The economy of China and the South-Pacific Island nations are complementary to each other. The Pacific Island nations have abundant resources and China possesses the technical skills and capabilities to exploit them equitably. The potential for mutual cooperation is great. [174]

China-Australia Relations
China and Australia signed eight inter-government agreements and documents, including an agreement for cooperation in the peaceful use of nuclear energy and an agreement on the transfer of nuclear energy. [175] Australia agreed to sell uranium, which amounts to US$4 billion to China for peaceful development of nuclear electrical power plants. Uranium imports from Australia will help fuel the thirty nuclear power

generation units that China plans to build by 2020. Nuclear energy is a key part of China's goal to reduce major pollutants by 10 percent in the next five years. [176] The signing of this agreement has signaled a breakthrough of Western trade barriers and prejudice against China. Also, Australia ships liquefied natural gas to China's southern city of Shenzhen. China is now the second largest trading partner of Australia after Japan.

China-New Zealand Relations

New Zealand signed a Trade and Economic Cooperation Framework following a visit by President Hu Jintao to this country in 2003. The two countries held six rounds of free-trade talks since December 2004 and continued discussions on a free-trade agreement with China more recently. [177]

China-Cambodia, -Laos, -Myanmar, and -Philippine Relations

Wen Jiabao received a warm welcome during his visit to Cambodia where he signed eleven bilateral agreements to strengthen the two countries' economic and technical cooperative efforts and to combat border crimes. China also promised to provide US$600 million assistance to Cambodia, out of which US$200 million is a low interest loan to be used to build two bridges. [178] "China is a powerful country, especially economically, and it plays an important role as member of the U.N.," according to Cambodian government spokesman, Khieu Kanharith. [179]

In summary, China has been eager to form stable friendships among nations in Southeast Asia by making large loans with attractive terms for large scale infrastructure projects. Such financial activities were once the sole preserve of the World Bank, the Asian Development Bank, the U.S., and Japan. In addition to a no strings approach, China is appreciated as a lender by poor countries because it is willing to take on complicated projects in distant areas under harsh conditions. For example, in Cambodia some Chinese engineers often had to work in temperatures as high as 106 degrees Fahrenheit.

Chinese government financings are secured without the expensive consulting fees common to Western projects. Cambodian Prime Minister

Hun Sen said that "China is a most trusted friend." [180] China is building roads, ports, and bridges in poor countries like Cambodia, Laos, and Myanmar, and offers loans to some countries like the Philippines which are relatively stronger economically.

China is the world's largest consumer of steel, grain, aluminum, copper, iron ore, and zinc, among other commodities. China's demand for natural gas is expected to rise 26 percent over the next five years and its crude oil demand is forecast to more than double by 2025 from the current 7 million barrels a day. [181] The huge demand for energy and other resources needed by China to feed its flourishing economy is creating a profitable bond with commodity exporters, helping to refresh global markets and trading alliances.

10. China's Multilateral Cooperation

In Asia and worldwide, China participates in over forty regional security and economic forums. China is also a U.N. Security Council member. China has diverse functions summarized as follows:

i) Asia-Pacific Economic Cooperation (APEC): APEC was established in 1989 in response to growing interdependence among Asia-Pacific economies and to address the need to advance economic dynamism and a sense of community. Another goal is to circumvent trade constraints imposed by the E.U. and North America Free Trade organizations. China joined the APEC in 1991. It now has twenty-one member economies: Australia, Brunei Darussalam, Canada, Chili, China, Hong Kong, Indonesia, Japan, South Korea, Malaysia, Mexico, New Zealand, Papua New Guinea, Peru, the Philippines, Russia, Singapore, Chinese Taipei, Thailand, the U.S., and Vietnam.

APEC has three official observers: the ASEAN Secretariat, the Pacific Economic Cooperation Council and the South Pacific Forum. APEC now covers about 60 percent of world economies and about half of the world trade volume. Asian nations were disappointed by the lack of U.S. support of APEC during the 1998 Asian economic crisis. The U.S. response was to sign separate free trade agreements with Asian countries and others, which weakened free-trade targets designated by

APEC. In addition, China stabilized its currency during the Asian financial crisis and this action prevented deterioration of financial conditions in many developing nations.

China continued to support APEC to help cure the economic crisis. China plays a major role in APEC today.

China and Australia held a fifth round of Free Trade Agreement (FTA) talks in Beijing on market admittance. [182] Australia earns billions of dollars annually from the sale of iron ore and other raw materials to the mushrooming Chinese economy. In 2004, China was Australia's second trade partner and export market next to the U.S. In late 2005, China became Australia's largest import country. Australian economists made statements suggesting that Australian living standards will depend on economic developments in China.

Speaking at the Asian Association in New York in September 2005, Australian Prime Minister John Howard said that development in China has not only benefited its own people, but is also good for the whole world. Recent economic development advanced the global economy and world trade growth. Although John Howard has been satirized as the deputy sheriff for the U.S. in the past and is a strong ally of the U.S., Australia is pursuing independent diplomacy to achieve its own goals.

In 2004, America expressed concern when Australian Foreign Minister Alexander Downer remarked in Beijing, that Australia was not bound to help the U.S. defend Taiwan. Prime Minister John Howard came to Downer's aid afterwards by saying, "America has no more reliable ally than Australia and I am not ashamed to say that. We have a separate, strong, growing relationship with China and it is not in Australia's interests for there to be in conflict between America and China and I will do everything I can, and Mr. Downer will do everything he can, to discourage that ever occurring." [183–184]

ii) Association of Southeast Asian Nations: ASEAN was created in 1967 in response to a growing conviction among Asian leaders that their region required a stronger independent voice in world affairs and a new forum without the preponderant role that had been played by the U.S. since World War II. [185] When formed originally, it had ten members: Brunei, Cambodia, Indonesia, Laos, Malaysia, Myanmar, the Philippines, Singapore, Thailand, and Vietnam, and another associated group known as ASEAN Plus Three, ASEAN+3. The latter included China, Japan, and South Korea. In 1992, ASEAN also initiated the ASEAN Free Trade Area (AFTA), which laid out a comprehensive program of regional tariff reduction to eliminate trade barriers of the member countries, and lately there are talks about establishing an Asian currency.

The Eleventh ASEAN Summit was held in mid-December 2005, in Kuala Lumpur, Malaysia. At the Summit, Kuala Lumpur signed a Declaration on the Establishment of the ASEAN Charter which was a new milestone in ASEAN's development as a mature regional organization. [186] At the same time, three new members were accepted in to the organization: Australia, New Zealand, and India. ASEAN is now a sixteen-nation association, with Russia as an observer. Fifteen of the sixteen countries are also APEC members. The official theme of this Summit is "one vision, one identity, one community."

During the ASEAN Summit meeting, Malaysia Prime Minister Abdullah Ahmad Badawi said, "Internally we need to take concrete and determined steps to guide ASEAN towards the realization of an ASEAN Community. ASEAN's credibility depends on how it manages to shape this Community," and "Externally, ASEAN is faced with the challenge of seeking ways and means to promote peace and stability in East Asia." [187]

The sixteen ASEAN countries also held their first East Asia Summit on December 14, 2005, at Kuala Lumpur. The sixteen countries cover half of the world population and their total gross GDP exceeds US$8,000 billion. [188] From the beginning, the Summit mapped out a progressive and exciting blueprint. Chinese Premier Wen Jiabao gave a speech at the Summit and indicated that China will not seek a dominant role at the East Asia Summit, but wanted to welcome the participation of Russia, the U.S., and other countries who wish to establish stronger ties with East Asia. [189]

The Kuala Lumpur Declaration clearly defines the leading role of ASEAN. The Declaration indicates that the Asian Summit will serve as a forum for dialogue on military strategies, political, and economical issues.

Wen Jiabao emphasized that China supports East Asian cooperation's transparency and openness, and opposes sealing up, excluding others. [190] The countries are also planning a unified Asian currency borrowing from the E.U. euro experience. But there is still a long distance to go before the birth of a unified Asian currency. [191]

China does not want to become a hegemon or a superpower, its aim at forming an economic partnership with ASEAN countries has shown great success in exhibiting a softer power in South-East Asia. China-ASEAN trade surged 28.2 percent in just the first two months of 2006. [192] In 2006, more than seventy ASEAN firms gathered at the exhibition Hall of Changchun Exhibition Center seeking partners at the second Northeast Asia Investment and Trade Exposition. [193] Taking advantage of geographical proximity, the ASEAN enterprises have already established long-standing economic relations with their counterparts in southern China.

iii) Shanghai Cooperation Organization: The SCO evolved from the Shanghai Five which was founded by leaders of China, Kazakhstan, Kyrgyzstan, Russia, and Tajikistan in 1996. After the inclusion of Uzbekistan in 2001, the members renamed the organization as SCO, with India, Mongolia, and Iran. Pakistan received observer status later. The original purpose of the SCO was to support member states by solving border conflicts and avoiding military conflicts. It was also charged with fostering anti-terrorism, and countering militant Islam. China and Russia held their first joint military drill, called Peace Mission 2005 in August. [194] The SCO recently reiterated the One-China Principle, resolutely opposing any form of separatism among member countries. It will support its member countries' territorial integrity and strengthen cooperation in this area to secure the regional peace, safety, and stability.

In short, the SCO has now become an active vehicle for regional cooperation to tackle the 'three evil forces" of terrorism, religious extremism, and separatism and perhaps hedge against undesirable U.S. influences. [195] China and Kazakhstan held their first joint anti-terror drill over two days in August 2006. The drill began in Kazakhstan's Almaty region with the aim of raising the security levels, protecting regional safety, and increasing border stability. Kazakhstan shares a 1,000 mile border with Xinjiang, where the Uigur people have settled. [196]

Apart from Russia, China has collaborated with Kazakhstan in building the Kazakhstan-China oil pipelines from Atyrau in Kazakhstan to Alashankou in the Xinjiang Uighur Autonomous Region. The first two sections were completed in 2003 and 2005. The feasibility study for the second construction phase of the third section from Kenkiyak to Kumkol is underway. Also, the second section, from Atasu to Alashankou will not reach its design capacity of ten million tons (about 36.76 million barrels) in 2007, if Russian companies do not become active in transporting oil. [197] China has provided a US$600 million loan to cooperate on constructing natural gas pipelines to connect to the pipelines that go from Kazakhstan to China. [198] China has also been interested in investments in other SCO member states.

iv) World Trade Organization: The WTO replaced the General Agreement on Tariffs and Trade in 1995. It is now an international, multinational organization, which sets the rules for a global trading system by promoting lower trade barriers and providing a platform for the negotiation of trade, and resolving disputes between its member states. China joined the WTO on November 11, 2001. Three years later, China became the second largest import and export nation surpassing Japan and began to play a lead role in balancing the power of this organization. The WTO has helped China transform its economy.

In 2005, the sixth WTO leaders' meeting was held in Hong Kong to develop an outline for a global treaty by the end of 2006. The mission was to lower or eliminate trade barriers in agriculture, manufacturing, and services. Nearly 6,000 delegates from the 149 member states attended the meeting. Negotiations got off to a rocky start when the E.U. would not change its offer of an average 46 percent cut in farm tariffs unless developing nations offered substantive reductions in their trade barriers on manufactured goods and services.

The U.S. offered to eliminate government export subsidies for U.S. farm products by 2010, and to reduce by 60 percent the amount of trade-distorting domestic support the government provides U.S. farmers over the following five years. The developing countries said that the U.S. offer was hollow because subsidy spending at current levels could continue and they needed wealthy nation aid so that they could strengthen their ports, roads, schools, and bridges. [199]

More than 4,000 protesters from all over the world gathered outside the meeting hall complaining about WTO practices including perceived unfair trade agreements. The situation was chaotic. [200] "Rich nations of the world should open up their markets and do more to protect and help the poorest, most vulnerable citizens of the developing world, or possibly face disaster," said Chinese Commerce Minister Bo Xilai. [201]

As discussed, despite China's rise as a trade power, it still is among the developing nations; of its 800 million farmers, one quarter live on less than US$1 a day. China is among a large group of WTO countries supporting a proposal to move ahead with granting tariff-free and quota-free treatment for products exported by the fifty least-developed nations, in an effort to help those countries that benefit from free trade. [202] China was a member of the G-20 group of developing economies and also part of the G-33 group, which seeks to protect agricultural production for subsistence farmers.

China has reduced its tariffs for farm products from 54 percent to 15.3 percent, and for industrial products from 42.9 percent to 9 percent. Beijing has also eliminated tariffs and quotas for forty-nine developing countries, and has given "special product" and "special protection mechanism" status as proposed by developing countries. [203] China speaks on behalf of the poor countries.

The WTO meeting was initially intended to approve a draft trade treaty known as the Doha round, but the plan was abandoned because of the differences between rich and poor members. [204] The Doha round of WTO trade talks was aimed at removing barriers to agricultural and industrial trade to help developing countries overcome poverty. Zambian Trade Minister Dipak Patel, who was the coordinator of the poorest WTO states, harshly criticized the U.S. and Japan for seeking exemptions to protect their own industries. After six days of intensive debate, trade representatives from all nations reached a compromised agreement based on the E.U. proposal to terminate all government export subsidies for farm products by 2013. Proposals were made to construct a framework for reducing trade barriers and creating subsidies for farm products and industrial products by April of 2006. [205] The much delayed Doha trade talks were back on track.

Unfortunately, the Doha round of WTO trade talks in Geneva was suspended on July 24, 2006, after fourteen hours of negotiations among the largest trade countries for failing to produce a consensus on free trade issues related to global agricultural and manufacturing products. The so-called G6 nations, namely Australia, Brazil, the E.U., India, Japan, and the U.S., with a total trade volume consisting of three-fourths of the world volume, worked vigorously to save the negotiations. E.U. trade representative Peter Mandelson told the British press that the U.S. refusal to offer to cut farm subsidies more deeply should be blamed, whereas the U.S. negotiator Susan Schwab accused the E.U. and other nations for their unwillingness to lower their trade barriers to American agricultural products. [206] The U.S. decided to stop the trade talks at that time. Resumption of the talks seems unlikely for at least another five years.

On August 30, 2006, the U.S. top trade official Susan Schwab called on Beijing to help revive the stalled Doha trade talks, explaining that Beijing had "an unprecedented stake in the successful conclusion of a robust Doha agreement," which could only be possible "with vigorous and positive Chinese participation." [207] China's Commerce Minister Bo Xilai said that Beijing is willing to help revive stalled WTO talks, but rich countries should first make "substantial contributions." [208]

v) The United Nations: The U.N. was founded in 1945 by fifty-one countries based on proposals worked out by the representatives of China (the ROC), the Soviet Union, the United Kingdom, and the U.S. in 1944. In 1971, the PRC replaced the ROC to become the United Nation Security Council Member representing the only legitimate nation of China in the world. On September 2005, Chinese President Hu Jintao announced at the U.N. summit that China would increase aid for developing countries to promote universal development to achieve common prosperity. The measures included zero tariff treatment for certain products from all thirty-nine less-developed countries (LDCs) with diplomatic relations with China. It offered to expand aid programs to the heavily indebted poor countries and LDCs, mostly in Africa and Latin America. China will continue dialogues with developing countries and expand cooperation with African and Arab nations under the framework of the China-Africa Cooperation Forum and the China-Arab Cooperation Forum. China plans, in addition, to promote relations with the Latin American countries. [209]

China has sent more than 3,000 military personnel, policemen, and civil servants on U.N. peacekeeping missions, with approximately 1,500 still working in eleven different countries and regions. Following the Indonesian tsunami of December 2004, China contributed more than US$20 million to U.N. agencies to support recovery and reconstruction efforts in the countries affected by this terrible tragedy. [210]

China emphasizes that it is still the largest developing country in the world and knows well that it faces many severe and difficult challenges. For this reason, prior to 2003, China did not agree to participate as a regular member of the G7 (G8, once Russia joined) composed of developed nations. Following ultimate participation in the G8 meetings, China assumed the dual roles of dialogue facilitator and observer.

The year 2005 marked the sixtieth anniversary of the U.N. The role of China in the U.N. has changed from its past passive and defensive approach to one that is increasingly proactively confident and strong. China agreed to the U.S. Security Resolution on North Korea and the Iranian nuclear issue, which surprised some nations. This illustrates that China is assuming a broader international role and is participating as a responsible stakeholder. In the future, China will be judged to a higher standard by the international community, and therefore, must increase its international role and responsibilities as it develops in economic and political strength.

11. Conclusions

This chapter has presented an overview of the dynamic economic, diplomatic, and political role of China today. As discussed, the PRC established a central government based on a constitutional system adopted by the NPC in 1982. During the first twenty-seven years of the Mao period, the PRC survived the difficult economic transformation of the Great Leap Forward which included experiments with communes. It was a major economic failure, because it constituted a fundamental attack on the institution of family, the most basic unit of Confucianism and the backbone of Chinese society. Chinese society was altered by Mao's version of Marxism and a planned economy in which the government provided food, housing, health care, schooling, and more to all the people.

While the Chinese people were often short of material comforts, crime rates were low and corruption was not tolerated. Unfortunately, during the last ten years of his rule, Mao initiated the Cultural Revolution that led to internal power struggles and immense suffering in China.

When Deng Xiaoping regained political power in 1976 he initiated an open door policy to improve the Chinese economy. Since then China formally entered the global market and moved quickly to privatize poorly-operated government-owned factories and businesses. The government permitted individual business ownership and embraced the concept of a market economy. This economic reform drastically altered the economic structure and helped establish China as the fastest growing economy in the world. Over the past twenty-eight years many of the largest companies in the world have been attracted to invest in China.

Most foreign companies realize higher profit margins in China. At the same time, China has been aggressively constructing badly-needed infrastructure including railways, bridges, highways, power plants, dams, and infrastructures throughout the country. China has lifted about 300 million people out of poverty over this period of time and plans to move 300 million more out of the rural areas into the cities in the immediate future. China faces the uphill task of job creation. Rapid growth is not without its costs. China has a serious pollution problem and depends heavily on imported oil. To become more productive, China is striving to develop advanced science and technologies by funding extensive research and development.

Since China instituted an open door policy, it has reached out to form bonds in the international community. China is interested in trade and peaceful cooperation with other countries and does not wish to impose its political ideology or system on other nations. China's economic progress and peaceful influence have steadily enhanced its use of soft power. This approach marks a return to the ancient values of Confucianism.

CHAPTER IV

Where Does America Stand Now?

This chapter provides an overview of American political systems, development, foreign policy, and evolving relationship with China.

1. A Comparison of Chinese and American Governmental Processes

The U.S. declared independence in 1776. The Declaration of Independence states:

We hold these truths to be self-evident, that all men are created equal, that they are endowed, by their Creator, with certain unalienable Rights, that among these are Life, Liberty, and the pursuit of Happiness. That to secure these rights, Governments are instituted among Men, deriving their just powers from the consent of the governed, That whenever any Form of Government becomes destructive of these ends, it is the Right of the People to alter or abolish it, and to institute new Government, laying its foundation on such principles, and organizing its powers in such form, as to them shall seem most likely to effect their Safety and Happiness. [1]

From this Declaration, it is evident that the founding principles of America 231 years ago were: Americans believe God made man, then, inspired by God, man made government, and that the government derives power from the consent of the governed. Alarmed by the European religious wars and the political power of churches, the First Amendment of the American Constitution requires a "wall of separation" between church and state so that the government is not unduly influenced by religious preferences. Freedom of religious expression is a right protected under the U.S. Constitution and the Bill of Rights because so many early settlers came to America to escape religious persecution. The Bill of Rights consists of Amendments 1–10 of the Constitution. [2]

The first U.S. President was George Washington who served two terms of presidency (1789–1797). His greatest contributions were his election as delegate to the First and Second Continental Congresses and his command of the American army during the Revolutionary War. America's great Presidents in early history include John Adams (1797–1801), more remarkable as a political philosopher than as a President, and two term president Thomas Jefferson (1801–1809) who drafted the Declaration of Independence, engineered the purchase of the Louisiana territory and maintained American neutrality in the conflict between France and Great Britain that led to the war of 1812.

While the Congress has the authority to declare war, recent presidents are said to have exercised too much power over all forms of legislation, controlled information to prevent criticism or legislative interference, engaged in covert activities domestically and abroad, and made war without sufficiently explicit legislative approval. [3] For example, the U.S. claimed that "Weapons of mass destruction in Iraq" posed a threat to international peace and security and, without U.N. Security Council authorization, began a war on Iraq. When U.S. forces failed to find "weapons of mass destruction," critics charged that the White House had misled the Congress and the public. [4]

The U.S. political system is democratic with two primary political parties, the Democratic and the Republican Parties. There are dozens of other parties including the Independent Party, the Green Party, the Libertarian Party, and the Communist Party. [5] None of the latter has succeeded in electing a President. However, governors, congressmen, and other elected officials have emerged from minor parties.

Every American voter has the right to vote for the political candidates he or she chooses to work for the people. In this popular governance system, the powers of government are derived from the people; the government must be accountable to the people for how it exercises those powers. American's cultural background of freedom, human rights, and individualism has empowered the American public to make decisions affecting their own political affairs. Since popular governance demands that bureaucracies and bureaucrats be held accountable for their actions, more time is spent responding to congressional inquires and holding public hearings to satisfy the demands of accountability. This often directly diminishes the capacity of the bureaucrats to accomplish their allotted responsibilities. [6] Although after the election, the two parties vow to work together and the president represents all the people, in practice, we see that many decisions are partisan and polls often show that an elected president receives less than a 50 percent approval rating (George W. Bush's approval rating dropped from 90 percent before the Iraq War to a low of 30 percent for his performance). [7]

Many choose not to vote. Often special interest groups, including large corporations, trade unions, and various professional groups invest in political campaigns and wield excessive influence on elected officials which affects decision-making and policies.

Despite some flaws, Americans are strong supporters of a democratic government and the imbedded principle of popular governance is based on the belief that "all Men are created equal," and political leaders are chosen by the people and for the people.

In contrast, in the Chinese political system, the CPC is China's sole incumbent political party, with its 70.8 million party members and 3.5 million party organizations, which makes decisions for the 1.3 billion Chinese population through the local and National People's Congresses. The Chinese political system does allow other parties to coexist with the CPC, and these parties work together with the CPC as active advisors. They are not opposition parties as in the Western democratic system. They do not propose presidential candidates, but they can participate in elections at the local level or be appointed as officials in the government.

The CPC members are the elite of Chinese society who are selected and trained by the party schools and systems to assume the responsibilities of government bureaucrats at various levels through planning and counseling. Advisory meetings are often held within the workplace to discuss political or administrative decisions by gathering all opinions and examining alternatives. There will always be different opinions, but final decisions are made as a result of group decision-making. In this "elite governance" system, the CPC is given extensive power and discretion. The president of the PRC is elected by the NPC. One important quality a leader must have is a great ability to negotiate and balance power from diverse power groups. Superb political skill and an excellent record of performance in government are essential. The Chinese system does not discriminate against women. Currently, Chinese Vice Premier Wu Yi is the highest ranking female official in China. She was appointed to combat the SARS epidemic in 2003, one of the most challenging jobs in China.

If the country has a good leader, and the morale of the bureaucrats is high, the Chinese government can achieve greater efficiency in the administration of its bureaucracies. Once a decision is made by the central government, there is the expectation that it will be executed effectively throughout the appropriate government agencies down to the community level. It is unclear how well the government system of checks and balances works. The Chinese legal system is not yet well developed and is lacking in effective enforcement mechanisms. Thus, for party members, legal decisions are first made by CPC rule.

Because of the lack of at least one powerful opposition party to mitigate corruption as in the American democracy, the Chinese system relies heavily on moral discipline and the skills and abilities of its national leaders and government bureaucrats. If a country has a brilliant leader like former Premier, Lee Kuan Yew, who ruled Singapore under an autocratic political system with strict regulations, it might flourish with effective and powerful leadership. If not, the political power and resources of the nation may be squandered in the hands of a small number of rich and powerful bureaucrats who infringe on the needs of the rest of the society.

Not unlike ancient Chinese rulers, the national leader of China today serves as the head of the national "family," who makes all the decisions with the recommendations of other political members for the family and assumes full responsibility for both success and failure. In order to unify and lead the nation in a chosen direction while maintaining control, stability, and authority, the Chinese government places limits on individual freedom in the areas of freedom of the press and the opportunity to choose leadership through democratic elections (direct elections are held in townships and villages, numbering over half a million throughout the country, to fill in the leadership vacuum left after the collapse of the people's commune system of the Mao era). China has thus established an authoritarian, paternalistic system of governance.

The Chinese political system stems from a cultural background within its society, which remains centered on Confucianism, and which has never promoted individualism. Historically, in the feudal society, Chinese people often place more faith in their government to determine the direction of the nation than in their own decision-making capability on the future of the country. But, as discussed in Chapter I, Mencius (BC 372–289), a follower of Confucius, proposed that "people are the most important, the country is the next important, and the emperor is the least important." His view was that it is acceptable for the people to overthrow or kill a ruler who ignores the needs of the people and rules tyrannically. This means: the people would like to place their faith in their government, but if they lose faith in government, they will not stand idle and do nothing. The spirit and drive of people seeking fair treatment from government is embedded in Confucianism.

China is gradually adopting political reforms as evidenced by the CPC proposal of a theoretical framework of "consultation democracy." This was the main theme of the eighty-fifth anniversary party celebration intended to meet growing demands for more democracy in China. This trend is a result of Westernization of Chinese society. [8]

Chinese leader Hu Jintao stressed the importance of his "for the people" political ideology. He has announced that the next, fifth generation political leader of China will not be appointed, but will be determined by elections within the CPC. This new development represents a shift towards a more democratic society which integrates Chinese cultural characteristics and is discussed further in Chapter V.

The key question is whether it is meaningful to ask which political system is better: the democratic model of the U.S. or the authoritarian elitist governance embodied by centralist rule in China. It appears to really depend on the particular leader that is elected in either system, not the system itself. Statistically speaking, over a long period of time, each political system can produce good and bad leaders. Critics may say that the difference is basic: In a democracy, a bad leader can be removed by the vote of the people. In China, the removal of a leader by revolution is justified.

The Chinese national leader can serve only two terms for a maximum of ten years and a new leader will be elected by the CPC. The old Chinese centralized government with its society built on the foundation of Confucianism has been tested for several thousand years. When the central government was weak, the Middle Kingdom was invaded, collapsed, or was destroyed by popular uprisings. To adapt to the modern world and undertake political reform, the new Chinese centralized government is "groping for stones to cross the river" as it did to achieve economic reform a few decades ago, as opposed to a more traumatic approach to change. In order to maintain social stability, China is both cautious and careful.

Throughout its turbulent history, China has developed without a Western form of democracy. Today it is thriving on a path of economic recovery. People in China now have more freedom than they had in the past and more than most Americans realize. [9] Encouraging steps have been taken by Chinese authorities to relax certain restrictions on foreign reporters covering China. Gradual openness is indicative of a more confident China that is willing to loosen some controls. At the same time, Chinese authorities are sensitive and concerned about receiving positive feedback from foreign reporters in order to maintain a commendable image in the international community. [10]

The American democratic system, with its roots in ancient Greece, has evolved for over 200 years since independence and the first election of President George Washington (1789–1797). America is a major superpower and has achieved a great deal in its relatively brief history. The United States has made enormous advances in many areas of human civilization including industry, culture, finance, science, and technologies.

Over the years, the U.S. has been critical of the Chinese political system. Will the American system last as long as the Chinese system for a few hundred or even thousand years more? Only future events and history will judge the merits and longevity of these distinct systems of government.

In commenting about differing approaches to government, former U.S. Secretary of State, Dr. Henry A. Kissinger, wrote the following about Lee Kuan Yew, the former highly effective leader of Singapore: [11]

> *Lee Kuan Yew would not be true to himself were he less than frank about his analysis of the difference between the individualism of the West and the priority for social cohesion in countries such as his and in much of the rest of Asia. He does not ask us to change our patterns, only to refrain from imposing them on societies with different histories and necessities.*

Nevertheless, there is no doubt that the Chinese political system is gradually evolving by blending into it the quintessence of Western political elements and preserving the Chinese characteristics.

2. The U.S. Economy before 1978

The U.S. economy developed rapidly after the Civil War (1861–1865). The U.S. remained a largely agricultural nation until the late nineteenth century. During the late 1900s, the U.S. entered a period of industrialization. Because of bountiful resources and cheap labor, the nineteenth and twentieth centuries brought explosive economic and industrial growths in America.

The evolution of U.S. industrial infrastructure included development of advanced scientific methods, management systems, and labor unions. This period encompassed the rise of American industrialists and business tycoons such as John D. Rockefeller in oil, Henry Ford with the automobile, Jay Gould in railroads, Andrew Carnegie in steel, and J. Pierpont Morgan in banking.

The Americans enjoyed the risk and excitement of business enterprise and potential rewards of power that business brought. Americans enthusiastically embraced the idea of moneymaking. By contrast, the Chinese slogan, "to get rich is glorious" emerged after 1978, approximately 100 years later. In America, military and non-military manufacturing industries thrived from the late nineteenth century to World War I (1914–1918), survived the Great Depression (1929–1940), lasted through World War II (1937–1945), and beyond.

After World War II, many Americans worried that the drop in military spending might lead to another period of economic hardship like the Great Depression. Instead, peace fueled exceptional economic growth in areas like the automotive industry and housing. The U.S. GDP grew from about US$200 billion in 1940 to US$300 billion in 1950 and to more than US$500 billion in 1960 with an average annual growth of nearly 5 percent. Despite the three-year-long Korean War (1950–1953), the American birth rate, known as the "baby boom," increased dramatically.

European countries aged by the war became markets for numerous U.S. goods under the Marshall Plan following World War II. It was during this period of 1945–1960 that the U.S. developed international monetary arrangements, consolidated firms into huge, diversified conglomerates and that labor unions won long-term employment contracts and other benefits. At the same time, the U.S. labor force underwent various transformations. By 1956, American workers held more white-collar jobs than blue-collar jobs and by 1998, U.S. farms employed only 3.4 million people, a dramatic reduction from 7.9 million in 1947. Henry Ford realized his ambition to democratize the automobile by manufacturing vehicles that were both reliable and affordable for working and middle class Americans. Widespread ownership of cars resulted in a population shift of Americans from urban areas to the less crowded suburbs. [12]

Following the turmoil and exhaustion of two major wars, World War II and the Korean War respectively, the 1950s are viewed by some historians as a period of re-growth and complacency. However, it was also during the 50s that the "Red Scare" and the U.S. government's fear of a Soviet nuclear threat reached a zenith. [13] The Cold War (1947–1991) began soon after World War II between the political camps led by the Soviet Union and the U.S.

In the 1960s, America struggled through a period of enormous turbulence as well as economic and social change emanating from the civil rights movement, the women's movement, and the anti-war movement.

In 1961, President John Fitzgerald Kennedy (1961–1963) created a volunteer organization within the State Department known as the Peace Corps. This government agency was established to help developing nations meet their needs for trained manpower.

Later President Lyndon Baines Johnson (1963–1969) set forth a legislative agenda of wide ranging domestic social programs designed to eliminate poverty and racial inequality; this program, known as the Great Society, was the most sweeping set of social measures implemented since Franklin D. Roosevelt's New Deal. Great Society programs included major Federal spending in areas including education, urban development, health care, and transportation.

The Vietnam War started in 1965 as a limited military action under President Dwight D. Eisenhower and later President John F. Kennedy mushroomed into a full-scale war during the Johnson presidency. By the end of the 1960s, the cost of the war in Vietnam contributed to inflation and diminished U.S. prosperity. The Vietnam War dragged on until 1975.

Finally, President Richard M. Nixon (1969–1973) was forced to resign following impeachment for obstruction of justice in what is known as the Watergate affair. The U.S. trade deficit swelled as low-priced, high-quality imports from automobiles to steel to semiconductors flooded into the U.S. market. Then a period known as "stagflation" arose in the 1970s. This included high inflation and unemployment, higher interest rates, and excessive government borrowing.

3. The U.S. Economy after 1978

Beginning in 1979, the U.S. economy went into recession. During the mid–1980s, farmers were particularly hard hit by natural disasters including droughts and flooding. In addition, scandals were exposed involving leading financial institutions including savings and loan organizations that engaged in unwise lending following partial deregulation.

President Jimmy Carter (1977–1981) tried but failed to reduce "stagflation." He also lost reelection to a second term to Ronald Reagan. During the eight years of Ronald Reagan's presidency (1981–1989),

America entered a robust economic expansion beginning in 1982. Under Reagan, supply-side economics, popularly known as "Reaganomics," was noted for huge cuts in income taxes, inflation reduction, interest rate reduction, increased military spending, increased deficits and national debt, and continued deregulation of business.

But the trade deficit continued to swell throughout the 1980s, forcing the Reagan administration to borrow heavily both domestically and abroad. By the end of his second term, the U.S. national debt rose from 26 percent of GDP in 1980 to 41 percent in 1989, the highest level since 1963. The U.S. owed more to foreign countries than it was owed, and changed to the largest debtor nation from the world's largest international creditor. Nonetheless, Reagan was credited with restoring psychological optimism to an America that seemed to be losing confidence. After Ronald Reagan, President George H.W. Bush (1989–1993) could not reduce the government debt and some people said that the economic stagnation cost him the 1992 presidential election to the Democratic candidate, William Jefferson Clinton.

In Asia during this period, China was in its second decade of open door economic development, while Japan entered a steady 5 percent annual growth period following several decades of robust post-war economic recovery beginning in 1945. In the 1980s, Japan became the second largest economic entity in the world. Its per capita GDP was only one-fourteenth of the U.S. value (US$131 vs. US$1,897) in 1950, but by 1987, its per capita GDP surpassed the U.S. In other words, the Japanese per capita GDP multiplied 151 times in forty years after World War II, and rhetoric regarding a "Japan threat" reverberated loudly within American industrial and financial communities. It was at this time that the U.S. pressured Japan to increase the value of the Japanese yen, which caused its appreciation by more than 40 percent against the U.S. dollar in a short period. The Japanese economy cooled as it failed to maintain its momentum and fell into a long recession that lasted over a decade. The Japanese economy started to grow again in 2003. It benefited significantly from robust Chinese economic development.

When President Clinton (1993–2001) took office, he cut government spending on welfare benefits and reduced the size of the federal work force. He continued the appointment of the highly respected

Federal Reserve Chairman, Alan Greenspan, to ensure confidence in the stability of the economy and related fiscal policies. During the Clinton presidency, more than 22 million jobs were created. In addition, he converted the largest budget deficit in U.S. history to the largest surplus of over US$200 billion, reduced the unemployment rate to a thirty-year low, increased income at all levels, increased the homeownership rate and increased stock ownership. The Dow Jones Industrial Average increased by 220 percent and the NASDAQ increased by 300 percent from 1993 to 2001. Many economists think that the massive rise in the stock market and increased employment coincided with the technology and dot-com boom. This may not be directly attributed to the success of the Clinton administration. Clinton was widely considered the most investigated President ever. He was plagued by attacks from extreme right-wing opponents and with scandals known as the Travelgate and Whitewater controversies. Investigations into the latter two failed to reveal any criminal activity. However, Clinton's denial of involvement in the notorious sex scandal with Monica Lewinsky tarnished his reputation and made him one of the three U.S. Presidents who have faced impeachment proceedings. He was personally reckless, but a strong, charismatic leader. Clinton is clearly a president that many Americans will recall with fondness for his leadership during a period of economic prosperity.

On the whole, with the end of the Cold War in 1991 and the fall of the Eastern Bloc including the Soviet Union and its allies in the late 1980s, the U.S. economy improved and trade opportunities expanded greatly. Innovation in the U.S., including technological advances in electronics, telecommunications, and computer systems, triggered a vast industry and revolutionized the world through information technology, the Internet, and instant communications.

The U.S. economy grew very rapidly under conditions of low inflation, strong corporate earnings, low unemployment rate, and surging stock market. The U.S. government budget deficit peaked at US$290 billion in 1992 but posted its first surplus in thirty years in 1998 due to the skyrocketing stock market and the high employment rate of the Clinton term perpetuated by the information technology and Internet industry. America's labor force changed markedly in the 1990s.

The number of small farms declined further, being replaced by large scale farming operations. During this period, many manufacturing jobs in steel, textiles, and shoes were replaced by service jobs in technology industries including telecommunications, computer systems, health care, and financial services. The American economy matured in the twenty-first century; whereas nations with low labor costs such as China, India, Mexico and Brazil absorbed much of the manufacturing industries (toy, textile, shoe, and steel industries). China, in particular, evolved as a world factory and assembly plant, with rapid economic growth that surprised the world. Both the U.S. and China have become the two locomotive engines that drive the world economic development forward.

President George W. Bush took office in 2001 (2001–present). As the world economy grows more rapidly due to high-tech development and globalization, the U.S. economy has been growing at a stable rate of 3–5 percent in the first six years of the twenty-first century. For example, growth rates were 4.4 percent in 2004 and 3.5 percent in 2005. The U.S. unemployment rate also dropped to 4.7 percent in March 2006, the lowest rate in four and a half years. [14]

However, the Iraq War which began in 2003 has strained the U.S. economy and increased heavy borrowing from China, Japan, and Saudi Arabia resulting in growth of the deficit. As of this writing, over 3,200 U.S. soldiers have died and more than 24,000 have been injured. Direct military expenditures have reached US$352 billion and the daily cost of the war amounts to over US$280 million. By the end of the 2008 fiscal year, the direct military expenses will reach US$532 billion, not including military equipment replacement, maintenance, medical treatment, and compensations, etc. More than 655,000 Iraqis have died thus far during the war and four million became refugees, including two million who escaped to the neighboring countries. On average, 3,000 Iraqis flee the country daily.

But war losses cannot be measured only by economic numbers. What hurts more is the loss of the American Dream for many families. Here are heartfelt words (in *USA Today*, October 26, 2005), left by Army Chief Warrant Officer Aaron Weaver who died in the Iraq war, about his dreams of the future for his fifteen-month-old child:

My Dearest Little Savannah,

I always knew that having children is special to a parent, but it means so much more than I ever imagined . . . You are the meaning of my life. You make my heart pound with joy and pride. No matter what happens to me or where we go, you will always know that I love you.

In another *Newsweek* article "Black Hawk Down: The True Cost of Iraq War," February 5, 2007, issue, Weston Kosova described the farewell telephone conversation of Cpl. Victor Langarich with his mother the night before a fatal helicopter fight; he seemed convinced that he would not leave the war zone alive. He was crying,

"I will remember you every second," he said.

In Great Britain, 81 percent of the British surveyed opposed the U.S. war in Iraq. [15] President Bush recently deployed 21,500 more U.S. soldiers to Iraq. The war entered its fourth year on March 18, 2007. The *CNN* reported survey findings by Opinion Research Corp., which showed that only 35 percent of Americans were confident about the Iraq War, declining from 83 percent at the outset; sixty one percent thought the war was not worthwhile. [16] Extensive government spending for the war is resulting in an enormous government deficit estimated to reach a total of US$11,200 billion by 2010. This is equivalent to a personal debt of about US$38,000 for each American regardless of sex and age. The interest alone for the estimated total national debt, by 2010, is US$561 billion. This is equivalent to the total current amount of U.S. defense and military expenditures. [17] American children and grandchildren will be burdened heavily by debt caused by the war in Iraq.

While a Federal Reserve Bank Research Report stated that in the next ten years, the slowdown of the U.S. economy will be much greater than previously predicted by economists, its overall trend must be re-evaluated. The Federal Research Board also reported in 2006 that the richest 1 percent of Americans owned one-third of the nation's wealth; and the next wealthiest 9 percent owned roughly another one-third of the nation's wealth. In terms of real value, the top 15 percent of Americans owned an average of US$831,600 in net assets. [18]

A substantial portion of this is due to investments in real estate which may fluctuate in value as economic conditions change. The rich-poor gap is a characteristic of capitalism. Because America is the wealthiest nation on Earth, its capitalist system can afford to support a huge middle and working class or even the poorest population. In underdeveloped or developing nations, the rich-poor gap, nevertheless, may be a life-threatening social issue. China, after more than a two-decade market-driven economy, is experiencing a serious rich-poor gap and addresses the problem seriously in order to maintain stability.

A more alarming matter is the huge U.S. government debt. In a worst case scenario, the U.S. government will have trouble sustaining the Federal Social Security Program and Medicare health care benefits for seniors in the near future when the large baby boom population retires.

On the private income side, a significant number of Americans have a near-zero saving rate and the huge U.S. trade deficit, in particular with China and Japan, has prevented the U.S. from making more rapid economic development. In 2006, the government deficit was about 3 percent of the U.S. GDP, but the trade deficit reached 6 percent of the GDP. In 2005, the U.S. total trade deficit was US$726 billion and China accounted for about US$202 billion, or roughly 28 percent; in 2004, China's share was US$161.98 billion, and in 2003, US$24.1 billion.

Both American individuals and government are accustomed to using credit and borrowing money. Americans borrow money from banks to buy homes, cars, boats, electronics, and to pay for tuition and health care. The American government is borrowing money from countries that have higher rates of saving such as China, Japan, and South Korea where about 40 percent of after tax income is deposited in a bank savings account. China had US$853.7 billion in foreign currency reserves at the end of February, 2006. China outdistanced Japan in 2006 to become the largest holder of foreign currency reserves. [19] The size of China's holdings has been increasing every month.

It is clear that America recognizes the rising economic power of China just as it understood the Japanese challenges in the 1980s. The U.S. manufacturing industries remain very strong; about 75 percent of manufactured products in China are made by the U.S. companies in China. However, this industry has declined in relative importance in the twenty-first century inside the U.S.; instead, the service sector has grown substantially, whereas manufacturing in China is just beginning to gain momentum.

America is the leading superpower in the world after winning two world wars and the Cold War. After World War II, the U.S. GDP was more than 50 percent of the world GDP; now it has stabilized at about 30 percent. More importantly, the U.S. has exploited the latest scientific breakthroughs for military purposes, thereby creating military supremacy over all other countries in the world. American military presence is everywhere on land and in the North and the South Pacific Oceans, the Indian Ocean, and the North and the South Atlantic Oceans. [20] The U.S. economic dynamism and military supremacy provide the precondition for the exercise of global primacy. Hence, it is important to review briefly and understand the influence of U.S. military and foreign policies throughout modern history.

Over the past twenty years, the U.S. growth rate has averaged just over 3 percent, a full percentage higher than Germany and France (Japan averaged 2.3 percent over the same period). [21] In 1980, the U.S. made up 22 percent of world output; today it has risen to 29 percent. The U.S. currently ranks as the first most competitive economy in the world according to the World Economic Forum, and is first in technology and innovation, technical readiness, company spending for research and technology, and in the quality of its research institutions.

China trails the U.S. by more than thirty nations in these important areas. In virtually every sector in which the U.S. competes with advanced industrial nations, its businesses lead the world in productivity and profits. [21] Among the twenty top world universities, eighteen are American; the U.S. invests 3.25 percent of its GDP in higher education, compared with 1.28 percent in the E.U., 1.1 percent in Japan, and 0.5 percent in China. [22] The U.S. spends 2.59 percent in research and development compared with 1.93 percent in the E.U., 3.15 percent in Japan, and 1.31 percent in China. Soon China will spend an estimated 2.2 percent by 2010. But China has few patents (E.U. 1.0 per 100,000 population; U.S. 2.02; China 0.50). America remains by far the most attractive destination for students, taking 30 percent of the total number of foreign students globally. Beijing University is aggressively hiring Western professors and is embracing virtual education. MIT offers courses free on-line, which means that access to great education is expanding via new technology. It is likely that China will establish comparable world class universities within a couple of decades. [21] At the same time, the American educational system will remain the most flexible and dynamic in the world for decades to come.

4. The U.S. Foreign Policy before the End of World War II

American foreign policy is driven by its national interests and by the leadership of the president, the Congress, and the political party in power. The American Civil War occurred over four years ending in 1865. From then until the end of the nineteenth century, the united nation was immersed in recovery and reconstruction. U.S. strength and military power increased very rapidly, surpassing many European nations. For some time, isolationism prevailed in American foreign policy. Then a few U.S. leaders began to dream of an empire that would include Canada and much of Mexico. It was hoped that the U.S. territory would extend deep into the Pacific Ocean. American leaders were tempted to increase political influence and power in the international arena. With the help of the Monroe Doctrine, U.S. leadership eliminated European and Russian control and dominance in key geographic areas of most of the Western Hemisphere.

By 1900, America began to extend its influence by supporting the invasion of China by Austro-Hungarian, British, French, German, Italian, Japanese, and Russian forces. China became a semi-colonial society under these foreign powers until Dr. Sun Yat-sen led a revolution to overthrow the last Qing Empire, which established the ROC in 1912. In the meantime, various countries in Europe fought wars against each other until World War I broke out in 1914. World War I, which ended in 1918, was known as the Great War or the war to end all wars because it was among the largest, bloodiest, and deadliest of wars in Europe up to that time, resulting in over ten million dead and twenty million wounded.

World War I was sparked by the assassination of Archduke Ferdinand of Austria by members of a Serbian terrorist group, but the real root causes are much more complicated. Almost all countries in Europe

116

became part of the Great War. The U.S. joined later with Britain, France, Italy, and Russia to fight against the Central Powers composed of Austria, Germany, and the Ottoman Empire that included Turkey. At the end of the War, Japan also joined with the Allies to gain control of the German colony in China. After the war, an international organization called the League of Nations was formed. It was U.S. President Woodrow Wilson's (1913–1921) concept aimed at preventing wars in the future. [23]

Theodore Roosevelt (1901–1909) was the first president to insist that it was in the U.S. interest and a duty to make its influence felt globally. If American interests collided with those of other countries, it had the obligation to draw on its military and economic power to prevail. He believed in Darwin's theory of survival of the fittest. To him, America had a mission as a great power. [24] Similarly, President Woodrow Wilson also recognized later that America had a crucial role to play in world affairs. However, Wilson advocated the position that America had an obligation to spread its moral principles and values throughout the world. [24] These principles included the foundational belief system in democracy, freedom, and human rights. Wilson's ideas, known as Wilsonianism, promote the notion that world peace depends on the spread of democracy. Further, President Wilson held that states should be judged by the same ethical criteria as individuals, and that the national interest requires adherence to a universal system of laws. [24] After World War I, this vision was the basis for the formation of the League of Nations. Both President Woodrow Wilson and Theodore Roosevelt changed the U.S. course from isolation to full engagement in world politics. Theodore Roosevelt's balance of power and Wilson's value-driven diplomatic strategies have profoundly impacted American diplomacy. To this day, these two approaches permeate American foreign policies and are the basis for actions in global politics. The following passages regarding Theodore Roosevelt illustrate his importance and influence as the twenty-first president of the United States:

> *The Presidential achievements of Theodore Roosevelt are impressive. In foreign affairs he led us into the arena of international power politics, thrusting aside the American tradition of isolationism, while on the domestic scene, he reversed the traditional federal policy of laissez-faire, and sought to bring order, social justice, and fair deal-*

ings to American industry and commerce. In all his policies as Chief Executive, he expanded the powers and responsibilities of the Presidential office, establishing the model of the modern Presidency which has been followed by most of his successors in the White House.

His specific achievements are numerous: including his work for forest conservation, "busted" trusts (also known as monopolies) bringing the large corporations under the control of the people, began the Panama Canal, established the Department of Commerce and Labor, negotiated an end to the Russo-Japanese War, and was the first American awarded the Nobel Peace Prize. In addition, he successfully mediated international disputes over Venezuela, the Dominican Republic, and Morocco. He was the first world leader to submit a dispute to the Court of Arbitration at The Hague, and he was the first head of state to call for the convening of what became the Second Hague Peace Conference at which he obtained for Latin American nations equal status with the rest of the world, and won the adoption of the Drago Doctrine, which outlawed the use of force in the collection of foreign debts.

Many of the policies he advocated during the Bull Moose years were adopted by Presidents Woodrow Wilson and Franklin Roosevelt.

Towards the end of his life, he was a major force for military preparedness particularly as World War I loomed. Much of what he achieved affects each and every American today and his name and personality have become part of the collective icon for what America stands for at its best.

— THEODORE ROOSEVELT: A BRIEF BIOGRAPHY,
BY TWEED ROOSEVELT, GREAT-GRANDSON
OF PRESIDENT THEODORE ROOSEVELT

The Allied Nations won World War I, and the League of Nations was founded after the Paris Peace Conference of 1919. Its aim was to prevent wars through collective security, disarmament, and settling disputes between countries through negotiation and diplomacy. However, the League did not have armed forces of its own and had difficulty relying on the Great Powers to enforce its resolutions. In the 1920s, America was ambivalent about internationalism and isolationism. It refused to commit itself to safeguarding the Versailles Treaty in Asia, when Japan invaded Chinese Manchuria in 1931. The U.S. condemned Japanese actions, but refused to participate in collective enforcement. In Europe, much worse was about to happen after Hitler gained power and became German Chancellor in 1933. In addition, the League failed to prevent aggression by the Axis Powers in the 1930s and the German invasion of Poland in 1939, which started World War II.

To prevent American involvement in war again, the U.S. Congress adopted the Neutrality Act between 1935 and 1937. The U.S. President Franklin D. Roosevelt (1933–1945), who sensed the danger of Hitler's dictatorship and renewed Japanese military aggression in China, made the famous Quarantine Speech on October 5, 1937, to raise awareness regarding global concerns. His speech fell upon deaf ears and was attacked by isolationists who demanded to know the President's intentions. Nevertheless, over the fierce opposition of the isolationists, President Franklin D. Roosevelt proceeded with de facto military cooperation with Great Britain in 1939 by moving the bulk of the U.S. fleet to the Pacific. The U.S. also supplied China, France, Great Britain, the Soviet Union, and other Allied nations with vast amounts of war material between 1941 and 1945 under the Land Lease program proposed by Roosevelt in January 1941. It began in March 1941, nine months before the Pearl Harbor attack by the Japanese air force. It ended soon after V-J Day, on September 2, 1945. [25]

The close friendship and working relations that developed between Franklin D. Roosevelt and British Prime Minister Winston Churchill were crucial in the establishment of a united effort to deal with the Axis Powers. In August 1941, Roosevelt and Churchill met for the first of nine face-to-face conferences during the war. Their meeting created the document known as "The Atlantic Charter," which set forth the concepts including self-determination, the end of colonialism, freedom of the seas, and the improvement of living and working conditions for all people.

Many of the ideas were similar to those proposed by Wilson's Fourteen Points, which were not accepted by the U.S. allies at the Versailles Conference at the close of World War I. [25]

After the fall of France, Franklin D. Roosevelt further stressed the imminent threat of the Axis Powers to U.S. security and increased the defense budget to show his determination in bringing about the defeat of the Nazis. In 1941, Roosevelt announced a state of emergency and made clear that "We will not accept a Hitler-dominated world," and "We will accept only a world consecrated to freedom of speech and expression."

In May 1940, 64 percent of Americans considered the preservation of peace more important than the defeat of the Nazis. Eighteen months later, in December 1941, just before the Japanese attack on Pearl Harbor that number dropped to only 32 percent. Under President Harry S. Truman, Roosevelt's successor, World War II ended in Asia after the U.S. dropped two atomic bombs on Hiroshima and Nagasaki, Japan, in mid–1945. The Japanese surrendered on August 15, 1945. Previously, Hitler committed suicide in his bunker in Germany on April 30. It was his Field Marshal, Alfred Jodl, who signed an unconditional surrender with the Allies on May 7, 1945.

Winston Churchill, Joseph Stalin, and Franklin D. Roosevelt made plans for post-war Europe at the Yalta Conference in February 1945, which resulted also in the formation of the U.N. The Yalta conference was severely criticized for delivering Eastern Europe to Stalin and was known for resulting in the division of Germany and other territories. The United States and Great Britain also agreed to recognize the autonomy of Outer Mongolia, which belonged to China since the Qing Dynasty.

Franklin D. Roosevelt's policy was a mixture of traditional American exceptionalism and Wilsonian idealism. Prior to his death on April 12, 1945, President Roosevelt played a major role in shaping the post-war world; a series of international conferences was established following the blueprints for the post-war world order. This included, for example, the U.N. that should make future wars impossible by fostering the ideal of collective security, the World Bank that would focus on financing to developing countries, and other organizations that would work for food and agriculture, for relief and rehabilitation, and for civil aviation.

Perhaps the most important U.S. foreign policy initiative following the devastation of Europe during World War II was the Marshall Plan, named for its lead sponsor, former Secretary of State George C. Marshall. Fanned by the fear of Communist expansion and the rapid deterioration of European economies in the winter of 1946–1947, the U.S. Congress passed the Economic Cooperation Act in March 1948 and approved funding for the rebuilding of Western Europe. [26] The Plan entailed a comprehensive financial and technical support program to rebuild Europe. It also institutionalized and legitimized the concept of U.S. foreign aid programs. The Marshall Plan generated a resurgence of European industrialization and brought extensive investment into the region. In the immediate aftermath of the defeat of Hitler and his Third Reich, the plan promoted the U.S. goal of European integration and recovery. [27] It was also a stimulant to the U.S. economy by establishing markets for American goods. [28]

5. The U.S. Foreign Policy after the End of World War II

The U.S. diplomatic policies after the World War II can be separated into two categories with the end of the Cold War in 1991 as the line of demarcation. Prior to 1991, the world experienced a long period of intense, limited military confrontations between two camps—the Soviet Union and the U.S.—for over forty years. Amid this fierce opposition, the Bay of Pigs took the U.S. to the brink of nuclear war and the significant losses on both sides during the earlier Korean War, and the proxy war fought in Vietnam resulting in the loss of over 55,000 U.S. soldiers. All these events affected policy.

After President Roosevelt, the new president, Harry S. Truman (1945–1953), could not hold the alliance together and by the end of his first term, the U.S. and the Soviet Union initiated the Cold War that lasted from 1947 to 1991 with the collapse of the Soviet Union. Knowledge of the devastating effect of atomic bombs during World War II prevented the Cold War from getting involved in direct armed conflict of the contested countries; instead it was waged by diplomatic maneuvering, economic pressure, intimidation, propaganda, assassination, low-intensity military operations, proxy wars, and an escalating arms race.

Since both the U.S. and the Soviet Union had nuclear weapons, each was locked in a military stalemate known as mutual assured destruction (MAD). Many scholars and policy analysts believed that MAD made the world relatively stable and peaceful because it induced greater caution in international politics and discouraged the use of nuclear weapons for resolving disputes, hence maintaining a "horror balance" and avoiding a World War III. [29] This scenario has been modified somewhat with the rise of Islamic militant terrorists bent on the total destruction of the U.S., the U.K., and other Western nations.

i) U.S. Foreign Policy during the Cold War Era (1947–1991)

During the Cold War, the U.S. was accused by the Soviets of being the paragon of capitalist imperialism and of supporting racism at home and fascism abroad. Its allies included France, Great Britain, West Germany, and other members of the North Atlantic Treaty Organization (NATO or the Western Alliance), Australia, Israel, Japan, New Zealand, the Philippines, Saudi Arabia, South Korea, and Thailand. The Soviet Union was accused by the U.S. of violating human rights, crushing independent movements in Eastern Europe, and supporting dangerous insurgents abroad. Its important allies included Czechoslovakia, East Germany, and Poland, other members of the Warsaw Pact, Cambodia, Cuba, Laos, Mongolia, North Korea, Syria, etc. Countries that maintained neutrality included Austria, Finland, India, Sweden, Switzerland, Sudan, and Yugoslavia. China under the PRC and Albania had their own version of Communism and opposed many policies instituted by the Soviet Union.

Two wars took place in Asia during the Cold War era involving the U.S.: the Korean War from 1950 to 1953 and the Vietnam War from 1965 to 1975.

a) The Korean War (1950 to 1953)

Korea was annexed by Japan from 1910 to the end of World War II in 1945. In 1941, the Soviet Union, allied with the U.S., broke the 1941 nonaggression pact with Japan, declaring war on the Japanese empire. The Soviets entered Korea from the North while President Harry S.

Truman ordered U.S. troops to the South. After Japan surrendered in 1945, the U.S. and the Soviet Union agreed to divide Korea along the thirty-eighth parallel and the Korean Peninsula was divided into zones of control in the North and the South by these two powers and was administered by them temporarily. The North formed a communist government and the South a government with elections. Later, in 1949, both Russian and American forces were withdrawn. This was the same year that Mao Zedong established the PRC on the Chinese mainland and ROC's Chiang Kai-shek fled to Taiwan.

In June of 1950, the North Korean military surprisingly crossed the thirty-eighth parallel and war broke out between the North and the South. President Harry S. Truman ordered U.S. Commander General and U.N. Commander-in-Chief for Korea, Douglas MacArthur, to use air cover to protect the evacuation of U.S. citizens and ordered the Seventh Fleet to protect Taiwan. Other Western powers quickly joined American troops to support South Korea. Among these were U.N. troops which fought fiercely against the North Koreans who were backed by the Soviet Union and the PRC.

The U.N. troops drove the North Koreans back past the thirty-eighth parallel. General MacArthur thought that spreading the war across the Yalu River bordering between the DPRK and China would be necessary, whereas Truman and other leaders disagreed out of concern that China would intervene. The PRC warned that they would intervene if any non-South Korean forces crossed the thirty-eighth parallel. On October 7, 1950, when American troops crossed the thirty-eighth parallel, Chairman Mao sent Premier Zhou Enlai to Moscow and got Stalin's assistance by providing air support, and the Chinese People's Volunteer Army (PVA) assault began on October 25, 1950. Both the Chinese and the U.S. forces suffered heavy casualties, and the withdrawal of the U.S. Eighth Army was the longest retreat of an American unit in national history.

On January 4, 1951, the Communist Chinese and North Korean forces captured Seoul. Both the American Army and the U.N. Corps were forced to retreat. The situation was so grim that MacArthur openly demanded a nuclear attack on China, much to the alarm of American allies. In March 1951, a revitalized U.S. Army drove the North Korean and Chinese troops from Seoul. MacArthur was removed from command by President Harry S. Truman on April 11, 1951. The rest of the war involved little territorial change but involved lengthy peace negotiations. Battles continued while negotiations were underway. Finally, a cease-fire was declared on July 27, 1953, and a DMZ was established in the proximity of the thirty-eighth parallel.

For many Chinese, fighting in a war is seen as an honor despite heavy losses. Although China had its own reasons for war, a common Western perception was that the Soviets used the Chinese as proxies because China had borrowed heavily from them to rebuild Chinese economy after the Chinese Civil War.

The U.S. estimated that 600,000 Korean soldiers died in the conflict, about 2.5 million people combined were killed in the North and South and one-half of the houses were destroyed. The North remained a pro-Soviet totalitarian Communist state and the South a pro-America dictatorial republic that democratized in the late 1980s. American troops remain in South Korea and the DMZ is still the most heavily defended border in the world. The official Chinese estimate for PVA casualties was 390,000. This included one of Chairman Mao's sons, Mao Anying, who was killed as a PVA during the war. The U.S. Defense Department reported a total of 33,686 deaths throughout the three-year war. Moreover, the U.S. concluded that it had been caught ill-prepared for the war and responded by boosting its military budget which doubled the size of the army. American soldiers were then deployed all over Europe, the Middle East, and elsewhere in Asia. The American view of their role in the Korean War echoed familiar Wilsonian precepts of freedom versus dictatorship, good versus evil, law rather than the ruthless exercise of power, and defense of universal principles. Such lofty principles have underpinned the U.S. rationale in numerous military actions in two world wars, in the Vietnam War in 1965 and in the Gulf War in 1991.

The end of the Korean War represented a distraction from the real war, namely the Cold War with the Soviets. Stalin proposed mutual recognition of two spheres of influence: one for America in Western Europe, the other for the Soviet Union in Eastern Europe with a unified, armed neutral Germany between them. Stalin died a year after he made the proposal, and shortly thereafter, Dwight D. Eisenhower (1953–1961) was elected. Winston Churchill (Prime Minister of Great Britain from

1940 to 1955) advocated negotiation with the new Soviet leader, but Eisenhower was not receptive to reopening talks with the Soviets.

By 1955, the Geneva Summit could not alter the fundamental reality that the U.S. and the Soviet Union were locked in geopolitical competition and the new Soviet leader Nikita Khrushchev was ready to challenge the West outside the Soviet sphere of interest, causing the Soviet-American conflict to move beyond Europe. The U.S. tried to dissociate from Europe and attempted to deal with the developing world through the U.N. The bloody suppression by the Soviet Union of the Hungarian uprising in 1956 proved that this nation was another victim of the Russian expansionism. But America did not risk another war to overturn the communist control of Eastern Europe. Although, right after World War II, America had a nuclear monopoly, the Soviet Union also began to develop its own thermonuclear weapons and inter-continental strategic missiles. It was beyond dispute that by 1958 a general nuclear war would already surpass the accumulated total casu-alties of both world wars. However, despite the 1961 Berlin Crisis that saw U.S. Army troops facing East German Army troops in a stand-off, the East German government eventually backed down to avoid the eruption of a real war.

Perhaps the worst nuclear standoff between the U.S. and the Soviet Union was the Cuban missile crisis which occurred in 1962 when John F. Kennedy was President (1961–1963). The crisis arose over Soviet deploy-ment of nuclear missiles in Cuba in response to U.S. deployment of fifteen Jupiter intermediate-range ballistic nuclear missiles in Turkey. The missiles in Turkey were considered a direct threat to cities in western sections of the Soviet Union. The standoff lasted for thirteen days and ended when Soviet leader Nikita Khrushchev announced that the instal-lations would be dismantled. However, the compromise satisfied no one. It was a sharp embarrassment for Khrushchev and he lost power two years later. Kennedy himself was assassinated the next year.

b) The Vietnam War (1965 to 1975)

During this war, the Democratic Republic of Vietnam (North Vietnam) allied with the Communist Soviet Union, China, Czechoslovakia, East Germany, and North Korea against the Republic of

Vietnam (South Vietnam) and its allies Australia, New Zealand, the Philippines, South Korea, Thailand, and the U.S. The peak years of the war ran from 1965 until the official U.S. withdrawal in 1973. It was conducted through three U.S. presidencies. The war ended on April 30, 1975, with the military conquest of the South by the North.

After gaining independence from French colonization in 1954, Vietnam was temporarily divided between the anti-Communist South and the pro-Communist North. In 1956, South Vietnam, with American backing, refused to hold unification elections as was agreed upon at the Geneva Conference. Fighting began in 1957 with Communist-led guerrillas known as Viet Cong supported by the Soviet Union and China against the U.S. backed South Vietnamese government. The conflict spilled over into the neighboring countries of Cambodia and Laos. The South Vietnamese government and its Western allies portrayed the conflict as based on a principled opposition to communism, namely to deter the expansion of Soviet-based control throughout Southeast Asia. This concept was known as the "domino theory." In contrast, the North Vietnamese and its Southern affiliated organization viewed the war as a struggle to reunite the country under a communist dictatorship and to repel a foreign aggressor.

With the Korean War as a precedent, the U.S. had feared that a reunified Vietnam would result in a Communist government. Soon after the Korean War, on February 12, 1955, to support the South's government, U.S. President Dwight D. Eisenhower sent the first few hundreds of American armed servicemen along with Central Intelligence Agency (CIA) agents to Vietnam as military advisors. Their number grew to 16,300 by 1963.

In 1961, President John F. Kennedy had a bitter disagreement over key U.S.-Soviet issues with Soviet Premier Nikita Khrushchev in Vienna and the Kennedy administration remained essentially committed to the Cold War foreign policy inherited from the Truman administration. Following continued losses to the Viet Cong, President Lyndon B. Johnson (1963–1969) escalated the war in 1965. President Johnson's strategy involved a "scorched-earth" policy commencing with air strikes on North Vietnam and the commitment of ground forces, which numbered 536,000 by 1968.

President Richard M. Nixon followed Johnson with a strategy known as Vietnamization. This entailed withdrawal of American troops and the provision of greater responsibility for the war to South Vietnam. With the escalation of the war, numerous large-scale anti-war and anti-draft protests took place all over America. Many demonstrations occurred at colleges and universities as protests against the mandatory draft. From 1968 to 1973, efforts were made to end the conflict through diplomacy. In 1973, U.S. troops were withdrawn from Vietnam. Two years later, South Vietnam surrendered to the North and Vietnam was reunited.

The Vietnam War may be thought of as the second Indochinese war. The first began in 1945 after World War I with the collapse of the Japanese Military Administration and ended in 1954 with the Geneva Peace Accord. The Vietnam War was one of the longest and most unpopular wars in American history. The Vietnam War cost the U.S. 58,000 lives and 350,000 casualties. As many as two million Vietnamese died in the conflict. Virtually every Vietnamese family was affected by the war. Persecution and poverty prompted an additional two million people to flee Vietnam as "boat people" over the twenty years following the country's reunification. The problem was so severe that during the 1980s and 1990s, the U.N. established refugee camps in neighboring countries to rescue and support the fleeing refugees.

In addition, Vietnamese and American clashes over the Cambodian border in 1970 made it a theatre in the Vietnam War. China supported North Vietnam; hence, it also supported the Cambodia regime at the time. President Nixon instructed Henry A. Kissinger to order "a massive bombing campaign of Cambodia." By 1973, half-a-million tons of U.S. bombs had killed over 100,000 peasants and devastated the countryside.

On May 2, 1973, the Khmer Rouge, led by "Brother number one," Pol Pot, came to power in Cambodia. The regime set about building a radical, peasant-dominated agrarian utopia. The capital and provincial towns were cleared and the inhabitants forced to march to the countryside to work fifteen-hour days with virtually no food. Many died of starvation or disease. Many thousands more comprised of intellectuals and the devout were tortured and clubbed to death in the "killing fields." An estimated 1.7 million Cambodians perished. The Vietnamese invaded and brought down the regime in January 1979. [30]

The Vietnam War had a powerful impact on U.S. sociopolitical opinion. After the war, the U.S. Congress enacted the War Powers Act in 1973, requiring the president to receive explicit Congressional approval before committing American forces overseas. Even today, many Americans question the American incursion in Vietnam. Was it a blunder, a necessary war, or a noble cause? For both supporters and critics, these opinions generated passionate discourse and divergent political positions with regard to U.S. foreign and domestic policy in the years that followed.

c) The Sino-Soviet Split and President Richard M. Nixon's Visit to China

As discussed, during the Cold War America fought two major wars in Asia: the Korean War and the Vietnam War. In each case, America fought against allies of China and the Soviet Union. During the Korean War, the Soviet Union provided military supplies and advice. Chinese soldiers had full responsibility for the actual combat.

Throughout the Vietnam War China and the Soviet Union provided both supplies and military advice without combat troops. In the late 1950s, China and the Soviet Union engaged in a major ideological conflict about the two countries' respective views of communist doctrine. By 1964, diplomatic relations between the CPC and the Communist Party of the Soviet Union were severed.

With the start of the Vietnam War in 1965, the Sino-Soviet split became a lasting reality. The only exception was Chinese permission to transport Soviet arms and supplies across China in support of Communist North Vietnam during the Vietnam War. The Chinese Cultural Revolution in 1966 resulted in severance of most contacts between China and much of the rest of the world. China was strategically isolated and vulnerable.

The Sino-Soviet conflict reached a peak in 1969 when armed border clashes broke out along the Ussuri River on Damansky Island. By 1970, Mao realized that he could not simultaneously engage in confrontations with both the Soviet Union and the U.S. while working to suppress internal disorder. Mao determined that the threat of the Soviet Union was greater due to its geographical proximity; he therefore sought an accommodation with the U.S. Mao concluded that this was the best policy in spite of the fact that the Vietnam War was at its height and anti-America rhetoric in China was at a peak.

For America, Wilsonian idealism enabled American leaders to play a global leadership role from the end of World War II until the 1960s. The Vietnam War and the domestic turmoil related to the anti-war and civil rights movements led to a shift to a more complex and balanced approach in international relations. In July 1971, the U.S. Secretary of State Henry A. Kissinger secretly visited Beijing and laid the groundwork for President Richard M. Nixon's visit to China in February 1972. This marked the beginning of the triangular relationship between the U.S., China, and the Soviet Union during the Cold War era. The break-through by Nixon and Kissinger was based on a revitalization of the concept of balance of power introduced by Theodore Roosevelt sixty years earlier. For the first time since the PRC establishment in 1949, the communist bamboo curtain had been raised.

Nixon's trip to China was the first by a U.S. president under the PRC government. At this time China did not maintain diplomatic rela-tions with the U.S. At the conclusion of his trip, the two leaders issued the Shanghai Communiqué setting forth their foreign policy positions, in which the U.S. declared: "The United States acknowledges that all Chinese on either side of the Taiwan Strait maintain there is but one China and that Taiwan is a part of China. The United States government does not challenge that position." Both nations pledged to work toward full normalization of diplomatic relations.

In the international arena, the ROC was originally recognized as the sole legitimate government of both the PRC and Taiwan by the U.N. and most nations. On 25 October 1971, following a visit by Henry A. Kissinger to Beijing, the U.N. General Assembly passed Resolution 2758, which in effect expelled the ROC. The PRC replaced the ROC on the Security Council and on all other U.N. organizational entities. Most countries today recognize that there is one China and that the PRC is the sole legitimate representative of China.

At present, the ROC maintains formal diplomatic relations with only twenty-four pocket-sized countries. On January 1, 1979, the U.S. and China promulgated a Joint Communiqué on the Establishment of

Diplomatic Relations between the People's Republic of China and the United States of America. The communiqué stated:

"The United States of America recognizes the government of the People's Republic of China as the sole legal government of China. Within this context, the people of the United States will maintain cultural, commercial, and other unofficial relations with the people of Taiwan. . . .

The government of the United States of America acknowledges the Chinese position that there is but one China and Taiwan is part of China."

The U.S. subsequently terminated its diplomatic relationship with the ROC, but later, in 1979, enacted a domestic law—the Taiwan Relations Act—to sell weapons to Taiwan, which had the effect of impeding progress towards improved relations with China. [31]

In order to solve the issue of the U.S. arms sales to Taiwan, the U.S. and the Chinese government conducted negotiations and reached an agreement on August 17, 1982. They unveiled the third Sino-U.S. Joint Communiqué, in which the U.S. government stated its position:

"It does not seek to carry out a long-term policy of arms sales to Taiwan, that its arms sales to Taiwan will not exceed, either in qualitative or in quantitative terms, the level of those supplied in recent years since the establishment of diplomatic relations between the United States and China, and that it intends to reduce gradually its sales of arms to Taiwan, leading over a period of time to a final resolution."

Although the U.S. has been firm on its one-China policy since the date it established a diplomatic relationship with the PRC, the U.S. often takes advantage of the subtle difference between "opposing" and "not supporting" Taiwan independence. In addition, for more than twenty years, the U.S. government has sold huge amounts of arms to Taiwan. The continuous U.S. arms sales to Taiwan has all along been viewed by the PRC as a barrier to solving the Taiwan problem, and also as sending the wrong message regarding Taiwan independence. The U.S. thus far has identified one explicit condition for the cross-strait political future and that is a peaceful "resolution," rather than a peaceful "reunification." These ambiguities have resulted in the U.S. walking a diplomatic tightrope with regard to the China/Taiwan issue. Also damaging is periodic saber rattling by the U.S., China, and Taiwan on the subject of the Taiwan Strait. [31]

Mao Zedong died in 1976. In spite of the efforts by the Soviet Union's Mikhail S. Gorbachev to restore normal relations with China, the Sino-Soviet split continued until the late 1980s. To cement improving relations, Gorbachev visited China in 1989 amid the June fourth Tiananmen Square Protests and the ensuing crackdown. The June fourth Tiananmen Square Incident is regarded as another power struggle within the CPC, but it looms large in the minds of Westerners who see the Chinese government as repressive even today. [32]

Because of the expense of the forty-year Cold War arms race with the U.S., the lack of a free market economy, and inefficient government-run monopolies, the economy of the Soviet Union was in shambles. By the late 1950s, both the U.S. and the Soviet Union had developed massive nuclear arsenals. The arms race had exhausted the economy of the Soviet Union and when Gorbachev embarked on political reform before reviving the country's economy, the communist party quickly lost its hold on power. Finally, in his 1991 Christmas speech, Gorbachev resigned as president of the Soviet Union. The collapse of the Soviet Union ended the Sino-Soviet split.

d) The Reagan Era (1981–1989) and the Gulf War of 1991

U.S. President Ronald Wilson Reagan was committed to anti-communism. Apart from his conservative economic policies, his foreign policy is noted for a military buildup and a shift from containment of the Soviet Union to confrontation. Some historians consider him a leading figure in orchestrating the collapse of the Soviet Union in 1991. Some Americans credit President Reagan with restoring the nation's optimism, replacing perceptions advanced by his predecessor Jimmy Carter, of a deep malaise. The Reagan presidency influenced the American psyche to such a great extent that the decade of the 1980s is often referred to as the "Reagan era."

President Reagan was followed by Republican George H. W. Bush (1989–1993). Two years later, the Gulf War began between Iraq and a coalition force of approximately thirty countries led by the U.S. The war, mandated by the U.N., was intended to liberate Kuwait that had been invaded by Iraq. The cause of the war was the unproven contention by Iraq that Kuwait was illegally slant-drilling oil across Iraq's border. The coalition force won a decisive victory driving Iraqi forces out of Kuwait with minimal human casualties. The operation was known as "Desert Storm."

ii) The U.S. Foreign Policy after the Cold War Era (1992–Present)

Although President George H.W. Bush triumphed militarily during the Gulf war, he lost his re-election bid to the Democratic contender William Jefferson Clinton (1993–2001). It was widely believed that the loss was due to poor domestic economic performance. The Clinton era ushered in a period that was economically robust and peaceful. This time of relative calm and prosperity was interrupted by the terrorist attacks on September 11, 2001, (9/11) on the Twin Towers at New York City's renowned World Trade Center, a symbol of U.S. economic and financial power. The attack, which involved the use of commercial aircraft as missiles, was part of a coordinated assault on other symbols of U.S. power; namely the Department of Defense and, reportedly, the U.S. Capital. The later attempt on the Capital was foiled through the heroic efforts of the passengers of United Airlines Flight 93. Nineteen of the twenty-one terrorists were Saudi Arabians, trained by fellow Saudi and Islamic militant, Osama bin Laden. The assault on the Towers was a catastrophe comparable to Pearl Habor in American history, as it occurred on the U.S. mainland and caused the death of over 3,000 innocent people.

The scale and impact of the 9/11 terrorist attacks completely transformed existing global strategic plans and the focus of the U.S. military. It was a watershed moment in world history. The attack of 9/11 was the work of Osama bin Laden and his terrorist organization, al Qaeda. Al Qaeda launched what it characterized as a holy war against the crimes and sins committed by the Americans listed in a fatwa—a religious ruling or declaration of war—by Osama bin Laden in 1998. The fatwa accused the U.S. of the following:

1) Plundering the resources of the Arabian Peninsula

2) Dictating policy to the rulers of those countries

3) Supporting abusive regimes and monarchies in the Middle East, thereby oppressing their people

4) Having military bases and installations in the Arabian Peninsula, which violates the sanctity of the Muslim holy land, in order to threaten neighboring Muslim countries

5) Intending to create disunity among Muslim states, thus weakening them as a political force

6) Supporting Israel, and wishing to divert international attention from (and tacitly maintain) the occupation of Palestine

The 9/11 attack has created a model and a mythology for the terrorists. It has left a dark shadow on the heart of Americans. Unfortunately, the anti-terrorist war seems endless, without clear war zones or visible enemies. America will be preoccupied for many decades.

In response to 9/11, the U.N.-approved war in Afghanistan was initiated to hunt for Osama bin Laden; then a pre-emptive invasion of Iraq (2003–present) took place, led by the U.S. and the United Kingdom, but without U.N. backing. The second Iraq incursion was justified on the basis of false intelligence regarding weapons of mass destruction. The White House claimed that Iraq had biological weapons despite evidence to the contrary. In addition, a recent report revealed that before the Iraq War, the Iraqi leader Saddam Hussein had not had any contact with the Al Qaeda leader Abu Musab Zarqawi who at the time was engaged in terrorist activities. [33]

This report makes the rationale for the American attack on Iraq even less convincing. America has sacrificed its prestige in the world and consumed enormous human, military, and financial resources on the war. However, President George W. Bush said that the national security of America "depends on the advance of liberty in other countries," and offered a broad defense of his goal of spreading democracy worldwide. He rejected the notion that his policies are "backfiring" in the Middle East. [34]

Presently, there are about 132,000 American soldiers and eighteen American air force bases in Iraq. Experts agree that Iraq is in a civil war due to the upsurge of Shiite-Sunni sectarian violence. President George W. Bush has approved an increase of 21,500 soldiers to Iraq for a total of about 157,000 soldiers to strengthen American security. [35–36]

The American public is expressing widespread reservations about the Iraq War and pessimism about the future. Many have lost confidence in President Bush whose approval rating of 30 percent is at a historical low. Earlier, a CBS survey reported that 66 percent of Americans thought that the country was on the wrong track. [37] When President George W. Bush was asked when he expected American forces to fully withdraw from Iraq, he answered, "That will be decided by future presidents." [38–39]

Ailing British playwright Harold Pinter was one among those who in 2005 opposed the current Iraq War. He used his Nobel Prize lecture to fiercely attack U.S. foreign policy and urge an unflinching pursuit of truth to restore "the dignity of man." He said that post-Second World War history was full of examples of Washington exercising "a clinical manipulation of power worldwide while masquerading as a force for universal good," and he said that the U.S. and its ally Britain – "its own bleating little lamb" - had traded in death and "employed language to keep thought at bay." [40] As the war entered its fourth year, protesters across the country raised their voices on March 17, 2007, against the U.S. policy in Iraq. [41]

After 9/11, President Bush created the Department of Homeland Security to raise the nation's alert level and to conduct security protection against terrorist attacks. This represents one of the largest restructurings of the U.S. government in contemporary history. At the same time, Congress passed the Patriot Act, which permits law enforcement to invade the privacy of citizens and limits judicial oversight over law-enforcement and domestic intelligence gathering. The Bush administration also initiated a secret National Security Agency operation to eavesdrop on telephone and e-mail communications—without a warrant—between the U.S. and people overseas. Some Americans think that their government has invaded the privacy of its citizens and violated their human rights. [42]

Although the world media condemned the 9/11 terrorist attacks, they also criticized the Bush government's attack on Iraq as a pretext for gaining control of oil resources. To many, the U.S. squandered worldwide support and sympathy in its fight against terrorism through its invasion of Iraq and made the world more dangerous. Major newspapers and media including the *New York Times*, the *Los Angeles Times*, *USA Today*, *The Economist*, the *Times of London*, the French newspaper *Libération*, the German business and finance daily newspaper *Handelsblatt* (Düsseldorf), and many Middle Eastern, Asian, and Arabic newspapers have criticized President Bush for his policies on Iraq and for over-extending executive power that domestically infringes on human rights. Some news media reports suggest that these policies undermine and severely damage the Western democratic value system.

Although Saddam Hussein was a brutal dictator, Iraq had no known connection with the 9/11 terrorists before the war. Now the conflict has become a breeding ground and hotbed for a new generation of terrorists. The fight of the Bush government against terrorism has lost focus, international respect, and support. Today, many Americans view the Iraq War as a serious mistake.

In summary, we have reviewed several major U.S. wars: the Korean War, the Vietnam War, the Cold War with the Soviet Union, and the two wars with Iraq in the Middle East. The first three may be considered wars fought in the national interest for political ideologies related to democracy, freedom, and human rights, whereas the two Iraq wars may be fought to protect interests in oil in the Middle East and to support Israel.

6. Conclusions

The U.S. is governed by a democratic system led by two major political parties. Every American voter has an equal right to vote to choose among the political candidates for the government positions. In this system of "popular governance," the power of government is derived from the people. The government must be accountable to the people for how it exercises its power. The cultural background of freedom, human rights, and individualism empowers Americans to make decisions to manage their own political affairs. The U.S. has the most powerful economic capitalistic system in the world.

After the Civil War, America's economy and industrialization progressed rapidly and by the early twentieth century, it became a major economic powerhouse in the world. On the political front, Theodore Roosevelt's concept of a balance of power and Wilson's value-driven diplomatic strategies had a profound impact on modern American foreign policy. The U.S. participation and victory in the two world wars after an early period of isolation established the American status as a leading world power. It has been a model for countries that support democracy and capitalism and an opponent of countries led by the Soviet Union which advocated Communism and planned economies. The confrontation between the former Soviet Union and the U.S., known as the Cold War, lasted over forty years. During this period both the Korean War and the Vietnam War took place as a result of Cold War tensions. Although the Korean Peninsula remains divided and the U.S. lost the Vietnam War, the Sino-U.S. diplomatic relationship was established and the Soviet Union collapsed in 1991.

After the Cold War, America became the leading world superpower. In the international arena, the U.S. government applied foreign policies perceived as biased in the Middle East. These policies unsettled the Muslim world and the U.S. became the target of some extremists from that region. The 9/11 attack reshaped America's perception of homeland security. Since then, the U.S. has been engaged in a war in Afghanistan to destroy the sanctuary of Osama bin Laden and other al Qaeda terrorists, and launched a preemptive strike in Iraq to search for weapons of mass destruction based on wrong intelligence.

The American antiterrorist strategy has met with numerous obstacles and it seems that the military has fallen into the trap of fighting a guerilla war in Iraq. In addition, there are many added complexities of U.S. involvement; for example, restoration of infrastructure, training of police and Iraqi soldiers, unemployment, health care, flight of the middle class, etc. Many mistakes were made by the U.S. in the early stages of the war that continue as problems now.

The U.S. is a strong ally of Israel and vice versa. Israel and Iraq are currently the two primary strategic targets of the U.S. in the Middle East. The U.S. government has borrowed billions of dollars per month to finance the war. Some analysts believe the U.S. is caught in a Catch-22 dilemma: if it withdraws troops, previous efforts will be in vain and its credibility will be hurt; if it continues to fight, it will remain embroiled in a dangerous Vietnam-like war without a foreseeable end.

However, it is important to acknowledge the tremendous contributions made by the U.S. in the Second World War and its contribution to the international community after World War II. Without America, no one could predict how long Nazi Germany would dominate and rule Europe. This was also the war that the Chinese and the Americans fought together against the Japanese invasion.

Without America, the U.N. would probably not exist. Its founding helped unite the international community, although many people do not have a positive view of the U.N.'s effectiveness. However, the pre-emptive strike of the U.S. against Iraq, a sovereign nation, without U.N. consensus, seriously damaged the U.S. reputation. It is unfortunate for both the U.S. and the rest of the world that the recent American unilateralism is built largely on geopolitical fantasy. U.S. military objectives and actions in Iraq have disrupted world order as well as damaged long-term American national interests. This unfortunate war has prompted some to think that America has become a "threat" rather than a peaceful force in world affairs.

CHAPTER V

Say "No" to China Threat Theory

In previous chapters, we discussed Chinese and American history and culture, their political systems, foreign policies, economies, and where these two great nations stand today. It is clear that the two countries are very different.

In the preface, four waves of enthusiasm towards China in recent U.S. history were reviewed. In between these positive periods, some China threat rhetoric has surfaced.

Although the Soviet Union, not China, started the Korean War, the China threat theory surfaced soon after the establishment of the PRC. The U.S. and other Western policies called for the containment and non-recognition of Beijing for more than two decades. [1] The China threat theory espoused by the U.S. raised the temperature of conflict during the Vietnam War (1965–1975), although China played an adversarial role only secondary to the Soviet Union.

After the Cold War, in order to maintain supremacy, the U.S. could not accept challenges from any other country, whether remote or potential. China has shown robust growth following its open door policy in 1978 and the shift to a market economy. In addition, the political and diplomatic position of China is gradually improving. The China threat theory intensified again, as the U.S. trade deficit with China went through the roof during the second term of President George W. Bush.

China bashing by the U.S. was compounded when the Japanese Foreign Minister Taro Aso stated that "I recognize that it (China) is becoming a considerable threat." Beijing reacted angrily to these remarks. "China sticks to a path of peaceful development," stated Chinese Ministry spokesman Qin Gang. [2] The *New York Times* responded to this rhetoric in an article entitled "Japan's Offensive Foreign Minister" for his "inflammatory statements" suggesting that China's military buildup represents a threat to Japan. The article concluded that Aso's "sense of diplomacy is as odd as his sense of history." [3]

We shall examine the China threat theory in great detail.

Part I

Refuting Japan's China Threat Theory

The Han Chinese did not try to conquer Japan. Twice the Mongolians attempted to invade Japan in the thirteenth century after they conquered China, ending the Chinese Song Dynasty. The allied armies of Koryo and Kublai Khan of the Yuan (Mongol) Dynasty (1279–1368) launched invasions of Japan in 1274 and 1281, but failed due to storms. [4] Japan adopted Chinese culture and a feudal system similar to that of China for several hundred years until the Meiji Restoration (1862–1869), which transformed Japanese political and social structures into a new modernized form. This was a direct response to the opening of Japan with the arrival of the ships of Commodore Matthew Perry.

The current Japanese imperial rule was established in which the emperor performed high priestly duties, while his ministers governed the nation in his name by adopting a Western democratic-style system. After the Meiji restoration, Japan's economic and military strength rose rapidly and eventually led to the unfortunate Japanese invasion of China, Korea, and other countries in Asia. Many Asian nations, invaded by Japan during World War II, continue to hold bitter memories of their war experiences.

1. The Bitter Memory of the Japanese Invasion of China

The first Sino-Japanese War broke out in August 1894. The Chinese Qing Court was defeated and forced to sign the Treaty of Shimonoseki in 1895. As a result, China paid a large indemnity and ceded to Japan numerous territories including: the Liaodong Peninsula, the Pescadores Islands, all islands appertaining to Taiwan, and the island of Taiwan.

In 1905, Japan defeated Russia and took control of Manchuria in northeastern China. Five years later, Japan successfully invaded and colonized Korea. The initial incursion by Japan into China was underway as early as January 18, 1915, a year after World War I broke out. Japan presented China with a secret ultimatum known as the "Twenty-One Demands," designed to give Japan regional ascendancy over China. [5]

In 1917, during World War I, China joined the Allies and declared war on Germany. However, after winning the war, China's demand to end foreign rule within its borders was ignored in the Treaty of Versailles. Instead, the former German concessions in China's Shangdong Province were transferred to Japan. [6] Then the second Sino-Japan War broke out in 1937 and lasted until 1945. Along with Chinese civilians and soldiers who were killed or wounded, millions of families were devastated. It was the Chinese men and women who held back the main Japanese force in the Asian battleground during World War II for eight years.

The triangular historical relationship among China, Japan, and the U.S. after World War II is complicated. But the source of China-Japan tension is mainly attributed to Japanese anxiety regarding the rapid economic expansion and development in China. Economic growth has created a new power balance in the Asia-Pacific region. During the 1980s and 1990s, the Japanese government concentrated on how to emerge from its own economic stagnation rather than focusing on international affairs. After the Asian economic crisis in 1997–98, Japan recognized her neighbor was no longer the weak country it had been in the past.

Nationalism has increased in Japan with its economic recovery. The Japanese government has adopted national policies in two strategic directions: first, it established a closer relationship to the U.S. to counterbalance China; second. it sought to normalize its international position by establishing independent national security policies.

2. Shrine Visits by Japanese Leadership Cause Tension

Former Prime Minister of Japan, Junichiro Koizumi repeatedly visited the famous Yasukuni Shrine in Tokyo, which memorializes fourteen Japanese war criminals among other war dead honored there. This signaled a return to Japanese nationalism, glorified the Japanese invasion of Asia, and was a way to gain domestic political support. Although more than 68 percent of the Japanese disapproved of the visit, an estimated 60 percent did not think that Koizumi should compromise on objections raised by China, South Korea, and the U.S. Strong nationalism in China and Japan has hindered each nation's ability to engage in friendly high-level dialogue. The Shrine visits are no longer a cultural issue. They have been transformed into a diplomatic source of contention. [7] The Sino-Japan diplomatic relationship reached the lowest point in recent history during Koizumi's term.

As Japan's strongest ally, it would be helpful and productive for the U.S. to intervene to thaw the troubled China-Japan relationship to improve and maintain Asia-Pacific stability. The U.S. House Committee on International Relations unanimously passed a resolution that urges Japan to assume responsibility for condoning sexual slavery during World War II. The resolution is the first of its kind, holding Japan accountable for sexual enslavement of women during the war. [8] Chinese and Korean "comfort women" were among those who suffered the most and many Chinese still have difficulty erasing these tragic memories of invasion, rape, and massacre by the Japanese. [9] In spite of recent economic and political ascendancy, the Chinese people remain somewhat insecure about national defense and security. They wish for peace, stability, and respect.

To date, the Japanese government has never issued formal apologies or shown remorse to the Chinese people or government regarding Japanese atrocities during the war. In addition, some Japanese school text books deny the brutality of Japanese soldiers during the war. [10] The new Japanese Prime Minister Shinzo Abe also denied the responsibility of Japan for using Asian women as sex slaves for Japanese troops in World War II. [11] This angered many Chinese and Koreans again, and called it "Japan's Shame" and "A Second Rape." [12] "The kind of atrocities, the kind of crimes – crimes against humanity – that the Japanese Imperial Army committed during World War II against the Chinese people were so huge, so horrendous, compared to the Opium War, or compared to anything that we have seen in history. . . . I mean the degree, the magnitude, the method, how they treated other human beings is beyond words," remarked Joseph Wong, a founder of the Canada Alpha Society that promotes public awareness and preserves the history of World War II in Asia. [13]

Sensitivity to the Shrine visits is also illustrated by a report of Brian Yam, a Chinese man married to a Japanese woman, who visited Yasukuni Shrine. His goal was to gain an appreciation for the reasons for so much tension on the issue: [14]

> *A few exhibits portrayed the invasion of Korea by Japan as being forced by China. Another referred to the Rape of Nanking as an "incident" with no mention of the number of deaths. [. . .] Another odd experience was seeing a room full of pictures of war dead referred to as "war gods" in Japanese. It was then that I truly understood how Japan became so reckless during World War II.*

Chinese Foreign Minister Li Zhaoxing said on November 15, 2005, at the Asia Pacific Economic Cooperation Forum in Busan, South Korea, that "The Chinese people want a real friendship with Japan but Japanese leaders ought not to do any more things that cause pain to the other Asian countries." [15] The China-Japan friendship could produce a mutually beneficial relationship or both would suffer.

For a few months, all high-level meetings among the leaders of

China, South Korea, and Japan were postponed because of the tense atmosphere. [16] Other than China and South Korea, Japan also has a territorial conflict with Russia over four islands in the north. Neither country wishes to compromise. [17]

Japan is becoming more isolated in Asia for four primary reasons: 1) Under the previous leadership of Junichiro Koizumi, Japan strengthened its relationship with the U.S. and Japanese right-wing politicians had a Cold War position on China; 2) Japan has assumed a strong opposition stance by freezing aid loans to China from March to June 2006, refusing to compromise on territorial disputes, endorsing distorted war history written in Japanese school text books and visiting the Yasukuni Shrine; [18] 3) Japan tried but failed to become a member of the U.N. Security Council in an attempt to broaden its international influence and has been pushing South East Asian countries into negotiating a FTA to increase Japanese dominance; and 4) Japan seeks to become a country of equal global stature by increasing its military buildup and by modifying the Constitution to strengthen and legitimize its security protection.

President Bush expressed some concern on this subject during his latest visit to Japan. [19] The U.S. Congressional Research Services reported that if Japan continues on this negative diplomatic path with China, it will damage and conflict with U.S. interests. Nevertheless, the military cooperation between Japan and the U.S. has been strengthened because of a shared concern about the economic rise of China and nuclear weapons development in North Korea, although tremendous progress has been made with the help of China regarding this issue.

3. The Strengthened U.S.-Japan Military Tie to Contain China

Japan and the U.S. signed a Mutual Security Assistance Pact in 1952 after Japan gained full sovereignty at the end of the allied occupation. This provided the initial basis for the Japan-U.S. security relations after World War II. The Pact was revised in 1960. The new Treaty of Mutual Cooperation and Security declares that both nations will maintain and develop their own military capacities to resist armed external attacks on territories under Japanese administration. However, Japan is relieved from defending the U.S. because the Japanese Constitution prohibits sending armed forces overseas (Article 9). Since the Constitution forbids the maintenance of land, sea, and air forces, and expresses renunciation of "the threat or use of force as a means of settling international disputes," Japan has forces only for purposes of self-defense. The Treaty also allows the stationing of U.S. forces in Japan.

Since the collapse of the Soviet Union, the U.S.-Japan alliance has become more influential in security matters in East Asia. The rapid growth of Chinese influence has gradually caused Japan concern about maintaining its dominance in East Asia. At the same time, the U.S. also regards China as a potential enemy by maintaining a Cold War mentality. To the U.S., the Soviet Union has been an irreconcilable enemy and Japan has been an economic rival, whereas China is the first nation that has the potential to challenge the U.S. on both ends. Hence, under the current Bush administration, the U.S. wants to continue to exhibit its importance in Asia by strengthening its relations with Japan (and Australia) to contain China.

In 1994, the Japanese government included the Taiwan Strait, Korean Peninsula, and the South China Sea, which is defined as the "neighboring area," into its geographic space for defense under the Japan-U.S. Treaty of Mutual Cooperation and Security. This means that if conflict breaks out across the Taiwan Strait, Japan has the obligation to send troops together with the U.S. The U.S.-Japan security alliance has entered a new stage which poses a threat to Northeast Asia, especially to the military security of China and its plans to recover the territory of Taiwan. [20] In 1997, the Treaty was revised again to expand the role of Japan in reinforcing U.S. military forces in the event of attacks in the "surrounding areas" of Japan. [21] Japan, in preparation for using its naval forces to push its strategic border into the China Sea, has moved to increase its military buildup by modifying its Constitution to strengthen and legitimize its security protection.

After World War II, Japanese foreign policy was conciliatory. Japan worked to improve its relationships with countries in Asia. But now Japan is changing its approach: in seven years, foreign aid from Japan decreased by 50 percent from US$15.5 billion in 1999 to US$6.8 billion in 2005. The exception is India because Japan wishes to keep India as an ally to contain China. [22]

In 2006, the Minister of State and Head of the Japan Defense Agency, Fukushiro Nukaga, went as far as demanding that the Japanese Self-Defense Force (SDF) assume an international peace-keeping role. The U.S. has encouraged Japan to develop theater missile defense (TMD) systems within the U.S.-Japan security agreement and Japan has acquired new technology including the in-flight refueling technique. [23] In addition, Japan has launched spy satellites and is considering lifting its weapons export embargo. Japanese military expenditures rank second in the world, after the U.S. All of these activities demonstrate that Japan wants to play a more active role in Asian and world security.

The strong Japanese economy over the past sixty years and its promising GDP trend for the future show that Japan is capable of pursuing aggressive foreign policies to contain China and suppress North Korea in order to protect its national interests. Judging from Japan's recent military build-up, economic strength (its GDP ranked second in the world in 2006), superior hi-tech capabilities, military aggression during World War II, and recent frantic political provocations, it would be more accurate to describe Japan as a threat to Asia and the world community rather than China, especially since China faces many domestic challenges ahead.

In February 2005, the U.S. and Japan held security consultations and clearly included Taiwan as their protectorate despite protest by China. Seeking to counter the new U.S.-Japan proclamation and warn against a Taiwan independence movement, Beijing passed the Anti-Secession Law (ASL) on March 14, 2005. Later a joint military drill was conducted with Russia. These actions by China have helped the U.S. and Japan understand both the Chinese military modernization and political determination to pursue sovereignty on the subject of Taiwan. In response, the U.S. and Japan deepened their military linkage to include future use of Japanese civilian ports by the U.S. military.

In the interim, the U.S. Aegis Destroyer Stethem has moved in and out of the Akita port from the Yokosuka port to become familiar with the area in preparation for any emergencies on the Korean Peninsula, the Taiwan Strait, or the East China Sea. Only an Aegis Destroyer can make a direct attack against missiles. The Stethem can track two hundred targets and attack more than ten targets simultaneously. Before the spring of 2009, Japan will complete the disposition of thirteen E-2C Air Surveillance systems. Missile information detected by the Aegis Destroyer can be transmitted instantaneously to an automatic control center at a Tokyo base. [24] Also, Japan will provide two air bases in Kyushu as U.S. Marine Corps midway staging posts. The U.S. agreed to move 8,000 soldiers of a total of 18,000 Marine Corps stationed in Okinawa to Quam [25] to reduce the friction with the local Japanese and to establish an offensive force that can act independently irrespective of Japanese government restrictions, provided that Japan pays for the relocation expenses. Japan's SDF will increase its control of the Okinawa base, which is at China's doorstep within about 1,000 miles.

The geopolitical containment of the coastal area of China can be described as an island chain stretching from Japan and South Korea at the north through Okinawa and Taiwan in the middle, and to the Philippines and South China Sea in the south. The U.S. and Japan will also start the disposition of NMD in East Asia. [26] The China dragon is completely encircled by the U.S. and Japanese joint forces. This forced China to break through the circle by announcing possession of DF-21 solid-fueled missiles initially developed in 1967, and reconfigured later, to break the NMD system. [27] From January 29 to February 8, 2007, the U.S. and Japan conducted joint exercises to prepare for any crisis that may break out on the Korean Peninsula or in the Taiwan Strait. A total of 1,350 SDF joined with 3,100 U.S. troops for the exercises, the second of their kind since February 2006. [28]

4. Deterioration in China-Japan Diplomatic Relations

The Cold War perspective involving policies of containment of China which have resurfaced in Japan is a key reason for the growing tensions between the two countries. The Bush administration, seemingly more suspicious of China than Japan, has pushed Japan to assume a more assertive stance against China by encouraging conservative Japanese politicians of the incumbent Liberal Democratic Party (LDP). The LDP is the biggest opponent to the Democratic Party of Japan. These right wing politicians have long wanted to turn the SDF into a full-fledged military power and revise the Constitution to allow for Japanese arms exports and dispatching troops to Iraq. Former Prime Minister Koizumi authorized passage of a special law permitting the deployment of troops to noncombatant areas in Iraq. This was considered unconstitutional by some critics. Such a deployment has helped strengthen the Japanese-American alliance and deepen their military ties.

Military expenditures by Japan are much higher than those of China. The naval force of Japan is particularly strong in detecting torpedo and anti-submarine activities. In order to revise the Constitution, rebuild the military, and recover national dignity after World War II, Japanese politicians have had to invent an external enemy. This has the effect of quelling criticism and pacifying the objections of Japanese citizens who love peace.

Although China-Japan diplomacy is at a low point, the two countries are not enemies and their security and military dialogue has never ceased. Despite some of the security issues, these difficulties can certainly be resolved through continued diplomatic effort. In December 2005, the Japanese Foreign Minister Taro Aso said that China has a population of over one billion, possesses nuclear bombs, and has had a double-digit annual growth rate in military expenditures for the past seventeen years. He said that China had gradually become a threat to Japan. [29] If Japan is making China a potential enemy simply for the sake of normalizing the nation to become a major military power, then this will reduce mutual trust and aggravate relations. The Japanese *Sapio* magazine has exaggerated submarine development by China as "a fascinating novel," describing it as the nation's main naval fighting resource. [30] This disregards the growing economic strength of China and the need to build a strong national defense to protect its resources and wealth.

In response to a question on Japan-Taiwan relations at a session of the U.S. House of Councilors Budget Committee on March 9, 2006, Taro Aso said that Taiwan "is a country that shares values with Japan," and he glorified Japan's past colonial rule there. His repeated remarks calling Taiwan "a nation" by distorting history has gravely undermined China-Japanese ties. [31]

Japan also worries about Taiwan's likelihood of reunification with the PRC, since 90 percent of Japanese oil imports come from the so-called Japan line which passes through Taiwanese waters (the line extends from the Caspian Sea, crossing the Indian Ocean, the strait of Malacca and Taiwan). The conflict over Taiwan is dangerous and a flash point for all the parties involved including the U.S. It could lead to a regional arms race culminating in a nuclear Japan. [32]

5. Japan's Recent Strong Stance against China

After World War II, Japan quickly rebuilt its society and economy with the help of the U.S. and became the second largest economic power in the world. After China started economic reform, it became Japan's major investment partner and its largest trade partner. Sino-Japan trade volume is one-fifth of Japan's total trade volume today. China's robust economic development has helped the recovery of a stagnant Japanese economy since the 1980s. Although the two nations' diplomatic relationship is at a very low point, the two economies are complementary. Separation of economic issues from politics has been the guiding principle for their diplomacy through the Cold War era.

But today this principle seems no longer valid. Since the 1990s, the relationship has deteriorated substantially and is continuing to decline. While there are many complications, a basic problem is that Japan cannot tolerate the rise of China. Historically, there has always been only one strong country in East Asia; China in the old days and Japan today. China is now becoming a strong country and the evolution of two or more strong countries (India is also rising in tandem) in addition to the existing U.S. superpower in East Asia is clear. Harvard Professor and well-known expert in East Asia, Ezra F. Vogel, has named the coming China-U.S.-Japan era in East Asia as comparable to the Three Kingdoms period of ancient China. [33] With these new conditions, conservative Japanese politicians are attempting to prevent Chinese progress by any means possible including spreading the China threat theory.

To be fair, development and economic progress are the birthright of any nation, which cannot be denied by another nation. If this matter can be viewed without prejudice, the contributions made by Chinese development must be acknowledged since it brings tremendous opportunities to Japan and helps with its economic recovery. It is puzzling that while Japan made huge profits from China, it persists in its opposition to the Chinese needs and requirements. Japan is also the nation that opposes China the most. From historical disputes to pragmatic issues such as Taiwan independence, the Japanese government promotes unilateral policies that are provocative and antagonistic towards China. This was especially true during the term of Junichiro Koizumi. The relationship between China and Japan is at a crossroads.

Improvements in relations will have a profound impact on the welfare of both nations in terms of basic benefits, regional peace and stability, and harmonious development of the Asia-Pacific region. China hopes that Japan will resolve the difficult historical issues and respect China's stance on Taiwan by not interfering with PRC plans for peaceful reunification. Many Japanese politicians recommend that the two sides break the current diplomatic stalemate and return to a more positive diplomatic relationship.

6. The China-Japan Territorial Disputes

China and Japan held the fourth-round talks on the East China Sea issue on March 6–7, 2006, in Beijing, but could not reach any agreement. China planned to start production at a new offshore oil and gas field in Pinghu by late 2006. The Pinghu field and the nearby Chunxiao field are west of a meridian line that Japan claims separates the 200 nautical mile exclusive economic zones defined for the two countries.

The Chinese do not recognize the meridian line unilaterally claimed by the Japanese and are dissatisfied with it. Beijing claims its zone stretches to the edge of the continental shelf near the Okinawa prefecture. Japan is concerned that China might siphon off resources that could be buried under waters claimed by the Japanese east of the line. [34] Japan refuses to accept the PRC proposal for a joint exploration in the north region of the East China Sea and the south region near the Diaoyutai Islands (Senkaku Islands). Both China and Japan are determined to wield a strong hand in the oil-rich seas and strategic shipping lanes that lie between them. [35]

The sixth-round talks on the East China Sea took place on July 8, 2006, in Beijing. After the meeting, both nations had serious disagreements, but decided to establish a hot-line communication mechanism as well as an expert team to conduct research on East China Sea oil exploration. [36] Shortly thereafter, the China National Offshore Oil Company, Ltd. (CNOOC) announced that it began production at the Chunxiao gas field. Tokyo protested and demanded China halt production work or else face retaliation, if China refused to stop. After confirming production activity by the Chinese, Japan is likely to also start its own production work near the meridian line in retaliation. [37]

Another territorial dispute in the East China Sea concentrates in the tiny uninhabited Pacific islets of Okinotorishima (the remote Bird Island). The islets are simply rocks above the sea surface. Japan will begin studying ways to foster the growth of coral reefs near two islets at the center of a territorial dispute with China. Japan is trying to use the islets to extend its exclusive economic zone far into the Pacific Ocean under the terms of the U.N. Convention on the Law of the Sea. But Beijing argues they are rocks, not islands, and that Tokyo cannot claim exclusive rights to the surrounding area or prevent China from exploiting nearby resources. The dispute came up after a Chinese research ship came twice within 370 km (about 220 miles) of the islets, triggering a diplomatic protest by Tokyo. [38]

The third area of dispute is the Diaoyutai Islands in the south of the East China Sea. A Japanese high school textbook identifies these islands as territory of Japan because it is under the control of Ishigaki City, an Okinawa prefecture. However, both the PRC and the ROC claimed Diaoyutai Islands as part of Daxi Village of Taiwan Province. The Diaoyutai Islands consist of five islets and three rocks of seemingly insignificant economic value. But recent studies suggest that the surrounding seabed might be rich in oil deposits. It became apparent that acquisition of territorial sovereignty over these islets might lead to a legitimate claim to the adjacent territorial sea including the valuable oil and mineral rights. Other issues of significance are summarized below:

The Chinese Claims

China claims that the Diaoyutai Islands were part of Taiwan dating back to the Chinese Ming Dynasty. These islands are mentioned in Chinese literature written in 1372 and documented by royal visitors traveling from Ming China to the Ryukyu Kingdom located in what is now the prefecture of Okinawa, Japan. After the Ming Dynasty, the Qing Dynasty gained effective control over Taiwan and its surrounding islands including the Diaoyutai Islands. After losing the First Sino-Japan War, China signed the Treaty of Shimonoseki in 1895 and ceded Taiwan and its surrounding islands to Japan although without explicitly mentioning the Diaoyutai Islands. China claims that after World War II, Taiwan and its surrounding islands were returned to Chinese sovereignty under the provisions of the Cairo Declaration, [39] the Potsdam Declaration, [40] Article 2 of the San Francisco Treaty, [41] and the Treaty of Taipei. [42]

The Japanese Claims

Japan claims that their government survey conducted in 1885 confirmed that there was no evidence that the uninhabited islands had been under Chinese control, thus refuting the Chinese claim of the islands during the Qing Dynasty. The Japanese government did not formally claim the islands at the time of the survey. It waited until January 14, 1895, in the middle of the first Sino-Japanese War, to do this. Japan then decided to erect a marker on the islands to formally incorporate them into its territory, just three months before the military defeat of the Qing Dynasty and the signing of the Treaty of Shimonoseki. This decision was not publicized until fifty years later.

What Actually Happened?

In 1945, Japan surrendered and returned Taiwan to the ROC, but privately turned the Diaoyutai Islands and surrounding islands that belong to Taiwan over to the U.S. Later after a U.N. scientific research team reported that the islands had an oil reserve of 1.4 billion barrels, or about 10 percent of the world's known reserve, Japan quickly destroyed Chinese signs on these islands and replaced them by Japanese signs and gave eight islands Japanese names. Finally, in 1969, the U.S.-Japan Joint Communiqué promulgated that the Diaoyutai Islands and surrounding islands belonged to Japan.

Since then, the Chinese people have protested against the communiqué. When China and the U.S. established a diplomatic relationship, the Diaoyutai issue was not included for discussion. In the 1978 China-Japan Peaceful Friendship agreement, the issue was shelved for future discussion. [43] Japan has unilaterally changed the sovereignty of the Diaoyutai Islands and surrounding islands. As a result, the protests of the Chinese people and governments on both sides of the Taiwan Strait have not ceased.

More Controversies and New Disputes
After World War II, Japan claimed the islands came under U.S. occupation as part of Okinawa. In 1972, the islands were returned by the U.S. to Japan. Taiwan rejected the Japanese claim that when U.S. forces were stationed on Taiwan during the Cold War, the U.S. military applied for Taiwanese, rather than Japanese permission, to conduct military maneuvers. This involved using the islands as aerial bombing targets. Also, as a result of heavy Chinese protests, the U.S. Department of State and the U.S. Senate made it clear that the return of Okinawa (including the disputed islands) to Japan did not affect the determination of sovereignty over the disputed islands. Their statement is shown below: [44]

... that the reversion of the disputed islands by the United States does not affect the legal status of the islands because the United States could not acquire through the San Francisco Peace Treaty more than what Japan possessed after her surrender in 1945. Nor could it return to Japan, under the Okinawa Reversion Agreement, more than what it had acquired from Japan in 1951.

This matter remains to be settled by China and Japan.
A survey in 1968 by the United Nations Economic Commission for

Asia and the Far East suggested that the seabed of the East China Sea could be one of the richest oil-deposit areas in the region. It is a reality that both China and Japan place priority on securing natural resources and there is the question of preserving national pride.

It is unlikely, however, that both nations will resort to the International Court of Justice (ICJ) to resolve this dispute for several reasons: first, it is not in the interests of either party to damage the growing economic partnership between the two nations; second, the potential economic benefits at stake are huge and both China and Japan probably would not want to risk an adverse decision at the ICJ. China has proposed a viable option for peacefully ending the dispute by creation of a joint Sino-Japanese venture to exploit the mineral and oil in and around the seabed and the subsoil. However, Japan not only rejected China's proposal, many Taiwanese media reported that Japan and the U.S. held a large scale military drill near Okinawa and Diaoyutai Islands from February 6–10, 2006.

The two countries are planning to hold another joint military drill in the summer of 2006, using Huang-Wei Yu and Chih-Wei Yu of the Diaoyutai Islands as the targets and China and North Korea as their assumed enemies. [45] Both Japan and the U.S. kept a low profile about these drills. It was apparent that both nations were treating China as their hypothetical enemy despite China's repeated proposal of a peaceful settlement of the East China Sea territorial disputes.

Ninety percent of Chinese imports and exports depend on sea transportation. Many of its strategic resources including 30 percent of its oil imports and 50 percent of its iron ore are transported by ship. Still, the strategically important Diaoyutai Islands and most islands in the South China Sea are controlled by other nations. If China loses the Diaoyutai Islands, the sea lanes in the south and north seas would be controlled by other nations.

7. Japan's Push for Increased Influence

There was a joint effort by nations known as the Group of Four to become the new permanent members of the U.N. Security Council (UNSC). The Group of Four includes Brazil, Germany, India, and Japan.

Japan faced possible opposition due to strained relations with China, and the U.S. was unlikely to change its reluctance about expanding the UNSC membership. [46]

Although the Japanese proposal was dead, a proposal resubmitted by Brazil, Germany, and India remained on the table. Japan's failure clearly indicates that the U.S. does not wish to "normalize" Japan despite close Japan-U.S. ties, and the U.S. is aware of the underlying ambition of the Japanese leadership to reshape its international influence and military capability.

Japan has been pushing for an East Pacific Agreement to sign FTA with ASEAN+6 (10 countries from the ASEAN plus Australia, China, India, Japan, New Zealand, and South Korea). This was the main theme of global strategies proposed by Japan in June 2006. The proposed inclusion of Australia, India, and New Zealand, which are not East Asian nations was considered a means to control China, thereby permitting Japan to assume a lead role in the ASEAN+6 communities. The ASEAN+6 include 50 percent of the global population with a total GDP greater than the sum of the North American FTA and the E.U., respectively. However, the Japan-South Korean FTA negotiation stagnated after 2004, and the China-Japan relationship also hit a historic low in recent years. The original purpose of the ASEAN was to support resolution of regional economic problems caused by globalization such as unemployment, bankruptcy, and poverty. The goal was to prevent manipulation of South-East Asian countries by international conglomerates in the midst of globalization.

Another primary objective was to deepen regional cooperation to meet development needs much like the model of the North American FTA, the Pan American FTA, and the E.U. Following initial objections the U.S. accepted ASEAN's existence, adding that non-Eastern Asian nations like Australia, India, and New Zealand would reduce Chinese influence in the region. Moreover, Japan frequently injected highly sensitive political issues in negotiations such as security protection in efforts to assert a leadership role. Japan's ASEAN+6 idea was not well received by the ASEAN representatives on August 25, 2006. They suggested that regional economic integration must be done step-by-step and the ASEAN+3 free trade negotiation must first be established in the Pan-Asian free trade region. The

ASEAN hopes a proposed major railway project linking Singapore to southern China will be ready in 2015 to facilitate the flow of goods and people across the region. The railway project is expected to improve linkages among the economies of the region and provide southern China with easy access to ASEAN markets. [47] New Zealand and China plan to conclude their free trade talks before April 2008. If successful, this will represent the first FTA for China with a developed country. [48]

8. China Is Very Important to Japan, Not a Threat

Despite the China-Japan saber rattling, China is, in fact, very important to Japan. After World War II, economic prosperity, a democratic political system, and strong competitiveness made Japan one of the best developed countries in the world prior to 1990. Highly developed nations including the U.S. and those in Europe felt the economic and financial threat and challenges from Japan. But, since the 1990s, the over-extension in investments and the drastic rise of the Japanese yen against the U.S. dollar led the Japanese economy into a long-term recession. No matter how hard the government worked towards recovery, it was unable to reverse the economically dispirited conditions. However, as Chinese market conditions grew, new vigor was injected into Japanese enterprises and the economy gradually recovered. By 2003, the Japanese GDP rose by 2.5 percent for the first time since the start of the recession. China is now the safe harbor for Japanese enterprises where they may avoid the trade wars encountered with the U.S. and the E.U. in the 1980s. Many products made in China are in fact from Japan or elsewhere, and assembled in China. Because of this situation, China is blamed for the huge trade surplus with the U.S. In reality, China earns only a small portion of the profit; most profits are returned to Japanese and American enterprises. It seems that China gets the blame due to its exaggerated trade surplus whereas Japan and U.S. get most of the profits. It is estimated that Japanese investment in China has contributed to growth of 0.8 percent in the Japanese GDP. [49] China is under pressure to raise its renminbi (RMB) exchange rate over U.S. dollar under political pressure from the U.S.

In 2005, Japan's total FDI in China was US$60 billion. Records showed that China-Japan trade has reached a mature stage and remains vigorous. Economic ties are considered strong enough to endure occasional political rifts between the two nations. Despite existing political problems, Japan's FDI with China will continue to increase due to expanding investments in banking and service industries. The Japanese market lacks vitality due to its aging population and declining population growth; hence, China becomes very important to Japan.

Japanese enterprises use China as their manufacturing base and source of cheap Chinese labor which boosts profits. Japan also relies increasingly on China as a major consumer market. Japanese merchandise manufactured in China can be sold in its vast market. Japan is an export economy and policy makers recognize the importance of Chinese purchasing power.

In 2005, the bilateral China-Japan trade volume reached US$188 billion, slightly lower than the Chinese trade volume with the U.S. In 2006, their trade volume increased by 11.5 percent. It is very likely that China will become Japan's biggest trade partner in 2007. The E.U. and China surpassed the U.S. to become two of the largest trading partners of Japan. This indicates that Japan is more dependent on China than the other way around, and that the "China factor" has special importance to Japan.

The 2006 GDP for China ranked fourth in the world after the U.S., Japan, and Germany. Its foreign trade ranked third. China has 173 manufactured products ranked first in the world and its contribution to global economic growth ranked second, after the U.S. China and the U.S. are the two locomotives driving the world economy forward. The foreign exchange reserve of China exceeded US$1,000 billion at the end of 2006, surpassing Japan to become the highest in the world.

All of these economic indicators show that China has a new image and its soft power has risen substantially. In addition, senior citizens comprise 17 percent of the Japanese population. By 2030, this number will increase to 33 percent. This means that in twenty years, Japan's economic growth will slow due to a labor shortage. It is possible that the Japanese economy may not be able to function normally by then. But if Japan relies on its neighbor China to supply the manpower, it could resolve the aging labor problem easily.

Through the preceding analysis, we may appreciate how China helped Japan emerge from an economic crisis. China helped Japan end a failed economic period and recover strength and confidence. China made it possible for Japan to embark on a new age of development. [50]

9. Japan's Economic Expert Was Spreading "China Grain Threat"

Recently Shibata Minfu, the Head of the Tokyo Marubeni Economic Research Institute made sensational statements intended to frighten people. He announced that China's rapid economic development and increase in grain imports might lead to "Sushi and beef steaks disappearing from Japanese dining tables to be replaced by rice and salted vegetables eaten during the era of starvation and the Japanese diet could be lowered to 1950's level." [51] He targeted China as the archenemy and potential cause of future starvation in Japan. He stated that increasing demand for meat and grains by China would cause rapid depletion of world food reserves. His viewpoint is very similar to that of American scholar Lester R. Brown, described in "Who Will Feed China?" in 1995. [52] Brown's theories received mixed reviews in China and internationally.

A more balanced view is given in the bestseller, *Will Famine Once Again Knock at China's Door? – A Wake Up Call for the World,* written by two Xinhua Press Agency journalists and a panel of specialists. These authors conclude that new methods for improving agricultural production combined with suitable levels of imports would solve the food shortage in China in the twenty-first century. On October 26, 1996, the State Council of China issued a white paper that stated it would be able to feed itself and set a target for China of 95 percent grain self-sufficiency under normal conditions by implementing several agricultural measures. The lack of water supply was generally considered by experts as the single greatest constraint on China's ability to increase its agricultural production apart from the low government prices paid to farmers.

Twelve years have passed since Lester R. Brown published his alarming prediction. In 2005, the U.N. World Food Program (WFP) made the decision to end its food aid to China in April of 2006. The U.N. WFP began providing food aid to China in 1979 to meet the immediate needs of more than thirty million poor mainlanders. The Chinese government has made tremendous progress in the alleviation of hunger and poverty and no longer needs U.N. help. China has not only put an end to its twenty-six-year history of receiving food, but has also become one of the strongest donor countries in the world.

With less than 7 percent of world farmland, China has managed to feed 22 percent of the global population. China has reduced the number of poor, through both governmental leadership and social participation, from 250 million to 26.1 million. This accounts for 70 percent of total poverty alleviation worldwide during the same period. [53] The U.N. agency reported in July 2006 that China became the third largest food aid donor in the world in 2005. In the same year, China stopped receiving assistance from the WFP while the U.S. and the E.U. remained the top two contributors and Japan was the fourth. Chinese foreign aid reportedly quadrupled in the past decade. [54] Ninety-two percent of the food China donated went to North Korea, contributing 49 percent of total food donations received by North Korea, according to the International Food Aid Information System. [55] This success can be attributed to improved policy, agricultural technologies, and dedication. [56] Chinese success in grain production and poverty alleviation answers the question "Who Will Feed China?" and puts an end to the negative implications of the China grain threat theory.

In fact, what is really alarming is the Japanese grain import trend. Japan is now the largest grain importer worldwide. It spent US$39.4 billion in grain imports in 1999, a third of total Asian grain imports. In addition, beef accounted for nearly 20 percent and pork was nearly 30 percent of total world imports. Japan represents only one-fiftieth of the world population. Japanese grain sufficiency dropped from 70 percent in 1970 to 41 percent in 1999, an average annual increase of 5.6 percent of grain imports. [57] Since it is unlikely that Japan will boost its grain production with its limited farm land, grain import remains the sole method for securing adequate grain supply. Mr. Shibata Minfu actually demanded that China reduce grain consumption in order to maintain Japan's disproportionately high levels of grain consumption.

10. China Is Still Lagging behind Japan in Many Areas

The following overview presents important facts and indicators, which demonstrate that China is in no position to threaten Japan:

i. In 2005, the Japanese GDP was about US$4,571 billion compared to the American GDP of US$12,486 billion. The average personal income in Japan was over US$30,000 which is among the highest in the world. In the same year, the Chinese GDP was about US$2,225 billion, the fourth in the world, and their average personal income of US$1,703 is at the lower end in the world. In other words, the average Chinese income was equivalent to about 5 percent of the average Japanese income.

ii. Japan's foreign exchange reserve at the end of February 2006 was US$850.1 billion, only a bit less than China's US$853.6 billion. [58] Both Japan and China have very high personal savings rates (over 40 percent) and are major U.S. creditors (holding about 15 percent of the total U.S. Treasury notes owned by foreign nations). [59] China's foreign exchange reserve exceeded US$1,000 billion in late 2006. However, Japan, which owns US$640 billion U.S. Treasury notes, is the world's biggest financier. [60] Its net asset value amounts to US$8,910 billion, more than four times that of Germany. China's total net asset value is unknown, but is perhaps only one-tenth of that of Japan.

iii. In technology, Japan is ahead of China by about twenty years. In terms of trade in technology products, trading volume in China is very small and is not at the same level as Japan. China still produces mostly low-tech products. In order to buy one commercial jet, China has to sell 100 million pairs of trousers. Japanese technical exports are second only to the U.S. In addition, Japan is active in acquiring scientific technologies, but very conservative in its technology exports to China. Japan is China's biggest trading partner and Japan has always had a trade surplus with China. Japanese exports to China are mostly value-added industrial output and high-tech products such as domestic use electronics, cars, and high-precision instruments. Many of these products consist of Japanese parts that are assembled and resold in China whereas Chinese exports to Japan are mostly labor-intensive or low-tech products.

iv. Japan has a very high quality educational system through which students complete 100 percent of elementary and junior high school. An estimated 96.8 percent complete high school and their illiteracy rate is zero. Nearly 50 percent of high school graduates enter university and college graduates make up 48 percent of the total population.

Japan has twelve Nobel Prize winners. Of these eight are in sciences. Japan plans to increase this number to thirty over the next fifty years. The total percentage of technically-trained workers was one-third of that in the U.S. in 1955, but exceeded the U.S. number in 1986, and became the first in the world (with 55.1 per 10,000 people in 1955 and 102.2 per 10,000 in 1986, respectively, in Japan). Japanese patent applications amount to 389,000 cases and now rank number one in the world.

The semi-illiteracy and illiteracy rate in China is over 15 percent of the total population and the educational budget is less than 0.5 percent of the national GDP, or the 149th in the world. One quarter of Chinese counties lack primary school education. In remote areas, only 30 percent of students attend junior-high schools and 10 percent attend high schools. The national average for high school entry is 44 percent. Less than 2 percent of eligible high school graduates enter university compared to the 16 percent worldwide average. Higher income nations average 42 percent of eligible students. Thus far, China has only one Nobel Prize winner, in the field of literature.

v. Japan has limited activities that produce negative environmental impacts. For example, Japan closed all the mines and stopped felling trees. Forests cover 67 percent of the land area and Japan meets its needs for minerals and lumber through imports. In contrast, forests cover a mere 12 percent of the land area in China, far less than the world standard of 22 percent. Nonetheless, Chinese merchants continue cutting trees for export of lumber and wood products that include one-time-use chopsticks. Rampant mining activities in China have depleted precious resources and also produced numerous mining incidents, injuries, and deaths. Although the death toll in coal mine accidents, for 2006 was down 21 percent, some 6,000 Chinese miners were killed in 2005 in fires, floods, cave-ins, and other disasters despite repeated official promises to improve safety. Many deaths were blamed on management indifference to safety rules or lack of required equipment. Corruption also hurt safety efforts. Data show that China produced 35 percent of the world's coal in 2003, but reported 80 percent of the total deaths in coal mine accidents. Coal mining has become the most deadly job in China. About 600,000 miners to date are suffering from pneumoconiosis, a disease of the lungs caused by long-continued inhalation of dust. And the figure increases by 70,000 miners every year. [61]

vi. Today, Japanese products ranging from toys to cars and electronics disseminate a powerful cultural influence around the world. For example, Pokemon, Hello Kitty, and Shonen Jump are known by children and teenagers everywhere. The famous Mandarake store in Tokyo is full of customers speaking English, Japanese, Spanish, French, and Korean. Most merchandise is sold for over US$30 per item.

Japanese sushi is nearly as popular as McDonalds. In São Paulo, the biggest city of South America, there are many restaurants selling sushi along with Brazilian barbecued beef. In Paris, sushi has become French people's favorite dish over the past two years. Japan is reinventing itself to become the "coolest" nation in the world following thirteen years of economic stagnation. Japanese artists, musicians, designers, movie stars, and singers permeate Western culture. [62] There are about 3 million foreigners learning Japanese, more than twenty times the number in 1997. Right wing politicians in Japan seek to spread Japanese culture to exert worldwide power and influence.

vii. Japan is the second largest economy in the world with a GDP more than two times that of China. It represents about 10 percent of the world's total GDP. The Japanese defense budget is about two and a half times that of China and has an estimated 250,000 military personal. Although at present Japan is not a large military presence, its recent military expansion is very disturbing. Yet, Japan has promulgated the China military threat theory by stating that the actual Chinese military expense is two to three times that of the official figure.

On December 13, 2005, Chinese Foreign Ministry spokesman Qin Gang refuted Japan's unfounded accusations by saying that Japan's land area is only one-twenty-fifth of China's, its population is also only one-tenth of China's, but Japan's 2004 military expense was 1.62 times that of China's (US$25.6 billion); the Chinese military expense per person was US$23, whereas the Japanese military expense per person was US$2,300. The Chinese military expense was US$13,000 per soldier, whereas the Japanese military expense was US$200,000 per soldier, over fifteen times that of China. The Japanese SDF is far better equipped and has more military capability. [63]

Moreover, as stated earlier, since 1994, the Japanese government has included the Taiwan Strait, the Korean Peninsula, and South China Sea also known as the neighboring area, into its sphere for defense coverage under the Japan-U.S. Treaty of Mutual Cooperation and Security. This means that if conflict erupts across the Taiwan Strait, Japan is committed to sending troops together with the U.S. The U.S.-Japan security alliance has entered a new stage, which poses a threat to Northeast Asia, especially to Chinese military security and China's endeavors to recover Taiwan. Although Japan has returned sovereignty to Taiwan, its actions have changed from strategic ambiguity to strategic clarity through the alliance with the U.S.

Immediately following the North Korean launch of seven missiles on July 5, 2006, Japanese Foreign Minister Taro Aso and several Japanese officials stated openly that Japan has the right to initiate a pre-emptive strike against another country. [64] This is the first time Japan made a clear pre-emptive strike warning to a sovereign nation since its surrender in 1945.

viii. As discussed previously, Japan has the strongest high-tech military in the Asia-Pacific region other than the U.S. Furthermore, Japan is under the nuclear protection umbrella of the U.S., and therefore, any attack against Japan could lead to U.S. nuclear retaliation. It is quite obvious that Japan does not have to worry about any serious military attacks. However, a recent public survey found that 80 percent of the Japanese Internet users supported the notion that "Japan should have the capability to attack an enemy military base." It seems that the Japanese people have revived a new form of nationalism and new conservatism that is no less fanatical than the views that existed prior to World War II. These attitudes shocked many foreign diplomats. [65]

China, on the other hand, is an enormous nation that has not yet completed national reunification. With growing economic strength, China must be concerned with national security to maintain a peaceful environment for sustained development.

After World War II, Japan kept a fixed exchange rate (360 Japanese yen = 1 U.S. dollar) for some time to concentrate on raising productivity, raising production quality, as well as manufacturing new products to expand its export base. By 1968, the Japanese GDP ranked the second in the world. In 1965, auto exports were only 13 percent that of Germany, but by 1974, within less than ten years, it became the world's largest auto exporter. [66] China is still far behind Japan in economic progress in many areas. In addition, recent rapid economic growth and progress by China has been made at the expense of the environment. While considerable environmental damage may take China years to remedy, Japan does not have such problems. Chinese lack of environmental controls is also a choice by government and a failure of leadership. This is a huge problem in the U.S. as well.

11. Can Japan Contain China?

Chinese criticism of Japanese Shrine visits by government leaders has remained at the level of verbal vitriol based on different moral principles and perspectives. Chinese leaders and diplomats alerted the international community of Shrine visits by Japanese leaders revived militarism and Japan's huge military expansion. Japan has developed advanced technology for electronic components required for modern warfare. From fighter jets to warships, 95 percent of the electronic parts used by American cutting edge weapons are all made in Japan. On the surface, the Japanese military force is not large, but its actual military strength is second only to the U.S. In certain specific areas, Japanese military strength has surpassed the U.S. Japan is seeking continuous military expansion and eventually its military strength will cause an imbalance in regional peace and stability. [67]

American policies designed to contain China have received political support by right wing conservatives in Japan. The once warm China-Japan economic relationship is now replaced by a cordial China-Europe economic relationship. It appears that the previous Koizumi government had not been wise in shaping its foreign policies related to the peaceful development of China in East Asia.

Political and diplomatic actions by Japan may have a negative impact in the future. As discussed, Japan has delegated its military leadership to the U.S. and has become more isolated in Asia. As a result, its ambition to become a world leader is diminished. This is supported by U.S. opposition to the Japanese attempt to become a U.N. Security Council member. The only dream Japan still has is to contain any further rise of China in East Asia. Even this may not be realistic.

Although Japan is the second largest world economy, its prosperity is dependent on exports. Present Chinese economic strength also relies heavily on exports, but its domestic market is much larger. China survived under a Western economic blockade for many decades, through-out the Cold War. It would be difficult for Japan to compete with China's economic structure in the long run. Finally, the right wing conservative politicians of Japan exhibit poor timing.

The U.S. is mired in conflict in Iraq and Afghanistan, and confronted by the Iranian and North Korean nuclear issues. U.S. resource constraints limit its ability to support Japan in its efforts to contain China. Moreover, because China has strong ties in the Middle East and on the Korean Peninsula that could be used to support U.S. policy, it would be wishful thinking for Japanese conservative politicians to expect America to confront China when intertwined interests are at stake.

12. Conclusions

On August 15, 2006, the sixty-first anniversary of the end of World War II, Koizumi made his sixth visit to the Yasukuni Shrine in Tokyo. He was supported by conservative politicians. China, South Korea, Singapore, and Malaysia all reacted with outrage. The Koizumi era ended in September 2006. He left his successor to quell the anger of Asian countries as well as international critics.

Both the Chinese leaders and the new Japanese leaders were prepared for the post-Koizumi China-Japan relationship. The Chinese Youth Joint Association invited the Three Thousand Japanese People's Delegation for a visit to China again. In 1984, when Chinese leader, Hu Jintao, was the chairman of this association, he invited three thousand Japanese youths to visit Beijing for the first time. [68] Japanese businesses continue to concentrate investments in China despite the objections of their conservative politicians.

The new Japanese Prime Minister Shinzo Abe made a landmark visit to China in October 2006, after both nations decided to shelve their differences and begin with a fresh start. China and Japan are moving forward toward a strategic relationship based on trust, and curators plan to clarify and soften the offensive language used in exhibits that refer to China at the Yasukuni Shrine. [69]

But Abe called for changes to Japan's pacifist Constitution. He accelerated the planned upgrade of the Japanese Defense Agency to a full Ministry of Defense. This signals movement away from postwar pacifism, which bars Japan from using force to settle international conflicts. [70] Despite mounting international pressure, Abe failed to acknowledge that Tokyo forced thousands of women into sexual slavery. [71] In addition, he has personally pressed French President Jacques Chirac not to lift the E.U. arms embargo to China and tried to engage India and Australia into the camp of containing China. [72] In 2007, Japan and Australia signed the Japan-Australia Joint Declaration on Security Cooperation to strengthen their strategic relationship. [73]

Historians from China and Japan have given up on the idea of collaborating to develop a single history of Sino-Japan relations in a joint study project sponsored by the two governments. [74] On March 30, 2007, the Japanese government announced that new high school textbooks would no longer acknowledge that the Imperial Army was responsible for ordering civilians to commit mass suicide during the battle of Okinawa in the final months of the war, another sign that Japan was pressing ahead in revising its World War II history. [75]

Improved Sino-Japanese ties are crucial and Abe could make or break this important bond. Abe has maintained strategic ambiguity on the Shrine visit issue and China has continued relations with Japan despite the sex slavery issue. But Abe and his right-wing politicians seem to return to a conservative stance by remarking that there is no evidence proving that Japanese soldiers coerced women into sexual slavery. These comments contradict the prior official position, which was contained in the 1993 Kono talk. [76]

The year 2007 marks the thirty-fifth anniversary of normalization of

China-Japan diplomatic relations, and Chinese Premier Wen Jiabao made a successful visit to Japan in April 2007, the first such visit in seven years. Wen described his trip as an ice-breaker trip. [77] Both nations are now eager to have a new start despite the aforementioned difficulties between the two nations.

Polls showed that Abe's popularity was in free-fall, plummeting by 30 percent, to a 37 percent approval rating. [78] If his approval rating continued to decline before the July election of the Upper House of Parliament, he would become a lame duck even if he wins. [79]

After I finished writing this book, Abe unexpectedly resigned on September 12, apparently tired of political battles over diplomacy and economics. Unlike Abe, the new Prime Minister Yasuo Fukuda is believed to be a foreign policy "dove" by principle rather than pragmatism, seeking friendlier relations with China.

A peaceful diffusion of the current diplomatic tensions would better stabilize the Asia-Pacific region and create a mutually beneficial environment for both nations. China and Japan should be friendly neighbors, not enemies.

Part II

Refuting America's China Threat Theory

The China-U.S. relationship is a very important one in the world. It is not only bilateral and regional, but also global. In the past, America seemed very distant to most Chinese because the two countries are separated by the vast Pacific Ocean and have distinctly different cultures and languages. In chapter I, we reviewed how, beginning in the mid-nineteenth century, Confucianism spread to the U.S., through poor Chinese immigrants fueled by news of the California Gold Rush. This occurred after the Civil War during the reconstruction which resulted in U.S. ascendancy as an industrial power.

With the newly acquired national strength, Americans began to explore East Asia including China. Many American priests established churches and religious schools in China to preach the Christian gospels to the local people. In 1900, America joined with the united armies of seven other nations to invade China.

China expert Susan Shirk's book, *The Political Logic of Economic Reform in China*, points out that while Mao Zedong's decentralization during the Great Leap Forward and the Cultural Revolution paved the way for China's later economic reform, no one could deny that the Chinese economy was in a state of collapse when he died in 1976. It was only by 1978, when Deng Xiaoping opened China and returned it to a market economy that the poverty-stricken economy shifted to a new, prosperous road. Within a brief time span of less than thirty years, China has become one of the two major forces in the world economy. In the face of these dramatic changes, the U.S. started to promote the China threat theory after the collapse of the Soviet Union in 1991.

In 1993, the *New York Times* reporter Nicholas D. Kristof, who once lived in Beijing, was the first to suggest that the PRC would fill the power vacuum left in the Asia-Pacific region after the retreat of the U.S. and Russia, and would further expand its interests in this area to become the dominant power. The U.S. Atlantic Council research analyst Mike Pillsbury stated that, when the national GDP of the PRC exceeds that of America in 2020 as expected (Goldman Sachs experts think this will happen in 2045), the PRC will be able to threaten U.S. interests. By then, the PRC could blockade Taiwan or initiate military attacks against Taiwan and severely threaten its neighboring countries in Asia.

For these reasons, the China threat theory has gradually taken hold, followed by the China containment argument which has appeared in international forums. Those who most often cited China as the greatest current danger to the U.S. were academic and think-tank experts (34 percent), followed by state and local government leaders (27 percent). Military leaders considered China and Iran equally dangerous (23 percent for each). [80] Many American reporters were among the China bashing groups and their articles have created powerful images of China.

As a large, populous country with vast territory, China has always been an object of interest for other countries. The China threat theory has historic roots. For a time, the "yellow peril theory" was prevalent.

Reasons for the pervasive China threat rhetoric are diverse in nature. Some are economic; others are political, military, and strategic.

The China threat theory encompasses concepts associated with a China military threat, the China economic threat, and the China cultural and political threat. The Chinese view is that the China threat theory is simply an attempt to oppose and contain development by China. The Chinese people view its development as natural and inevitable after being crushed by Western powers for over one hundred years and suffering domestic turmoil for a few decades. Peaceful development by China should be regarded as beneficial to the world rather than harmful.

The primary proponent of the China threat theory is the U.S. because it fears that China may become a rival for influence in Asia and worldwide.

In the following sections, the China threat theory is refuted from cultural, political, economic, and military perspectives. Recommendations are set forth, which propose ways to bring about a peaceful and harmonious relationship between two great world powers in the future.

Section I. China Is Not a Cultural or Political Threat to the U.S.

Ever since Samuel P. Huntington published his book, *The Clash of Civilizations and the Remaking of World Order*, [81] Western academics, politicians, and media have had heated debates on whether the Islamic-Confucian world, from the Middle East to China, would someday declare war on the West because of a cultural clash. In Robert D. Kaplan's provocative piece, "How We Would Fight China: The Next Cold War," [82] he writes, "The Middle East is just a blip," and an inevitable war "will link China and the United States in a future conflict that may stretch over several generations."

In another piece, "Supremacy by Stealth," he observes that a world managed by China would be infinitely worse than the world we have now, and the highest morality must be the preservation of American power; hence, America should manage the world using military force, covert operations, the planting and guiding of in-country functionaries (spies and intelligence assets), terrorism, and assassination. [83]

Kaplan is not alone! His warmongering statements are not unusual among the many hawkish policymakers, military-utopian intelligentsia, and neoconservatives with high positions in the U.S. government. However, it is also the Kaplan-type neo-conservative school of thought that has influenced the current Bush Administration's foreign policy with disastrous results in Iraq.

Is China a threat to America? This issue is analyzed through a review of various aspects of the China threat theory after we analyzed these two nations from different angles in the previous four chapters. Whether China can develop peacefully will depend heavily on American cooperation.

1. Chinese Culture Embraces Family Values, Tolerance, and Morality

When people travel, they discover that in many areas of Asia, traditional Chinese culture permeates almost all aspects of daily life, from family values to social consciousness. The Western style of individualism was never promoted in traditional Chinese culture. The value of the individual rests mainly upon responsibilities to the family, society, and country (in the U.S., the individuals are encouraged to excel themselves by competing as hard as possible with less emphasis on enhancing "interrelationships"). People are willing to work very hard, endure long-term hardships, and make sacrifices for their families, friends, superiors, and countries. And more importantly, while they are accustomed to an authoritarian political system, they expect their leader to think for them and protect them by acting as the head of the household so that they may prosper as in a big family. They believe that a nation is like a family, and that such decisions are rarely made by voting, but by consensus or out of respect for the head of the household. This is an important difference between Confucian and Western cultures. People should consider this difference to better understand Chinese and other, similar Asian political systems.

In addition, Chinese traditional culture is especially tolerant of religious preferences. Western culture, religion and morality arrived in China through trade. The U.S. was established as a nation in 1776 when China was on the verge of a decline. When American priests arrived at China in the late Qing Dynasty, they were not only amazed at the poverty of the Chinese people, but also at their lack of a Western-style God. When in China, American diplomat Chester Holcombe recorded his vivid impressions of Chinese culture in his book, *The Real Chinaman.* [84] He condemned ancestral worship as a form of idolatry. Of course, this was a purely Western viewpoint and even today many Chinese would not agree with this notion.

For the Chinese, ancestral worship is a way of showing respect and appreciation for the forefathers who made the continuation of generations possible. Placing a memorial tablet of an ancestor in the home reminds the younger generation of their responsibility to follow in the footsteps of the deceased with their blessing. The Chinese people do not regard this kind of worship as a religion or as in conflict with the Western belief in one God. An estimated 80 to 100 million Chinese Christians or Catholics practice their faith in China today. Approximately 12 million Catholics attend some 6,000 churches. [85] Every year about ten million bibles are printed. Often, these people also worship their ancestors at home. At the same time, hundreds of millions of Chinese engage in traditional folk religions, worship local gods, heroes, and ancestors. As mentioned in an earlier chapter, a recent poll by East China Normal University estimated that 31.4 percent of Chinese sixteen or older are religious, putting the number of believers at roughly 400 million. [86]

Considering the different religious and cultural backgrounds, it is possible that Americans might not understand certain Chinese religious expressions and are inclined to judge the Chinese culture solely based on American experiences and values.

In addition, China has millions of Muslims who have lived together with the Han for hundreds of years. For this reason, the Chinese people may understand the Muslims much better than the Americans do and have no intention of exploiting them. Although millions of Muslims live in the U.S., the foreign policy of the U.S. in the Middle East does not bring peace to Muslims who do not live in the States. What went wrong? Did the conflicts originate from sources other than religion? Does

America hold a double standard for Muslims in the United States versus those in the Middle East? Or do conflicts arise from the U.S. ambition of controlling the world energy resources and maintain hegemony, as stated in *The Grand Chessboard* by Zbigniew Brezinski? [87]

China is home to numerous, diverse religious groups: 8 percent are Buddhist, 1.5 percent are Muslim, several hundred thousands are Taoists and hundreds of millions follow traditional folk religions. In addition, many Chinese practice Western religions: There are an estimated 0.4 percent Catholics and an estimated 0.4–0.6 percent, unofficial (worship in private homes) Vatican-affiliated Christians. There are also an estimated 1.2–1.5 percent followers of the Protestant faith. Of these, 2.5 percent worship in Protestant churches, independent of government control.

In China, many local folk gods or goddesses are widely worshipped by commoners for good luck. We can say that Confucianism is a very practical philosophy. It is this practicality that makes the Chinese people very tolerant of different religious beliefs. Chinese society on the whole is not ruled by religious power but by values like" benevolence, righteousness, etiquette," "love others as love themselves" and "do not impose on others what you do not want imposed on you," to maintain social stability and harmony. One must understand this important difference between Chinese and Western cultures.

Confucius demanded the devotion of rulers to their people and that they achieve perfection themselves, thereby spreading their own virtues to the people instead of imposing proper behavior through laws and rules. In Confucianism, the best government is one that rules through rites and belief in the natural morality of the people, rather than by use of bribery and force. These concepts are so deeply rooted in Chinese minds and belief systems that there is not yet a different political philosophy practiced successfully in China today, although rule of law is needed in China today to complement the Chinese moral discipline due to complications in modern society. Confucian teachings on how to manage a society and a nation are different from the approaches of the neo-conservative Bush government. The Bush administration appears to prefer confrontational methods such as sanctions and military conflict over negotiation and compromise. At the same time, the current U.S. government seems to impose a moral double standard on other nations.

Historically, China was separated into different kingdoms, but these divisions could never become permanent as in many other ancient empires in the world. Western scholars are struck by this unique aspect of Chinese civilization and attribute it to the great continuity of Chinese history and the high level of cohesiveness of Chinese civilization. China is a unified multinational country with fifty-six nationalities who live in harmony and whose equality and unity are protected by its Constitution.

The minority nationalities that conquered China through history have all been absorbed by the Chinese melting pot. The Chinese people have learned that only by "seeking agreement and leaving aside differences" through tolerance, making friends, and co-mingling, can society remain peaceful and harmonious. Apart from emphasizing family values and morality, the most special characteristic of Chinese culture is its tolerance of other cultures including religions and nationalities. Culture clash never lasted in Chinese history, because sooner or later different cultures blended together. Hence, China thought of itself as the center of the world, the one and the only, for a few thousand years.

Changes occurred when China confronted Western military might during the First Opium War. At that point, the dynasty struggled and collapsed. Chinese complacency and refusal to accept Western ideals, as well as its view of Western civilization as barbaric, in part caused Japan and the Western powers to engage in brutal wars against China. It tumbled in a whirlpool for more than 100 years only to find, in the end, that it had to shake off cultural prejudice and arrogance accumulated through five thousand years of history. China has since worked diligently to absorb new cultural elements from the West.

2. China Adopts Western Values to Avoid Clash of Civilizations

The concept of clashing civilizations is not new to China and the West. Such clashes may be avoided by learning from the Chinese experience. The promotion of war and hostility is not only immoral, but potentially catastrophic, especially in a nuclear age. The Chinese people confronted Western aggression and cultural clashes the hard way during the Qing Dynasty, but have since learned to avoid these conflicts. They have paid a high price for this precious lesson. The Chinese people will not let a similar clash encountered over 150 years ago reoccur. China also wants the world to learn from its past failures and suffering.

China has a very long history; time has smoothed many of the sharp edges of its culture. The Chinese have learned to become very flexible. China wishes to preserve its cultural quintessence while integrating foreign cultural elements. The adjustment process has been long and painful for the Chinese of the nineteenth and twentieth centuries requiring the experience of defeat in many wars, soul-searching cultural movements, and political and economic reform. However, China has finally found its own way and is on the correct path to restore its past glory in the twenty-first century through peaceful means.

Official Chinese data shows that there are thirty million people learning Chinese worldwide and an estimated twenty-four hundred schools in the U.S. plan to offer Chinese language courses. Reportedly, there are not enough teachers to meet the demand. [88] This is a good indication that Americans are trying to understand the Chinese people and their culture.

In American families, Chinese has become the third most popular language to speak at home followed by French and German (U.S. Census 2000). However, there are far more people in China trying to learn English. In 2001, China established English as a mandatory course to be taught from the third grade on. In large cities such as Beijing and Shanghai, English is taught in the first grade. In his report "English Next," British linguistic scholar David Graddol estimates that there are currently about 176.7 million Chinese attending regular English language classes.

In preparation for the 2008 Olympic Games in Beijing, the Chinese government ruled that all police under age forty must learn to speak English. In preparation for the 2010 World Exhibition, the Shanghai government has established a goal for all residents to speak English. In addition, China is training more than twenty million talented students in English. Perhaps in a few years, the English speaking population in China will exceed that of India. [89]

Some Chinese people are enthusiastic about becoming Americanized or Westernized by adopting Western habits and cultures. Development of this interest often includes learning English, worshiping

American movie stars, converting to Catholic or Protestant faiths, dying hair blonde, eating at McDonalds, or drinking coffee at Starbucks. Others attend U.S. schools and universities, read English books, listen to American music, and become permanent American residents or citizens. They enjoy living the American dream.

At the academic level, Chinese scholars are busily studying various topics related to the U.S. At the government level, Chinese thinkers enthusiastically compare American ideals to Chinese thought and perceptions. Chinese government officials are eager to learn how the American government operates. School children are speaking English better than their parents and grandparents. Many Chinese are working vigorously to understand Western culture, American thinking and way of life.

The *New York Times* reporter, Joseph Kahn, wrote that the world history textbook of a middle school in Shanghai mentions the late Chinese leader Mao Zedong only once and predicts that "Bill Gates Replaced Mao Zedong." Topics including changes in political power and the Communist revolution are covered superficially. Instead, the focus is on economics, science and technology, social customs, and global developments. [90] Although these new texts are a source of controversy among the mainland academics, many scholars support the new direction of the teaching materials. [91] Perhaps this can be interpreted as evidence that China is more interested in a progressive, open and harmonious society than it is in adherence to old Communist doctrines.

Relatively speaking, far fewer Americans want to learn the Chinese language or read a book written by a Chinese author. Although many nations are grateful for the level of aid provided by the U.S. over the years and understand that the Marshall Plan rebuilt Europe in the aftermath of World War II, some U.S. actions were motivated by self interest. U.S. foreign policy over past decades has not always been positive.

Many in the Bush administration appear chauvinistic, exhibiting an attitude of "the American way, or the highway," in the execution of foreign policy. Perhaps it is time for the Americans to think about the need to learn more about other cultures and the perspectives of other nations. The ugly American problem of the past is a trend that can be changed dramatically by the baby boomers and newer generations who travel and who are intensely curious about the world.

It is undeniable that the Chinese people are living in a global world led by the Americans and that American influence is ubiquitous. The Chinese people must "catch up" to understand the international agenda promoted by Americans and the West. However, it is inaccurate to assume that China wants to become totally Westernized or abandon its traditional culture.

China has no wish to mimic the rest of the world. In Chinese history, all foreign invaders were assimilated within two generations without exception. This has had a powerful influence on Chinese culture not only in China but throughout Asia, except India, which has an ancient civilization and a huge population as well. Nevertheless, China has absorbed Buddhism from India and it has evolved to become the most important religion in China.

The Chinese people are becoming adept at absorbing American culture and integrating it into a new Chinese culture. For example, the PRC has invented a language conversion system called Ping Ying so all Chinese names can be pronounced using the English alphabet. This is a bold and useful step taken by the Chinese government to show its determination to connect to the Western world and also a way for the rest of the world to better understand China. China's strength and influence is rising and its impact in the world is becoming more evident. China is striving to understand the U.S. culture. If America minimizes the importance of other cultures as China did 150 years ago, another clash of civilizations may occur. If this happens, the U.S. would be responsible, not China. China is working to avoid this.

It is evident that there are far more Chinese people who understand America than Americans who know China. Americans need to learn more about the Chinese. Americans should learn, most importantly, that Chinese culture is not invasive and its people are not warmongers. Based on their own experiences and wisdom, the Chinese know that sanctions, suppression, aggression, colonization, and war only produce disastrous consequences.

Differences associated with history and culture exist, but any clash or conflict may be avoided by more tolerance, understanding, integration, and a strong focus on peace for coexistence. Though still far from complete, the Chinese people have augmented their traditional culture with the Western culture, and China's new wisdom can help avert problems and inject new hope for the future.

3. Democratization with Chinese Characteristics

While some Americans perceive the government in China as authoritarian, very few within China view the political system as strictly Communist anymore. In his book, *Blueprint for Action*, [92] Thomas P.M. Barnett writes that the CPC is not really in control of much of real importance inside the country today. China, by virtue of its size and status, is facing enormous pressures to continue its rapid pace of economic growth unmatched elsewhere in the world. In fact, China's economic development is so vast that it is beyond the CPC or any other groups' capacity to manage directly at this point. Still, China is essentially a single-party state. It is anticipated that ongoing experiments with grass-roots political reforms should eventually transform China into a democracy according to Li Junru, Vice President of the Party School of the CPC Central Committee. [93]

The CPC celebrated its eighty-fifth founding anniversary on July 1, 2006. Chinese leader Hu Jintao reiterated his concept of "putting people first" and insisted on "governing for the people and supported by the people." He repeatedly stressed power for, sympathy with, and benefit for the people to be his own "three people principles." He then proposed four practical measures to carry out his putting people first policy to: 1) earnestly determine the conditions of the people; 2) listen carefully to the opinions of the people; 3) increase prosperity for the people; and 4) assiduously ensure and protect the safety of the people.

"The people have to be put first" was CPC's basic principle advocated by Mao Zedong during the Yanan period. Later, it became the primary political concept and standard of conduct, but its promotion suffered a severe setback during the Cultural Revolution. [94] Now it is important to examine the position of Hu Jintao on the ideal of "Putting people first" following nearly three decades of economic development.

Hu Jintao's concept of putting people first basically replaced the class struggle theory of Karl Marx and the continued revolution theory of Mao

Zedong in Chinese political ideology. It has rekindled Confucianism and its policy of benevolence by installing a good government and moral, benevolent leaders.

Benevolence means loving people in Chinese. Approximately one hundred years after the death of Confucius, Mencius (BC 372–289), a disciple, philosopher, and sage proposed that "people are most important, country is next in importance, and the emperor is least important." It is acceptable for people to overthrow or kill a ruler who ignores the needs of the people and who rules tyrannically. It is quite remarkable that early in Chinese civilization, the idea of people having the right to overthrow a tyrannical emperor existed over two thousand years before the French enlightenment movement in the eighteenth century that proposed "people's rights are given by God" and "all men are created equal." [95]

But conceptual differences exist between West and the PRC with regard to democracy. In Western democracy, there must be at least two political parties in competition and each can nominate political candidates for specific positions. In the U.S., politicians are elected by people through voting whereas in the PRC, democracy means the wielders of power (the highest political bureau consists of nine members to form group leadership) are chosen by the members of the CPC to work for all the people including non-CPC members. Other political parties act as advisors instead of opposition parties and do not get elected as the nation's leaders. The Chinese democracy is representative and collaborative. It operates as a one-party internal democracy or as a form of democratic centralism.

China has managed its internal democracy since 1994, under which Party members and ordinary people are invited to play a role in decision-making at the local township and village level. In other words, China is not aiming to implement an American-style democracy in the near term by having at least two opposing political parties, which nominates political candidates for local, state, and national political positions. A new internal democratic reform was launched in early 2006 by the PRC as a two-year program to reshuffle leadership at provincial, municipal, county, and township levels.

The Chinese model is consistent with deep-rooted Confucianism to preserve social harmony and ensure the smoothness of the democratic process. The Chinese people remember the lesson learned during the

Chinese Civil War between the CPC and the KMT, which led to the cross-strait separation. China is one of the very few nations that are still not unified today. It will not tolerate any political party promoting separatism in the name of democracy. However, the CPC has tried to introduce competition to local elections by inviting non-members of the Party to participate in these elections.

Although Confucius advocated that the best government is one that rules through rites and natural morality, modern Chinese society has more complicated structures and regulations that lack the characteristics of ancient peasant society. The rule of law is essential in addition to rule of rite. In spite of all the reform efforts, in its eleventh Five-Year Plan, China recognized that it has a long way to go before fully attaining the rule of law.

The key to accelerating management reforms is to streamline the role of each unit and boost the moral standards of the public as well as officials. Guidelines introduced by the central government in 2004 detailed the shift to a rule of law as follows: [96]

- A separation of government and business
- A set of administrative and local rules in line with the Constitution and legal procedures
- A fair and transparent system in which the public can reflect its views
- An efficient and low-cost system to solve social conflict
- A separation between the administration of power and profits, and an administration to support and respect the rule of law

Equally important, the eleventh Five-Year Plan is a crucial tool for developing the rule of law as a means of eliminating corrupt officials.

Although many people outside of China do not support the Chinese one-party democracy or the Chinese form of democracy, the political system is well matched to the historic and cultural background of China. It provides political and social stability for sustainable economic development desperately needed by the nation.

When Hu Jintao visited the U.S. in April 2006, he gave a speech to

Yale students on China's theory of democracy. They supported Hu's theory that "There is no socialism without democracy, and there is no democracy without socialism." One student remarked: China's democracy has to progress at its own speed; for a big country like China, change cannot be too fast. Another student said: the most important and urgent matter for China is to develop its economy and meet basic human rights including the economic right to work and prosper; later China may develop additional political reforms and individual freedoms based on a strengthened economy. Already, the kind of freedom the Chinese people have now is much more than they had in the past. [98, 99]

The U.S. political system is designed with three branches of government that are intended to be separate in a system of checks and balances. The power of each branch is limited, but the total power of the government can be unlimited despite the opposition of the American public. For example, the majority of the American people are now against the continuation of the Iraq War, and the Senate recently passed (218 vs. 212 votes) a US$122 billion measure which would require that Bush begins bringing home some troops within four months of its passage, setting a nonbinding goal of having all combat troops out of Iraq by March 31, 2008. [100] Bush vetoed this war-funding bill on May 2, 2007. [101] Voters must wait perhaps until the next election to stop this war, although prominent Republican Senators are speaking out against the scandal-plagued White House and talk of impeachment has moved from the margins to the mainstream. [102] The war deaths and injured are mounting for both the American and the Iraqis.

This is different from the Chinese situation. Mencius gave Chinese commoners the right to overthrow their government, even if this process could be violent. In Chinese history, there have been several revolutions initiated by the people who successfully overthrew their emperors. This historical precedence exerts great pressure on the Chinese leaders to perform well and avoid uprising by seriously putting the people first in their governance.

Two major political struggles have occurred during PRC history. The Cultural Revolution reviewed in Chapter I and the June 4th Tiananmen Square Incident in 1989. The latter problem stemmed from the discontent of the Chinese people over the rampant corruption among some

Chinese officials. After a decade of open door policies some politically-connected Chinese became rich through inequitable and dishonest means. The leaders who favored political reform could not control the angry students who demanded immediate political change. Finally, Deng Xiaoping made the decision to end their protests through forceful suppression. After the incident, China faced sanctions from many Western nations and was once again in isolation diplomatically and economically. The E.U. also imposed an arms embargo on China that remains to this day.

The Tiananmen Square Incident was a precursor of an uprising. Although the Chinese leadership has since remained mute on the subject, the incident did make them more diligent and effective in their governance, and subsequently, resulted in more freedom for the people. The June 4th protest will be recorded in Chinese modern history as a serious warning to the government, causing a quick, necessary correction in the direction of the nation.

With the increasing rich-poor gap, the number of protests is increasing in China despite rapid economic growth. Often, forceful suppression is used by the local governments to silence the villagers who object to government-approved land grabs and the lack of freedom of the press. The official Chinese press fails to report these incidents or attempts to cover them up. The CPC newspaper, the *Study Times*, urged local governments to refrain from using force when dealing with protests. [103] This is a sign of new progress.

The Transparency International Corruption Perceptions Index that was reported in London/Berlin on October 18, 2005, gave China a score of 3.2 and rank 78 among 159 nations surveyed. The U.S. received a score of 7.6 and rank 17, Hong Kong 8.3 and 15, and Singapore 9.4 and 5. Two thirds of the nations scored less than 5 out of a clean score of 10, indicating serious levels of corruption. These numbers point to a strong correlation between corruption and poverty. Since corruption traps millions in poverty, anti-corruption laws must be enforced to cure the problem. China has set up a special taskforce to tackle the problem of corruption. In 2006, the Ministry of Supervision moved forward with an administrative investigation to weed out civil servants who accept bribes including various commercial cases in the banking, insurance, publishing, sports, tele-communications, and energy sectors. The *Washington Post* reported that China executed a former director of its food and drug agency Zheng Xiaoyu on July 10, 2007, for approving fake medicine in exchange for cash. The government encouraged the public to report cases of malfeasance. This illustrates that Beijing is very serious about tackling product safety.

From August 2005 to June 2006, the Chinese taskforce investigated 6,972 commercial cases and government auditors uncovered misuse of US$3.7 billion in the first half of 2006. [104] A total of 252 people were accused of embezzlement or other misappropriations of government money. [105] Several famous anti-corruption cases were unveiled and resulted in the removal from office of Shanghai Mayor Chen Liangyu and several other high-ranking Chinese officials. Experts reported that the investigation may have exposed only the tip of the iceberg and that the Chinese government must work harder to crack down on corruption through regular legal oversight and criminal prosecution. The Chinese Communist party school is adopting an anti-corruption textbook for the first time to avoid public anger that could undermine their grip on power. [106] The Central Party School is the training center for high ranking members of the party.

Within the Chinese system, the national leaders are elected by professional politicians in the NPC, and the NPC deputies are elected from a group of professional politicians in the provinces, autonomous regions, and municipalities or the armed forces. Unless the candidate is truly exceptional and capable of overcoming political obstacles and balancing power, there is no chance of effectively leading 1.3 billion people.

Nevertheless, even if exceptional national leaders are elected, they may face many obstacles and challengers in their own party. Moreover, Chinese political power plays are very complicated and lack transparency. Most people have difficulty grasping the full complexity of the acquisition and management of political power and its implications.

For example, in an article published in February 2007, entitled "A Number of Issues Regarding the Historic Tasks in the Initial Stage of Socialism and China's Foreign Policy," Chinese Premier Wen Jiabao promoted the concept of socialist democracy, but made it very clear that the time was not right for sweeping political reforms. Later, the 162 words of his speech concerning democracy were deleted by the Central

Propaganda Department before broadcast to Chinese audiences in the mainland. [107] This clearly indicates that, at the present time, stability is the highest priority of the Beijing government.

When Wen answered a question about how long it might take China to become a democracy, he stressed that "China was still, and would be in the primary stage of socialism for 100 years." Mr. Wen's remarks were aimed at staving off rising pressure from the right and left. [108] While the "leftists were accusing the leadership of abandoning socialism, and blaming the system for breeding rampant official corruption and other social problems," "the party reformists and liberal intellectuals were stepping up pressure for the leadership to undertake bolder political reforms following the passage of the Property Law." Wen Jiabao was telling the left that the current socialist system was "imperfect and immature," and corruption and social injustice were "not because of the leadership abandoning socialism," but "the inevitable results of an 'imperfect and immature socialist system.'" [109] This showed that there is continuing party infighting related to the political direction of China.

Nevertheless, some success has been achieved. The fifth generation of the Chinese national leaders will be elected based on nominations as opposed to previous appointed successors, in order to practice internal party democracy and party-faction co-management. [110]

American democracy has already reached a mature state after more than 200 years of development. Its strengths and weaknesses have become more transparent. The weakness of the democratic elections in the U.S., to a great extent, is driven by money. American political candidates need votes, and very often "more money" means "more votes." During the mayoral election of New York City in November 2005, billionaire Mayor Michael Bloomberg spent US$77.89 million of his fortune for reelection. That came to more than US$100 per vote. The election was termed by the Associated Press as the most expensive mayoral reelection in history. In the race for governor of New Jersey, dueling multimillionaires spent US$75 million combined, with US$40 million by Jon S. Corzine, who won the election.

Taking into account the US$60 million he spent on a Senate seat in 2000, Corzine had spent US$100 million in five years for elections. According to a survey, in Washington D.C., a U.S. senator needs about

US$20 million to keep the seat in the Senate. The *Washington Post* crit-
icized the U.S. political system in an editorial, reporting: "A political
system that turns elective office into a bauble for purchase is not a healthy
one." Decisions of the U.S. Congress and the Administration are also
deeply influenced by money. It is known to all that in the U.S., various
firms and interest groups hire public relations and consulting firms to
lobby Congress and the Administration, spending money to influence
their decisions and win government contracts. [111]

In 2004, lobbying expenditures at the Federal level amounted to
US$2.1 billion. Campaign costs for presidential and congressional
campaigns reached US$3 billion. On Oct. 24, 2005, a national public
opinion survey released by the *U.S. News and World Report* revealed that
73 percent of Americans believed their leaders were out of touch with the
average person; 64 percent of Americans felt that their leaders were
corrupted by power; 62 percent thought that leaders seek increases in
personal wealth. A joint Gallup Poll by the *USA Today* and the CNN
found that the job approval for Congress, which had a Republican majority, fell to 29 percent, the lowest level since 1994; 49 percent of American
adults said that they believed "most members of Congress are corrupt."
Former U.S. Attorney General Ramsey Clark said that it is an offense to
democracy to describe the United States as a democracy. [112] His words
bear truth even though some may criticize his radical views.

In the American democratic system, the president is elected directly
by electors, and therefore, indirectly by each voter. The weakness of the
system is, first of all, that not everyone chooses to vote; secondly, most
voters are not professional politicians and they rely on superficial TV
advertisements, brief debates, or propaganda. Furthermore, if voters have
been grossly manipulated by false information, biased religious beliefs,
misguided patriotism, or irrational exuberance, then true democracy
cannot prevail and Americans can be stuck with a president for four to
eight years.

The strength of the American system is the direct elections of
Congress (i.e., Congressmen and Senators), as well as state governors,
town council members, and so forth. In addition, the role of a free press
and freedom of speech against the state play an important role in
American politics. For example, the Walter Reed Hospital scandals [113]

were exposed by the *Washington Post*, which also brought down President Richard M. Nixon in the 1972 Watergate scandal.

The latter showed that no one in America, not even the president, can be above the law. American people also are vigorous in spirit and actions, and keep on fighting for what they believe is right. Lately, there were massive demonstrations against the Iraq War in major cities calling for "End the War," "Bring the Troops Home," and "Tell the Congress." [114] Thousands gathered at the Pentagon to protest the war. They sang songs like "The Battle Hymn of the Republic." [115] While the U.S. democracy is far from perfect; it is vastly different from the authoritarian government of China. In China, there are many more protests today, and both the protesters and the local police often engage in violent clashes that sometimes result in death and injury.

Clearly, neither the American democracy nor the Chinese one-party system is panaceas capable of solving all problems. The weakness of the one-party Chinese system is the lack of freedom, checks and balances in the political process, and the extreme concentration of political power in the hands of a few people. The Chinese leaders are constantly under pressure to perform to maintain their power and control of the CPC. The Chinese system is evolving, and gradual political reforms have been implemented. It remains to be seen whether the Chinese government can maintain the stability of its governance while facing numerous domestic challenges at the same time. Both nations should understand the strengths and weaknesses of their respective political systems and strive for the best.

In the international arena, one aspect that deserves special attention is the policy of each government towards foreign nations. When China conducts international business, it always respects the sovereignty of other nations without setting political preconditions for a given relationship, except acceptance of the One-China Principle. Perhaps the current U.S. administration has been overzealous in imposing its democratic system on other nations through foreign policy initiatives, often demanding that other nations follow the American way. This approach is undemocratic and unpopular among many nations in the world, especially in the Middle East and Latin America. It would be wise, therefore, for the U.S. to reexamine its own foreign policy and exhibit a spirit of true democracy towards other nations worldwide.

In March 2007, *Time* magazine presented findings from a survey of individuals from twenty-seven nations who responded to a question on what they thought were the most admired and least admired nations in the world. Here are the results:

The five most admired nations were: Canada (54 percent), Japan (54 percent), France (50 percent), Great Britain (48 percent) and China (42 percent); the five least admired nations were: Israel (56 percent), Iran (54 percent), the U.S. (51 percent), North Korea (48 percent), and Russia (40 percent).

This survey suggests that the current Bush administration has misread the world by placing the American national interest above all else and acting according to his own wishes, while the people of the world want peace, equality, and justice to develop a prosperous economic environment. [116]

4. China Issued Its First White Paper on Democracy

On October 19, 2005, the Information Office of China's State Council issued a white paper on democracy. The document, entitled "Building of Political Democracy in China," is the first of its kind in China, providing a detailed account of the inception, development, and substance of a socialist political democracy and the principles that the country follows. [117] The document mentioned the problems the country has to overcome in building a democracy and the major steps to be taken to reform its political system. It is divided into twelve parts including the people's congressional system, the system of ethnic regional autonomy, grassroots democracy in urban and rural areas, and respecting and safeguarding human rights.

The white paper states: "Democracy of a country is generated internally, not imposed by external forces," and "the political system a country adopts and the road to democracy taken must be in conformity with the condition of that country." It states, "Without social stability, smooth economic development cannot be expected" and it described China's political system as "the people's democratic dictatorship. . . . Criminal activities, such as sabotage of the socialist system, endangering state security and public security . . . are penalized according to law," and "because situations differ from one country to another, the paths the people of different countries take to win and develop democracy are different."

Other highlights of the paper are briefly summarized as follows:

- The socialist legal system has to be strengthened so that democracy could be institutionalized. Socialist political democracy has to be developed and socialist political civilization has to be built.

- The "socialist political democracy" means a combination of the basic principle of Marxist theory and the useful achievements of the political civilization of mankind including Western democracy, the assimilated democratic elements of China's traditional culture and institutional civilization. Thus, China's socialist political democracy shows distinctive Chinese characteristics.

- China's democracy will not be manipulated by a small number of people, but be managed for the overwhelming majority of the people.

- China's democracy has democratic centralism as the basic organizational principle and mode of operation. When democratic centralism is practiced, it requires that we give full rein to democracy and discuss matters of concern collectively, so that people's wishes and demands are fully expressed and reflected. . . . The practice of democratic centralism also requires that "the majority be respected while the minority is protected."

- China is a vast country with a large population. There are great disparities in development between urban and rural areas and among different regions. It is of unusual significance for China to have a stable state power. . . . Only then can unnecessary and unwanted internal political strife be minimized so that all positive factors can be exploited to the fullest, and all resources, strength, and wisdom can be pooled to tackle major problems. These elements have a major impact on the national economy and the livelihood of individuals, and are essential to ensure sustainable social and economic development.

- Deputies to the local people's congresses at county and township levels are elected directly by their electors. Over the years, the population that has enjoyed the right to vote and participate in elections has accounted for more than 99 percent of citizens eighteen and older.

- The people's congresses have four main functions and powers: legislation, supervision, appointment and removal of officials, and decision-making on major issues. These features are a major reflection of the way the Chinese people exercise their power as masters of the states through the system of a people's congress.

- The NPC and its standing committee exercise the legislative power of the state, mainly to amend the Constitution, and enact and amend the basic laws concerning criminal offenses, civil affairs, state agencies, and other matters. The people's congress at the provincial level and its standing committee may enact local regulations under certain preconditions.

- Democratic elections, democratic decision-making, democratic management, and democratic supervision are the major contents of villagers' self-government. By the end of 2004, some 644,000 villagers' committees had been established throughout the country, with most of the provinces, autonomous regions, and municipalities directly under the central government having elected their fifth or sixth committees. This has been the method China uses to build its grassroots political democracy in rural areas.

- The conference of workers and staff is a basic system ensuring the democratic management of an enterprise or public institution by its workers and staff members. By the end of 2004, more than 1.7 million enterprises and public institutions had established trade unions and 369,000 had set up conferences of workers and staff, covering more than 78 million employees.

• In March 2004, an amendment to the Constitution was adopted by the Second Plenum of the Tenth National People's Congress, which included the statement that "the State respects and safeguards human rights," aimed at guaranteeing: 1) people's rights to subsistence and development; 2) citizens' civil and political rights; 3) people's economic, social, and cultural rights; 4) legitimate rights and interests of special groups of people including women, the aged, minors, and under-privileged groups such as the disabled; and 5) rights of the ethnic minorities.

• For democratic rule by the CPC, the following improvements must be carried out: 1) reform and improvement of the leadership system; 2) development of intra-party democracy; and 3) expansion of democracy in government and business enterprise.

• The Chinese government is the government of the people. It must strengthen its performance by 1) promoting administration in accordance with the law; 2) accelerating the transformation of government functions; and 3) decision-making in a scientific and democratic manner.

• China's judicial structure and system are important components of the country's system of socialist political democracy. Chinese judicial practices abide by a: 1) system of open trials; 2) system of people's jurors; 3) system of people's supervisors; 4) system of lawyers; 5) system of legal assistance; and 6) system of people's mediation.

• The history and reality of human political civilization have proved that there is no single, absolute democratic system in the world that is universally applicable. To determine whether a political system is democratic requires assessment of the degree to which the will of the majority is fully reflected. Democracy is intended to preserve the rights and freedoms of the people.

The white paper explains that China's path is one with its own characteristics, which has "realized the Chinese people's demand to be masters of their own country." China's political system is multi-party including nine political parties, today. They operate through cooperation and political consultation under the leadership of the CPC. This is different from the two-party or multi-party competitive systems of Western countries and the one-party systems practiced in other countries. The cooperation between the CPC and other political parties is based on the basic principle of "long-term coexistence, mutual supervision, fair and honest treatment, and sharing in prosperity and misfortune.

According to the white paper, building a political democracy in China will involve the following principles:

- Upholding the unity of the leadership of the CPC, the people as the masters of the country, and ruling the country by law

- Giving full expression to the characteristics and advantages of the socialist system

- Being conducive to social stability, economic development, and continuous improvement of the lives of the people

- Safeguarding national sovereignty, territorial integrity, and state dignity

- Conforming to the objective law of progress in a systematic way

The white paper stresses the importance of the reform in several key areas including administrative management, the judicial system, personal systems, and in control and exercise of power. As in any nation, the development of democracy is a process.

China's political system has experienced many internal reforms not publicized to the outside world. Recently, in an open letter to the NPC and the central government, the former first secretary for trade at the Chinese Embassy in Tokyo Tang Chunfeng said that the NPC had largely failed to have its voice heard on key bilateral issues:

"The international community wrongly believes that China is still a communist dictatorship because of some misconceptions over how power is distributed in the country," "Even top leaders and lawmakers are afraid of speaking out, leading to some criticism of our political system." [118] He called for an introduction of a mechanism to allow lawmakers to speak out on important international and bilateral issues so that the international community could be updated on political changes in China as well. His proposal indicates that China is a country still in the midst of progressive change. It will take some time for the outside world to understand more about its globalization efforts, trade, economics, and governance.

The U.S. did not begin as a full democracy. Women, Native Americans, and men without property could not vote. From 1863 when President Abraham Lincoln reevaluated the meaning of "All men are created equal" to 1963 when Dr. Martin Luther King presented his "I have a dream" speech, the American concept of democracy evolved further. It took the African Americans 100 years to win the right to vote. Similarly, China, a nation of 1.3 billion people, may need that much time or even longer to achieve true democracy. When the U.S. was undergoing rapid economic expansion in the 1820s, it had a population of ten million. China's present population is 130 times that and social stability plays an extremely important role in critical political reform. China must keep a cool head to avoid speed traps in the reform process.

5. China Issued a Sharp Retort to U.S. Report on Human Rights

The U.S. is a frequent critic of China's human rights record despite much improved conditions today. In the spring of 2006, the U.S. State Department issued the "Country Report on Human Rights Practices for 2005." The section of the U.S. report dealing with China said that human rights conditions had worsened in 2005, reversing a modest trend of improved respect for rights that the department had observed earlier. It cited "increased harassment, detention, and imprisonment" of people viewed as threats to the government. The report also criticized tighter controls on the Chinese press and more assertive censorship of all kinds of media, including the Internet. [119] The 2006 report is similar in scope to the 2005 report and said "the government's human rights record remained poor, and in certain areas has deteriorated." [120–121]

To refute the U.S. report, China immediately issued a response on March 9, 2006, on the "Human Rights Record of the U.S. in 2005" commenting "As in previous years, the State Department cited human rights violations in more than 190 countries, including China, but kept silent on the serious violations of human rights in the United States." [122] Beijing urged the U.S. government to stop "provoking international confrontations" on the issue of human rights [123] and raised many human rights violations by the U.S. [124–136] The report urged the U.S. government to look squarely at its own human rights problems, reflect upon what it has done in the human rights field, and take concrete measures to improve its own human rights status. This would require calling a halt to international confrontation on the issue of human rights, and making a fresh start to contribute to international human rights cooperation and the healthy development of international human rights.

China is a developing country, whereas the U.S. is a developed nation. Naturally, China has a lot to catch up in many areas including the human rights issue. But clearly, the two nations also have very different views on human rights practices derived from their different culture and history.

In the U.S., human rights, as given by God, is extremely important since "individualism" is emphasized; whereas in China, "collectivism" may take higher priority in society and people are more willing to sacrifice personal freedom and rights for the country's sake. The more important issue is: while the U.S. human rights records are far from perfect, is it constructive to continuously criticize human rights practices of other nations? Moreover, if such accusation is used as a political attack against another nation, then it is not surprising for China and other nations like Russia to show strong anger and respond in similar ways. All nations should work hard to improve human rights practices before pointing fingers at each other.

Thanks to the U.S. free press that recently revealed a serious government scandal: President George W. Bush admitted that the U.S. had secret overseas prisons to detain and try terrorists. He said that fourteen important suspects involved in the 9/11 terrorist attack had been turned over to the Defense Department and transferred to Guantanamo prison, a U.S. Navy detention center. In 2002, the U.S. authorized the use of these secret prisons to detain and try terrorist suspects, but kept it concealed. In 2005, the administration acknowledged the existence of such secret prisons in Eastern Europe. European countries were angry and condemned the U.S. for having violated international guidelines related to the Treatment of Prisoners of War. [137]

At the twenty-first round of the China-E.U. Human Rights Dialogue in Vienna on May 27, 2006, an E.U. official stated that China made progress in human rights protection and promotion. [138] The dialogue that began in 1997 is held every six months. China recognizes that it must do more to protect the human rights of its people to become a truly great country in the twenty-first century.

On July 29, 2006, thirty Wal-Mart workers in Jinjiang, in east China's Fujian Province, established a trade union. This represents a new milestone in the struggle for rights by Chinese workers. In less than two weeks, nine of fifty-nine Wal-Mart stores in the mainland of China established trade unions. The speed of this achievement was unprecedented in China. Wal-Mart entered the Chinese market in 1995; it resisted the concept of unions, but relented under pressure by Hu Jintao. [139] Negotiations between Wal-Mart and the All China Federation of Trade Unions have led to the successful formation of nineteen trade unions since late July 2006.

The "Human Rights Record of the U.S. in 2006" by China shows similar contents except that it mentioned more human rights violations caused by the U.S. war in Iraq; for brevity this will not be discussed further. [140]

6. The Beijing Consensus vs. the Washington Consensus

On August 1, 2006, British Prime Minister Tony Blair delivered a speech in Los Angeles, California, in which he remarked that Britain is increasingly engaged in diplomatic activities with both China and India. He predicted that many developing countries will become more prosperous. Over the next twenty to thirty years China would emerge as a new superpower and the world would be reshaped by new political authorities including China, India, and Russia. He concluded that it is therefore necessary for Britain and the U.S. to adjust their policies. Shortly thereafter, twelve scholars spoke at the U.S. Senate Hearing on "China's World Role: A Responsible Stakeholder?" They attempted to analyze the rapid development in China, which brings new strength to the world and new challenges to U.S. foreign policy. [141]

The U.S. is striving to understand this immense Asian nation and its role in the world. Most scholars presented their views from the standpoint of U.S. strategic planning on how to contain rather than how to cooperate with China. China is writing its own version of what it wants to accomplish. China intends to create a new splendid civilization without resorting to war and conquest. China plans to demonstrate that different countries can coexist peacefully and work together to solve common problems related to energy, pollution, poverty, and so forth.

China must learn to grasp opportunities to facilitate peaceful development and avoid falling into the traps of hegemonic power camps. Namely, the Chinese people's deep love for peace and harmony and their confidence in the Chinese culture remains the cornerstone behind its developing principles. In order to understand this point of view, the basic ideologies that comprise the latest Washington Consensus and the Beijing Consensus are examined here.

The Washington Consensus emanated from Washington, though doubts linger whether it was really a consensus, especially within Asia. [142] However, it is interesting to know that the Beijing Consensus did not originate from Beijing, but through Joshua Cooper Ramo, a former Foreign Editor of *Time* magazine. He is currently managing partner in the offices of John L. Thornton. In addition, he is Professor and Director of the Global Leadership Program at Tsinghua University in Beijing and a Senior Advisor to Goldman Sachs. He is well-known for his work entitled "The Beijing Consensus" issued in 2004. He attended many meetings in China and spoke with numerous Chinese government officials. The two consensus reflect differing positions as well as the different paths taken, and diverse related impacts on the world, in particular, the third world, which includes underdeveloped and developing countries. China is adapting to Western methods of business enterprise as it develops economically while preserving its unique identity and character.

What Is the Washington Consensus?

The Washington consensus is a set of policies promulgated by the neo-liberal economists in the U.S. as a direct result of the neo-liberal revolution that swept the globe beginning in the 1990s. It has been pushed aggressively by the neo-conservative Bush administration as the basis of globalization and a formula for promoting a socioeconomic and political movement towards free markets and free societies worldwide. The political philosophy unpinning the neo-conservative Washington Consensus encompasses economic competition, political democracy, and social liberalism. It is designed to make the target economy more like that of first world countries such as the U.S. A more detailed review follows:

i) Economic Impact

The Washington Consensus has been the subject of sharp criticism by many Latin American countries including Argentina, Bolivia, Brazil, Chili, Cuba, Peru, and Venezuela. Opponents perceive the consensus as representative of the jaws of imperialism and hegemony which have gripped these countries. One problem of the Washington Consensus is that it was developed by Western bankers, economists, and policy makers based on the First World economic concepts. It imposes economic structures in the underdeveloped world intended to enhance the interests of multinational companies and the international monopolies. Critics believe that it fails to consider the environment of the underdeveloped economy and needs of the people. The agenda of the Washington Consensus was promoted deliberately and systematically. Participants of the Washington Consensus reached a consensus based on acceptance of neo-conservatism.

When first world countries impose neo-liberal policies on economically vulnerable Latin American countries through organizations such as the World Bank and the International Monetary Fund (IMF) and through political pressure or bribery, often, no great economic boom occurs. Instead, severe economic crises and high debts result. The critics of the North American FTA of the 1990s and the Dominican Republic-Central America FTA passed by the U.S. Congress in 2005 blame the agreements for depleting jobs of the U.S. working class and for exploitation of Mexican laborers because free trade permits the movement of goods across borders as opposed to labor which cannot move as freely. Goods produced cheaply in underdeveloped economies are sold at much higher prices in the first world countries to the benefit of the large multinational corporations and the consumer, but not to the benefit of the producers. As a result, the rich-poor gap between the first world and the underdeveloped countries has widened.

Similarly, the Washington Consensus plunged Southeast Asia into financial, economic, social, and political chaos during the 1997–98 Asian financial crises. The Washington Consensus is a Washington-knows-best approach designed to dictate to other nations how to run their countries. [143] Many economists consider the Washington Consensus as an arrogant policy for the U.S. and a suicidal policy for third world nations.

ii) Political Impact

The Washington Consensus also pushes for political democracy and social liberalism in the underdeveloped nations in the Middle East as manifested by the Bush administration foreign policies since 2000. Neoconservatives believe that the U.S. should not hesitate to use its unrivaled power – forcefully if necessary – to promote its values around the world. Some even speak of the need to cultivate a U.S. empire. Neoconservatives believe that modern threats facing the U.S. can no longer be reliably contained and therefore must be prevented sometimes through preemptive military action. They have revived the older Wilsonian tradition, but they no longer consider the U.N. relevant.

In fact, the neo-conservatives (neocons) think that the U.N. gets in the way to some degree. Instead, they employ a high-minded approach and are more concerned about basic American values. Most neocons believe that the U.S. has allowed dangers to gather by not spending enough on defense and not confronting threats aggressively enough. [144] The current Bush administration imposes this mode of conducting foreign policy and engages in war as necessary to achieve its aims. Democratizing Iraq and building a New Middle East by preemptively invading Iraq are recent examples of their tactics. This is an incredibly tall order and it might consume much time and resources without a positive outcome. Not everyone in the U.S. wants to make these sacrifices, which lead to the loss of American and Iraqi lives, injuries, and bloodshed. Furthermore, it is unclear whether the Iraqis really want an American-style democracy. The war in the Middle East endangers world peace and the U.S. role deserves an in-depth examination:

Iraqis were coerced through war to install an American-style democracy. The Israel-Hezbollah conflict in the summer of 2006 has rekindled the old antagonism in the Middle East and the Iranian nuclear crisis cannot be eliminated through traditional U.S. threats of economic sanctions. To resolve these problems, a basic understanding of the Middle East, is essential.

The History of Conflict in the Middle East

Many recognize that the Middle East has been an area of tension since the end of World War II in the aftermath of the creation of Israel. The Middle East crisis originated with the passage of U.N. Resolution Number 181 in 1947. The resolution, backed by the U.S., emphasized the interests of Israel and enraged Arab nations including Egypt, Iraq, Jordan, Lebanon, the Palestine and Syria,. In 1948, the First Middle East War was fought and won by Jews who wished to establish a homeland in Israel. This displaced many Palestinians and led to an enormous refugee problem and planted the seeds for a war-ridden Middle East.

A second Middle East war was fought in 1956 over ownership of the Suez Canal. This dispute was between Egypt and a joint force from Britain and France. The Third Middle East War broke out on June 5, 1967, when it became known that Egypt had concentrated large-scale forces in the Sinai Peninsula based on a false report spread by the Soviets. [145] This concentration of forces gradually led the Arabs to believe that an opportunity had been created to realize their nineteen-year aspiration to destroy Israel. In the light of this development, Israel had no choice but to preemptively strike. [146] This is known as the Six-Day War and entailed a sudden attack by Israel against Egypt, Jordan, and Syria. Its aim was to destroy the Arab dream of establishing a confederated Arab nation advocated by President Gamal Abdel Nasser of Egypt. Israel's decisive victory diminished the military power of its Arab neighbors and tripled its territory.

After Egypt lost the war, the concept of a secular confederated Arab nation quickly weakened and the principles of religious Islamic fundamentalism, popular in Afghanistan, emerged as mainstream thinking. The battered Arab societies facing their own corrupt societies and governments, wars, and international pressures needed the spiritual relief and support they could find in Islamic fundamentalism and they began to regard the Palestine liberation war as a jihad (Jihad usually refers to military exertion against non-Muslim combatants. In broader usage and interpretation, the term has accrued both violent and non-violent meanings. It can refer to striving to live a moral and virtuous life, to spreading and defending Islam, and to fighting injustice and oppression, among other interpretations. Jihad is also used in the meaning of struggle for or defense of Islam.)

The Fourth Middle East War erupted in September 1973 when Egypt and Syria took revenge through a sudden attack on Israel, which recaptured some of the land lost in the prior Middle East war. After this war, both Israel and surrounding Arab nations felt military methods geared to annihilation of the enemy would fail and began to seek compromise solutions to bring about peaceful coexistence. Unfortunately, Israel initiated a fifth Middle East war in June 1982 in an attack against the Palestine Liberation Army and Syrian soldiers in Southern Lebanon. After the Fifth Middle East War, the Palestinian Liberation organization was weakened substantially and its leader, Yasser Arafat, reluctantly accepted the 1947 U.N. Resolution 181 recognizing the new nation of Israel. [147]

The U.S. Role in the Middle East and Afghanistan

The U.S. was praised by the international community for support of the return of the Suez Canal to Egypt during the Second Middle East War. However, following withdrawal of British and French colonial powers from the Middle East, U.S. and Russian influence became more pervasive. The U.S. Middle East policy traditionally favored Israel because of the many successful Jewish Americans represented in business, finance, education, media, politics, the arts, and many other areas. The U.S. did not object to the Israeli refusal to accept U.N. Resolutions 242 and 338 to return occupied land to the Arab countries.

The Palestinian refugees have lived in the refugee camps without land, assets, democracy, or freedom since losing their home in the First Middle

East War. They experienced anger and hatred towards the Israelis and the Americans. After the 1960s, the Palestinians organized terrorist activities around the world to seek revenge against Israel and its supporters. This was the backdrop and one of the possible sparks for the 9/11 terrorist attack in the U.S. by the Arab Islamic fundamentalist, Osama bin Laden.

A review of the U.S. voting record on the Palestinian issue in the U.N. over the past few decades reveals why many Arabs hate the U.S. After World War II, Israel repeatedly refused to accept U.N. resolutions in support of Arab interests and, because of U.S. pressure, the U.N. has never imposed any sanctions against Israel. Both the U.N. and the E.U. have condemned the intransigence of Israel and claim that it is the biggest barrier to peace in the Middle East.

Before World War II, many Arab leaders admired the Western system of government and hoped to introduce democracy into their political systems. Following the failure of the free elections in Syria in 1943, Arabs began to doubt whether the Western form of democracy would be suitable for the Arab society. [148]

In addition, the U.S. criticizes Middle East terrorists for opposition to democracy and freedom while supporting the Israeli invasions and ignoring world opinion.

Today, the U.S. anti-terrorist war in Afghanistan continues. There are about twenty thousand American troops in Afghanistan and fifteen thousand NATO troops assumed command of military operations from the U.S. forces in volatile southern Afghanistan. The goal is to crush resurgent Taliban forces. [149] Military operations have been underway for six years because of the 9/11 terrorist attack.

When Iraq invaded Kuwait in 1990, the U.S. convened a multinational military coalition force to oust Iraq from the country. The current Iraq War has entered its fourth year with no end in sight and with no discovery of weapons of mass destruction. The American public is turning against this war. A recent Gallop Poll showed that support for President Bush and advocacy of his antiterrorist foreign policies has dropped to 30 percent. [150] This is an all time low for his presidency.

Top U.S. commanders in the Middle East appeared before the Senate Armed Services Committee on August 3, 2006, where they reported to a Senate panel that the wave of sectarian violence between rival Shiite and Sunni Muslims in Iraq was pushing the country towards an all out civil war. [151] The number of U.S. soldiers in Iraq has been increased to over 150,000 to deal with the Sunni insurgency and a possible resumption of problems with Shiite militias. [152]

The Israel-Hezbollah Clash

In July 2006, Lebanese Hezbollah guerrillas captured two Israeli soldiers, igniting a relentless Israeli attack and bombardment of southern Lebanon's civilians, hospitals, and infrastructure. This led to the skyrocketing crude oil prices to US$78 a barrel that summer. As a result, neo-conservative idealism regarding democratization of the Middle East became less appealing worldwide.

The U.N. estimated that about one million Lebanese were displaced by the conflict. One thousand Lebanese died and Israelis suffered serious casualties causing a burgeoning humanitarian crisis in Lebanon and Gaza. Popular support for Hezbollah rose from 50 percent before the clash to 85 percent. [153] The *London Times* criticized Bush and his advisors for refusing to consider international pressure to back an immediate ceasefire. The lack of action prompted Lebanon Prime Minister Fouad Siniora to lash out in despair at the meeting in Rome on July 26 that "Is the value of human life less in Lebanon than that of citizens elsewhere? Are we children of a lesser God? Is an Israeli teardrop worth more than a drop of Lebanese blood?" [154]

Israel has invaded and occupied Lebanon seven times over the past thirty years and the Hezbollah have been fighting to regain the lost territory. Palestinian Liberation Organization Chairman Mahmoud Abbas commented that Palestinians absolutely cannot accept any unilateral Israeli resolution. He reiterated that only by establishing an independent Palestinian nation based on the 1967 border definition and through fair resolution of the Palestinian refugee issue and illegal Israeli occupation, could there be a real possibility of disentanglement from the Palestinian-Israeli conflict. [155]

On July 24, 2006, an Israeli guided missile hit a U.N. observer post in southern Lebanon, killing four U.N. observers from Austria, Canada, China, and Finland. Israel ignored ten warnings by the U.N. not to launch missiles near the post. [156] The U.N. Secretary General Kofi

Annan and China expressed "deep shock" and "strongly condemned" such an unfortunate incident and urged an immediate ceasefire. [157]

As international pressure mounted, the Bush administration grew concerned that the situation in Lebanon would further inflame anger towards the U.S. in the Arab world. Secretary of State Condoleezza Rice changed her tone at a meeting in Rome, but repeated again that she would only work towards a "sustainable" truce. [158] On July 25, when the first U.S. humanitarian shipment arrived in Lebanon, homeless Lebanese refugees showed little appreciation towards American generosity. Instead, they angrily scolded the U.S. for providing bombs to Israel. [159, 160]

The Israel-Lebanon military clash, the Iran nuclear crisis, the Iraq chaos, the continuing fight in Afghanistan, and the North Korean missile tests have placed severe pressure on U.S. foreign policy advocated by the Bush administration and its neo-conservative supporters. Some experts believe that the U.S. was fighting for influence in the region using Israel and Lebanon as battlegrounds. China would like to see a peaceful Middle East and supports international nuclear non-proliferation. China insists on resolving the current Middle East crisis through political and diplomatic negotiations. It seems that the U.S. would not be able to control the situation unilaterally over the long-term. It is likely that terrorist threats against the U.S. will not subside without major changes in U.S foreign policy.

On August 11, 2006, the U.N. Security Council unanimously passed a resolution calling for an end to Hezbollah attacks on Israel and to offensive military operations in Lebanon by Israel. China supported the U.N. resolution and hoped the concerned parties would strive for its implementation. Chinese deputy representative to the U.N., Liu Zhenmin, said that "This formed a good basis for future efforts to achieve a long-term political solution to the Lebanon-Israel issue," and hoped that, through the principle of "land for peace," the Middle East peace process would be revitalized. Both Hezbollah and the Lebanese government accepted this cease-fire resolution with reservations on August 12. [161] After enacting the cease-fire agreement, the Chinese government decided to increase its troop level in the U.N. peacekeeping force in Lebanon to 1,000 and provide aid worth US$5.04 million. Chinese Premier Wen Jiabao said that "China is concerned with the situation in

Lebanon, and hopes all sides will observe Resolution 1701 of the U.N. Security Council to facilitate the early settlement of the conflict." [162]

The famous American reporter and Pulitzer Prize winner, Seymour Hersh, wrote in the *New Yorker* that the Bush government was closely associated with the Israeli attack in southern Lebanon as a military drill in preparation for a war against Iran. [163] If this is true, it would have a negative impact on the image of the U.S. and Israel and result in increased turbulence in the future.

The new Middle East policy of President Bush faces serious problems. Although the number of Americans who have died in Iraq is far fewer than that of the Korean or Vietnam wars, the drain on the U.S. economy has escalated quickly. The Iraqi people are suffering daily. A change in U.S. foreign policy is the key to the recovery of Iraqi stability.

If Iran were willing to cooperate with the U.S., the unrest in Iraq would be relieved quickly. Otherwise, Iraq could become a muddy trap for the U.S. for a long time. If the U.S. stays in Iraq, its soldiers will continue to die. Iran, by providing weapons to insurgents in Iraq, can use Iraq to torment the U.S. by making it confront increasingly violent religious factional conflicts. If Iran intervenes against the U.S., any attempt for peacemaking among the religious factions would be doomed to fail. If the U.S. retreats, then Iran could take over Iraq and control the Gulf region. This would mean a tremendous loss for the U.S. in the Middle East.

Iran has not concealed its intention to eliminate Israel. The provocation of Israel by Hezbollah was designed to promote resistance to Israel. It seems that Iran may be the biggest winner of the current Hezbollah-Israeli clash. Of course, the U.S. can always attack militarily, but what would the U.S. gain? Does America want another Iraq?

What Is the Beijing Consensus?

Joseph S. Nye, Jr., former Dean of the Kennedy School of Government at Harvard University, was the first to introduce the term "soft power." It describes a kind of influence that a nation should use to get others to willingly adopt similar goals, foreign policies, political values, culture, and economic objectives, rather than operating through economic domination and military suppression. Basically, soft power produces influence in four areas: culture, ideology, systems, and diplomacy.

In the past, China's culture prevailed for centuries from the Hang and Tang Dynasties to the mid–Qing and its neighboring countries were willing to become geographic peripheral tributaries of China. After the fall of the Qing Dynasty, China was consumed with a fight for the nation against foreign partition over the next 100 years. Later, a continuous bitter domestic power struggle between the CPC and the KMT raged for over a decade on the mainland. Finally, the CPC succeeded and established the PRC in 1949.

During much of the Cold War, China was totally isolated. Through the first twenty-nine years of PRC rule, the poverty-stricken nation sought the means to survive in spite of domestic and international turmoil. Mao Zedong pursued centrally planned economic programs guided by Marxism and his own brand of communist ideology. Many of these seemed to fail. When he died in 1976, China was on the verge of economic collapse.

However, Deng Xiaoping initiated an open door policy in 1978 to embrace a market economy that integrated a form of "socialism with Chinese characteristics." China has "groped for stones to cross the river" instead of dramatic change through a form of potentially dangerous shock therapy. It pursued a own course to develop its rapidly growing economy. It has also adopted a pragmatic approach to handle international relations based on the principle of non-interference in domestic affairs. The whole package is termed as the Beijing Consensus by Western scholars and politicians.

The Beijing Consensus has attracted attention and won respect from many underdeveloped and developing countries. It seems that the Chinese policy is seen favorably because China is also a third world nation that has fought imperialism and has stood with the third world against Western pressure. The Beijing Consensus offers hope to developing countries worldwide. A survey in 2006 by Russia and the U.S. on China reported that it was viewed as the fourth most influential nation in the world after the U.S., the E.U. and the UK. The survey offered ten nations as choices. More specifically, possible selections included: Britain, Canada, China, the E.U., France, India, Italy, Japan, Russia, and the U.S. Sixty-eight percent of Americans interviewed thought the influence of China would increase notably and be comparable to the U.S. over the next ten years. [164]

Instead of imposing drastic economic, political, and social reforms promoted by the Washington Consensus, China has emphasized stability as the foundation of its economic and political reforms and its foreign policy. Based on these criteria, a Beijing Consensus has emerged with distinct attitudes towards politics, economic development, and the global balance of power.

In the words of Joshua Cooper Ramo, who originated the phrase, the Beijing Consensus is: 1) driven by a ruthless willingness to innovate; 2) a strong belief in sovereignty and multilateralism; and 3) a desire to accumulate the tools of "asymmetric power projection"—just as in armed conflict, the weaker party must avoid fighting on its stronger opponent's terms and exploit the latter's foibles. The Beijing Consensus was brought forward spontaneously by international opinion against the background of fast economic development and rising international influence of the Chinese since reform. It does not have universally recognized documents and its content is still under debate due to the rapidly changing nature of Chinese society. [165] A simple description of Ramo's definition of the Beijing Consensus is as follows: [166]

> *China is making a path for other nations around the world who are trying to figure out not simply how to develop their countries, but also how to fit into the international order in a way that allows them to be truly independent, to protect their way of life and political choices in a world with a single massively powerful center of gravity, I call this the new physics of power and development of the Beijing Consensus . . . It does not believe in uniform solutions for every situation. It is defined by a ruthless willingness to innovate and experiment, by a lively defense of national borders and interests and by the increasing thoughtful accumulation of tools of asymmetric power projection. . . . Most importantly, it is both the product of and defined by a society that is changing so fast that few people, even those inside China, can keep up with it.*
>
> *The Beijing Consensus is as much about social change as economic change. It is about using economics and governance to improve society. . . . It also remains fraught with contradictions, tensions, and pitfalls. Yet many elements of the country's rise have*

engaged the developing world. China is writing its own book now. The book represents a fusion of Chinese thinking with lessons learned from the failure of the globalization culture in other places. The rest of the world has begun to study this book.

. . . They [The Beijing Consensus] are about politics, quality of life, and the global balance of power. . . . Or as one summary of Chinese thinking explains, "The present world is plagued by serious problems such as the widening gap between the North and South, a worsening environment, international terrorism, and international drug trafficking. A shift from power politics to moral politics should be expedited." Continuing U.S. failure to meaningfully address these problems will only accelerate the acceptance of a Beijing Consensus. . . . This is not to say that the Chinese government has some master plan to challenge the United States for hegemony and is using this ideological doctrine to finesse that power shift. In fact, many Chinese leaders now argue that what China needs is a "Peaceful Rise" (. . .). But even this will demand a shift in the physics of international power. That shift is now underway.

Is China's development following the Beijing Consensus? A summary analysis follows:

i) The Ruthless Willingness to Innovate: A Path to Prosperity for Poor Countries

Today, the Chinese people understand fully that change driven by knowledge, such as the information revolution, will promote rapid growth and development. One popular approach to development in China is creation of high-growth economic hubs. [167] A few vital statistics on innovation in China are summarized below:

- China now has 110 million Internet users and over 390 million mobile phone subscribers. By 2010, the number could reach 250 million. [168]

- Ninety-eight percent of provincial leaders in 2002 attended college. This was up from 20 percent in 1982. The number with post-graduate degrees grew from 12.9 percent in 2001 to 29 percent in 2003. Two-thirds of the "fourth generation" leaders under the age of fifty-four hold Masters or Ph.D. degrees. [169]

- Adult literacy rate in 1977 was 66 percent. By the mid-1990s, it was over 80 percent. [170] The nationwide illiteracy rate average was approximately 10.9 percent in 2003. In 2004, more than 93 percent of the country achieved nine years of basic education. There were 2,236 institutions of higher education in 2004, with a total enrollment of twenty million students. All rural children are expected to receive nine years of free education by 2010. [171]

- China awarded 12,000 Ph.D. degrees in 2004 and will exceed the U.S. annual rate of Ph.D. graduate rate of 40,000 per year by 2010, although the quality and academic standards of these degrees are not as high as those of U.S. institutions.

- The World Bank estimates that China has lifted 300 million people out of poverty with improved farming techniques that boosted grain productivity.

- China's GDP in 2005 ranked fourth in the world. China plans to quadruple its GDP by 2020, a goal can only be achieved with innovation-led growth.

- Nearly 9 million students are taking annual national examinations to enter universities, but only 2.6 million can be accepted. A strict Confucian value system is applied to the educational system to assure fairness and safeguard against corruption and backroom dealing.

- In China 150 million entrepreneurs and independent professionals are being recognized as important along with other workers, farmers, and intellectuals. They are regarded as a new pillar of socialism with Chinese characteristics. They contributed one third of the tax revenues. Over the past decade, private enterprise in China created nearly six million new jobs annually, representing approximately 75 percent of the nation's annual total. [172]

- China has overtaken Japan in 2006 as the third-largest U.S. export market and its fastest-growing exports market. [173] China alone accounted for about 12 percent of global trade growth in 2005, whereas in 2000, it accounted for less than 4 percent of the global trade.

- Global high-tech exports in 2005 approached US$220 billion and accounted for almost one-third of its total exports, a stunning 100 fold increase since 1989.

- The eleventh Five-Year Plan proposed by the CPC Central Committee states that in the industrial sector, the main task is not expansion in scale, but structural upgrades to convert large industries into powerhouses.

- Innovation created 6.08 million jobs in urban areas and resulted in reemployment of 2.36 million workers who were laid off in the first half of 2006. As a result, the official urban jobless rate was 4.2 percent at the end of the second quarter, lower than the government projection of 4.6 percent for 2006. [174]

- Eighty-six percent of notebook computers sold worldwide come from China. By 2008, this figure will reach 90 percent; today, almost no computer is without components made in China. [175]

- The market share for Chinese cars is growing in South America, Europe, and elsewhere worldwide. Sales growth for cars in South America and Europe rose by 520 percent and 117 percent in value in the first six months of 2006. The primary auto export market for China is Asia, Europe ranked second, Africa third, and South America fourth. In 2005 China exported 125,500 motor vehicles to 171 countries and regions. This was an increase of 68.8 percent over the same period a year before. [176]

- The value of auto exports reached US$1.255 billion, up 115.1 percent. The Chery QQ model in Venezuela sells for under US$10,000. This was less expensive than the Chevrolet Spark, its nearest competitor. [177] Overall Chinese automaker profits rose by 76 percent in the first half of 2006. [178] China aims to export US$70 billion worth of autos and auto components by 2010. In 2005, the car and auto parts exports hit US$10.9 billion, up 34 percent over the previous year. [179] However, its market share in world auto and auto parts is still less than 1 percent.

- Dalian, a port city in northeast China, announced plans on August 11, 2006, to build the first commercial Chinese-made high-speed magnetic levitation (Maglev) train. This would be the second commercial Maglev line. The first system, located in Shanghai, was built with German technology and Chinese labor. The newest system will cost half that of the foreign-made system. An accident in 2006 on the Shanghai Maglev system raised doubts about the reliability of the German technology. Chinese scientists and engineers have spent twenty years in research on the Maglev technology and possess the capability to produce the Maglev train independently. The Chinese people are confident that, within five years, their technology will be competitive. The Chinese government has also approved the construction of a high-speed Shanghai-Beijing rail line. Chinese-built high-speed trains capable of speeds of up to 150 mph started on runs from Shanghai to two nearby cities, Hangzhou to the southwest and Nanjing to the west. The new trains operate at an average speed of 100 mph. [180]

- Rapid economic growth will drive as many as 300 million farmers to the cities over the next twenty years. This is the world's largest urbanization movement. China has 1.3 billion people of which 800 million are farmers. [181] The new work force will enter into emerging industry sectors that have higher economic values than farming. It is estimated that by 2010, the urban population in China will exceed the rural population and, by 2050, that number will be 70 percent of its total population. [182]

- Chinese telecom equipment companies like Hua Wei Technology Co., Ltd. in Shenzhen have hired 7,000 engineers and invested US$558 million in research and development. Fifty-seven percent of its sales in 2005 were in overseas markets, and sales increased by 15 percent in Asian markets and 9 percent in Latin American markets. [183]

- Suntech Power Holdings Co., Ltd., a solar energy manufacturing company, designs, develops, manufactures, and markets a variety of photovoltaic cells and modules, which are devices that convert sunlight into electricity. The firm successfully launched an initial public offering at the New York Stock Exchange on December 24, 2005. The five-year old Suntech spent US$20 million annually on research and development. It is targeting all PRC families as customers for solar energy in the future. [184]

- As much as US$77.5 million was invested by Silicon Valley venture capitalists in China in the first half of 2006. [185] In the past, Silicon Valley investors rarely focused their attention in the PRC. They now look to China for the next Chinese Baidu, a Chinese search engine, to win a better market share than Google. China now contributes 12 percent of world's published scientific papers annually. [186]

- China vows to upgrade its trade structure over the next five years to gradually shift from a labor intensive growth pattern to technology-intensive development pattern. Advanced technology exports experienced robust growth increasing by a factor of 4.9 times in 2005 over the previous year, accounting for 31.7 percent of China's total processing trade. This refers to business activities of importing all or part of the raw and auxiliary materials, parts and components, accessories, and packaging materials from abroad in bulk, and re-exporting the finished products after processing or assembly by enterprises within the mainland. [187]

From this overview, it is evident that China has made tremendous progress in improving education and emphasizing innovation. It has successfully lifted a huge portion of its population out of poverty. However, this is not to suggest that China has succeeded in catching up with the major industrialized nations. China has a long way to go to become a completely modernized nation and a leader in advanced technologies. For example: in 2003, China owned only 0.3 percent of international patents, far behind the U.S. (36 percent) and Japan (26 percent). Also, a closer examination shows that international firms performed much of the scientific and industry research in China. Foreign organizations filed two-thirds of all Chinese patents. Fifty percent of the patents filed abroad for inventions made in China belong to foreigners, almost half are owned by Americans. [188]

Only 5.2 percent of 1.3 billion Chinese population have a university degree, whereas one-fourth of the Americans have university degrees. [189] In addition, China imports high value-added components from Japan, South Korea, and Taiwan for assembly and exports the finished products to the West. Products manufactured by foreign companies in China are about 60 percent of the exported products. These largely outnumber those made by indigenous companies (40 percent). In other words, "assembled in China" would be a more appropriate description than "made in China" for Chinese exports. Taiwanese companies currently account for 80 percent of global notebook computers, but rapid migration of Taiwan companies to the PRC in recent years has made the vast majority of notebook computers Chinese exports. [190]

China has vowed to shed its image as a world-class economy with poor homegrown high technology. Chinese President Hu Jintao reviewed his ambitious plans at the opening of the Fourth National Conference on Science and Technology on January 9, 2006. Hu said that the country must pursue a path of scientific and technological innovation with Chinese characteristics. "Technological advancement has become the focus of international competition and the key to a country's drive to modernization. . . . But as international practice has shown, key technologies that are the lifeline of the national economy and security cannot be purchased." Despite some technological breakthroughs in the manned space missions and increases in grain production, China still lagged behind leading world powers in terms of innovation, and the central government would issue a document on the implementation of science and technologies. [191] China is confident of becoming an innovation-oriented country by 2020 despite many arduous tasks ahead. Statistics show that China has 38.5 million scientific and technological workers, including 1.09 million in research and development, ranking first and second in the world, respectively. [192]

While China has a long way to go to become a high-tech nation, it is undeniable that it has succeeded in overcoming the post-Mao slump and the associated failed planned economy which lacked a strong industrial base. In a few decades, it has created a favorable environment for accelerated development of an innovation-led market economy. In addition, China has a long historical and cultural tradition that emphasizes education, language, collectivism, and the accumulation of knowledge and education. These are favorable conditions for the promotion of innovation. No wonder developing nations view China as a role model and want to emulate a similar development program. For example, bilateral trade between China and Africa has increased more than 300 percent since 2000 and now exceeds US$40 billion a year. Many African countries have declared a "Look East" policy and turn to China for economic and political salvation.

ii) A Strong Belief in Sovereignty and Multilateralism: A Determination to Find Its Own Route

The Chinese mentality and international perspective have changed substantially from the closed door, Great Wall approach of the past to embrace the world. China wants to develop to achieve prosperity and supports democracy in its international relationships by respecting sovereignty and advocating multilateralism among world nations. This is viewed as the best method for collaboration and problem solving. In order to achieve globalization with Chinese characteristics, China needs to build a stable, peaceful local environment to assure growth. By using economics and governance to improve society, China aims to influence economic forces by applying timely strategies to deal with problems.

After the Cold War, the U.S. became a major world superpower.

Although the U.S. government presents itself as a human rights advocate and the most democratic nation in the world, it has engaged in numerous undemocratic and unethical global interventions and wars since 1945. Writer William Blum in his book, *Rogue State* calls it "The American Empire." He lists on fifty-nine pages (pages 162 to 220) U.S. interventions after World War II in over sixty nations in the world. He compares the U.S. to the Roman Empire as follows: [193]

There was no corner of the known world where some interest was not alleged to be in danger or under actual attack. If the interests were not Roman, they were those of Rome's allies; and if Rome has no allies, the allies would be invented. When it was utterly impossible to contrive such an interest—why, then it was the national honor that had been insulted. The fight was always invested with an aura of legality. Rome was always attacked by evil-minded neighbors . . . The whole world was pervaded by a host of enemies, it was manifestly Rome's duty to guard against their indubitably aggressive designs . . . .even less than in the cases that have already been discussed, can an attempt be made here to comprehend these wars of conquest from the point of view of concrete objectives. Here there was neither a warrior nation in our sense, nor, in the beginning, a military despotism or an aristocracy of specifically military orientation. Thus, there is but one way to an understanding: scrutiny of domestic class interests, the question of who stood to gain.
—JOSEPH SCHUMPETER, 1919

America is today the leader of a worldwide anti-revolutionary movement in the defense of vested interests. She now stands for what Rome stood for. Rome consistently supported the rich against the poor in all foreign communities that fell under her sway; and, since the poor, so far, have always and everywhere been far more numerous than the rich, Rome's policy made for inequality, for injustice, and for the least happiness of the greatest number.
—ARNOLD TOYNBEE, 1961

From William Blum's writing, it is apparent that the U.S. government has acted as a dominant force, not unlike the Romans in the third century. This includes actions in the three-year war on the Korean Peninsula against China and North Korea, the Vietnam War, and the on-going war in Iraq and Afghanistan. While strongly condemning some rogue nations, the U.S. itself has become a rogue nation to some degree. The entire world worries—which one will be America's next military target?

After nearly three decades of economic globalization, the Chinese gradually developed an awareness of its place in the world in the twenty-first century. Under Deng Xiaoping, foreign policy was guided by the idea that China should "hide its brightness." The goal for the Chinese is not conflict, but conflict avoidance. This reflects a deeply-held Chinese belief that armed conflict is a sign of failure. [194] The American approach of imposing sanctions or suppression through military force has created a chaotic world and made many enemies. China does not want to follow the American footsteps.

China does not intend to join in the group of countries that use colonization and war to achieve status as big nations. China threat theory advocates reflect the mindset of inherent ownership. Chinese leaders would like to reestablish the nation in a superior position and transform international power politics into morality politics. This is rooted in ancient Chinese culture and the teachings of Confucius to rule by virtue.

China holds a strong belief in sovereignty and multilateralism, and a determination to find its own route to prosperity compatible with the principle of non-interference in the domestic affairs of other nations. This principle does not mean China rejects political and economic reform in the third world including India, Brazil, and especially Africa. China recognizes that good governance and political reforms are extremely important to the long-term development of African nations. China has always given what it could in financial aid and technical support to African nations with no political preconditions other than affirmation of a one-China policy. China has successfully exported its economic development model with Chinese characteristics to its African trading partners by encouraging them to develop their economy through trade, investment, and infrastructure development without dictating terms for political or economic reforms. [195] Critics have been saying that China is also interested in African oil and strategic minerals, and China is a commercial partner with Darfur. To these criticisms, the African people said clearly that Africans have African interests too; when both interests met, a mutually beneficiary cooperation flourished. As for Dafur, China initially did not want to get into Sudan's internal politics, but decided later to send a special envoy to help the Darfur situation.

Another example of Chinese economic multilateralism is evident in the regionalism of ASEAN countries. Over the past ten years, China has worked extensively with the ASEAN. As a result, their multilateral and bilateral trade relationships have flourished. Size and geographic proximity facilitate these relationships. Their best option is a mutually productive relationship with China.

The ASEAN countries signed nuclear nonproliferation agreements with China and invited it to participate in their regional discussions on the subject. In terms of military power, China is much weaker than the U.S., so the ASEAN is not concerned that it represents a security threat.

iii) A Desire to Accumulate the Tools of Asymmetric Power Projection to Control Their Own National Destiny

The last piece of the Beijing Consensus puzzle is control of China's national destiny. China has departed from the doctrine of modestly hiding one's capacities while biding one's time, or hide its brightness, first promulgated by the late Deng Xiaoping in 1989. What Deng meant, at the time, were that China need not play a major role in the world. It was a policy suitable for the period of the 1990s and should not be viewed mistakenly as a permanent diplomatic strategy. Now China has joined the international system and is making a substantial contribution.

Rather than building a U.S style power base, bristling with arms and intolerance of other world views, China is emerging as a power based on its own model, the strength of its economic position and the rigid defense of its national sovereignty. During the recent East Asian Summit in Kuala Lumpur, sixteen East Asian leaders gathered to try to envision a new integrated Asia. China's political and economic presence and influence was overwhelming. Equally significant was the number of small neighboring countries that did not consider China a threat. Also, according to a

PricewaterhouseCoopers global CEO survey in 2006, almost 80 percent of the 1,410 CEOs view China as the most significant market opportunity in the future. [196]

On other international fronts, China does not wish to instigate conflict or war, nor does it have the intention of entering an arms race. Instead, it intends to project enough asymmetric power to limit U.S. political and military pressure on China through fostering good international relations. [197] China has won many friends through trade and innovation in Africa, Central Asia, Europe, Latin America, and the Middle East. China, Kazakhstan, Kyrgyzstan, Russia, Tajikistan, and Uzbekistan of the SCO member states, and India, Iran, Mongolia, and Pakistan, which are SCO observing members are working together to solve border conflicts and to avoid military conflicts, terrorism, and to counter militant Islam.

No country can affect Chinese fortunes more directly than the U.S. The U.S. is the only country with the capacity and ambition to exercise global primacy and it will remain so for a long time to come. America is a global leader in economics, education, culture, technology, science, and military capability, and China can learn much from America. While the U.S. definitely would not want any nation to challenge its supremacy, China has to find a way to achieve its own prosperity by avoiding any strategic pressure or clash with the U.S.

The 9/11 terrorist attacks changed destiny for America and China. They have completely transformed U.S. global strategic and military plans. The U.S. made a pre-emptive strike against Iraq without U.N. support and with the explicit opposition of a majority of world nations including traditional allies, such as France and Germany. This has made the U.S. a lonely superpower and a target for hatred by the Islamic world. The entire Iraq episode including the bombing, the crushing of Iraqi civilian lives, and the revelations about Iraqi prisoner torture by the U.S. soldiers has damaged the U.S. image throughout the world and substantially eroded its soft power. Nonetheless, the U.S. hard power is rising through increases in military spending, which is roughly half of all military spending worldwide.

Global challenges confronting the U.S. currently include:

• Future terrorist attacks on the U.S. territory

- Iran nuclear development crises

- The on-going Iraq War

- Tensions with Islamic countries in the Middle East and else-where

The U.S. is a superpower with vulnerabilities. Its use of military supremacy and technology as a dominant force in foreign policy has driven other nations to develop asymmetrical forces. This response may be characterized as a "horror balance" through the development of nuclear capabilities. America, Britain, China, France, India, Israel, Pakistan, North Korea and Russia all have nuclear weapons. In addition, Iran is suspected of developing nuclear weapons.

This hinders the U.S. in its exercise of military supremacy wherever it wants and damages illusions of unlimited military power. Economically, the U.S. is one of the major global economic powers. Politically, it must use diplomacy and negotiation to achieve its goals. The Iraq War is a classic example: America is a powerful giant, but the world nations do not like to deal with a giant who acts like a bully throwing its weight around. Therefore, it is unlikely that the U.S. will be able to maintain global hegemony.

The world needs someone who can bring harmony, peace, and balance, not hegemony, to remedy conflicts. The U.S. needs a strong and peace-loving country like China to help resolve issues related to counterterrorism, nuclear nonproliferation, the reconstruction of Iraq, the maintenance of stability in the Middle East and the Korean Peninsula. The Chinese people believe that in the long run, the decline of U.S. supremacy and a subsequent transition to a multi-polar world are inevitable. However, in the short term, Washington's power is unlikely to decline and its position in the world affairs is unlikely to change. [198]

From a Chinese perspective, U.S. geopolitical superiority was strengthened in Central Asia by its victory in the Afghan war, in the Persian Gulf, and on the Arabian Peninsula by the Iraq War. It was also enhanced in East Europe and the Black Sea through the successful U.S. backed color revolutions, or "Flower Revolutions"—names given collectively to a series of related movements that developed in post-communist societies in Central and Eastern Europe, and Central Asia, and are possibly spreading elsewhere including some places in the Middle East. Some observers have called the events a revolutionary wave.

Each time massive street protests followed disputed elections and led to the resignation or overthrow of leaders considered to be authoritarian in the Ukraine and Georgia. In the Northeast and Southeast Asia, American influence increased through the strengthened U.S.-Japan security alliance. These developments provided China with limited opportunities. Beijing wisely recognized the pressure exerted by U.S.-China asymmetry in strength and realizes that it must not challenge the international order and the institutions favored by the Western world. [199] The Chinese wish to accumulate the tools of asymmetric power projection to control their own national destiny as follows: [200, 201]

- China uses its own success and impressive size to exhibit its power projection or soft power to the rest of the world.

- The China-U.S. relationship should not be a relationship of confrontation and rivalry for primacy, but a relationship between equals.

- Since there is a tremendous gap between the two countries in national power and international status, the fundamental differences between their political systems and ideology have prevented the U.S. from viewing China as a peer. China's political, economic, social, and diplomatic influence on the U.S. is less than the U.S. influence on China. It is, therefore, only natural that in their diplomatic and cultural exchanges, the U.S. has assumed an offensive role while China has played a more defensive role.

- The China-U.S. relationship is based fundamentally on mutual interest. The positive and negative factors between the two are closely interwoven and frequent clashes may be avoided.

- China's rise is inevitable. Any U.S. attempt to hinder economic modernization in China would hurt both countries. Although American motives for developing economic ties with China may be self-interest, such ties also help

China by spurring its economic prosperity and technological advancement.

- China and the U.S. each face a similar paradox. Because of increasing interdependence, economic decline in either country would have a negative effect on both economies.

- History shows that the U.S. is not a permanent enemy of China, nor does it want the U.S. to view it as a foe. The leadership in China has established goals to achieve prosperity by the middle of the twenty-first century; with Washington's cooperation, there is little to stand in its way.

China advocates the "Four Noes" policies which include: no hegemony, no power politics, no alliances and no arms race as an alternative to the U.S. Cold War approach of containment. The Chinese idea is to appeal to other nations to adopt these concepts and encourage the U.S. to reexamine its policies.

As discussed, China is creating a roadmap for other nations that are trying to develop their countries economically and define an appropriate international position. Other developing nations aim to be truly independent, protect their way of life and secure political choice and stability in a world with a single, massively powerful center of gravity, namely the U.S. [202] Most foreign experts believe that in twenty years China will become a "near peer" power with the U.S. The Chinese are optimistic about a future of peaceful, cooperative development with the U.S.

In August 2006, Chinese President Hu Jintao met with Ted Stevens, formerly acting president of the U.S. Senate, and pledged to further Sino-U.S. ties. Hu stated that as stakeholders and constructive cooperators, China and the U.S. should enhance exchange and understanding, expand cooperation and common strategic interests, and manage sensitive issues and mutual concerns through bilateral agreements. [203] There was an exchange of views on a wide range of issues, including Sino-U.S. relations, the Taiwan question, parliamentary exchanges, peaceful development, trade, energy, the Beijing 2008 Olympic Games, and other regional and international issues of common concern. A consensus was reached on many issues.

Section II. China Is Not an Economic Threat to the U.S.

America is the richest country in the world and the current U.S. economy is healthy. Its economy grew at a stable rate of 3–5 percent in the first five years of the twenty-first century. For example it grew by 4.4 percent in 2004, 3.5 percent in 2005, and 3.3 percent in 2006. This is much larger than the corresponding figures for the Euro-zone (2.0 percent, 1.6 percent, and 2.7 percent for 2004, 2005, and 2006, respectively). The U.S. unemployment rate also dropped to 4.7 percent in March 2006, the lowest rate in four and half years. The U.S. has the largest GDP in the world. Right after World War II, its GDP was more than 50 percent of the world GDP; now it has stabilized at about 30 percent. The size of the U.S. economy as a proportion of the global economy is likely to increase in the years to come. The following is a tabulation showing GDP in 2005 for the top five nations in millions of U.S. dollars:

GDP (nominal) *(millions of USD)*		GDP (PPP) *(millions of USD)*	
United States	12,485,725	United States	12,277,583
Japan	4,571,314	China (PRC)	9,412,361
Germany	2,797,343	Japan	3,910,728
China (PRC)	2,224,811	India	3,633,441
Great Britain	2,201,473	Germany	2,521,699

GDP = consumption + investment + government spending + (exports – imports).

PPP = purchasing power parity, which takes into account the relative cost of living, and inflation rates between countries, rather than just using exchange rates which have the potential to distort the real differences in income.

The tabulation shows that the U.S. GDP (nominal) was about 5.6 times that of China excluding Hong Kong and Macao, although China's GDP (PPP) was almost 77 percent of the U.S. value. However, the U.S. GDP (nominal) per capita (GDP divided by the average population) was US$41,399, whereas China's was only US$1,703; the GDP (PPP) per capita was US$42,101 for the U.S. and US$7,204 for China. The Chinese average GDP per capita is very low in comparison with the U.S. value.

Assuming a steady annual growth rate of 4 percent for the U.S. and 8 percent for China, it would take China about forty-five years to reach the same GDP (nominal) as the U.S. It would be a miracle if China sustains its current high grow rate for another forty to fifty years without any unexpected economic downturns, given the many problems that have emerged already as serious potential impacts. Such problems are discussed in great detail later in this book.

1. The Three Stages of China's Economic Development

According to a global survey of over 207,910 people by the University of Maryland in 2005, seventy-four percent of Chinese thought that a market economy was the best and most promising economic system in the world, followed by 73 and 71 percent of the Philippinos and the Americans, respectively. [204]

Frequently, globalization is viewed as an exclusively Western phenomenon, an aggressive force that often endangers cultures and ways of life. But Robbie Robertson pointed out that this view is inaccurate. "Globalization is not about rampant capitalism, technology, or homogenization," instead, "It is about the changed environments people create and manipulate as their societies globally interconnect." [205] If his statement is correct, then it is apparent that China has done very well in adapting to the globalization trend in the late twentieth century and has benefited from economic reform that blends Chinese characteristics.

Chinese enthusiasm for a market economy has evolved in three stages: 1) the development of a market economy by implementing an open door policy to welcome foreign investments in the mainland; 2) the connection of Chinese economic development to global economic systems; and 3) an extension of Chinese economic activities and influences to the rest of the world. [206]

In the first stage, China invited foreign governments and businesses to invest in Chinese markets to boost economic growth and development. This was a very successful policy which quickly ended international isolation and created significant momentum for domestic economic development. As a result many entrepreneurs, business owners and a new middle class emerged under an authoritarian political system. At the end of 2004, foreign investment capital in China was six times that of Japan and ten times that of South Korea. [207]

Chinese government officials were told to make economic development a top priority in their governance. This guideline transformed government administrators into Western style Chief Executive Officers, making them aggressive in the pursuit of commercial contracts in their jurisdictions. Corruption, however, is very common at all government levels and has been considered by some as a temporary, short-term stimulus and economic benefit.

Nonetheless, there is a serious potential negative long-term impact inherent in social unrest which may be attributed to the diversion of funds from proper usage. This sort of corruption may be viewed as a temporary necessary evil which must be closely monitored and abated. Nevertheless, Chinese economic development was much more successful than that of East European countries, Russia, and other developing countries. The open door policy was welcomed by Western capitalists, since it provided much needed new markets, low-cost labor, and material resources. Hence, capitalistic economies like America, Europe, and Japan all had a positive attitude regarding economic reform in China at this stage.

In the second stage, China began its globalization by connecting its domestic economic system with the world. Capitalists monitored developments in China, recognizing that issues related to market size could have a major impact on the world economy. During this phase of economic reform, China not only joined the WTO, but also became a member of almost all the important regional and international economic organizations. The "connection" conforms to the U.S. global strategic plan to absorb China into the existing world system designed by the U.S. after World War II so that it can be contained. This connection is also a most rational strategy.

After years of economic development, China has accumulated its own capital markets and produced many entrepreneurs. It is ready to enter the world market for investment purposes. This adds new momentum to the development of the global capitalistic system with many positive effects. The world knows that foreign exchange reserves in China now rank first, oil consumption second, trade third, and the GDP fourth in the world. This is the so-called 1,2,3,4 of China.

This all seems normal and plausible, but as Chinese economic development enters the third stage designed to extend activities and influence globally, a level of discontent and confrontation is apparent from existing economic powers, in particular, the U.S. The China threat theory is rampant once again in the American media and among politicians, scholars, and later with the general American public. It is difficult for the Chinese people to understand these attitudes in light of the contributions made to the global economy, in particular, hundreds of millions of Chinese people still live at the poverty line on a meager income of US$1-2 a day.

China understands this is a common phenomenon throughout history. Any rise in economic power by a nation is often perceived as threatening by other powerful nations. For the Americans, it would be better to think of China's reemergence as strong nation as positive and well-deserved, especially after the Chinese people suffered so many years of turmoil and strife. China is no longer merely a regional power or a dilapidated colonial state. Healthy competition between China and the U.S. is inevitable and should be viewed as a stimulus to progress. More importantly, competition is both constructive and common among world powers.

The next section provides an overview of the economic impact of China on the U.S. Included is an examination of areas where the two nations have differences that must be resolved through dialogue and negotiation combined with understanding and patience.

2. The Background of the Sino-U.S. Trade Disputes

The economic strength of China is important to the world for a basic reason: profit potential. Over the past twenty-eight years, China's GDP growth averaged 9.4 percent annually. In 2006, China's GDP grew 10.7 percent. Export trade amounted to two-thirds of GDP growth rate. Two-thirds of its foreign trade is with the U.S. Chinese products are cheaper and of reasonably good quality for the price. "China cost" is defined as work performed at one-third of the price of production for foreign in house manufacturing. The "China cost" advantage is due to low labor costs as well as the lower overhead costs including office and factory rents, taxes, and material costs. This is why the "Made in China" labels are ubiquitous in world markets today.

A Goldman Sachs study concludes that by 2045, China will be the largest economy in the world, replacing the U.S. Another report predicts a much earlier date of 2020. No matter how rosy these theoretical predictions may be, China still faces many challenges and uncertainties ahead. First of all, within China, experts forecast that an annual growth rate of 7 percent over forty years must be sustained in order to meet the target of building a moderately prosperous society across the country. Also, China needs to rapidly ramp up the rate of innovation to quadruple the current per capita GDP by 2020. [208]

The blueprint for China's economic and social development over the next five years contains the important goal of reducing energy consumption per unit of GDP by 20 percent by the end of 2010, based on 2005 figures. [209] Western regions of the mainland consumed up to five times more energy to produce each unit of gross domestic product than their counterparts in southeastern coastal regions, according to a Chinese government report. The national average in 2005 was 1.22 tons of coal equivalent per 10,000 yuan (about US$1,250) of GDP, and 2.59 tons of coal equivalent in producing each 10,000 yuan of value-added industrial output in 2005.

This is a very ambitious plan that will require effective new strategies to change the national economic growth pattern by upgrading technology, restructuring and implementing industrial policies to promote reductions in energy consumption. A quick fix to excessive energy consumption would be to impose taxes and hike energy prices. Chinese businesses are spreading across the world and are changing their operations with an amazing speed. This is an unstoppable historic trend.

China's trade surplus with the U.S. was US$201.6 billion in 2005, which was about 28 percent of the U.S. total trade deficit of US$726 billion. China's GDP was US$2,224.81 billion, an increase of 10.2 percent over the year 2004, government revenue exceeded US$3,750 billion, an increase of US$65.4 billion over the year 2004, and the consumer price index rose by a meager 1.8 percent. The Chinese economy was robust and characterized by rapid growth, improved economic returns, and stable prices. [210] China's GDP grew by 10.7 percent in 2006 and its trade surplus increased to US$232.5 billion. [211] However, these trade surplus estimates are U.S. calculations.

The Chinese trade surplus calculations give US$102 billion and US$177.5 billion for 2005 and 2006, respectively. [212] The issue is the totally different estimates of the bilateral trade imbalance by the two countries. The main difference is how to treat Chinese exports to the U.S. and U.S. exports to China via Hong Kong. There is a clear discussion of this subject in "U.S.-China Trade Issues after the WTO and the PNTR Deal: A Chinese Perspective" in 2000 by Jialin Zhang. The U.S. data will be used throughout this book for consistency in explaining the underlying trade issues.

In 2006, China replaced the U.S. to become the largest manufactured goods exporter. U.S. exports to China also grew by 31.7 percent over 2005 to $55.2 billion in 2006. In 2005, the U.S. exports to China totaled US$41 billion, an increase of 25 percent from 2004. These data showed that China-U.S. bilateral trade was growing rapidly and the China-U.S. economies are deeply intertwined. Yet, China's large trade surplus has become a target that triggered a list of disputes over currency rates, intellectual property rights and auto-parts trade. [213] China urged the U.S. not to politicize the trade issues and to avoid further complications.

On February 14, 2006, the U.S. government unilaterally set up a trade representative office to supervise China's condition of complying with international trade regulations. In March, the chief legal consultant of this office, James Mondale, pressured China on issues of intellectual property rights, the auto-parts trade, and China's new responsibilities in the WTO. At the same time, seventeen Chinese wood floor enterprises were subject to 337 difficult investigations by the U.S. International Trade Committee. This is evidence that the U.S. trade dispute against

China is growing more intense, and that the U.S. has made assessments of violations of trade regulations which disfavor China. [214]

The Chinese government thinks that the two sides should develop bilateral trade with a strategic vision and move in the correct direction through negotiations—not threats, to promote development of bilateral relations. Major trade disputes are summarized below:

1) The Textile, Anti-Dumping, Auto-Parts, Higher-Tariff Issues, and WTO Cases

China has the second largest economy in Asia; its US$1.42 trillion in imports and exports in 2005 was the third largest in the world after the U.S. and Germany. This rapid trade expansion drove China's economy but, at the same time, intensified friction with global trade partners. For example, if China's textile exports continue to grow at an annual rate of 21 percent whereas Bangladesh, Pakistan, and Cambodia climb an average of 5 percent, China would take over more than 80 percent of the textile export market of developing nations by 2020. [215] China will conform, as needed, to improve commercial ties to other nations. It will complement trade policies by increasing foreign aid, waiving debt, and expanding imports. Additionally, China will manage trade disputes with developing countries effectively.

Official data revealed that between 55–60 percent of all Chinese exports were carried out by firms supported by foreign investments or low-end processing companies. For example, although China is a major DVD exporter, only nine of the fifty-seven core DVD production technologies were developed by Chinese manufacturers. It is obvious that Chinese workers remain low on the world trade ladder. [216] The fact that Chinese exports tend to be concentrated in certain low-tech industries has caused increased trade friction in the areas including textiles, shoe manufacturing, and auto parts. Each of these issues will be discussed in turn:

The Textile Issue: Dissatisfied with a dramatic increase of over 50 percent in Chinese textile exports, the U.S. instituted a temporary quota system in 2005 against textile exports by applying the WTO's Clause 242. The PRC currently has twenty million textile workers, most of whom have low income. For China, the textile industry is highly sensitive and critically important to social stability. The U.S. and China began seven rounds of textile trade negotiations during the summer and fall of 2005 to set limits on various kinds of textile imports. In this uncertain climate, Chinese textile companies faced the prospect of damaging order cancellations and many workers lost their jobs.

By November 3, 2005, in the eighth round of negotiations, the U.S. acknowledged "tangible progress" by both sides in many areas. [217] Finally, after more tough negotiations on November 8, both Chinese Minister of Commerce, Bo Xilai and U.S. trade representative, Robert Portman, signed a textile trade memorandum aimed at developing a stable trade environment over the next two to three years. Portman said that this was a fair agreement, but Bo Xilai's attitude was more reserved. While affirming a positive outcome, he added the agreement did not meet all expectations. The agreement would become effective on January 1, 2006, and terminate on December 31, 2008.

The agreement provided for a quota on twenty-one types of Chinese textile imports to the U.S. (the U.S. State Department listed as many as thirty-four types). Imports will increase by a percentage amount over the previous year, namely, 10 to 15 percent for the first year, 12.5 to 16 percent for the second year, and 15 to 17 percent for the last year, 2008. Although the Chinese textile companies were not entirely satisfied, they were willing to accept the outcome of the negotiations. [218]

With the recent, rapid Chinese currency revaluations, the textile industry indicated that it will lose money if the yuan continues to appreciate. "With average profit margins of 3 percent, textile companies will no longer be able to absorb the cost of the rising yuan," according to the National Development and Reform Commission. A one cent appreciation in the yuan would lead to a loss of two cents in profit margin. [219] Domestic textile exporters can earn an average of 30 U.S. cent per shirt. The appreciation of the yuan has underscored the need for textile manufacturers to sustain their competitiveness through technical innovation and intellectual property rights protection rather than through price cuts. The growth rate of textile exports by China has slowed but it still ranks as the largest worldwide. From January to July 2006, textile exports reached US$27.05 billion, up 18.7 percent from the year 2005. [220]

Anti-dumping Duties on Leather Shoes: The European Commission announced in late March 2006 that it would place anti-dumping duties on leather shoes from China and Vietnam, despite the fact that only three countries voted in favor of the tariffs. Ten voted against and eleven abstained. [221] Chinese shoe exports comprise two-thirds of the world total and include a full range of footwear products including sneakers, leather, and artificial leather shoes. However, imported shoes from China and Vietnam are only 9 percent of the total shoes purchased by Europeans. More than 150 shoe manufacturers in China formed an alliance and selected fifteen member companies to form an executive committee to carry out further steps against the anti-dumping move. The alliance argued that the proposed anti-dumping sanction lacks fairness and legitimacy, and will drag shoemakers down from their advantageous position and make it hard to compete and to survive. [222]

Recently, the alliance made a joint declaration to oppose E.U. sanctions using a "no injury defense." They reported that according to WTO protocol, any anti-dumping prosecution should have fifteen injury indicators; however, the E.U. sanctions are only based on six indicators. They added that the duties will encroach upon interests of importers, retailers, equipment suppliers, and consumers in the E.U. [223] The E.U. trade representative, Peter Mandelson, said that the Chinese and the Vietnamese governments were involved in unfair competition by providing low-interest loans, tax incentives, and low-cost land to subsidize their shoemakers. Both governments denied such accusations and blamed the E.U. trade protection policies. [224]

Despite the anti-dumping duties, the European dealers and retailers remain interested in lower cost Chinese shoes. More importantly, "Chinese industries can do better in terms of design, workmanship, and technological innovation," according to Massimo Donda, President of Federcalzature, a 120–year-old Italian footwear retailers' association which represents 11,000 Italian retailers. These remarks were made at the 99th Chinese Export Commodity Fair in April 2006. [225]

Duties on Chinese shoes were 4.8 percent beginning on April 7, 2006, and would rise to 19.4 by the end of the year. Donda said that it is groundless for some E.U. shoemakers to blame increased imports from China for the business decline in certain European industries. His comments are supported by several facts: 1) The total output by European shoemakers fell by 46 percent between 1995 and 2003, while footwear imports climbed by

73 percent; 2) Imports make up 82 percent of all the shoes on sale at the E.U. market, while only 18 percent are made locally in Europe; 3) It is difficult for domestic industries to meet local demands without importing from other countries; most high-end Italian shoes are for export; 4) Italian-made shoes make up only 3.11 percent of the world total but its export accounts for nearly 4 percent, which means the Italian industry still has room for development despite the fierce competition from China, Vietnam, and India; and 5) Imports have lowered retail prices on the E.U. market. [226] The European retailers are hoping that the temporary restrictive measures will not remain in place over the long-term.

In the meantime, the large Chinese shoe manufacturers will suffer severe losses or pass on increased overhead to the E.U. consumers. Numerous small and medium-sized firms will probably not be able to bear the sharp ups and downs of the international market, and thousands of Chinese workers will lose their jobs. This would be similar to the loss of jobs among other nations in the E.U. and North America. The shoe industries in the U.S. and Britain have been devastated. Many suffered there as well. But this is the essence of capitalism and globalization, namely, price matters, and businesses always look for the best price to make the most profit.

Tariffs on Imported Car Parts: The U.S., Canada, and Europe threatened to seek a WTO inquiry into tariffs levied by China on Chinese imported car parts just days before high-level Sino-U.S. trade talks were to take place in Washington on April 11, 2006, followed by a visit to the U.S. by Chinese President Hu Jintao on April 20, 2006. [227] The joint complaint gave China ten days to respond, and sixty days to resolve the issue through negotiations. China was the subject of a previous formal WTO complaint, in which the U.S. sought a review of a tax rebate on semiconductors. In that case, China backed down before both parties began a formal dispute resolution.

The market for the car part exports to China was about US$600 million in 2006. Car makers have flocked to China to set up joint ventures to make vehicles. Among these were the Ford Motor Co., General Motors Corp., Peugeot Citroën, Volkswagen, and Fiat. [228] A tariff was introduced in 2005, which required car manufacturers to provide detailed information on the parts used for the vehicles they assemble. If the value or number of imported parts exceeds 60 percent of the complete vehicle then the imported parts are taxed at the same rate as a finished car—28 percent rather than the 10 to 14 percent charged on parts. "China claims this is meant to stop the smuggling of complete cars by importing what they call complete knock-down kits, but if you set the standard too low, you are discouraging assemblers from using imported parts," according to Edmund Sim, Partner of the law firm, White & Case.

The U.S. and E.U. thought some Chinese rules on car import tariffs are not in line with WTO rules, putting European and U.S. car manufacturers at a disadvantage compared to local producers. The U.S., Canada, and E.U. officials thought that the rules appear designed to help Chinese car parts makers. China's Ministry of Commerce has expressed regret about the plans to file a WTO complaint against China over auto parts. [229]

Under the WTO rules, if a resolution is not developed in sixty days, then the E.U., the U.S., and China may ask a WTO panel to rule on the dispute. The WTO dispute resolution process usually takes about two years.

Potentially Steep U.S. Tariffs: The Bush administration proposed to reverse the twenty-three-year old bipartisan policy of not applying the countervailing duty (CVD) law to China to impose potentially steep tariffs on Chinese manufactured goods on the grounds that China was illegally subsidizing some of its exports. [230] The U.S. government regards China as a "non-market economy." The new duty was proposed by the U.S. NewPage Corporation. The immediate effect would be felt by two Chinese makers of high-gloss paper, one at 10.9 percent and the other 20.4 percent. The duties would be effective immediately. This would lead to higher costs for American consumers. The formal decision will be due in October 2007. China thinks that the U.S. unilateral trade action has violated the mutual consensus of the two nations in resolving their trade disputes via dialogues. China urges the U.S. to quickly change its decision since China will not accept these new duties. [231] This was the second action the U.S. would take to the WTO.

More WTO Cases Filed: On February 2, 2007, the U.S. filed a WTO case against China's subsidies saying incentives hurt U.S. exporters. Two more requests were filed on April 9, 2007, with the

WTO by the U.S. The first accused China of setting "excessively high thresholds for launching criminal prosecutions" against distributors of pirated products. The second challenged China's insistence that some of the pirates' chief targets—books, DVDs, CDs, and video games—be distributed solely by state-owned importers, a policy that may delay distribution and potentially create an opening for pirates to prosper. [232]

Chinese Vice Premier Wu Yi led a senior Chinese delegation in May 2007 to meet with U.S. Treasury Secretary Henry Paulson in Washington. At that time, Beijing announced a series of new measures to boost U.S. exports to China. The Chinese were urging American critics to take a more global view of economic relations and see trade problems within the context of the region and globalization. [233] Wu Yi said that China will actively respond according to the relevant WTO rules to the cases filed by the U.S. against China.

2) The Exchange Rate Issue

There are at least fifteen bills on the U.S. legislative books seeking to impose sanctions on China for allegedly keeping the Chinese currency "yuan" artificially low. The U.S. attributed the huge China trade surplus in 2005 to the under-valued Chinese yuan, estimated (by the U.S.) as much as 40 percent, which has made Chinese goods artificially cheaper to American consumers.

Chinese officials have hinted that if pushed too far, they might shift their billion-dollar reserve out of the U.S. Treasury Bonds, which could trigger a U.S. and global recession. Both sides have too much to lose. Former U.S. Treasury Secretary Lawrence Summers once called this "the balance of financial horror." [234] In fact, Chinese exchange rate policies are not responsible for the current global trading imbalances. Global imbalance is a result of globalization and macroeconomic policies implemented by each country and, most importantly, the wage differences and spending habits (a demand issue). A revaluation of the yuan will not reduce the U.S. trade surplus by an appreciable amount. This was already evidenced by the continuous increase of China's trade surplus after the yuan exchange rate against the U.S. dollar was raised in July 2005 and then continued to appreciate.

A review of the exchange rate issue follows:

i) The China Exchange Rate System and Yuan Appreciation Pressure: China had a fixed yuan exchange rate regime before July 2005. Its central bank pegged the yuan exchange rate to the U.S. dollar at around US$1 to 8.28 yuan since 1996. This implicitly guaranteed that any investor could exchange their RMB assets for dollars at the prevailing exchange rate. If investors suspected that the government would not or could not maintain the rate, they could abandon the RMB for other more stable currencies. This capital flight would delete the dollar reserves and force the devaluation of the RMB. This is the risk associated with setting exchange rates. But since China's foreign exchange reserve is over US$1.3 trillion, the risk is small.

China's foreign exchange assets are composed of its trade surplus in the current account and FDI in the capital account. The capital account is still under strict control, whereas the currency became convertible for current account transactions at the end of 1996.

The Chinese private sector and official foreign exchange assets have been growing in recent years at a rate much faster than the GDP growth rate, whereas the outflow of capital is negligible. The foreign exchange earned by export firms and the continued influx of FDI, plus the speculative money that rushes into China in anticipation of the yuan's appreciation cause the supply of foreign exchange to significantly exceed demand. This results in mounting pressure for yuan appreciation.

Jialin Zhang, a visiting scholar at the Hoover Institution has offered perhaps the best explanation of the Chinese exchange rate system summarized below: [235]

In China, any foreign exchange income earned from either exports or FDI should be sold to the central bank. The nation has in this way accumulated an incredibly large amount of foreign exchange reserves, currently over US$1.3 trillion. The central bank or People's Bank of China (PBC) must intervene in the foreign exchange market to buy excess dollars, expanding the monetary base by printing more currency and making foreign exchange the main channel of base money projection. Because of the multiplier effect of base money, the broad money supply, M2, builds up rapidly, which caused Chinese financial institutions to engage in excess lending. The rapid surge of money supply has distorted the real domestic economy. The real estate market and stock market are overheated, while the overall price level remains relatively stable.

To overcome the economic imbalance, the PBC sold billions of yuan in bonds to curb the huge upsurge of money supply and to mop up excess liquidity. This sterilization cannot continue indefinitely, since paying the bond interest alone is a drag on government finance. In short, the central bank has limited scope to sterilize foreign exchange inflows.

The PBC has also raised the bank's reserve requirements. It is estimated that the reserve requirement will remove a few hundred billion yuan base money and several times more M2 from the banking system, and thus prevent another build up of bad loans. By raising the reserve requirement, the central bank has sent a signal that it could absorb excess foreign currency without adjusting the value of the yuan.

The current yuan's exchange rate can be described as follows: 1) Foreign exchange-earning enterprises, while allowed to retain a part of their earnings, must sell all remaining foreign exchange to, or buy needed foreign exchange from, licensed banks to conduct their foreign exchange business; 2) The central bank controls the turnover of the foreign exchange of these banks according to an imposed limit. When foreign exchange exceeds or falls short of the limit, the central bank must buy from or sell to the foreign exchange market. Thus, supply and demand have been designed for the foreign exchange market, and the central bank quotes the midpoint rate of the yuan against the dollar, the Japanese yen, and the Hong Kong dollar on the previous day's rate in the foreign exchange market.

This mechanism implies that the Chinese foreign exchange market is not a market in the real sense, since supply and demand in that market are determined and controlled by the government rather than by the market mechanism. Transactions are made through bidding. Given the obligatory selling of foreign exchange to the state and the restrictions on buying foreign exchange from the state, the supply of foreign exchange has always exceeded its demand in the market, leading to pressure for yuan appreciation. China's current exchange rate is based on an inter-bank market, not on the market of national supply and demand.

Chinese state-owned enterprises and state-owned financial institutions are not responsible for their own losses and bankruptcies, nor do they have any incentives or other controls needed to make the best investments. Therefore, before the foreign exchange market is liberalized and the exchange rate floated, the foreign exchange regime should be reformed, and the state-owned enterprises should be restructured as independent entities responsible for their own profits and losses. Only then can the obligatory buying and selling of foreign exchange be abolished and the exchange rate truly determined by the market. Since the yuan faces both external and internal pressure for revaluation, it would be sensible to change the exchange systems itself rather than the yuan value.

The Chinese financial system is fragile and a sudden currency revaluation could lead to a banking crisis that could spell disaster for the world economy. In recent years, China's banking system has undergone reform. The Bank of China and the China Construction Bank have been recapitalized and went public in the Hong Kong stock market.

In conclusion, China's financial sector should be opened, recapitalized, and reformed. Bad loans must be fully provisioned and state-owned companies' runaway indebtedness curbed. With accelerated economic growth and expansion, yuan stability will be more difficult to maintain. International experience shows that most countries that have adopted a fixed exchange rate at a certain time have transitioned to a more flexible exchange rate. The yuan will eventually adopt a free-floating exchange rate, although this may take several years. Developed countries must first help China to: 1) fix its state-owned enterprises, especially in the banking sector; 2) establish a real foreign exchange market; and 3) create a true market economy. Financial reform in China is moving in these directions. In a few years, concrete results may be expected.

The PBC has broadened the yuan daily fluctuation band to increase the cost of yuan manipulative activities. On September 15, 2006, the daily yuan fluctuation was as high as 2.01 percent. So, while the yuan revaluation trend is mounting, the broadened daily fluctuation range will discourage currency speculators, effectively reducing the "hot" money inflow. The PBC is also considering relaxing the restrictions, which allow enterprises to wire or carry U.S. dollars out of China as a way of reducing foreign reserves that have surged and increased pressure for yuan revaluation.

ii) Different Savings Rates: The American personal savings rate has been very low (typically one or nearly zero percent of the total GDP). The Chinese save 40-47 percent of their after tax personal income. The Chinese government spent nearly 50 percent of its revenue on infrastructure development, one-fourth on real estate investment and 15 percent on manufacturing and industry, leaving very little for social security protection of the people. Different spending habits are the major cause of the trade imbalance. The American consumers should learn to adjust their spending habits and raise their savings rate and the Chinese people should be encouraged to increase domestic personal consumption. [236]

iii) "Assembled in China:" China is the end-product assembly plant for parts produced in Asian countries like Hong Kong, Japan, Malaysia, Singapore, South Korea, Taiwan, the E.U. and America. In August 2006, China's trade surplus increased by 28 percent relative to July to reach US$18.8 billion, a historic monthly high. This increase followed an accumulated yuan rise of approximately 4 percent after July 2005. The U.S. trade deficit in July 2006 was also at a historic monthly high of US$68 billion. [237] The underlying reasons for this continued Chinese trade surplus can be explained as follows: Exports by multinationals accounted for 58.5 percent of the mainland's total trade volume and the processing trade was 50 percent of the mainland's total foreign trade. While China posted a US$201.6 billion trade surplus in 2005, its processing trade recorded a surplus of US$142.5 billion for the period. [238] This indicates that Chinese enterprises have more capability to adjust to currency fluctuations than previously thought by the government, and the plummeting price of imported raw materials and intermediate products caused by the yuan's appreciation in the processing trade could offset the decrease in export profits due to yuan's appreciation.

Balancing the China-U.S. trade surplus and deficit would be very difficult because 90 percent of the products the U.S. imports from China today are no longer made by Chinese domestic companies. The actual trade surplus for China was much smaller than it appeared. In 1994, total exports from East Asia accounted for 41 percent of U.S. imports. Today, that ratio is only 34 percent. The difference is accounted for by increased East Asia exports to China followed by Chinese growing exports to the

U.S. Most of the previously mentioned East Asian trade partners have a trade surplus with China.

In 2005, the U.S. international trade imbalance reached US$726 billion or about 5.8 percent of the U.S. GDP. Of this, about 28 percent was attributed to China's contribution. But a closer examination shows that a big portion of this trade surplus must be used to pay for China's trade deficit with the East Asian trade partners as just said, and another big portion is taken away by the foreign enterprises abroad or inside China. China's real gain from its trade surplus with the U.S. is much smaller. This has prompted a saying: China gets the trade surplus, foreign enterprises get the profit. In a globalized world economy, it does not make sense to talk about bilateral trade surplus or gain. In fact, it is closer to reality to re-label Made in China as Assembled in China.

A simple example is that for a Barbie doll selling for US$20 in the U.S., Chinese manufacturers receive only thirty-five cents. In 2006, the *New York Times* published an article entitled, "Some Assembly Needed: China as Asia's Factory," by David Bardoza, who cited research by a Massachusetts Institute of Technology professor as follows: Although the U.S., European, and Japanese multinational companies moved their factories to the PRC beginning in the 1990s, they still tightly controlled profits. Quick appreciation of yuan values has a serious impact on the viability and the ultimate survival of Chinese enterprises. For example, many Chinese exports including shoes, textiles, ships, and automobiles have a net profit margin of less than 5 percent. A sharp rise of the RMB will wipe out the small profits and affect the livelihood of tens of millions of workers.

The *Wall Street Journal* reporter Andrew Higgins wrote in his article, "As China Surges, It Also Proves a Buttress to America Strength," the following: The retail price of Wanda Wireless Mouse, a bestseller by Logitech, is US$40, out of which Logitech takes US$8, the retail merchants or wholesale merchants take US$15, Motorola and other parts manufacturers take another US$14 and the mainland Chinese factories in Suzhou get just US$3. The three dollar amount covers all expenses such as rent, utility bills, and wages. The 450 employees' total salary in the North America sales office is more than the 4,000 Chinese workers' total wages. This also includes the compensation of high-level factory managers. These two examples illustrate what a pitiful wage the Chinese workers receive. [239] The huge Chinese trade surplus only converts to tiny tangible benefits for Chinese workers.

iv) A Misleading Job Loss Blame: The China threat theorists blame China for the loss of 3 million U.S. jobs since 2000. This is misleading. U.S. job loss can be accounted for by the following factors: 1) The global decline of overseas market demand reduced U.S. manufacturing production and job generation; and 2) U.S. productivity has increased, reducing job creation. The U.S. production output since 1994 has increased by 50 percent. This trend also exists in many other countries including China. The reduction of manufacturing jobs from 1995–2002 was 11 percent in the U.S., but that number was even higher in China and reached 15 percent. According to estimates by the U.S. Labor Department, the annual job loss in the U.S. caused by expanded trade with China was only 1 percent of the total job loss of fifteen million. [240]

v) Trade Tariffs Negative to Both: U.S. Senators Charles Schumer and Lindsay Graham proposed to collect a 27.5 percent tariff on Chinese goods sold to the U.S. market, if China refuses to allow the yuan to appreciate. However, their proposal would hurt the American poor and middle class, since a higher yuan would increase the cost of the imported Chinese goods and contribute to U.S. inflation pressure. The U.S. Federal Reserve Bank has increased its lending rate 17 times to 5.25 percent in less than two years trying to curb inflation pressures. [241] When interest rates are too high, the U.S. may experience a recession. In addition, politically pressuring China to raise the yuan and the imposition of unreasonable tariffs may also trigger trade retaliation by China.

The mutual trade benefits between China and the U.S. are obvious; trade protectionism or isolationism does not provide any advantage. The unbalanced global trade issue can be resolved through various measures, but in consideration of China's current trade ratio as part of the total U.S. trade deficit, even if the yuan appreciates by 10 percent, it would only affect the U.S. trade deficit by about one percent. The trade issue could be politicized and this did happen in 1985 when the Japanese yen was forced to appreciate substantially under U.S. pressure, but this kind of political solution is no longer suitable in today's globalized world. It would be better for China to make its own decisions based on its needs and pace the adjustment of its currency to the market, rather than force an appreciation in response to threats by a trade partner. Once a trade war erupts, the global economic system will suffer serious damage, and yet the basic problems remain unresolved.

vi) The "Hot" Money: Beijing is afraid that yuan's appreciation will attract a more speculative "hot" money flow into China. In addition, the RMB revaluation will hurt the PRC manufacturing industry, since its profit margin is very thin.

Nobel Economic Prize winners Professor Joseph Stiglitz and Robert Mundell as well as Stanford University economist Ronald McKinnon believe that China should not ease control of the yuan. Because a rapid yuan revaluation would cause a large influx of "hot money" into China, increase the unemployment rate as a result of reduced exports, and send China into the kind of deflationary slump that hit Japan in the 1990s. This would slow the Asian economy and cause a financial crisis. [242] Stiglitz remarked further that American consumers would probably buy their imported goods from some other countries if the yuan rises sharply. This would hurt American consumers and possibly instigate inflation in the U.S. "The problem of our trade deficit is not going to be solved by China's exchange rate. Cutting the Federal budget deficit would be more effective." [243] In August 2006, the U.N. Conference on Trade and Development concluded that yuan revaluation should be gradual rather than abrupt in order to maintain economic stability. [244]

vii) The Weak Dollar Issue: There are fundamental objections to a significant revaluation of the yuan argued by PBC academic member, Fan Gang. He stated that "The U.S. dollar, rather than the yuan, is a major source of instability." A yuan revaluation would not help solve the bilateral China-U.S. trade deficit of over US$200 billion. [245]

Fan Gang blames inflation on the weakened U.S. dollar and on loose monetary policies of the U.S. government. Only if China continuously prints more money, can the trade imbalance be reduced. But the inflationary cost of printing money is high and would cause serious inflation in China. He also said that the U.S. congressmen blaming China for the currency imbalance "understandably aren't familiar with either the complicated currency issues or domestic policies in any other country." [246] He argued that neither the high rate of savings in China nor the overspending in the U.S. were behind the global imbalance; "while there might be a case for American overspending, there is not necessarily a comparable situation in China in the sense of the international balance of payments," he said, noting that China spent much of its savings on capital investment, which was constructive.

He theorizes that China might well have contributed to global imbalance through slow wage growth when compared with productivity growth. He stated that since the 1990s, labor productivity in China had increased more rapidly than wages. Furthermore, "The yuan, in this context, could be undervalued at about 1 percent a year." He commented that Beijing had to step up to its responsibility to address global currency imbalances, but also had to consider the plight of the mainland's rural poor. [247]

viii) The Weak Banking Sector: The weak Chinese banking system is unable to sustain RMB turbulence for various reasons including: 1) The Chinese banking system needs modernization and improved systems and infrastructure; 2) Banks are unable to absorb bad debts in the event of bankruptcy in U.S. government assets over the next three years; 3) They face savings and lending rate adjustments and lending risks; and 4) China lacks a sophisticated financial services industry to assist Chinese enterprises in investment. [248]

In the financial sector, Chinese capital markets are immature with banks assuming risk and playing a large role in underwriting debt. In 2003, banks disseminated 85 percent of their capital in the form of loans. Banking institutions in China are vulnerable to the financial turbulence that would result from currency fluctuations.

The level of risk is exacerbated by banking methods. Typically, Chinese banks retain a small amount of customer deposits, lending most of their money in order to make a profit. Should a financial crisis precipitate a run on deposits, few would survive the huge wave of withdrawals. China is well aware of the financial crisis experienced by the asset price bubble in Japan in the 1980s based on excessively optimistic expectations with respect to the future. [249]

Chinese banks are even more vulnerable to financial turbulence since numerous bad loans were generated through government interference. Political interference in bank lending operations is widespread and many loans are based on unsound business practices. The nonperforming loan ratio for all banks was 8.6 percent at the end of 2005 and 8 percent by the end of March 2006. [250] Chinese banks have been under pressure to cut lending and curb the growth of potential bad loans. This includes avoiding lending to certain highly speculative, risky ventures. Chinese commercial banks reduced their ratio of bad loans to total lending—a key measure of banks' financial health—to 7.5 percent in June 2006.

Chinese economist Xu Zhenqing stated that when the level of Chinese savings drops by 2012–2015 as consumer domestic spending increases over the next decade, a weakness in the Chinese banking system will then be exposed. [251]

Historically, financial crises have occurred in many countries worldwide. Specific dates by country follow:

a. 1929: The Crash of 1929 in the U.S. was one of the most devastating stock-market crashes in history. The crash marked the beginning of widespread and long-lasting consequences for the U.S. and the world, and some regard it as the start of the Great Depression and the cause of Hitler's taking power.

b. 1982–1983: In August 1982, Mexico announced that it could not meet its regularly scheduled payments to international creditors. Shortly thereafter, Brazil and Argentina were in the same situation. By spring 1983, about twenty-five developing countries could not make regularly scheduled debt payments.

c. 1980s: The Japanese yen appreciated excessively under U.S. political pressure and Japan experienced an assets bubble and a period of zero growth that lasted until the beginning of the twenty-first century. Many banks collapsed, exports plummeted, and the manufacturing industry suffered greatly.

d. 1992: In the fall of 1992, a wave of speculative attacks hit the European Monetary System. Before the end of the year, five countries—Finland, Italy, Norway, Sweden, and the United Kingdom floated their currencies.

e. 1994: On December 20, 1994, the Mexican government announced its decision to devalue the peso against the U.S. dollar by 14 percent. It touched off panic selling of pesos, thereby compelling the Mexican government to float the peso. Other Latin American currencies—Argentina (peso), Brazil (real), Peru (new sol), and Venezuela (bolivar)—collapsed immediately.

f. 1997: A currency crisis erupted in Thailand. It spread from there to Indonesia, South Korea, and to Russia, then to Latin America. This Asian crisis had pushed one-third of the globe into recession during 1998. [252]

g. 1998: The global recession of 1998, which started with the Asian financial crisis in July 1997, exacerbated the Russian economic crisis. World commodity prices declined sharply. Because 80 percent of Russian exports were oil, this had severe economic consequences for Russia. The pressures on the ruble, reflecting the weakness of the economy, resulted in a disastrous fall in the value of the currency. [253]

h. 2001: In the first week of December 2001, the IMF decided to withhold a loan of US$1.3 billion approved for servicing Argentina's US$142 billion external debt. The Argentinean government embarked on a tougher round of cuts, which included freezing public bank accounts and limiting withdrawals to US$250 a week. It was at this point that the people of Buenos Aires rose up against the government. [254]

Yuan appreciation has occurred through minor adjustments and fine-tuning in small incremental steps to help stabilize expectations about the RMB. Chen Dongqi, Vice President of the National Development and Reform Commission Research Institute, reported that an increase of 3 to 4 percent per year is appropriate. A slow appreciation would undermine the flow of speculative money in and out of China. In addition, a slow appreciation would provide enough time for Chinese businesses, banks, and the public to make proper adjustments and avoid a financial crisis which could result in a collapse of the Chinese economy.

ix) The Japan Lesson: China wants to avoid the horrible experience of the Japanese following the drastic rise of the yen in the 1980s. In a situation similar to that of China today, the GDP of Japan in 1980 reached close to 50 percent of that of America. At that stage, the U.S. organized five other nations to pressure Japan to sign a G7 agreement, known as the Plaza Accord. This forced dramatic appreciation of the Japanese yen.

The yen exchange rate against the U.S. dollar was 240 yen to one U.S. dollar before the agreement was reached in September 1985. The yen then appreciated to 160 yen against one U.S. dollar in May 1986. By early 1988, the yen appreciated to 120 yen to one U.S. dollar. Between February 1993 and April 1995, the Clinton administration policies pressured the yen further in order to correct Japan's automobile trade surplus. This caused a rise in the yen from 100 yen against one U.S. dollar to 79 yen against one U.S. dollar by April 1995. After 1995, Japan's GDP trend fell behind the U.S., dropping to about 32 percent of the U.S. value in 2005. [255]

What happened in the short ten years between 1985 and 1995? The yen exchange rate against the U.S. dollar rose from 100 percent to 329 percent and the speculative U.S. dollars that went into Japan before the yen appreciation gained 229 percent. When the yen was strong and the dollar weak, the Japanese enterprises went abroad to invest in American real estate property and manufacturers moved out to set up new production centers. The Japan threat rhetoric was as rampant in the U.S. as the China threat rhetoric is today. But when the "hot" money pulled out of Japan, and the U.S. real estate prices plummeted in the late 1980s and the 1990s, Japanese businesses lost money and went bankrupt, banks were stuck with many defaulting loans, and industries lost jobs because of a substantial reduction of exports. The strong yen made Japanese products more expensive. Manufacturers were exporting their products at zero or negative profit to keep the market share. In short, the Japanese economy was doomed for more than ten years and lost an enormous amount of money to the U.S. More recently, rapid economic development in China has provided Japan with a new opportunity for economic revival that began at the turn of the millennium.

Now the yen-dollar exchange ratio is stabilized at around 140: 1, roughly the same as it was thirty years ago. The temporary devaluation of the U.S. dollar has not hurt the international status of the U.S. dollar. Similar tactics were applied by American and European consortia against Asian currencies during the Asian financial crisis. The abrupt rise and fall of the exchange rates of Asian currencies against U.S. and European currencies were induced by the enormous influx and outflow of speculative "hot" Western capital that resulted in the collapse of Asian stock and real estate markets in the years 1997 and 1998.

In the meantime, trade relations between the U.S. and Japan have proven that trade problems cannot be solved simply by letting the exchange rate rise or fall. Japan continues to enjoy a trade surplus with the U.S. despite the sharp appreciation of the yen over the past two decades.

The underlying cause of U.S. effectiveness in currency manipulations against Japan was a global economy dominated by the U.S. dollar. U.S. military and economic strengths supported the position of the dollar in the world financial market. The financial crisis experienced by Japan in the 1980s and 1990s taught China to resist any drastic appreciation in the yuan to avoid similar currency and economic problems.

3) China's Mounting Foreign Exchange Reserves

Foreign exchange reserves in China are now over US$1.3 trillion. These reserves are projected to continue to rise by roughly US$17 billion a month. As discussed, the huge wage difference between the Chinese and the U.S. workers is one of the dominant causes for China's large trade surplus. Unless this can be adjusted, the yuan revaluation will not reduce the trade imbalance appreciably since history indicates that currency manipulations never control trade effectively. [256] In addition, a yuan appreciation by 15 percent would already wipe out the profits of many investments now being made in China. However, the mounting Chinese foreign exchange reserves exert significant pressure for RMB appreciation. The Chinese government is fighting hard to reduce the size of its foreign exchange reserves. The ever-increasing reserves bring risk such as a depreciation or collapse of the dollar. A big portion of the reserves has been invested in highly secure U.S. Treasury Bonds.

The following are key areas for Chinese government focus:

i) Encourage domestic consumption and demand U.S. relaxation of export regulations on high-tech products to reduce exports and increase imports.

ii) Encourage Chinese companies to invest abroad. China's direct overseas investment in 2005 hit a new high of US$12.26 billion, an increase of 123 percent over 2004. Aggregated direct overseas investment reached US$57.2 billion by the end of 2005, but represented only 0.59 percent of the total overseas investment. [257] The U.N. Industrial Development Organization Director General,

Kanden Yumkella, estimated that China's direct overseas investments are likely to reach US$60 billion by 2010. [258] Most of China's direct foreign investment went to Asian and African countries.

iii) Buy U.S. dollars and force banks to help sterilize dollars by buying low-interest RMB denominated bonds.

iv) Set real interest rates versus artificially low rates for deposits to defer the "hot" money betting on a yuan revaluation.

v) Set aside funds for a social security system and increase spending on education, health care and hygiene, science and technological development, and environmental protection.

vi) Encourage corporations to invest in a strategic petroleum reserve and buy strategic raw materials in places like Africa and other resource rich areas.

vii) Encourage Chinese insurance companies and pension funds to invest in foreign bonds and securities.

viii) Buy blue chip stocks and banks.

ix) Continue to buy U.S. Treasury Bonds.

x) Establish venture capital funds to encourage development and financing of innovative, technology-based businesses.

xi) Continue to reform the banking system to introduce modern retail banking and consumer lending practices.

xii) Diversify foreign exchange reserves by increasing the reserves of South Korea, and other foreign currencies, while reducing the reserves of the U.S. dollars.

Cheap money still flows into factories and property developments of state-owned enterprises. As discussed, this is a source of the large volume of loans in default and a weak banking system. The World Bank and the International Finance

Corporation reported that China has accelerated its rate of reform, ranking fourth in terms of ease of conducting business among 175 countries and regions. Specific areas of reform include: a) speeding up the business registration process; b) easing access to credit; and c) strengthening investor credit protection. China is the top reformer in this area. [259]

China is fighting a war, not an opium war as in the past, but one against speculative capital and mounting political pressure from the U.S.

4) Measures Taken by the Chinese Government

There are 561 anti-dumping cases against China from thirty countries, which represents 16 percent of all the cases worldwide. Given China's total trade share of 6 percent in the world, the 16 percent ratio is high, but not unusual. Trade partners should work together closely to understand each other before filing legal complaints. China should also work more effectively to educate its accountants and merchants so that they can better understand international markets. Revaluation of the yuan will reduce the trade surplus to a slight degree. History demonstrates that nations cannot use currency to control trade in the long run since improper currency revaluation produces many negative impacts on the economy and market stability.

China is such a vast and dynamic nation that many factors influence the economic playing field. Its fiscal policies, including tax policy reform and balancing the budget are handled more effectively today, whereas, its monetary policies on the RMB exchange rate, interest rate modulation, and inflation control remain problematic. There are three major driving forces in the Chinese economy. They are: 1) exports; 2) infrastructure spending; and 3) domestic consumption.

Currently, GDP growth relies heavily on exports. Exports and imports account for 64 percent of China's GDP, while in the U.S. and Japan, it is about 30 and 30–35 percent, respectively. About 2 percent of the Chinese GDP growth derives from trade surplus. China should have an economy led by domestic consumption. In the U.S., domestic consumption accounts for about 75 percent of its GDP. [260] The same consumption percentage is much lower in China. The absolute value of Chinese domestic consumption, one trillion U.S. dollars, is very large, but small when compared to domestic savings. The frequently discussed trade surplus with the U.S. is also much smaller than domestic consumption. However, the speed of the trade surplus increase in the first and second quarters of 2006 from 36 percent to 63 percent over 2005 is astonishing. Certainly, the trade surplus is important to China. Therefore, trade disputes are worth further examination.

Proportionately, the Chinese trade economy is not as large as its domestic consumption, but its growth trend has been alarming. Many manufacturers prefer to sell their products in the international markets rather than the domestic markets to avoid fierce competition and significantly lower profit margins. A major future challenge for China will be determining how to balance the sources of economic growth through tighter monetary policies or other economic measures. Apart from encouraging Chinese domestic consumption, other approaches for reduction of the trade surplus with the U.S. are relaxation of the restrictions on China for high-tech exports by the U.S. and lower trade restrictions for imported goods by China.

China implemented drastic macroeconomic measures to strike a balance between reining in explosive growth and avoidance of an economic crisis that could hurt millions of workers through job loss. Among these are RMB revaluation, interest rate hikes, a one percent increase in commercial banks' reserve requirement, tighter controls over bank lending and land supply. In addition, stringent market access requirements were imposed on companies planning investments and new real estate regulations were developed. Local officials failing to adhere to central government directives are being punished by sentencing them to jail or even execution.

These economic measures are showing some preliminary signs of slowing down the economy. For example, in 2006, growth in urban fix-asset investments dropped 6.1 percent to 27.4 percent in July, down from 33.5 percent in June.; industrial output expanded by 16.7 percent in July, down from 19.5 percent in June. The Chinese government will not impose further drastic controls except to support implementation of the current economic policies. [261]

In September 2006, Tyler Cowen wrote an article in the *New York Times* entitled, "China Is Big Trouble for the U.S. Balance of Trade,

Right? Well, Not So Fast," in which he presented opinions that conflict with popular thinking. He argued that when the yuan appreciates, American consumers have to buy Chinese products at higher prices or from other nations that sell at higher prices. Consequently, the U.S. trade deficit would even be higher. Now Chinese products are cheaper than those from South Korea, Japan, Mexico, and the U.S. Buying goods from China at current, lower prices has actually reduced the U.S. trade deficit. More discussions on RMB valuation can be found in references. [262–267]

After years of consideration, the Chinese leaders see the need for moderate appreciation of the RMB as in the national interest. On July 21, 2005, the first increase by 2 percent of the yuan from 8.27 yuan per U.S. dollar and its linkage to a basket of foreign currencies occurred. The rate of appreciation is a source of perpetual debate. The central bank favors a more aggressive timetable, whereas the Ministry of Commerce, representing exporters, requests small changes. It is the State Council that must make a final decision. Such a decision is complicated by Chinese banks that are choked with US$500 billion in bad loans. Any drop in exports would likely diminish deposits and trigger a financial crisis.

U.S. manufacturers still contend that the yuan is undervalued, making U.S. goods more expensive in China and Chinese products cheaper in the U.S. [268] The yuan appreciation pace has been speeding up, breaking the psychological hurdle of eight yuan to one U.S. dollar in mid-May 2006. On March 29, 2007, it reached a new high of 7.7303 yuan against one U.S. dollar, the eighteenth time that old records were erased within the short three months of 2007; it is still rising at the time of writing. [269]

China's exchange rate reform has not created instability, because the overall economy is still performing normally. Some economic problems do exist, but they are not serious. [270] Maintaining stability is not just a political slogan used by the CPC to control the nation, it is a fundamental cornerstone needed to keep the gigantic Chinese economic machine running smoothly, and to promote financial stability throughout the world.

Fortunately, despite the high growth rate over recent years, China's consumer price indices (CPI) were relatively stable (China's CPI grew by

1.8 percent in 2005 over 2004, 1.5 percent in 2006 over 2005, and is expected to climb by 2.5 percent in 2007, according to a forecast of the Ministry of Commerce, whereas the producer price index was higher), which indicated moderate inflation. Some experts argue that the CPI is no longer a good indicator for certain economic sectors. Even though, there is no immediate threat of inflation, the high GDP obviously shows an overheated economy in certain sectors that require great attention. The 2006 GDP growth of China was 10.7 percent. [271]

If China lets the yuan rise by a substantial amount, it would immediately lose more billion dollars on the U.S. treasury notes and other U.S. investments totaling US$800 billion. [272] However, under the current situation, urban fixed asset investment in China soared by 30.5 percent in the first seven months in 2006, up 3.3 percent over the previous year, driving the economy to the verge of over stimulation. [273] China tried two approaches to solve this problem.

In the first approach, a gradual rising of the bank interest rate in a more controlled manner is most beneficial to the overall health of the economy. Also, raising the bank interest rate would force foreign businesses to increase wages for Chinese laborers, thereby improving their living standards. This would help shrink the gap between rich and poor and boost domestic consumption, so long as Chinese business investments remain profitable. Moreover, increasing production costs would encourage businesses to become more efficient, streamline operations, innovate, and develop new technologies.

On March 18, 2007, China made a third interest hike in less than a year to make its one-year loan rate to 6.39 percent and one-year deposit rate to 2.79 percent to curb inflation. However, China cannot continuously raise the interest rate. The side effect is the attraction of more "hot" money into the country. In addition to the yuan revaluation, the PBC announced a one percentage point hike to 4 percent in the required reserve ratio for foreign currency deposits to tighten credit and cool the economy. However, this measure would only drain an additional US$1.6 billion out of the banking system which had foreign currency deposits of US$161 billion at the end of June, 2006.

Consumer prices rose 2.7 percent in February 2007, picking up from a 2.2 percent rise in January 2007, while industrial production soared 18.5

percent in January and February combined. [274] The Chinese trade surplus rose surprisingly to US$23.76 billion in February 2007, a sharp increase from US$2.5 billion a year earlier. Premier Wen Jiabao worried and warned that the Chinese development was unbalanced, uncoordinated, unstable, and unsustainable. [275]

The second approach deals directly with China's growing trade surplus. This is a very serious challenge. According to U.S. calculations, the trade surplus for 2006 was US$232.5 billion. Due to the Chinese government's tight control of the yuan exchange rate, reserves have proportionally increased. A US$120 billion trade surplus would incur a RMB expansion of nearly one trillion yuan resulting in an increase of bank money supply to a few trillion yuan in one year.

Should this trend continue for several years, would China be flooded with RMB currency? How can China avoid skyrocketing stock and real estate prices? China must take much stronger measures to control its growth and reduce its trade surplus by increasing imports and reducing exports.

Importing high-tech products will upgrade industrial production, productivity, and technical skills. Importing large quantities of foreign consumer goods will also stimulate domestic competition for improved production which will benefit consumers. By increasing imports alone, China will be able to reduce the trade surplus and related pressure to appreciate the yuan. China should also encourage domestic spending on imported goods and services to reduce savings so that its stock and real estate markets will not balloon into dangerous bubbles.

The Shanghai stock market had a sharp plunge of about 9 percent on February 27, 2007, after former U.S. Federal Reserve Board Chairman Alan Greenspan warned that the U.S. economy might enter into a recession at the end of the year. [276] The plunge caused jitters around the world. This market rose 150 percent in 2006 and is bound to decline at some point. The plunge showed how vulnerable and closely linked world economies are today. While Chinese import growth falls from 22 percent to 18 percent, Chinese export growth is expected to slow to 18 percent down from 26 percent in 2006, according to the Asian Development Bank. [277]

Finally, it is important to emphasize that although China has an economy that is market driven, it does not yet have a fully-developed market economy. Management of the RMB exchange rate against foreign currency is a sovereign right that can only be determined by the Chinese government. The primary goal of the currency policies adopted by the Chinese government today is maintenance of financial and social stability.

5) The Trade Imbalance

Worry over rising economic influence in China is unwarranted because China is far behind in scientific innovations and Chinese profits are astonishingly low.

First, statistical records indicate that only 0.3 percent of Chinese businesses own independent intellectual property rights and due to a lack of core technologies, foreign patent rights represent 20 percent of the sale price of Chinese-produced mobile phones, 30 percent of the PC sale price, and 20–40 percent of digitally controlled machine prices. The Chinese PC profit margin was only 5 percent and DVD end profits were only US$1, whereas the sale price was US$30.

The net profit for a TV set was less than ten Chinese yuan, or US$1.25, which is less than the cost of a cup of coffee in the U.S. This level of profit is minuscule when compared to that of the real estate market in China. Investors including universities and research institutes pursued the real estate market aggressively.

Chinese industries rely on foreign technologies. For example, foreign technology is pervasive in airplanes, cars, trucks, manufacturing equipment, metallurgical industries, graphic equipment, and aviation control. Chinese production efficiency was only 5 percent of that of developed nations such as the U.S., Japan, and Germany. The equipment manufacturing industry fell seriously behind developed nations; more than 90 percent of fiber-manufacturing equipment, 85 percent of the integral circuit wafer manufacturing equipment, 80 percent of petrochemical equipment, and 70 percent of auto industry equipment, digital machines, and textile machines were imports. [278] Although the Chinese GDP rose, risks also increased. China has sacrificed its natural resources and polluted its environment to such a significant degree, that long-term, sustainable growth would be difficult to maintain without fundamental improvement in science and technologies.

Second, the Chinese trade surplus was due to the collective effort of the huge Chinese population. In 2003, the average yearly wage for Chinese laborers was US$1,708. If China's growth rate is 10 percent annually, it would take more than thirty years for Chinese wages to rise close to the average American wage in 2003 of US$17.75 per hour or about US$35,000 a year. The average U.S. wage is twenty times higher. If the growth rate in China is 6 percent and the growth rate of the U.S. is 3 percent, it would take over 100 years to match the U.S. wage. During this period, even if the yuan tripled its value, by 2030 the gap between the Chinese wage and the U.S. wage would still be thirty years. [279] It is apparent that no matter how much the yuan is revaluated, there is no way to balance the wage difference between the two countries for many years, which is the real cause of the cheaper "China price." Therefore, the currency revaluation is not the major source of the trade imbalance issue between China and the U.S. From this analysis, we understand that China's trade surplus will continue to increase for a long time until its GDP volume aligns roughly with its population.

6) The Intellectual Property Rights (IPR) Issue

The U.S. has criticized China's inability to curb the export of pirated products. China vigorously defended its record of protecting IPR, stated that pirated goods comprised only a tiny portion of Chinese exports to the U.S. In 2005, Chinese exports to the U.S. were valued at US$162.9 billion, while pirated goods seized by the U.S. customs had an estimated worth of US$63.97 million, less than 0.04 percent of total Chinese exports. [280] Nevertheless, U.S. trade representative Rob Portman said that the U.S. will establish a China Enforcement Task Force to ensure that the PRC abides by the WTO regulations. [281] China urged the U.S. not to politicize trade issues.

China has responded to U.S. criticism and launched an anti-piracy program. For example, at the Tenth China International Fair for Investment and Trade in September 2006, Chinese Vice Premier Wu Yi said that the Chinese government will continue to strengthen law enforcement in IPR protection and severely punish those who break the law. China is the third largest trading partner of the U.S. and its fourth largest export market, while the U.S. is China's second largest trading partner and its biggest export market. The Vice Premier hopes that the

U.S. will lift restrictions on exports of certain goods to China and increase bilateral trade in the high-tech area in order to diminish the imbalance in bilateral trade. [282] China's anti-IPR-infringement efforts include the following:

- China has striven aggressively to crack down on piracy. In 2005 alone, China investigated 1,210 IPR violation cases worth US$12.47 million. From 1996 to 2005, Chinese customs investigated 5,571 IPR violation cases that were worth US$91.25 million. Since China joined the WTO, the investigations of IPR violation cases increased by 30 percent each year. In addition, China established IPR service centers in fifty major cities in 2006 to investigate reports of infringement and other IPR complaints. Shanghai plans to set up the mainland's first such center.

- China developed an IPR protection action plan for 2006, which included: 1) tightening laws and regulations, strengthening law enforcement, and cracking down on IPR infringements; 2) improving the IPR protection mechanism and enhancing international exchange and cooperation; and 3) increasing publicity on IPR protection awareness of the whole society. [283] China also warned overseas Chinese citizens and companies not to sell or rent pirated movies and music, and to abide by local laws on IPR to avoid problems. [284]

- On March 17, 2007, more than 1.81 million pirated CDs and DVDs were seized in a production factory in Guangdong Province in south China, which was the largest single crackdown on CD and DVD piracy in the country's history. [285]

- When Hu Jintao visited Microsoft Chairman Bill Gates in Seattle on April 20, 2006, he said, "I would like to reassure Mr. Gates that we will diligently protect intellectual property rights. We will honor the pledges we made. China has stepped up legislative efforts and law enforcement to protect intellectual property." The day before, Lenovo, the mainland's biggest computer manufacturer, agreed to buy US$1.2 billion worth of

Microsoft software for installation on its computers. [286]

- At their annual meeting in 2006, delegates representing foreign entrepreneurs at the Boao Forum for Asia reported that they appreciated Chinese efforts to protect IPR. Chinese Minister of Commerce, Bo Xilai, stated that IPR protection has become a basic national policy. [287] During his visit to the U.S., Bo Xilai asked the U.S. government for understanding and patience in the Chinese efforts to crack down on violations of IPR. [288]

- Chinese authorities have closed 3,014 shops for selling pirated DVDs, software, and other products as the government launched a 100-day crackdown. "We are giving shopkeepers a harsh lesson to make it clear that selling pirated products will lead to strict penalties," according to Liu Binjie, Deputy Director of the State Press and Publications Administration. [289]

- China and the U.S. are coordinating efforts to protect IPR. The U.S. plans to hold more training programs to bring together Chinese officials at provincial levels along with U.S. government officials to learn methods of copyright protection. [290]

Despite efforts by the Chinese government, Beijing has a long way to go to meet its WTO commitments according to the May 2006 annual report by the American Chamber of Commerce in China. [291] If China cannot effectively curb its infringement of IPR, even Chinese businesses would be unwilling to invest in research and development to produce needed core technologies for high-tech industries.

In short, China will remain its own victim of infringement of IPR and will be unable to revive its innovative capabilities. Since China is so vast, it is difficult to correct IPR problems as the developed nations expect. However, despite the existing problems, the Chamber praises the Chinese government for increased awareness of the IPR issue and efforts to resolve related problems.

3. The American Problems in the Trade Issues

In addition to the trade disputes reviewed previously, a 2006 study by Oxford Economic Forecasting (OEF), an economic consulting firm, concluded that the trade relationship with China has been a huge blessing for the U.S. economy. The OEF report estimated that 1) trade and investment with China will add 0.7 percent to U.S. GDP by 2010 by stimulating productivity growth and U.S. exports; 2) the U.S. annual average household income has risen US$500 since 2000, and will be US$1,000 higher by 2010; 3) U.S. consumer prices would have been 0.5 percent higher in 2005 had China not embarked on the sweeping economic reforms that made its export explosion possible, and that gap will reach 0.8 percent by 2010; and 4) the long-term benefits to the U.S. of trade with China are substantial. [292]

The report also provided data on the much disputed job losses in the U.S. and on China's trade surplus as follows:

About 205,000 manufacturing jobs in the U.S. were lost since 2000 when China exports began to explode as China prepared to enter the WTO. That number will reach 500,000 by 2010.

Many new service jobs have been created through China trade and the actual net loss in U.S. jobs is marginal.

The swelling U.S. current account balance poses substantial potential risk, but China is not solely to blame because U.S. exporters have lost market share in most of the world.

The Chinese share of U.S. imports has risen dramatically from 8.2 percent in 2000 to 14.8 percent in 2005 largely because Japanese, South Korean, Taiwanese, and Singaporean companies began shifting production en masse to the mainland in 2000 in anticipation of China's entry into the WTO. As a result, the U.S. imbalance with all of East Asia has remained basically the same; estimated at 29 percent over a five year period. [293]

If Beijing allowed the yuan to strengthen by 25 percent, it would provide a small boost to U.S. exporters and reduce the U.S. overall trade deficit by US$10 billion to US$15 billion per year because Chinese factories would absorb lower profits or lose orders to other low cost Asian producers.

Another U.S. economic issue is that the richest Americans have become comparatively wealthier through tax breaks and globalization in contrast to average U.S. workers whose income has grown only 9 percent over the past thirty years, while productivity is up 80 percent. The inflation-adjusted median U.S. household income dropped between the years 2000 and 2004. [294]

The argument about China trade boils down to the basic debate over whether gains for the U.S. economic growth benefit all Americans or whether the U.S. is consuming beyond its means; neither of these issues is a problem caused by China. During a speech in Beijing in March 2006, U.S. Commerce Secretary Carlos Gutierrez commented that the U.S. "draws significant benefits from its commerce with China. . . . U.S. exports to China grew by 20 percent last year, which built on 22 percent growth from prior year," he stated further. The yearly trade is nearly US$250 billion today and involves significant commercial resources and many new jobs. China maintains that trade friction and other problems between China and the U.S. should be properly handled through negotiation and not be politicized. "This is a point of view with which we both agree," said Gutierrez. [295]

4. The Energy Issue

The world fossil fuel reserve is limited and the world will face severe energy resource challenges in this century. America has only 5 percent of the world population, but consumes 25–30 percent of the energy resources on Earth. According to estimates, crude oil reserves may be used up in forty to sixty years, but the production rate will drop before that.

America is the world largest oil importer and consumer. Chinese energy demands also increased dramatically after the open door policy of Deng Xiaoping, initiated in 1978, which embraced a market economy. China was self-sufficient in oil resources until 1993. By 2006, Chinese oil resources met only 53 percent of the nation's energy demand. According to estimates, by 2030, 75 percent of Chinese oil will be imported. [296]

There are many reasons for the surge in oil demand in China. When China joined the WTO in 2001, its economy blended well into the global economy when increased productivity drove the strong demand for crude oil. China is the world's second largest oil consumer and the third crude oil importer. It is estimated that, by 2020, China's oil imports will nearly double from its 2005 level and its natural gas imports will triple in the same period. However, despite the pressing demand for energy, the Chinese average per capita energy consumption is only one-twelfth of America's. [297]

Currently, China's main energy source is coal, which provides 77 percent of its energy needs; the rest comes from oil, hydro-energy, natural gas, and nuclear energy. Faced with explosive growth in China, the Bush administration launched a series of political, economic, and military initiatives to control world oil resources.

There are really only five countries worldwide with significant oil resources, namely: Iran, Iraq, Russia, Saudi Arabia, and Venezuela. [298] It is estimated that, by 2030, one-third of China's imported oil will come from Russia. China and Russia are planning to construct an oil pipeline to ship oil from Siberia to China.

At present, Iran is China's major source of oil. China and Iran recently signed agreements to cooperate further on oil exploration. China is planning to construct a pipeline to ship oil by land from north of the Caspian Sea to pipelines in Kazakhstan and the Chinese western province of Xinjiang. The plan is to reduce dependence on shipping oil by sea since the U.S. Navy now controls the Malacca Strait. At present, 90 percent of Chinese oil imports arrive by shipping, 80 percent of it passes through the Malacca Strait.

When President Bush reached a historic nuclear pact with India, while denouncing the Iranian nuclear program, some experts speculated about the U.S. administration's strategic motives. It is obvious that whoever controls the Indian Ocean may succeed in carrying out an economic blockade against China and whoever controls the Middle Eastern oil resources will be able to disable economic development by China. In order to protect its stability and economic development, China must ensure its energy resources and energy security. To this end, Beijing plans to build oil pipelines that pass through Far Eastern Russia to China. An alternative is to build a deep water port in West Pakistan to pipe oil directly across Central Asia to other cities in the mainland via oil pipelines that pass through Xinjiang Province.

5. Has America Gained More Oil from the Iraq War?

Many people worldwide believe that the U.S. invasion of Iraq was not intended to destroy terrorists, search for weapons of mass destruction, or transform Iraq into a democracy. Rather, they think the U.S. sought control of Iraqi oil. After paying a huge financial price for the war and suffering severe damage to its image in the world, the U.S. has failed to benefit from cheaper Iraqi oil. U.S. policy makers have not succeeded in containing access to oil by China in the Middle East, nor are Americans feeling safer. A few pertinent facts follow:

- During the thirty-five months before the start of the Iraq War, America received an average of 640,000 barrels crude oil from Iraq per day.

- During the thirty-five months after the start of the Iraq War, America accessed an average of 580,000 barrels crude oil from Iraq per day.

- Since the beginning of the Iraq War, Middle East crude oil supply to the U.S. declined from an average of 2.757 million barrels per day in 2001 to 2.384 million barrels per day, which was 25.3 percent and 18.5 percent (for the first half of 2006), respectively, of America's total oil import per day; whereas China's imports from the Middle East increased dramatically from 800 thousand barrels in 2001 to 1.62 million barrels for the first half of 2006, an increase of 102.5 percent. It is remarkable that prior to the Iraq War in 2002, Saddam Hussein only exported eleven thousand barrels of crude oil to China per day, but in 2005, after he was ousted, China was able to import about thirty thousand barrels per day. Does this mean that China's peaceful energy policy is more effective than the U.S. method of instigating war?

- Before the U.S. attacked Iraq the price of crude oil was US$27 per barrel. In the fall of 2006, it was above US$70 per barrel. For every US$10 increase per barrel, gasoline prices in the U.S. rise by about twenty-five cents a gallon. Since many believe that the crude oil prices are determined by the New York Stock Exchange, the oil companies have made huge profits since the beginning of the Iraq War.

- Iran has filled the power vacuum left by the fall of Saddam Hussein in Iraq. Furthermore, following the fall of the Taliban in Afghanistan, Iran has effectively controlled Iraq through manipulation of the Shia Muslims and has gained substantial power in war torn Afghanistan. The U.S. invasions of Afghanistan and Iraq have helped Iran by clearing its enemies from these two countries. Iran is the biggest beneficiary of America's anti-terrorist war in the Middle East. [299] The U.S. seems prepared to attack Iran using its nuclear uranium enrichment program as a pretext. If this plan succeeds, the U.S. would control both Iraq and Iran, and consequently, China's energy life line. Now that the U.S. is confronted with strong resistance on the nuclear issue, will it pursue aggression against Iran? This remains to be seen.

- James Baker, former U.S. Secretary of State and Treasury Secretary, visited Hong Kong in March 2006, where he commented on China-U.S. trade relations. He said that the energy issue might trigger competition, but the global energy supply is actually sufficient; the only problem is the price. [300] He may be correct, however, continuous price escalation has already triggered global competition for oil resources among developed countries like Japan and the U.S. as well as developing countries like China and India.

6. The Chinese Energy Strategies

Energy demand in China has, to some extent, altered the people's ancient emotional tie with the land known as the "Great Wall Affection." Now the Chinese people fondly remember the amiable Ming Dynasty General Zheng He as their role model whose advice was to sail across and embrace the ocean. Although most live on the mainland, many modern Chinese have become twenty-first century Venetians crossing oceans and straits to visit Europe, the Middle East, Africa, North America, Latin America, Australia, and the South Pacific Islands. Many have settled overseas.

In order to secure energy resources, the Chinese government has made comprehensive adjustments in politics, diplomacy, and military relationships. The guiding principles are: Treat business as business, and leave political ideologies behind. Maintaining harmony with neighbors and "energy diplomacy" in the twenty-first century have replaced the previous renowned ping-pong diplomacy of the 1970s. To tackle the energy resource issue, China has aggressively pursued peaceful solutions as follows:

China is accelerating plans for construction of renewable energy projects across the country with goals of developing hydropower and wind power capacity to 180 gigawatts (1 gigawatt = 1,000,000,000 or 10^9 watts) and 5 gigawatts, respectively, by 2010. By 2020, hydropower and wind power capacity will total 300 gigawatts) and 30 gigawatts, respectively. In the same year, China also plans to build up biogas installed capacity of 30 gigawatts and solar installed capacity of 1.8 gigawatts. China's electricity installed capacity was 508.41 gigawatts at the end of 2005, with the percentage of coal-fired electricity installed capacity reaching 75.6 percent, hydropower, 22.9 percent and nuclear power, only 1.35 percent. China plans to raise electricity installed capacity for renewable energy to 10 percent of its total power capacity by 2010, and 20 percent by 2020. [301]

The Chinese government is establishing a special fund for the development of renewable energy including biological, solar, hydroelectric, and wind. [302] Further, China is increasing renewable energy development by charging a tiny fraction of consumer electricity rates, 0.1 cent per kilowatt hour to be used to develop renewable energy. [303] The push for renewable energy sources is not only driven by energy concerns, but also by a strong desire to generate "Green GDP," since China ratified the Kyoto Protocol in May 1998 and wants to demonstrate that it is a responsible member of the global family.

China is accelerating exploitation of coal-bed methane, also known as coalmine gas, to satisfy increasing demand for energy. China started to explore and use coal-bed methane in the 1990s. With improved technology and investment, the use of coal-bed methane will increase rapidly. For example, in 2005, one billion cubic meters of coal-bed methane was used. Usage rose to 1.4 billion cubic meters in 2006. It is shocking that 1.3 billion cubic meters is emitted, but unused, each year. One cubic meter of coal-bed methane is equivalent to 1.13 liters or 0.3 gallons of gasoline. It retails at less than half the price of gasoline.

China's thirty-seven trillion cubic-meter reserves of coal-bed methane are the third largest in the world followed by Russia and Canada. This is equivalent to forty-five billion tons of standard coal. Sixty percent of the gas is stored in coal beds over 1,500 meters deep, easily mined and developed. Coal-bed methane is an effective alternative energy source for China, but it is also a major type of greenhouse gas. The Chinese government has approved a five-year plan for the development of coal-bed methane to increase annual gas output to ten billion cubic meters by 2010. The plan involves establishing an industrial system to develop coal-bed methane and offers a series of preferential policies along with foreign and domestic investment opportunities to exploit this industry sector. [304]

Recently, ONGC Videsh of India and CNOOC of China spent US$800 million to own jointly 50 percent of Omimex de Colombia Oil Company. Each has a 25 percent share of the business. [305] This was the second time that the two nations cooperated on an investment in foreign oil for mutual benefit. Some experts felt that although both countries have rapidly growing economies, each has a capital shortage and lack of political clout to compete in the international oil markets. Through collaboration and joint venture, economic and political risk is shared and mitigated. Moreover, these arrangements promote closer diplomatic ties.

China is working to reduce energy consumption per unit of GDP by 4 percent annually. Unfortunately in the first year, 2006, that number was reduced by just 1 percent, making the goal impossible to achieve as it appears.

Chinese President Hu Jintao in his address to a G8 working meeting in 2006 urged international energy exporters and consumers to cooperate and develop a new energy security concept to maintain stability and the safety of global resources. He called for 1) encouraging research and development of sustainable energy; 2) stepping up of oil and natural gas exploitation to boost supplies for global demand; 3) strengthening policy coordination and improving mechanisms for monitoring the international energy market and responding to energy emergencies; and 4) stressing the importance of energy conservation to ensure long-term global energy security.

China welcomes collaboration and joint energy projects with the U.S. in oil and gas exploration. The crude oil output of China's offshore oil projects, in which U.S. oil companies participate, reached 15.53 million tons (about 57.09 million barrels) in 2005, amounting to 56 percent of the total output of the CNOOC. [306]

7. Challenges Faced by China

Despite China's impressive economic development record over the past twenty-nine years, there are serious problems in balancing the need for economic and social development with issues related to population growth, resource conservation and environmental protection. [307] Major problems China confronts today include the following:

- China is in the midst of one of history's greatest urbanization movements. Nearly 300 million farmers will move to cities over the next twenty years. Urban areas are growing at breakneck speed and yet efficiency is low. Furthermore, Chinese cities have high population density which results in problems related to sustainable development.

- University graduates face a tough job market. The number of university graduates increased from 2.12 million in 2003 to 2.6 million in 2004. The number increased to 3.2 million in 2005 and to over 4 million in 2006. The existing job market has the capacity to hire only 1.5 million a year now. The government could add another 0.75 million jobs to support development in western China or to work as military police, security, or military personnel. The resulting

shortfall means that more than two million university graduates were jobless in 2006. One example of the tight job
market and extreme job competition follows:

- On July 17, 2006, Huzhou City in Zhejiang Province was
recruiting 147 toll collectors. More than 1,600 applied for the
job. Of these, 720 were university graduates. Annual salary
and benefits for this position was 2,000 yuan or about
US$250. The job crisis is so extreme that many graduates are
willing to accept zero income for the first year of employment.
China must address this challenging job shortage problem
since university graduates have extensive intellectual capital
to contribute to the growth and success of the nation. [308]

- Deputy Finance Minister, Lou Jiwei, issued a report that the
gini-coefficient, which indicates income disparity, had
reached the dangerous level of 0.46. The gini-coefficient
ranges from 0 to 1 and a level of 0.4 is considered alarming.
[309] Some researchers believe the real gap is much greater
and could have reached 0.5. It is embarrassing for China to
have the second largest poor population in the world, after
India. A major contributing factor to the poor-rich gap in
China is serious corruption.

Deng Xiaoping's slogan "to get rich is glorious" reshaped the
economic landscape of China and created impressive prosperity. It also
caused a widespread moral degeneration among government officials. A
recent Chinese official report showed that more than 90 percent of
Chinese billionaires are high level CPC associates, their children, or rela-
tives. Some funds were taken by the People's Liberation Army whose
subsidiary enterprises are as rich as some giant Western multinational
companies. [310] It is clear that substantial tax revenues went into pock-
ets of a minority, elite group who have special political connections. The
corrupt bureaucrats are like the eunuchs in ancient China staying in
power even when the emperor and dynasty changed.

In 2001, *Forbes* reported that fifty of the wealthiest Chinese had a
combined net worth equivalent to the income of fifty million peasants.

[311] If China cannot effectively abate rampant corruption, public resentment and social unrest will erupt and escalate to an uncontrollable state. This was often the reason for the collapse of many Chinese dynasties throughout history.

Under the leadership of Hu Jintao this problem is being taken seriously. Several high-ranking government officials including the Shanghai Mayor and Beijing Vice Mayor have been fired for corruption and related misconduct. This may be only the tip of the iceberg. To ensure clean government and long-term stability and prosperity, China needs to establish an independent legal mechanism that is above the CPC authority, to systematically crack down on corruption at all government levels. In August 2006, Beijing issued new regulations to curb nepotism among senior politicians and prevent high-level leaders from serving in the same post for more than ten consecutive years. [312] This demonstrates government commitment to combating corruption.

Other key initiatives include parliament approval of a rural reform plan in March 2006, to address the rich-poor gap along with official corruption, especially land grabs, which entail appropriation of peasant lands without reasonable compensation, and rising social unrest in the countryside. [313] The Chinese government issued new rules aimed at tightening land supply in a bid to prevent overheating of the economy. The new rule included increased compensation for evicted residents and a requirement for more land to be sold through auction. It also warned local leaders that they will be penalized for failure to stop, or investigate illegal land sales in areas under their jurisdiction. Under the new rule, the use of farmland for construction purposes will no longer be approved by the State Council for each project, but should be reported to provincial governments and submitted to the State Council for approval on an annual basis. [314] The passage of the Property Law in March 2007, which deepens Chinese privatization, also provides more protection for peasants and property owners.

Alarmingly, China's rich-poor gap implanted serious discontent among the civilian population. Chinese bureaucrats at the local government level often fail to follow central government policies. Bureaucrats have wasted huge sums of government revenues. For example, in 2004, expenses for government vehicles amounted to US$51 billion and restaurant bills amounted to US$25 billion. The combined sum of these two items amounted to one-fifth of the national budget and aroused much criticism and anger among citizens. [315] The central government has a difficult challenge ahead managing widespread corruption among government officials. Many of them have departed from the moralistic path of Confucianism. It is tragic to see that after the Cultural Revolution, some of the most precious core values of the Chinese culture have suffered degradation.

To demonstrate serious commitment to combating rampant corruption, the Chinese Central Government launched a program to overhaul all fifty-two provincial governments and state business representative offices in Beijing by the end of 2006. Li Jinhua, the nation's top auditor, accused senior officials in the capital's regional offices of widespread financial corruption. One unconfirmed figure estimated that as much as US$2.5 billion was spent each year on securing contracts with central government agencies. In Beijing, there were as many as 520 municipal government agencies or representative offices and more than 5,000 county government agencies. Their future survival is now in doubt. [316]

Fairness in the distribution of health care and medical services in China ranked 188th out of the 192 world nations in the U.N. General Assembly in 2005. China only spent 17 percent of its total medical funding on public health, which was 45 percent of the amount spent by the U. S. In order to ameliorate this situation to meet higher public medical needs, China has to spend about US$187.5 billion to US$250 billion annually, which is about 5–7 percent of China's total government revenue or 1–1.5 percent of its GDP in 2005. [317] China is planning to change its radical market-oriented health reforms that have led to gross injustice in the distribution of health resources and attracted much criticism. [318] Eighty-seven percent of the peasant population has spent personal income for medical expenses, whereas only 44 percent of urban population must pay for health care. China announced that its new rural cooperative medical system would cover 396 million farmers, about 44.7 percent of the total rural population. [319]

Although in 2003 China launched a trial rural cooperative medical care system in some provinces that covered 671 counties and 177 million residents, Chinese farmers are very much concerned about the expense of medical treatment. China has about 800 million rural residents. High medical costs and inadequate health care have plagued the vast population of Chinese farmers, who were supposed to share in the fruits of rapid economic development to the same degree as urban residents. However, farmers learned that finding a well-equipped, low cost rural clinic was not easy. The Chinese government decided to double the government health care allowance of US$2.5 in 2006 for each farmer participating in the rural cooperative medical care system. The government allocated more than US$2.5 billion to be spent over the next five years to renovate hospitals in rural areas. By 2008, the basics of a rural Health Care Service System should be in place in all non-urban areas. [320]

China's per capita supply of energy (oil and natural gas are 8.3 and 4.1 percent of world reserves, respectively), water (only 25 percent of the world nation average among countries), and land (farming land is only 40 percent of the world nation average among countries) is becoming increasingly scarce. [321] Problems related to resource distribution and the environment are pressing after three decades of economic development. [322] In recent years many natural disasters occurred in China. There were typhoons in the southeast coastal areas, and severe heat and drought in the southwest provinces. Crops dried up and animals and people were thirsty. These problems, the demand of urban growth and industrialization, contributed to long-term water shortages in many regions of China. Clean water supply is an area of major concern since reportedly an estimated two-thirds of China's rivers and lakes are contaminated by waste water and industrial pollutants. In order to access water, wells were drilled deeper and deeper, resulting in a significant drop in the underground water level. Between 2000 and 2004, the per capita supply of water dropped by one-eighth to 1,856 cubic meters. [323]

Morgan Stanley's Chief Economist, Stephen Roach, in his article "Will the Global Economy Reverse Its Course?" warns that the Chinese economy is seriously overheated In the first half of 2006, China's GDP grew by an annual 10.9 percent, total export trade reached US$795.7 billion (a growth rate of 23.4 percent), trade surplus was US$61.4 billion, and in June, industrial production increased by 19.5 percent relative to the same period in the previous year, setting a new growth record. What attracted the most attention was the 29.8 percent increase in fixed asset investment. The China Bank loaned US$250 billion, which was a 150 percent increase over lending in 2005. Speculative foreign investment reached US$25.5 billion from February to May 2005. [324] China has little choice but to decelerate its growth and tighten monetary policy to avoid external protectionism. It has to encourage domestic private consumption as well as government spending in areas including education, hygiene, social security, and health care.

In 2005, the personal consumption rate was only 38 percent of its GDP, much less than the average rate of 50 percent in the world. [325] The oversupply of high-priced residential homes and the increase in nonperforming bank loans are of considerable concern. The debates among economists who support rapid GDP growth and those who advocate limited and balanced GDP growth will definitely continue for quite some time.

Forty percent of China's crude oil comes from imports. This fraction is estimated to grow to 54.4, 57.4 and 59.7 percent in 2010, 2015, and 2020, respectively. By 2030, it will rise to 75 percent. China consumes about one-third of world oil resources each year, of which imported crude oil is about 7 percent of the total world exported oil. China will spend US$400 billion annually on imported oil. The price of world crude oil in 2006 has tripled its pre-war value in 2003 after the U.S. invasion of Iraq. There is a significant potential risk of an energy crisis with such a high level of dependency on foreign oil. In 2005, China tried to find new oil resources around the world. This search has been successful since thirty percent of Chinese crude oil imports are now from Africa. It appears that securing energy resources will remain one of China's major challenges for future economic development. China must develop alternative energy resources and methods of energy conservation.

China has paid a high price for its economic miracle. The government admitted that in 2005 it was the world's largest producer of sulfur dioxide, which is a primary cause of acid rain. A total of 357 of 696 mainland cities and counties participating in a national monitoring program were affected by acid rain in 2005. Over one-third lacked sewage treatment facilities. [326] Fortunately, the scope of acid rain pollution has not increased. [327] On the mainland, sulfur dioxide emissions originate from coal-burning power plants. Coal accounts for most energy consumption and China is the world's largest coal producer. Environmental officials calculated economic losses caused by sulfur dioxide emissions to be about US$6.38 billion in 2005 with related health care costs accounting for the major share of this expense. The problem is that the environmental regulations, laws, and standards are not adequately implemented or enforced. [328]

However, the impact of Chinese pollution on other nations has been erroneously reported by the American media in July 2006. A report by the U.S. Environmental Protection Agency estimated that on certain specific dates, 25 percent of the micro-pollutant particles above the Los Angeles sky could be traced to China. In fact, only about 1 percent of these pollutants came from Asia. [329] Another report by Reuters stated that China actively engages in projects that convert coal into a clean fuel. [330] The Chinese State Environmental Protection Administration (CSEPA) plans to bypass local protectionism and strengthen its power to handle pollution accidents and environmental disputes. [331] Eleven monitoring centers are to be set up in major cities and in areas near nuclear facilities. [332]

Two indicators reported by the CSEPA showed that 1) the amount of chemical oxygen used to estimate the amount of organic matter in waste water rose 4.2 percent; and 2) discharges of sulfur dioxide were up 5.8 percent. Reportedly, the ecological environment has deteriorated further in the first half of 2006. [333]

China's rivers are badly polluted as well. The National People's Congress Standing Committee reported that the pollution problem of Chinese rivers can be described as "shocking." [334] Can China sustain its economic development without seriously combating these hazardous environmental conditions? This remains a great challenge to policy makers and Chinese businesses.

Since China is the world biggest emitter of sulfur dioxide, producing more than twenty-five million tons in 2005 that caused economic losses of US$62.5 billion through acid rain, the government is ordering mainland power plants to pay for rights to emit sulfur dioxide from as early as 2007—at an annual cost of US$875 million based on current output. The plan is to cut emissions of sulfur dioxide by 10 percent by 2010. The money raised would be spent on promoting renewable energy development and energy efficiency. [335]

By 2009–2010, China will overtake the U.S. as the world's largest carbon dioxide emitter. The Chinese government says that the country lacks the technology to significantly reduce emissions. Also, shutting down old factories or power plants could wipe out jobs in poor areas. Australia pledged to help China clean its heavily polluted air by working intensively with China on developing clean coal technology. By 2030, seventy percent of Chinese energy will be generated by coal-fired power stations. Australia and the U.S. are the only two major industrialized countries to reject the 1997 Kyoto Protocol, which commits thirty-five nations and the European community to reducing greenhouse gas emissions to 5 percent below 1990 levels by 2012. [336]

An inspection by the NPC found that the mainland has made little progress in controlling water and air pollution and treating industrial waste. It was estimated that pollution cost the mainland economy about 3 percent of GDP in 2004, but the actual cost is much higher. [337] Chinese Premier Wen Jiabao announced earlier in 2006 that by 2010 the central government planned to cut air pollution emissions by 10 percent. [338] Chinese local authorities are blamed for the blind pursuit of economic growth while paying little attention to meet environmental targets. In 2006, China launched investigations into six of the country's most notorious sources of pollution for illegal dumping of about ten cubic meters of chemicals into the Mangniu River in the northeast Jilin Province. Chinese authorities closed a factory and detained seven suspects following the spill. [339]

In his article entitled "China: Think Again!" in the March/April 2007 issue of *Foreign Policy*, China expert Harry Harding commented that pollution is the biggest problem in China today. Eight of the world's ten most polluted cities are in China. Overcoming the pollution problem is a formidable obstacle confronting the Chinese government and people.

Since China joined the WTO, its economy has maintained a high growth rate. The level of exports in China was under 50 percent of its growth up to 2003. Today, this ratio is approaching 80 percent and China has become a world factory. This means that Chinese foreign trade has grown rapidly. However, domestic consumption remains very weak relative to savings and the economy is very fragile. The high GDP growth (over 90 percent in ten years) has not produced enough job growth (only 10 percent in ten years). In order to achieve high GDP growth, China opened its production to foreign advanced technology businesses, which did not generate enough jobs. Large numbers of China's rural population went to cities and became migrant urban workers increasing the urban unemployment population. The huge numbers of migrant workers lack job security; therefore, boosting their consumption rate is difficult. China needs to develop its service industry and establish indigenous industries to generate more jobs to increase domestic consumption.

China's financial sector is confronting nine major potential risks:

   i. China's M2/GDP continues to climb and reached 185.48 percent in 2004. There is a significant potential risk of financial crisis in the banking sector.

   ii. In 2005, unrecoverable debts among banks reached US$225 billion.

   iii. Local governments have accumulated at least US$125 billion in debts, about 5–10 percent of the GDP. The local debt crisis may threaten China's financial security and social stability.

   iv. Due to the low efficiency of the national banking system, an underground financial system has flourished in China that represents about one-third of the legitimate national banking system. It threatens and undermines the existence of the official banking system.

   v. China lacks effective control of investment capital. High risk speculative manipulation of investment capital is commonplace.

   vi. Real estate speculation is rampant and 55 percent of construction loans are provided by banks.

   vii. Chinese financial institutions have RMB exchange rate risks.

   viii. The RMB exchange mechanism may fail.

   ix. The Chinese financial sector may suffer a "Latin-

American style" crisis. [340]

The Chinese population in 2006 was slightly over 1.3 billion. According to recent estimates, over the next twenty years, approximately 300 million of the rural population will relocate to urban areas. At the same time, each year an estimated forty million people will need jobs. Unemployment will be a long-term source of concern for China in the twenty-first century. China's rapid economic growth has not solved the unemployment problem. For example, from 1996 to 2000, for every percentage point of GDP growth, there was only 0.3 percent growth in the employment rate, and from 2001 to 2005, the job creation rate year-by-year dropped to 0.11 percent. One of the main reasons for the sluggish job creation is that capital-driven and innovation-led growth requires fewer workers. Another factor is the impact of restructuring and closing down state-owned enterprises. For example, in 1995 there were about 112.6 million people working in state-owned enterprises; this number dropped in 2005 to 64.88 million. In 1991 there were 36.28 million people working in collectively-owned sectors, but by 2005 the figure slumped to 8.1 million. Although the official unemployment rate was 4.2 percent at the end of June 2006, the actual unemployment level was believed to be much higher. [341]

China's one-child policy has achieved important birth control objectives. However, one problematic consequence is the increasing size of the aging population. Currently, there are 100.55 million over the age of sixty-five, which represents 7.7 percent of the total population. By 2010, that number will reach 170 million or 12.5 percent of the total population. By 2020, 243 million or 17 percent of the total population will be over sixty-five. [342]

By 2030, Chinese senior citizens aged sixty and over will increase to 400 million, about the total population of fifteen European countries. [343] The total Chinese population will reach its peak at 1.5 billion in the 2030s and decline from that point on. [344] The recent labor shortage in southeast China is the result of the decline in the more youthful population. China will be the only country in the world that grows older before becoming rich. China's present pension system is already running short of funds. How China will build an effective social security system to support its aging population in the future remains a huge problem that must be resolved. Also, as an aging society, China will have to face the impact of labor shortages and possibly slower economic development, unless it succeeds in replacing workers with robotics and other advanced technologies. [345]

While the Chinese Central Government enjoys a healthy revenue stream, rising from 22 percent in 1993 to 54.9 percent in 2002 of the national income per year, the local governments suffer serious budget deficits, which amounted to over US$37.5 billion at the provincial level. Other shortfalls were an estimated US$37.5 billion at county and city levels and US$75 billion at the village and township levels in 2003. [346] The situation has not improved since then.

Because of these staggering debt figures, the budget shortfall at the local government level appears to be out of control. In recent years, particularly, local governments have been enthusiastically involved in investment, and related debts have mounted dramatically. A key reason for this debt escalation is an unhealthy political system. Poor investments have placed a heavy burden on local government resources and slowed effective economic development which has been under funded by the central government. Moreover, current local government administrators are given short terms of job assignments, which adds pressures to pursue infrastructure projects with political rather than practical merit. Finding ways to correct shortsighted government decision-making and reduce the local debt is another pressing barrier to development. To help solve this problem, the Chinese Central Government is allowing the local governments to issue treasury bonds under certain conditions to increase local government income. [347]

According to financial data, global hedge funds are managing about 1.5 trillion U.S. dollars. Other speculative funds manage a few trillion U.S. dollars. If 1 percent of this capital were invested in China, it would amount to hundreds of millions of U.S. dollars or a few billion Chinese yuan. Since a RMB rise is widely rumored, considerable speculative money has entered the Chinese market. In the first ten months of 2006, more than 103 billion yuan (US$12.3 billion) flowed into residential projects in China, a 28.4 percent increase over 2005. [348] Large increases in speculative foreign money have caused China's foreign reserve to rise continuously. The overheated Chinese economy has attracted international attention. According to statistics, the first new banking loans in the first quarter of 2006 were US$157.5 billion. This was the target for the first six months of the year. The risk of inflation is on the horizon. [349]

Increased dollar holdings in China resulted in an increase in U.S. debt, since the U.S. continues borrowing money from China to fund U.S. spending. If this situation continues, the dollar will depreciate on a larger scale. Huge U.S. government and trade deficits have caused an imbalance in the global economy because the U.S. dollar has dominated the global economy. If the U.S. depreciates the dollar to pay international debts, a global financial crisis may erupt.

China must raise the quality of its products through innovation and improved technology to compete with products produced by developed nations on the international market. China should not continue indefinitely as the world's factory since the inevitable rise of the yuan in future years will gradually diminish China's cheap labor advantage. Asian countries such as Vietnam and the Philippines will eventually replace China as a source of low-cost labor. Whether China is able to transform into a truly industrialized nation over the next few decades remains a question and challenge that will test Chinese determination, strength, creativity, and ability to innovate.

China has an enormous existing shortfall of funds for social security and for the massive levels of future funding requirements. At the same time, booming exports have generated huge foreign exchange reserves. Now it is over US$1.3 trillion. Managing such huge reserves exacerbates pressure for a revaluation of the RMB and is increasingly a source of concern for Chinese financial authorities. Experts have estimated that foreign exchange reserves of US$700 billion should be appropriate for China's current economic condition. It is possible that additional foreign exchange reserves could be used as a national pension fund. [350]

On March 5, 2006, Chinese Premier Wen Jiabao delivered the "Report of the Work of the Government" at the Fourth Plenum of the Tenth National People's Congress, in which he delineated important tasks required to build a moderately prosperous Chinese society as follows: 1) solve major problems affecting economic performance; 2) promote economic restructuring and changes of the pattern of economic growth; 3) deepen economic restructuring and open China further to the outside world; 4) accelerate the development of social programs; 5) strive to increase employment and improve social security work; and 6) strengthen democracy and the legal system.

The fulfillment of these promises will be an indicator of the effectiveness and success of the Chinese government and Chinese people in the next couple of decades.

Section III. China Is Not a Military Threat to the U.S.

The U.S. neo-conservatives and the defense establishment often view China as a military threat. This perspective misleads some in the U.S. and has shaped a "contain China" strategy. In fact, anyone who studies Chinese history discovers that China was often economically strong, but neglected building its military strength because of a love of peace and social harmony that is deeply rooted in the culture. In 1820, during the Qing Dynasty, the Chinese GDP was about 30 percent of the world total, far higher than that of Great Britain and Japan at 5.2 percent and 3.1 percent, respectively. Nonetheless, China was defeated by the British and Japanese military in wars later.

Even today, Chinese military capability does not match its economic size and diplomatic position. Perhaps this is due to several factors including Chinese illusions regarding U.S. foreign policy, optimism about post Cold War international politics, or a passive response to China threat rhetoric. However, past experience demonstrates that peaceful development is not realized through dependence on other countries.

The U.S. has been a strong and dominant force since 1945 and the only superpower after the Cold War. It is understandable that America wants to maintain that position. It is, therefore, not surprising that the U.S. Defense Department's Quarterly Defense Report (DDQDR) in 2006, cited China as a potential military power and announced that the U.S. is investigating this possible future threat from China. The Pentagon report expressed concern over increased military spending on equipment to project power beyond Chinese borders.

As discussed previously, China is surrounded by fourteen neighboring countries and is relatively close geographically to several powerful countries including Australia, India, and Japan. Some of these nations possess nuclear power. In contrast, the U.S. is neighbor to weaker, peaceful countries and protected by the Pacific and Atlantic oceans. The two countries' geopolitical environments are vastly different.

China's official military budget for 2005 was US$30.96 billion following a decade of double digit annual increases. The U.S. DDQDR stated that the actual level of spending was several times higher. Pentagon estimates for 2005 put the figure at US$50-US$70 billion, which it said was the third highest military budget worldwide. [351] The DDQDR of 2006 differentiates between Chinese intentions and military capabilities, and between economic goals and development. It stresses that China is still at a crossroads. If properly guided, China may avoid any confrontation with the U.S. Fareed Zakaria of the *Newsweek* explained that the great debate in the 1970s was between the exceedingly low, but more realistic estimates of Soviet military power versus the more night-marish neo-conservative scenario. In his article, "The Year of Living Fearfully," [352] Zakaria reports that, in reality, even the lowest estimates of Soviet power were gross exaggerations.

China rejected the U.S. characterization of its military might as groundless. Beijing views U.S. accusations regarding the national defense development in China as interference with the nation's domestic affairs, increasing tensions, and misleading the public. Chinese Foreign Ministry spokesman, Kong Quan, responded, "We are an important force that promotes the peace and stability of the Asia-Pacific region and the world. . . . The United States should correct its wrong view and treat China's peaceful development in an objective and positive manner." [353] Beijing believes that U.S. government accusations harm efforts to improve China-U.S. cooperation. America should understand that in order for China to become a responsible stakeholder in world affairs, it must establish a military force that is proportionate to its defense needs and international status.

China's official 2006 military budget is US$35 billion. Comparing with the U.S. military budget of US$419 billion, about 50 percent of the world military spending, China has a relatively small military expense. Percentage-wise, China's figure is about 1.5 percent of its GDP and is lower than most of the industrialized nations' defense budgets of 2.5–5.0 percent. [354–359]

U.S. diplomacy has adopted a position that combines "contact" and "containment." On the "contact" side, China and the U.S. vow to restore comprehensive military ties. This was confirmed in a meeting between Chinese Defense Minister, Cao Gangchuan, and the Commander of the U.S. Pacific Command Admiral William Fallon, when they met in Beijing in May 2006. [360] Fallon said that the two forces would step up exchanges and contacts at all levels and promote mutual understanding and trust. Urging the U.S. to clearly oppose Taiwan independence, Cao called for an end to U.S.-Taiwan military contact and U.S. sales of weapons to Taiwan. "As the Taiwan issue has a bearing on the core interests of China, it will ensure the peace and stability of Taiwan on the basis of the One-China Principle and improve the relations across the Strait," Cao said. Here are the topics that deserve further analysis:

1. High-Level Military Exchanges

The mainland's top military officer, General Guo Boxiong, met briefly with President Bush and U.S. Secretary of Defense Donald Rumsfeld at the Pentagon in July 2006. This was the highest level military exchange between the two nations since a mid-air collision over Hainan in 2001 which strained relations. The meeting highlighted Sino-U.S. cooperation on issues such as North Korea and military matters, a sign of warming ties and closer military links. [361]

To enhance a high-level military exchange, mainland warships Qingdao, a Luhu-class guided missile cruiser, and the Hongzehu, a refueling ship, were scheduled to sail into Pearl Harbor, Hawaii, on September 6, 2006, for an exercise with the U.S. military. This was the first visit by a Chinese navy ship to a U.S. State in six years. China is responding to the U.S. demand to exhibit more military transparency so that common language, common protocols and common procedures can be built to avoid future problems. [362] The U.S. military leaders hope that the Qingdao's visit and other U.S.-China exchanges will give them further insight into China's military development. [363] Both Beijing and Washington agreed to continue military ship visits to each other's ports.

In 2006, the *New York Times* reporter, David Balvosa, wrote that

General Peter Pace, Chairman of the U.S. Joint Chiefs of Staff, played down any threat by China, saying more business ties with the U.S. will help prevent conflict. "I am very optimistic about the future. There [in business] the two countries share much in common."

Pace visited China in March 2007 to meet with China's top military authority. He toured military areas and institutions and reported that he did not perceive China as a threat. He commented further, "When you analyze potential military threat, you look for two things: capacity and intent. Clearly, both China and the United States have enormous military capacity. But neither has the intent to engage in war." [364]

China put forward proposals to strengthen communication between the two sides, including sending Chinese cadets to West Point, as well as participating in joint humanitarian and rescue-at-sea exercises. Pace urged his Chinese counterparts in meetings to provide more information about the aims of their military buildup. He called the meetings "encouraging," but said he did not get concrete answers. [365]

2. A Military "Horror Balance?"

During the first Taiwan Strait Crisis in 1954 and 1955 between the PRC and the ROC, U.S. military commanders supported Chiang Kai-shek in Taiwan and threatened to use nuclear weapons against the PRC. In the 1960 U.S. presidential campaign, the issue of whether to use nuclear weapons against China if the PRC invaded the Nationalist outposts was a matter of serious debate between the candidates, Nixon and Kennedy. Then, the PRC detonated its first atomic bomb on October 16, 1964. China became the fifth nuclear power following the U.S., the Soviet Union, Great Britain, and France. The official announcement in Beijing by the Chinese government stated:

> China exploded an atom bomb at 15:00 hours on October16, 1964, and thereby conducted successfully its first nuclear test. This is a major achievement of the Chinese people in their struggle to increase their national defense capability and oppose the U.S. Imperialist policy of nuclear blackmail and nuclear threats.

To defend oneself is the inalienable right of every sovereign state. And to safeguard world peace is the common task of all peace-loving countries. China cannot remain idle and do nothing in the face of the ever-increasing nuclear threat posed by the United States. China is forced to conduct nuclear tests and develop nuclear weapons.

The atomic bomb is a paper tiger. This famous saying by Chairman Mao Tse-tung [Zedong] is known to all. This was our view in the past and is still our view. China is developing nuclear weapons not because we believe in the omnipotence of nuclear weapons or because China plans to use nuclear weapons. The truth is exactly to the contrary. In developing nuclear weapons, China's aim is to break the nuclear monopoly of the nuclear powers and to eliminate nuclear weapons.

The Chinese Government hereby solemnly declares that China will never at any time and under any circumstances be the first to use nuclear weapons . . . .On the question of nuclear weapons, China will neither commit the error of adventure nor the error of capitulationism . . . .

We are convinced that nuclear weapons, which are after all created by man, will be eliminated by man.

On June 17, 1967, China tested the first hydrogen bomb, only thirty-two months after its first atomic bomb. Today, about sixty years later, its nuclear capability has improved substantially. China now has missiles that can carry nuclear warheads to western cities of the U.S. Nonetheless, China maintains a relatively small nuclear weapons arsenal. In contrast, because of the arms race with the Soviet Union during the Cold War from 1947 to 1991 and on-going development activities, the U.S. has accumulated enough nuclear weapons to destroy the entire Earth seven times.

On September 6, 2006, Beijing called on the E.U. to lift its seventeen-year-old arms embargo in advance of Premier Wen Jiabao's visit to the Asia-Europe Meeting in Finland. Chinese officials believe that the E.U. arms embargo on China is a legacy of the Cold War and they want to eliminate political discrimination as opposed to increasing arms sales.

Italian Prime Minister Romano Prodi said that his country was siding with France in support of an end to the E.U. ban on arms sales to China.

An arms embargo was imposed on Beijing after the 1989 Tiananmen Square crackdown. The twenty-five-member E.U. was divided on the issue. Many eastern European nations and Britain sided with the U.S. in supporting the continuation of the embargo. China views the lifting as a way to help forge closer ties with the E.U. in a constructive strategic partnership. The E.U. was the PRC's largest trading partner in 2004 and 2005, with total trade in the first half of 2006 of US$121 billion, up 21 percent over the previous year. Beijing was optimistic about the lifting of the arms embargo in 2005, but was disappointed later when the E.U. yielded to political and economic pressure exerted by the U.S.

Since the U.S. considers China a potential military adversary, both nations should manage the Taiwan issue with special care. China views the Taiwan issue a domestic affair left over after the Chinese Civil War between the CPC and the KMT, whereas the U.S. considers Taiwan its protectorate and maintains that its dominant presence in the Asia-Pacific arena is in its national interest.

The new U.S. Pacific Commander Navy Adm. Timothy Keating told reporters that many analysts and policy makers in Washington cast a wary eye at China: "While they [China] may achieve improved combat effectiveness in certain limited areas, their overall near peer status is a long way away. . . . We are watching carefully. We will work with them to the extent that is appropriate so as to be able to evaluate their military strategy and doctrine, tactics, techniques, and procedures, and stay ahead of them." Keating is responsible for U.S. military operations in an area stretching from New Zealand to North Korea. In contrast, U.S. Defense Secretary Robert Gates stated that he does not consider China a strategic adversary. [366]

3. A Possible Accident in Space

America is developing a series of weapons in space including some future laser weapons. China and the U.S. have many issues of concern to discuss on the topic of advanced space weaponry to avoid a future crisis there. When China initially wanted to participate in the international space station project, the U.S. rejected the request stating that China lacked the needed capital and technology.

But when China's technology improved to a level where it could contribute to the space station project, the U.S. rejected its request again. China was refused an opportunity to collaborate even though Brazil was accepted. Brazilian technological advances are not equal to those of China. On October 12, 2005, China successfully launched the Shenzhou-6 spacecraft. Most other nations congratulated China on this success, but the U.S. response was lukewarm and, in some cases, critical. Some conservative analysts regarded this event as a Chinese military equivalent of the Trojan horse. [367]

Despite these problems, Russia and China are actively cooperating on various space projects. The two nations are developing a set of 2007–2008 space cooperation guidelines. [368] After China launched the Shenzhou-6 spacecraft, Russia proposed to collaborate further with China on space projects. The core plan is to land on the moon jointly. During Hu Jintao's April 2006 visit to the U.S., both nations also agreed to collaborate on a space project to explore the moon [369] and Mars. [370] Russia plans to launch a spacecraft in 2009 that will carry Chinese made survey equipment. It will collect samples on Mars and its nearest moon. [371] China plans to launch Shenzhou-7 in September 2008, with three astronauts. [372] Under the manned space program, Chinese astronauts will conduct "module operations in outer space" including space walks and rendezvous, during the second stage of the program. [373] China also plans to place astronauts on the moon to collect soil samples in 2017. [374]

The *Christian Science Monitor* reported that the U.S. plans to send astronauts and materials to the moon and this project is expected to be completed before 2020. China shares a similar goal. [375] The U.S. said that it was interested in collaborating with China, but its deeds have not matched its words. The U.S. continued to practice a "China containment" policy. It rejected China's request for space collaboration and regards its space activities as suspicious. But keeping China isolated in space technology will not be effective, since China can get what it needs through collaboration with Brazil, Canada, Russia, and some European nations.

On January 11, 2007, China fired an anti-satellite missile that successfully destroyed one of China's own defunct satellites in space. In 1975, the Soviet Union successfully temporarily blinded two U.S. satellites that flew near Siberia by firing land-based anti-satellite laser weaponry. The Soviets were the first to launch a satellite into orbit around the Earth. There are an estimated 795 satellites in space today; of these 413 belong to the U.S. [376]

The White House waited a week until news of China's anti-satellite firing leaked and then issued only a mild expression of concern. Experts said that the test came as no surprise to the U.S. military, which had anticipated that China would develop an anti-satellite capability to put U.S. spy satellites at risk in the event of a conflict over the Taiwan Strait. Earlier missile shots failed to hit their target. U.S. countermeasures are cloaked in secrecy and difficult to assess. [377] "From what I understand, everybody knew that the Chinese were working on that and they [the U.S. military] had already taken the appropriate measures," said Vincent Sabathier, a senior fellow at the Center for Strategic and International Studies (CSIS). [378]

The virtual silence of the Pentagon regarding the Chinese test "is hard for me to understand except to conclude they already felt they had already dealt with this problem some time ago," said John Like, Director of GlobalSecurity.org. [379] According to some of the U.S. research information, the U.S. military had already combined its military research with space technologies. For example, there is the development of lighter than 10 kg nano-satellites, which can be launched into space for surveillance purposes, and as needed, can be reassembled robotically to change their function. [380]

China claims that its space research is intended for scientific and peaceful purposes. In a nationally televised news conference, Chinese Premier Wen Jiabao said that China favors a treaty banning the use of arms in space. "China's position on the peaceful utilization of outer space remains unchanged," and "China targets or threatens no other country and breaches no international treaties in its anti-satellite tests in outer space," he said. [381–382] However, judging from the rising risk of a military conflict in the Taiwan Strait, an anti-satellite missile test signals that China is prepared to deter any foreign intervention on this issue. [383]

China has been a strong supporter of the Outer Space Treaty, which aims to prevent nuclear weapons or any other weapons of mass destruction being put into orbit. "What China has been doing is taking the lead for about ten years now, trying to strengthen the Outer Space Treaty to reserve space for peaceful uses. At the United Nations, China has been in the lead in trying to press this forward, and in fact, at the U.N. General Assembly committees, has repeatedly, year after year, voted for this," according to Professor Noam Chomsky. [384]

In the summer 2004 issue of *Daedalus*, the Journal of the Academy of Arts and Sciences, strategic analysts John Steinbruner and Nancy Gallagher warned that the aggressive militarism of the Bush administration, particularly, and U.S. policy generally, is driving the world towards what they call ultimate doom. [385]

" . . . and you develop a capacity to attack them. How are they going to respond? They'll respond by defending themselves, and the defense is, in fact, developing offensive weapons capabilities. So, sure, that is an action-reaction cycle, continuing escalating the threat of war. In this case, war would be terminal," said Professor Noam Chomsky. [386]

President Bush authorized a new U.S. National Space Policy on August 31, 2006. The new policy rejects arms-control agreements that might limit U.S. flexibility in space and asserts a right to deny access to space to anyone "hostile to U.S. national interest." [387] The Henry Stimson Center, a nonpartisan think tank that follows the space-weaponry issue, said that the policy change will reinforce international suspicion that the U.S. may seek to develop, test, and deploy space weapons. A number of nations including China and Russia have pushed for talks to ban space weapons, and the U.S. has long been one of a handful of nations opposed to the idea. In October 2006, the U.S. voted for the first time in U.N. history against a call for negotiations of a space weapon ban—the only "no" among 160 "yes" votes.

It would be very short-sighted for the U.S. to monopolize space related technologies and other advances. Although the U.S. is still the giant in research and development worldwide, failure to collaborate with China is not in its best interests. Productive collaboration benefits both nations. To avoid any potential future crisis, the world countries should abide by the Outer Space Treaty signed (effective on October 10, 1967) to ban the signatories' placement of nuclear weapons or any other weapons of mass destruction in orbit around Earth, and engage in dialogue to build trust for world peace.

4. The Taiwan Issue

As discussed, the Taiwan issue has been a thorn in China-U.S. relations. Viewed superficially, Taiwan is a triangular issue among China, the U.S., and Taiwan. It is, in reality, a China-U.S. issue, or more precisely just an American issue. In fact, losing Taiwan does not threaten core U.S. national interests, since Taiwan does not possess energy or other strategic resources that merit military conflict. For China, however, Taiwan is of major importance. No Chinese national leader could still stay in power, if the PRC let Taiwan succeed in establishing formal independence.

From the Chinese point of view, China without Taiwan is one of the two countries in the world that are not unified completely. As China grows in strength, the demand of its 1.3 billion people for a unified nation increases significantly. Eventually, the U.S. must determine how it will manage this critical issue. In the meantime, China will pursue its extraordinary economic development opportunity. China has acquired substantial new power and authority in the world economy. To avoid conflict, much of the world opposes independence for Taiwan. Currently, there are 169 world nations that recognize the PRC as the one and only China and Taiwan as part of it; whereas just twenty-four nations have formal diplomatic relationships with the ROC in Taiwan. Since 1949, America has been the strongest supporter of Taiwan.

A brief summary of the major China-U.S.-Taiwan events since the end of World War II follows:

1948–1949 The U.S. supported Chiang Kai-shek: The U.S. assisted Chiang Kai-shek in a conflict against the Chinese communists on the mainland of China.

1950 An attempt to assassinate Mao Zedong failed: The CIA plotted an assassination attempt to bomb Mao Zedong's train on his way to the Soviet Union. Taiwanese spies were implicated.

1950 The U.S. recognized the ROC as China: While the U.S. recognized Chiang Kai-shek's government in Taiwan (Formosa) as the sole legitimate government for all of China,

President Harry S. Truman announced on January 5, 1950, that the U.S. would not become involved in the dispute regarding the Taiwan Strait and would not intervene in the event of an attack by the PRC. However, after the outbreak of the Korean War on June 25, 1950, Truman declared the neutralization of the Straits of Formosa and sent in the Seventh Fleet of the U.S. Navy to prevent any conflict between the ROC and the PRC, effectively putting Taiwan under American protection. In August 1950, the U.S. Thirteenth Aviation Regiment was stationed in Taiwan.

1953 The Korean War ended: A few months before the end of the Korean War on July 27, 1953, President Dwight D. Eisenhower lifted the Seventh Fleet's blockade on February 2, 1953.

1954–1955 The first Taiwan Strait crisis took place: Following the declaration by PRC Premier Zhou Enlai that Taiwan must be liberated, a war broke out between the PRC and the ROC from August 11, 1954, to May 1, 1955. On September 12, 1954, General Douglas McArthur recommended the possible use of nuclear weapons against the PRC. In November, Chinese airplanes bombed the Tachen islands. U.S. President Dwight D. Eisenhower, however, resisted pressure to use nuclear weapons or involve American troops in China's civil conflict. Instead, on December 2, 1954, the U.S. and the ROC agreed to a mutual defense treaty which did not apply to islands along the Chinese mainland, while the PLA and the Nationalist Army continued fighting until February 1955.

The U.S. Secretary of State, John Foster Dulles, stated publicly that the U.S. was seriously considering a nuclear strike against China. British Prime Minister Winston Churchill and NATO Foreign Ministers warned against such action. In late March 1955, Eisenhower was planning to "get rid of China's military potential." Finally, due to the lack of a nuclear defense capability and the willingness of the Soviets to threaten nuclear retaliation for any attack on the PRC, the PRC backed down under the U.S. pressure.

1958 The second Taiwan Strait crisis took place: This was a continuation of the first Taiwan Strait crisis. This time the PRC was accused by the ROC of initiating the shelling of the islands of Quemoy (Kimen) and Matsu in the Taiwan Strait on August 23. The war continued for forty-four days and cost approximately 1,000 lives.

Faced with a stalemate, the PRC called a unilateral cease-fire on October 6 and issued a "Message to the Compatriots in Taiwan," which called for a peaceful solution to the Taiwan issue and all Chinese to reunite against the "American plot to divide China." Afterwards, the two sides continued a propaganda assault on alternate days of the week and this strange informal arrangement continued until the normalization of ties between the U.S. and the PRC in 1979.

1971 The One-China Principle was acknowledged: The ROC was originally recognized as the sole legitimate government of both the mainland and Taiwan by the U.S. and most other nations. However, on October 25, 1971, the U.N. General Assembly passed Resolution 2758, which in effect expelled the ROC and placed the PRC in the China seat on the Security Council and all other U.N. organs. Most countries now recognize that there is one China; Taiwan is part of China; and that the PRC is the sole legitimate representative of China.

1972 The Bamboo Curtain was lifted: During the Cold War against the Soviet block, the U.S. realized that, to change the tense predicament, it must collaborate with China. This strategic change resulted in the legendary visit of President Richard M. Nixon and Secretary of State Henry A. Kissinger to Beijing in February 1972 and the development of a triangular political relationship among the U.S., China and the Soviet Union. The lifting of the bamboo curtain in 1972 enabled comprehensive participation by China in the economic globalization and benefited the U.S. and the world economy tremendously.

1975 Chiang Kai-shek died: His son Chiang Ching-kuo became president in 1978. Later he embarked on educational reform as well as infrastructure and industrial development that transformed Taiwan from an agricultural economy to a commercial and industrial one. Taiwan earned itself a spot in East Asia as one of the four economic powers along with Hong Kong, Singapore, and South Korea. Chiang Ching-kuo lifted martial law in 1987 that had been imposed on Taiwan since 1949 and allowed formation of other political parties. In 1986, the Democratic Progressive Party (DPP) was inaugurated as the first opposition party in the ROC.

1978 China sought a market economy: Deng Xiaoping visited the U.S. where he announced opening China as a market economy and encouraged foreign investments. Sino-U.S. trade increased annually and by 2005 America became the second largest trading partner of the PRC. China invests a huge portion of its foreign exchange reserves in U.S. Treasury Bonds and had US$232.5 billion trade surplus with the U.S. in 2006.

1979 The Joint Communiqué on the establishment of diplomatic relations between the PRC and the U.S. unveiled: The U.S. and the PRC agreed to recognize each other and to establish diplomatic relations as of January 1, 1979. "The United States of America recognizes the government of the People's Republic of China as the sole legal government of China. Within this context, the people of the United States will maintain cultural, commercial, and other unofficial relations with the people of Taiwan. . . . The government of the United States of America acknowledges the Chinese position that there is but one China and Taiwan is part of China." The U.S. subsequently terminated its diplomatic relationship with the ROC.

1979 The Taiwan Relations Act passed: On April 1, 1979, about three months after the U.S. and the PRC established diplomatic relations, the U.S. Congress passed the Taiwan Relations Act. This was designed to continue the relationship between the U.S. and the Taiwanese people. The Taiwan Relations Act eliminated the Mutual Defense Treaty. However, the Act stated that "The absence of diplomatic relations or recognition shall not affect the application of the laws of the United States with respect to Taiwan, and the laws of the United States shall apply with respect to Taiwan in the manner that the laws of the United States applied with respect to Taiwan prior to January 1, 1979."

The U.S. government has adhered to this law and has continued to provide Taiwan with arms and has guaranteed Taiwan's security. According to this Act, the American Institute in Taiwan (AIT), which operates in Washington, D.C. and Taiwan, organized the Coordination Council of North American Affairs (now known as the Taipei Economic and Cultural Representative Office) in the U.S. to handle matters on both sides. On April 16, 1979, the AIT office in Taipei officially began operations.

1982 China-U.S. August 17 Communiqué unveiled: In order to solve the issue of the U.S. arms sales to Taiwan, the U.S. and the Chinese government have conducted negotiations and finally reached an agreement on August 17, 1982. Both unveiled the third Sino-U.S. Joint Communiqué. In the Communiqué, the U.S. government stated that "It does not seek to carry out a long-term policy of arms sales to Taiwan, that its arms sales to Taiwan will not exceed, either in qualitative or in quantitative terms, the level of those supplied in recent years since the establishment of diplomatic relations between the United States and China, and that it intends to reduce gradually its sales of arms to Taiwan, leading over a period of time to a final resolution." However, for more than twenty years, the U.S. government has sold huge amounts of arms to Taiwan. The continuous U.S. arms sales to Taiwan have all along been viewed by the PRC as a barrier to resolving the Taiwan issue.

1988 Chiang Ching-kuo died: Lee Teng-hui became the President of the ROC (1988–2000). Under Lee, Taiwan underwent a process of localization and de-Sinicization (eliminate Chinese influence) in which only local culture and history were promoted and the cross-strait relations suffered serious setbacks. [388]

1995–1996 The third Taiwan Strait crisis took place: The PRC launched a series of missile tests in the waters surrounding Taiwan including the Taiwan Strait from July 21, 1995, to March 23, 1996. The first set of missiles was fired in mid to late 1995 intending to send a strong signal to the ROC government under the pro-independence Lee Teng-hui government. Lee's act was seen as moving ROC's foreign policy away from the One-China policy. The cause was the U.S. approval of a visa for Lee to visit Cornell University as an alumnus. This was after the U.S. initially assured the PRC that a visa for Lee would be "inconsistent with [the U.S.'s] unofficial relationship [with Taiwan]." The U.S. response to the missile tests was low key: The USS Nimitz just passed through the Taiwan Strait in December 1995.

The second set of missiles was fired in early 1996 when Lee was running for reelection. It was intended to intimidate the Taiwanese electorate in the run-off for the 1996 presidential election. In this case, the USS Nimitz Carrier Battle Group, steamed at high speed from the Persian Gulf sending two carrier battle groups which displayed a readiness to fight on the part of the U.S.

1999 Lee Teng-hui revealed the Taiwan independence stance: The 1999 Taiwan confrontation began on July 9, 1999, when President Lee Teng-hui responded to questions by saying that "The Republic of China has been a sovereign state since it was founded in 1911. Moreover, in 1991, amendments to the Constitution designated cross-strait relations as a special state-to-state relationship. Consequently, there is no need to declare independence. The resolution of cross-strait issues hinges on the issue of different systems. [. . .] The Chinese mainland's 'one country, two systems' formula for Hong Kong and Macao is irrelevant to Taiwan . . . Formosa is a sovereign, independent state." In response, President William J. Clinton reiterated that Washington's One-China Principle had not changed.

2000 Chen Shui-bian was the first non-KMT president elected (2000–present): The DPP replaced the aging KMT to become the ruling party, thus completing Taiwan's peaceful political transformation. In Chen's inaugural speech, he said that he would not declare independence nor do anything else that China might consider provocative as long as Beijing does not use force against the island. This was the main content of his "Four Noes and One Without."

2002 Chen Shui-bian proposed "One Country on Each Side:" Cross-strait relations deteriorated further with this proposal. The Chen Shui-bian government completely ignored the fact that the mainland of China had become Taiwan's primary source of economic support. Taiwan's GDP growth had been over 8 percent annually for over fifty years, but after Chen Shui-bian became the president, it grew at most 3–4 percent annually and had a decline in 2001. For the past seven years (from 2000 to 2007), the DPP government produced serious budget deficits and incurred heavy debts. According to a rough estimate, the national total assets have shrunk about US$1 trillion. [389] Today, the Taiwanese trade surplus is derived almost entirely from the mainland and its economic growth lags behind the other three Asian economic powers like Hong Kong, Singapore, and South Korea. Most businesses have moved to the mainland of China to survive and make profits. Taiwan is facing economic, political, and diplomatic isolation.

2005 KMT Chairman Lien Chan traveled to the Chinese mainland: During his visit, the KMT and the CPC ended six decades of hostility. The Hu-Lien meeting reached consensus on five issues for the cross-strait peace exchange and the KMT's popularity reached new heights. The Taiwanese attitude towards the PRC changed and cross-strait tensions gradually relaxed.

2005 China as a "Responsible Stakeholder" was proposed: On September 21, 2006, the U.S. Deputy Secretary of States Robert Bruce Zoellick spoke in New York at the National Committee on U.S.-China Relations. The subject was "Whither China: From Membership to Responsibility," which shed new light on U.S. expectations on merging China into the international community and on ways for China to become a responsible stakeholder. [390] Zoellick may represent those who wish to integrate China into the Western community using a less aggressive approach by pushing it to follow the game plan defined primarily by the U.S. after World War II. Others recommend that the U.S. maintain a containment strategy. Unilateralism and pre-emptive militarism have regained popularity in the Bush administration, a decade after the end of the Cold War.

2006 Hu Jintao visited the U.S.: On April 20, 2006, Chinese President Hu Jintao made his first visit to the U.S. As a result, China-U.S. relations improved and a new level of understanding was reached.

2006 Chen Shui-bian abolished the National Unification Council (NUC) and the National Unification Guidelines (NUG): This was a symbol of abolishing the aim of reunification with the mainland of China.

2007 Chen Shui-bian made new pledge of "Four Wants and One Without:" The Pledge broke the "Four Noes and One Without" promise in his inaugural speech on May 20, 2000 (please see Exhibit 2). Taiwan's stock market dropped precipitously the next day. His pledge infringed upon American national interests as argued by various politicians and scholars including John Warner (Republican Rep; Va.), Jeffrey A. Bader (Brookings Institution), and Bonnie Glaser (CSIS).

Exhibit 2

Sets forth evolving political and policy changes from 2000 to 2007

— THEN — Four Noes and One Without Year 2000	— NOW — Four Wants and One Without Year 2007
1. Taiwan will not declare independence	1. Taiwan wants independence
2. Taiwan will not hold referendums on Taiwan's nationhood	2. Taiwan wants a new Constitution
3. Taiwan will not change its national title	3. Taiwan wants to rectify its title
4. Taiwan will not enshrine "state-to-state" relations with China in the Constitution	4. Taiwan wants development
5. Taiwan will not abolish the NUC and the NUG	5. There is no left-right political axis in Taiwan, just the question of independence or unification

2007 A Draft of the Second Republic Constitution was proposed: The draft states that Taiwan's jurisdiction "covers Taiwan, Penghu, Kimen, Matsu, and offshore islands," and "any change to the political relationship between the Republic of China and the People's Republic of China must be decided by negotiations between the two sides based on equality and peace, pending the Taiwanese approval." The draft sparked fierce disputes in Taiwan. [391] The basic principle of the Second Republic Constitution is to seek *de jure* Taiwan independence. If it were passed, the Chinese mainland would have no alternative, based on the ASL, but to resort to non-peaceful methods to resolve the Taiwan problem. [392]

Modern history illustrates that the U.S. treated Taiwan as a protectorate. However, for the PRC, Taiwan is part of China, and the long separation of the mainland and Taiwan is a domestic issue. America does not have to get involved in China's domestic affairs, if America so decides. The Sino-U.S. developments have converted relations from hostility to an economic partnership with shared mutual interests. Nonetheless, the Taiwan issue remains a problem that has persisted over fifty years. Chen Shui-bian's stance has put the U.S. in a precarious position. [393] While U.S. military strength is far superior to China's, America can no longer be assured of military success despite its dominant role in international affairs. Sooner or later, the U.S. must decide how it wants to manage this sensitive problem to avoid a nightmarish confrontation with China.

5. From Strategic Ambiguity to Strategic Clarity

U.S. handling of cross-strait affairs has been consistent for over a decade. Although varying slightly, the U.S. has not deviated from the One-China Principle. Any variance was based totally on U.S. self-interest and needs.

President Clinton remarked that the One-China concept is an important policy accepted throughout seven presidential terms and by both political parties. In the 1990s, facing increasingly complicated and sensitive cross-strait relations, American experts on the Taiwan Strait suggested that keeping a vague strategy of "no reunification, no independence, and no war" would conform best to the American interests. It could keep Beijing in the dark about Washington's true intentions and simultaneously, scare Taiwan away from acting rashly. [394] Furthermore, by playing the "Taiwan card," the U.S. could intimidate the PRC. However, this kind of policy has encouraged Lee Teng-hui, provoked the 1995 Taiwan Strait tensions, and led eventually to the Taiwan Strait crisis in the spring of 1996.

In 1997, Clinton proposed the Strategic Alliance concept with the PRC and in 1998 he espoused the Three Noes. All these actions were an attempt to revise the policy of strategic ambiguity. In July 1999, after Lee Teng-hui unveiled the two-state theory, the Taiwan Strait rhetoric surfaced again and Washington soon replaced strategic ambiguity with strategic clarity.

During the reelection campaign of President Bush in 2000, neo-conservative advisors Paul Wolfowitz and Richard Lee Armitage, openly acknowledged the necessity of a clear strategic policy on Taiwan, since Chen Shui-bian had pressed ahead aggressively to develop Taiwan as an independent, sovereign country despite the risk of war with China. [395] They proposed that, if Taiwan declares independence unilaterally, it should not expect U.S. support; if the PRC attacks Taiwan without cause, it would face retaliation from the U.S.

In April 2001, the China-U.S. mid-air collision incident occurred. The newly elected President Bush stated that he "will try all he can to help Taiwan's self-defense." The U.S. Senate and House subsequently passed bills supporting Taiwan to become an observer member of the WHO. At this stage, China-U.S. relations were at a low tide. In less than two years, the attitude of President Bush had apparently changed. When he first met the new Chinese leader Hu Jintao, he reiterated that he would not support Taiwan independence, but on the subject of Taiwan, he said that "If necessary, the U.S. would help make possible Taiwan's self-defense."

Regardless of what these theories were, all people acknowledged that the current U.S. Taiwan Strait policy was "one China, two principles," namely, not in support of Taiwan independence and opposing the use of force. This is the *status quo* of "no reunification, no independence, and no war" defined by Washington.

Following the growing political and economic strength of the PRC, the U.S. realized that if Sino-U.S. relations continued to deteriorate due to the unsettled Taiwan issue, American economic and security interests would suffer. For this reason, the U.S. places increasing emphasis on Sino-U.S. relations rather than on Taiwan-U.S. relations. The U.S. clearly realized that the only situation that could derail Sino-U.S relations is military confrontation across the Taiwan Strait. If the U.S. were to still support "two Chinas" or "one China on each side," the ensuing trouble would outweigh any benefits. Although the U.S. continues to sell arms to Taiwan and opposes the use of force by the PRC, the U.S. is more concerned that an independence movement by Taiwan would compel the U.S. into an unnecessary military confrontation with the PRC.

6. The Cross-Strait Relations

During the fifty-eight year separation between the PRC and the ROC, the PRC's policy towards Taiwan has undergone different stages to minimize U.S. control: From the first stage of militarily liberating Taiwan in 1949–1970, through the second stage of peaceful liberation that lasted until the late 1970s, to the peaceful reunification and "one country, two systems" stage after the 1970s up to the present. [396] The PRC has never renounced the use of force in resolving the Taiwan issue.

The conditions that the PRC has developed that would trigger the use of force to recover Taiwan are summarized as follows:

If Taiwan should declare independence

If Taiwan should descend into turmoil

If Taiwan should develop nuclear weapons

If Taiwan should become a base for foreign military forces

If Taiwan should refuse to negotiate for unification within a
reasonable (yet undefined) time frame

To curtail the Taiwan independence movement and counterbalance
the Taiwan Relations Act, the PRC announced the adoption of the ASL
at the Third Plenum of the Tenth National People's Congress in March
2005. It is intended to clearly delineate acceptable parameters on the
Taiwan issue.

The adoption of the ASL by the PRC is, in its spirit, similar to the
U.S. 1861 stipulation of Anti-Secession Resolutions of the New York
legislature, which dealt with the eight southern states that tried to break
off from the Union (passed by the New York State Assembly,
01/11/1861). Chinese President Hu Jintao and other leaders have
portrayed the new law as a needed check on Taiwan's independence
activists including President Chen Shui-bian. Without the law to impede
him, officials have said that Chen could take one step too many to
produce a military conflict nobody wants. [397, 398]

7. Chen Shui-bian Plays with Fire

Chen Shui-bian's term as president will expire in 2008. Before he
loses the grip of power, he continues to provoke Beijing over Taiwan
independence, thus playing with fire:

- On January 1, 2007, Chen's New Year message proclaimed
  that "Taiwan is a part of the world, not China." This seriously violated the One-China Principle recognized by the
  world community. China condemned his remarks and
  warned the U.S. that 2007 would be the most dangerous
  year for sustaining cross-strait peace and stability. It is regret-
  ful that following Chen's declaration, the U.S. granted him
  transit permission to stay in San Francisco and Los Angeles
  en route to Nicaragua.

- On February 2, 2007, Chen said that Taiwan should "act

now" to draw up a new Constitution; otherwise it "cannot be called a normal, complete, and progressive new democracy." U.S. Deputy Secretary of State John Negroponte said that there is a "distinct possibility" that such a proposed new charter would be at "cross purposes" with America's one-China policy.

- On February 8, 2007, Chen began a new round of de-Sinicizing moves by eliminating the words "China" or "Chinese" from the island's government-run organizations, enterprises, and from certain laws and regulations. While 55 percent of the Taiwanese people did not support this move, only 21 percent showed approval; 64 percent thought it would incur huge social cost. On February 9, 2007, U.S. State Department spokesman Sean McCormack rebuked Chen's move stating that his act was "unhelpful," and "the United States does not support changes in terminology for entities administered by Taiwan authorities." He avoided addressing the question of whether or not Chen's action altered the status quo unilaterally. Chen's interpretation of the low key U.S. response was that the U.S. government "does not support (his actions), but proffers tacit approval." In other words, lack of support does not mean opposition.

- On March 18, 2007, Chen Shui-bian accepted a draft of the Second Republic Constitution. The draft states Taiwan's jurisdiction covers Taiwan, Penghu, Kimen, Matsu, and offshore islands. The draft sparked fierce disputes in Taiwan. The basic principle of the Second Republic Constitution is to seek *de jure* Taiwan independence. If it is passed, the Chinese mainland will have no alternative, based on its ASL, but to resort to non-peaceful methods to resolve the Taiwan problem.

- On July 6, 2007, in an interview with the *Washington Post* reporter Edward Cody, Chen Shui-bian said that Taiwan will press ahead with a controversial referendum on whether the self-ruled island should apply for U.N. membership under the name Taiwan, dismissing U.S. objections. [399]

At Chen's request, the U.S. Government approved a US$421 million sale of Advanced Medium Range Air-to-Air missiles and Maverick missiles to Taiwan to support his government. These weapons will enable Taiwan to launch attacks reaching as far as China's Yangtze River Three Gorges Dam. The U.S. is also making active war preparations by shifting major military forces to the Asia-Pacific region. Meanwhile, Beijing's sudden willingness to showcase its sophisticated weaponry may be a belief that only a credible military threat can deter Taiwan's independence movement.

In his new book, *Rising Star: China's New Security: Diplomacy and Its Implications for the United States*, Bates Gill, describes Beijing's new policy towards Taiwan as a "combination of intensified carrots and intensified sticks." Beijing is trying to create a new diplomatic strategy" so that it can realize national reunification, preferably through diplomatic and economic means." At the same time, "under the rubric or umbrella of a more benign and constructive set of policies," Beijing is moving ahead aggressively to build its military "to use that option if it needs to." Will Washington be able to rein in Chen Shui-bian? Or will it continue to sell advanced weapons and send the wrong signals to Taiwan to increase the tension?

Dissatisfied with Chen's provocative political activities that have increased the cross-strait tension, the U.S. government is responding to its State Department request to temporarily suspend the sale of 66 F-16s fighter jets to Taiwan. Under the worst situation, the deal will be delayed until the 2008 presidential election in Taiwan is over. [400]

8. Chen Shui-bian Has Neither Integrity Nor Political Merit

Corruption accounted for the DPP's defeat in Taiwan's 2005 local elections. But this was only the tip of the iceberg for much larger and more widespread scandals directly related to Chen Shui-bian were discovered a few months later. Chen Shui-bian is under investigation over the alleged embezzlement of NT$36 million (about US$1.11 million) in state funds. His son-in-law, Chao Chien-ming, is sentenced to a seven-year prison term for insider trading. Chen's wife, Wu Shu-chen, is being investigated over allegations that she accepted NT$5 million (about US$150,000) in department store gift vouchers in exchange for securing favors. And Chen Shui-bian's former chief aide, Chen Che-nan, has been charged with corruption. [401] The people of Taiwan can no longer tolerate Chen Shi-bian's kleptocracy; they think that he should assume responsibility for corruption and scandals by stepping down.

In 2006, he survived a major protest known as the One Million People Campaign to Oust Corruption led by Shih Ming-teh, the former chairman and founder of the DPP. He also survived several attempts to oust him: 1) a legislative vote to oust him initiated by opposition lawmakers on June 27, 2006; 2) demands made by several people and a larger group established by Shih Ming-teh, for Chen's resignation. [402] The DPP's basic support rate was a relatively low 35 percent, but Chen remains in power.

Chen Shui-bian has done very poorly in his six years of leadership of Taiwan. There are five characteristics of his government: 1) inept governance; 2) lack of understanding of economic principles; 3) poor diplomatic skills; 4) failure of leadership of the DPP; and 5) corrupt practices. Further, he is adept in methods of inciting ethnic hatred, and provoking the Chinese mainland. [403]

Taiwan's recent TVBS survey showed that more than 50 percent of the Taiwanese people did not support Taiwan independence and 56 percent worried about the cross-strait tensions. As *Time* Magazine's Man of the Year, Chen Shui-bian was portrayed as having a corrupt government and as a "trouble maker generally acknowledged by the international community." A meager 16 percent of the population was satisfied with his performance. Taiwan's opposition party KMT warned that Chen moves towards step-by-step, *de jure* independence. If he succeeds in stirring a military clash with China and drags America into war, he could call off the 2008 presidential election and declare himself to be the first President of the Republic of Taiwan. But what will be the fate of the

Taiwanese people? Will Chen's son and daughter be willing to fight a war for Taiwan independence?

The current political situation in Taiwan shows that social and political chaos will prevail in the absence of democratic elections and without the rule of law, a judicial system, a leader with integrity, and executable anti-corruption regulations. Perhaps the U.S. is also feeling somewhat embarrassed to see Taiwan's present political crisis, since America once praised democratic progress and the development of Taiwan as a role model for other Asia-Pacific nations.

Taiwan's trade surplus with the PRC reached US$58 billion in 2005 and climbed to US$70 billion in 2006, which constituted about 80 percent of Taiwan's GDP in recent years. The officially registered Taiwan investment in the PRC is US$42 billion, but the actual investment far exceeds this amount. There are about 700,000–800,000 Taiwanese businessmen residing in the mainland. The number of Taiwanese residing in the mainland may be closer to two million, if family members are included. Clearly the Taiwanese economy depends heavily on the PRC. Although political differences continue to hinder the reunification of China, other trends indicate economic integration with the mainland as the only solution to prevent any marginalization of Taiwan in the future. It would not be surprising to see a *de facto* cross-strait reunification before a *de jure* one in the foreseeable future. Unless the Taiwan pro-independence political leaders step over the "red line," there is no reason to speculate that the PRC would take over Taiwan through military means.

9. Will There Be a Taiwan Strait Crisis Again?

To stymie Taiwanese independence, the U.S. government, thus far, only issued mild verbal rebukes to Chen. On the contrary, there was proposed legislation Resolution 73 by Representative Thomas Tancredo and others on February 16, 2007, expressing "the sense of Congress that the United States should resume normal diplomatic relations with Taiwan (the Republic of China)."

Moreover, U.S. Pacific Commander Admiral Timothy Keating

emphasized that the U.S. should be prepared to step in to protect Taiwan should the need arise, even though some members of Congress warned that Taiwan has sometimes gone out of its way to provoke a hostile confrontation with China in an attempt to declare independence. [404] It is unfortunate that members of the U.S. administration support Taiwan. This explains why Chen Shui-bian promotes Taiwan independence and holds on to power. If China is treated as an enemy, it will become a real adversary.

Ernest Hemingway, the Nobel Literature Laureate, published *For Whom The Bell Tolls*, a best seller in 1941, in which he described his experiences in the Spanish Civil War. Many European countries were dragged into this war by taking sides. Will a similar military conflict take place between Taiwan and China, which would include the active participation of the U.S. and surrounding nations for the discredited Chen Shui-bian? If it were to happen, Taiwan would naturally suffer the first and heaviest blow and the Chinese and the Americans could unfortunately become enemies for generations to come.

Under the worst scenario, war could develop between the U.S. and China with Taiwan as the battleground in several ways: 1) military intimidation; 2) limited local war; 3) full scale war; and 4) nuclear war. War typically begins with military intimidation, as each side prepares for war. Next, a limited local war breaks out. If the PRC quickly seizes control of Taiwan's airspace, before U.S. intervention, a larger conflict may be avoided.

If after twenty-four hours U.S. aircrafts arrive and control Taiwanese airspace, Japan will become involved because of the U.S.-Japan security alliance. As soon as conflict begins between China and Japan, limited war will cease and a comprehensive attack could begin against the PRC or vice versa. Once the war reaches the state of a full scale war, there is a real danger of escalation to a nuclear war. [405–409]

It is questionable whether the U.S. could handle multiple battlegrounds that would include Iraq, Afghanistan, Taiwan, and Iran (a possibility) at the same time without vulnerability to Middle East terrorists. But whether the U.S. attacks Iran can be used also as a barometer for predicting the likelihood of a Sino-U.S. war, if Taiwan declares formal independence in 2008. The price to pay for a war against China would be unimaginably high and lack any real gain in energy or other resources that could compensate for its cost. Moreover, how would the world manage the millions of war refugees in East Asia? The destruction to U.S. soil could be the worst ever in history. For Taiwan, the cost of war would be so high that any gains will be outweighed by losses. China and Hong Kong would be devastated and it could take years to recover their infra-structures, economies, and external trade links.

China cannot be compared, in a meaningful way, to Iraq or Afghanistan in terms of military strength, size, technical, and human resources. Thus, any accurate estimates of relative military capabilities would be irrelevant and misleading. What we do know is that a war between China and the U.S. would have no winner. Therefore, a peaceful resolution of any conflict across the Taiwan Strait should be the only effective solution to disentangling the Taiwan issue.

10. Conclusions

China is not a cultural, political, economic, or military threat to the U.S. It is far behind the U.S. in terms of national strength on many levels. China's greatest priority today is advocacy of a peaceful and harmonious society to enhance coexistence and economic development.

New studies by the Chicago Council on Global Affairs entitled "Global Views 2006: China Topline Report" was published on October 11, 2006.

The survey reveals that 1) Asians, including Indians, South Koreans, and Australians, are quite comfortable with the rise of China. However, these countries and the Chinese still want the U.S. to remain engaged in Asia though they express low trust in the U.S. to act responsibly; 2) Americans see China catching up with the U.S. economically, and don't favor trying to stop it; 3) In China, a very large majority is enthusiastic about playing an active role in world affairs (87 percent) and nine in ten favor China becoming more powerful economically and militarily; 4) Chinese see themselves as the second great power in the world today and becoming the equal of the U.S. within ten years; 5) Seventy-eight percent of Chinese see their government structure as an economic advantage; 6) Majorities in all surveyed countries believe that at some point the U.S. will be equaled or overtaken by another country in power; 7) Sixty-one percent of Americans believe that China will ultimately catch up with the U.S. economically; 8) Americans also seem to accept the rise of China: 54 percent think it would be equally positive and negative if China's economy becomes as large as the U.S. economy and only 26 percent say that the U.S. should actively work to limit the growth of the China's power. Seventy-five percent favor friendly cooperation and engagement with China; 9) Seventy-five percent of Americans believe it would be mainly negative if China became significantly more powerful militarily; and 10) Eighty-eight percent of Americans and South Koreans, and 72 percent of Indians think the growth of Chinese military power will be a potential source of conflict between major powers in Asia. (For more information on this survey, please visit www.thechicagocouncil.org for "Global Views 2006: China Topline Report").

Americans distinguish clearly between rising Chinese economic power, with which they are comfortable, and military power, with which they are less comfortable, despite America's own military supremacy. A forty-seven-nation survey on global opinions released on June 27, 2007, by the Pew Global Project Attitudes project reported that 1) China is generally viewed favorably in Asia, the exception is Japan; 2) Europeans have become much more critical of China; 3) In the Americas, views of China are either favorable or mixed; in the U.S. the public is split evenly with 42 percent favorable and 39 percent unfavorable; 4) Across Africa, favorable views of China outnumber critical judgments. Most of the public surveyed view China's growing military power with concern, but continue to see China's economic growth as a good thing for their own country.

After reading this book, hopefully, people of the world can better understand the necessity of China's military modernization for the purpose of guaranteeing a secure environment for its peaceful development and deterring Taiwan independence activities.

The goal of the book is to discredit the China threat theory from cultural, historic, economic, political, and military perspectives. An examination of the political background and history of the China threat theory demonstrate that the rhetoric is largely propaganda without solid foundation. What, then, is the best option for the U.S.?

In his book, *Blueprint for Action*, Thomas P. M. Barnett presents a brilliant strategy and analysis of the economic progress and growing strength of China. [410] In addition, he sets forth an effective plan for peaceful cooperation with China. In referring to the rise of China, he writes:

> The sight of such rising power has and will naturally generate much fear in the West, but this fear is misguided . . . .
>
> If the United States is committed to winning a global war on terrorism by defending globalization's progressive development of the planet, then our blueprint for action must obviously list somewhere near the top the following task: locking China in at today's prices. By that I mean securing a long-term strategic partnership with China on security affairs now, while Beijing's prices remain relatively low, rather than putting off the inevitable for another twenty years only to pay through the nose at some later date . . .
>
> In a generation's time China will dominate the global economy just as much as the United States does today. The only way to stop that is to kill this era's version of globalization, and Taiwan is simply not worth that outcome . . . .
>
> America needs to take its defense quarantine to Taiwan off the table, and do it now, before some irrational polarization in Taipei results in a war between two nuclear powers. . . . I say, let's lock in a strategic alliance with rising China at today's price, because that cost has nowhere to go but up over the coming years . . .

If Barnett's blueprint for action can be put into practice, the Taiwan issue would disappear as a hindrance to peaceful coexistence between China and the U.S. Taiwan has been as much an obstacle to China-U.S. relations as the Middle East is between the U.S. and the Islamic world. The resolution of the Taiwan matter would raise China-U.S. relations to a new, highly constructive level. Taiwan, without the military backing of the U.S., will have no choice, but to quickly and naturally come to the negotiation table to meet the PRC for a peaceful reunification.

CHAPTER VI

The Future Is in America's Hands

The main theoretical basis for the China threat theory is the belief of some individuals that throughout history the rise of any nation must be accompanied by war and expansion. For example, the rise of Germany and of the Japanese Empire in the twentieth century supported this line of thinking. This kind of myopic thinking leads to the conclusion that it would not be possible for China to advance peacefully. However, like the failed China collapse theory and China grain threat theory, there is no evidence to support the China threat theory since development in China has been peaceful and China has consistently advocated peaceful solutions to international crises. When speaking to people in the mainland of China, few understand why the Chinese people, who work very hard for low wages, could be seen as a threat by some Americans.

When President Bush first assumed office in 2000, he did not seem interested in confronting the rise of China in a positive way. However, after the 9/11 terrorist attack, he found it useful to collaborate with Beijing to launch his anti-terrorism program. Things have changed in the intervening years since the attack. Americans increasingly recognize the CPC will continue to govern China in the foreseeable future. Sheer size and rapid economic development in China play an increasingly larger role in the global balance of power. In short, China has earned a unique position in the modern world. The exercise of independent foreign policy by China has enabled realistic responses to the volatile changes in international affairs.

China's special geopolitical position has enabled it to play a crucial role in maintaining global balance. With rising economic and political influence, any significant Chinese problems will affect global stability. It is doubtful that any foreign power can influence internal stability in China today. The CPC, with 70.8 million members in 2006, has effectively ruled the PRC for fifty-eight years. China recognizes that as long as it effectively implements measures to balance domestic development and maintains stability, it will function confidently on the international stage. In this sense, China's peaceful development would exert an important, positive impact on civilization and inspire other nations to pursue independent development. Under these circumstances, the U.S. would be wise to maintain friendly relations with China, treating it as an ally, not a threat.

For almost fifty years, U.S. foreign policy was geared towards containing the power and influence of the Soviet Union through Cold War thinking and strategies. Since the collapse of the Soviet Union, U.S. actions suggest that its leaders needed a potential enemy to ensure the viability and strength of the military industrial complex. Certainly, the Defense Department continued to operate on a Cold War scale. At that time, Russia was weak economically, Europe lacked economic unity, and Japan was an ally that needed U.S. protection; thus, the only real potential rival was the rising China, with its entirely different political system. No matter how China advances, the neocons and the Pentagon view China as a military threat and an economic threat, as an extension of this thinking.

However, it is important to understand that the Cold War era is gone and the electronic age and globalization have connected all nations economically and culturally, breaking barriers of space and time. Confrontational Cold War thinking is obsolete and warmongering strategies no longer fit a world where multilateralism would become a tenet of the twenty-first century. Collaboration is the most effective way to produce a positive outcome and peaceful coexistence. Military confrontation invites retaliation and contributes to the proliferation of an estimated 31,000 nuclear weapons worldwide, which is alarming. [1] Even if only one thousandth of these were misused, the consequence would be an unthinkable human disaster!

Political, economic, or military unilateralism by the U.S. may force other nations into temporary submission or change, but will not produce lasting peace. The reason is simple: Military might may vanquish, but not govern. Once the soldiers and generals leave, unrest would resurface, unless the military action has achieved what the majority of the people want. It is essential to reexamine American foreign policies: Why do so many people around the world dislike the Americans? Why do many once friendly countries now oppose the U.S.? By treating China as an enemy or threat, does America wish to develop another enemy, rather than a friend? Can America's foreign policy become more benevolent so that in 50 or 100 years, Americans will enjoy fruitful lives and coexist peacefully with the rest of the world? Can the U.S. avoid adherence to a destructive path by misusing its military might possessed today?

The truth is that the Chinese people are rebuilding their country and homes once again from the ashes of war. Should we not be cautious in assuming that the emerging role of China is comparable to that of imperial Germany, implying that strategic confrontation is inevitable and the U.S. had better prepare for it? Are not those who spread rampant China threat rhetoric both dangerous and wrong?

American hegemony is the most advanced in the world's history. It does not intend to kill all the people and destroy nations, nor does it require occupation or seizing of territories. What it demands is the obedience of other countries to its objectives and conformance to its position on global security and economics.

Japan conformed to the U.S. and allied demands after losing World War II and received needed U.S. support so it could evolve into a prosperous country.

But, do American generals and politicians truly understand the comments made by former Secretary of State, Madeleine Albright? "To any U.S. government, China is too big; America cannot overlook it or embrace it. China is difficult to control, because it has enormous pride in itself," she said. [2] However, were China not a country deeply committed to peace and harmony, there would not have been the Silk Road which spread Chinese civilization to the rest of the world. In the early fifteenth century, China had the world's largest fleet equipped with the most advanced cannons, but it did not attack other countries or seize their territories.

This proves that peace, harmony, and "love others as they love themselves" derived from Confucianism had a profound influence on the Chinese culture and political philosophy then, as it does today. Moreover, which country has forgiven an adversary like Japan in spite of the cost of its invasions during which thirty-five million Chinese died or were injured? Anyone who assumes that the rise of China is comparable to imperial Germany or Japan lacks understanding of Chinese and world history. The China of today cannot be treated as the "new kid on the block."

The years 2005 and 2006 have been important for the China-U.S. relations. There has been political, economic, and contentious diplomatic rhetoric surrounding the bilateral relationship in areas including the Taiwan Strait, the North Korean nuclear development, the RMB valuation, the failure of Chinese oil company CNOOC in acquiring America's ninth largest oil company Unocal, and the trade controversy. Many top U.S. officials including President Bush, former Federal Reserve Bank Chairman Alan Greenspan, Secretary of the Treasury John W. Snow, former Deputy Secretary of State Robert Bruce Zoellick, former World Bank President Paul D. Wolfowitz and former Secretary of Defense Donald H. Rumsfeld visited China. President Hu Jintao also made his first visit to Washington, D.C.

Frequent high-level dialogue indicates that both sides want to strengthen relations, establish mature diplomatic methods of communication and minimize distrust. Both sides are dedicated to developing effective bilateral relationships. Currently, there are five main forces influencing the direction of U.S. policy on China. These include unions, advanced technology industries, religious organizations, military defense industries, and financial and other private sector businesses. Some experts view China as an economic paradise, a gigantic market, and a great business opportunity; others oppose China because they believe it drains jobs away from the U.S. through cheap labor and has serious human rights problems. Some perceive the complexity of China, a nation presenting a mix of problems and opportunities.

On September 21, 2006, the former U.S. Deputy Secretary of State Robert Bruce Zoellick made remarks which shed new light on U.S. expectations for merging China into the international community and providing incentives for it to become a responsible stakeholder. [3] While Zoellick may represent those who want to integrate China using a soft approach in the direction favorable to U.S. interests, other forces promote a containment strategy. It is possible that U.S. unilateralism and preemptive militarism have gained preeminence under the Bush administration. But with the dim outlook for the Iraq War, American politicians are also leaning towards compromise in both North Korea and Iraq. Nevertheless, the China containment idea remains in place.

Here are some of the ways in which the U.S. continues to attempt to contain China, regionally and globally:

- In Central Asia, the U.S. has succeeded in "color revolutions" by financially supporting opposition factions to overthrow governments in several countries such as Ukraine and Georgia to establish pro-U.S. rule and to ensure dominant U.S. influence to the west of China (in Ukraine, the success was only temporary; now they have a compromise government, partly pro-Washington, partly pro-Moscow).

- In the Middle East, the U.S. has occupied Iraq and supported Israel in its clash with Hezbollah in Lebanon. This is viewed as a prelude to a potential move by the U.S. to launch a preemptive attack to destroy Iranian nuclear installations. If the U.S. succeeds in gaining control over Iran, America would dominate the entire Middle East and threaten China's oil supply.

- The U.S. is attempting to establish a small NATO in Asia starting with Australia in the south, Taiwan in the middle, and Japan in the north. India and Mongolia are the new U.S. targeted interests that would encircle China from its west and north.

307

- The U.S. has pressured the E.U. to continue its arms
  embargo against China initiated in 1989 and has engaged in
  dialogue to formulate joint strategic plans against China.

The world has changed dramatically since the end of the Cold War.
Worldwide economic globalization over the past three decades has interconnected disparate countries to a degree that is unparalleled in history.
The interdependence of different economies is mutually beneficial and
replaces confrontational militarism.

World War II, the most destructive war in history, cost more than
sixty million lives. The next war among great powers would cost
hundreds of millions or billions of lives. In his article, "China's Rise Need
Not Bring Conflict," [4] Martin Wolf clearly warns that the huge increase
in the expense of war is not the only reason to avoid it at all costs. In
addition, to combat the growing world-wide terrorist threat, America
would need a strong ally like China.

Additional territory, people, and other resources cannot bring prosperity without the development of markets, the investment in human
and physical capital and openness to international trade. Adam Smith,
the Scottish father of economics in the eighteenth century, has written
that in a world of liberal trade, empires are both unnecessary and burden-
some. Only peaceful commerce can achieve our desired levels of prosperity. China and the U.S. can actively collaborate in many international
organizations such as the U.N., the WTO, the ASEAN summit, and the
APEC. Peaceful development within China need not be interpreted as a
threat; instead, it is an opportunity and challenge.

Martin Wolf said that "the experience of the Chinese people in the
past half-century has been a superb demonstration of these propositions."
China has adopted the correct policies by establishing domestic economic
development as a priority and conducting friendly economic diplomacy
internationally. In this way, China has paved the way towards peaceful
development, multilateralism and friendship with neighboring countries.

China is not interested in an arms race with the U.S. Its aim is to
maintain sufficient military strength to defend its territory against any
external assault over the independence of Taiwan or other threats to its
sovereignty.

It is well-known that economic prosperity has been the strongest source of national strength including the historic rise of European nations like the British Empire, France, Portugal, and Spain, and more recently, the U.S. superpower. There is no exception. The collapse of the Soviet Union was not due to a military weakness, but a shattered economy. Throughout history, rising powers began with strong economic prosperity and collapsed once their economies weakened. America should understand its strength and vulnerability. Its strength is built upon an economic power that attracts exceptional talent from around the world. Economic opportunity and skill propelled American prosperity further. American values emphasize individual freedom and human rights. U.S. strength is built, also, on economic opportunity regardless of race, sex, religion, or ethnicity.

In response to the 9/11 attack, the U.S. abandoned economic multilateralism and pursued militarism. It used American values to promote the Bush administration's preemptive doctrine and unilateralism. The disastrous results prove that America has stepped on a wrong path.

The truth is: It is much easier to achieve an advantageous position through economic multilateralism rather than militarism. For this reason Chinese economic, political, and diplomatic influence has spread rapidly throughout Asia and the rest of the world. It seems that the price that America has to pay for containing China will grow larger and its effectiveness will be much reduced. Why would different countries wish to sacrifice their own economic gain in exchange for any political and military alliance to contain China? This seems not a difficult choice to make. History shows that U.S. cooperation with the ASEAN only resulted in seven projects over the past thirty years; whereas in the past ten years China and ASEAN's cooperation has led to approximately thirty projects. [5] The ineffectiveness of U.S. containment policy is apparent.

China has become a new strong presence in East Asia in the twenty-first century. Chinese trade with Australia, the Philippines, Thailand, and other East Asian countries is increasing rapidly. In 2005, China's trade volume with the South East Asian countries increased by 20 percent to US$130 billion. Any country in that region takes into account the economic influence of China in the development of trade policies. The Chinese do not criticize the U.S. or try to discourage East Asian nations in relations with the U.S. China simply wants to collaborate with other countries amicably. Along with trade, evolving international relationships extend to student exchange, tourism, and other areas.

In addition, the quintessence of traditional Chinese culture exhibits a spirit of tolerance and benevolence. Because of tolerance, China is happy to absorb American culture. This is a sign of the confidence the Chinese have in their own culture. And because of benevolence, China strives to build a harmonious atmosphere in its own society while pursuing world peace in the international community. Most countries treat China as both an economic and strategic partner. It is, therefore, evident that the U.S. containment will not work effectively in the future and Chinese influence will continue to increase.

The U.S. overreaction to economic growth in China is understandable to a degree, but unnecessary. It seems that the foreign policy of the Bush administration is guided by fear. Although the overall strength of the U.S. is unmatched internationally, Americans are feeling increasingly threatened by external and perceived enemies. According to the Bush administration, problems caused by Middle Eastern terrorists are compounded by the so-called rogue states, or the axis of evil, which includes North Korea, Iran, Syria, and Cuba. Even China, the E.U., and Russia could threaten American interests under this scenario. It seems that since Nicholas D. Kristof wrote in 1993 that the PRC might fill the power vacuum left in the Asia-Pacific Region, the China threat theory gained credence and popularity among some U.S. politicians.

U.S. military intervention in the Middle East, in particular, has generated much anti-Americanism. The U.S. government demands compliance with its foreign policy objectives from other nations, but fails to recognize that cooperation bought or coerced will not last.

It is remarkable that the U.S. has succeeded in achieving a position of world supremacy, but seeking absolute dominance in the world may be dangerous to other countries and to itself. Henry A. Kissinger's balance of power diplomacy, which may be considered a precursor of modern international multilateralism, has played an extremely important role in U.S. foreign policy during the Cold War era. It also implanted the seed for the open door policy later in China. The lofty Wilsonianism that shaped early international order and American thought, namely, "What we do, we demand also of others," has been adopted by the Bush government and neo-conservatives. They seem to use guns and bibles forcefully and carelessly as means to secure world dominance. In the long run, such actions are in opposition to U.S. national interests, and aggressive American militarism is an important reason for a jittery international community.

It is not surprising to find that the U.S. is now considered by many countries and people in the world as a greater threat to world peace than Iran or North Korea, yet the Americans themselves are living in constant fear. Fareed Zakaria, the *Newsweek* editor writes, "Can everyone please take a deep breath?" in his recent article, "The Year of Living Fearfully," on the subject of Americans' fear of war with Iran. [6] He correctly points out that Washington has a long habit of painting its enemies (or an imagined enemy) ten feet tall and crazy.

When the Hezbollah-Israel war broke out in 2006, former Speaker of the House Newt Gingrich immediately announced that mankind had entered the initial stage of World War III. U.S. Politician Bernard Lewis boldly predicted in the *Washington Daily News* that the world was at the threshold of a new world war and it was going to break out on August 22, 2006, in the Middle East region. [7] These are the voices of extreme right wingers. Americans need more people who promote balanced views just as loudly.

Of course, world war has not erupted, but inflammatory right wing rhetoric reflects American anxiety. Further analysis of reasons for American fearfulness may be found in a book by Kevin Phillips entitled, *American Theocracy*. Do we need the imagined China threat theory to exacerbate American fears? Don't Americans deserve peace of mind and a tranquil existence with the Chinese as well as the rest of the world?

The competition that exists among strong nations in the world can have a positive, healthy outcome. During a China tour in September 2006, U.S. Assistant Secretary of State Christopher Hill made very positive remarks about the Sino-U.S. relations as follows: "It is not a zero-sum game, since the two countries have close economic links and share common interests in many areas; hence, they will rely on each other for a long period of time." [8] He also said that China has contributed a great deal to the resumption of the six-party talks, and further, that the U.S.

will not pressure China to persuade North Korea to come back to the talks, although he voiced the hope that China would continue its effort along the same line in the future. His wish has been realized. As detailed earlier, the North Korean nuclear issue was near resolution in early 2007, through painstaking intervention and negotiation mostly by China, and on July 14, 2007, Pyongyang announced that it began closing down its main nuclear reactor. [9]

China does not need to react to every move made by America. As long as China builds an adequate, modern defense capability and continues peaceful economic development, the China threat theory will have no audience. In time, the U.S. will realize the true benefit of having China as a friend.

China is in the midst of a revolution again and it is a peaceful one. We are witnessing an unprecedented Chinese migration from rural to urban areas. We are also witnessing the Yangtze River Water Dam project which will change the course of the river and reshape the map of China.

It is correct to bring China, a rising power, into the global tent, making it an international stakeholder, not an outsider, and providing the nation with incentives to help create and reshape international norms and rules. However, it is also apparent that the Chinese social environment needs a strong government for some time to enforce a successful economic, social, and eventually political transformation. Governance by political elites who work for the people has been a successful formula for the country both historically and at present.

A top priority for China today is to substantially reduce its peasant population and the wealth gap, and transform its economy from labor intensive manufacturing to a balanced mix of enterprises in technology, services, and agriculture. China can leave the political responsibilities to the elites who work with discipline and professionalism; but they must be controlled, checked, and challenged to improve and excel in their jobs. Corruption must not be tolerated and should be punished fairly and severely to set standards of behavior and warn bureaucrats at all levels of the importance of maintaining a clean and just government. This task can only be carried out by the Chinese themselves. In fact, the world should appreciate the effectiveness of China in limiting its population growth and striving, for the past fifty-eight years, to solve its own problems of employment, food, lodging, crime, and other civil issues without burdening the world.

Chinese Premier Wen Jiabao recently pledged progress on sustainable economic growth, currency reform, and democracy, but stressed changes will be gradual rather than radical or rapid. Wen sought to flex Chinese diplomatic muscles by urging Iran to heed international concern over its weapons programs. He also stressed that resolving conflicts ranging from the economic to the diplomatic in a harmonious manner was critical to China's sustainable development. "We need peace, we need friends and we need time," he said in advance of a visit to Finland, Britain, and Germany. [10]

Despite all the challenges ahead, Wen was confident about China's future. He said, "We are in a position to ensure continued and fairly fast growth of China's economy for a considerable period of time to come, and we have full confidence in our ability to do so. . . . We will continue to deepen reforms of the RMB exchange rate mechanism. . . .This means that the floating of the exchange rate will be determined mainly by market supply and demand, and the floating band will be gradually expanded. So there will be no more 'surprise' adjustments to the RMB exchange rate." Wen also acknowledged that China's conditions are not ripe for direct elections at a higher level, but a Chinese version of democracy is practiced in 680,000 villages.

China, as a nation, suffered deeply throughout history. China was invaded, bullied, and humiliated. The Chinese people suffered with their country, but learned self-respect, self-reliance, and self-determination. Still, China has a long way to go. History will document the actions of the Chinese people just as history recorded the greatness of Americans with their technological breakthroughs and visions that changed the world in the twentieth and twenty-first centuries.

China is a large country with a vast population, a weak economic foundation, and regional development imbalances in energy, social, economic, technology resources and in environmental protection. It must work and diligently to sustain long-term growth. Economic success in China will bring hope to underdeveloped nations and opportunities to the developed countries of the world. China and the U.S. should work hand in hand, engage in continuous dialogue, rather than counterproductive conflicts, since neither would withstand the severe consequences of a cataclysmic confrontation. It is better to look ahead and avoid the trap of the China threat theory, which could result in an unnecessary and futile war with China. America has the great power and ability to shape this world. The future is in America's hands.

About the Author

Dr. Sheng-Wei Wang, born in Taiwan, is a scholar, writer, entrepreneur, media figure and political activist. She graduated from National Tsing Hua University with a B.S. degree in Chemistry and earned a Ph.D. degree in Theoretical Chemical Physics from the University of Southern California in 1976. She was awarded an Alexander Von Humboldt Postdoctoral Fellowship in 1977-78 to further her research work in Munich University under the guidance of Professor Gerhard Ertl, the 2007 Nobel Laureate in Chemistry. She became a staff scientist at Lawrence Berkeley Laboratory after many years of scientific research at Caltech and Stanford Linear Accelerator Center. Prior to founding in 2006 the China-U.S. Friendship Exchange, Inc., in Northern California, and co-founding in 2007 the Golden Happiness Ltd. in Hong Kong, she was also a self-made California real estate developer for 15 years.

She considered herself nonpolitical until Taiwan's 2004 presidential election with its shooting incident. She used her physics research skills to write a JFK-conspiracy-exposé arguing that President Chen Shui-bian's minor skin wound must have been staged. She briefed the U.S. State Department about her findings in May 2004 and was interviewed by KTSF 26 TV host Jay Stone Shih for three nights from 05/26/04 to 05/28/04. This investigation made her a well-known Chinese-American media figure.

In order to strive for peace across the Taiwan Strait, she is devoting her efforts to China's peaceful reunification. She has sent monthly newsletters to the U.S. Congressional members from 2005 to promote cross-strait reunification and good Sino-U.S. relations. She published many articles in both Chinese and English and was again interviewed by Chinese Dialogue360 TV host Jay Stone Shih on 06/15/07, 06/18/07, 11/30/07 and 12/03/07 (see www.dialogue360.net). She was also interviewed by Dr. Gianni Hayes' Radio Show on 02/27/08 from 9:00 to 10:00 PM EST.

Her translated English book, *"One Country, Two Systems" in Taiwan* (a Chinese book by Taiwanese writer Hsing Chi), was published in the U.S. in 2006 by International Publishing House for China's Culture. Her earlier article, "The Answer My Friend Is Blowing in the Wind," was published in the ELM magazine on February 1, 2006. Her latest essays, "For Whom the Bell May Toll?" and "The Blue Danube on Gulangyu Islet," appeared in American Chronicle's May 1 and May 12, 2007, issues. Her second English book, China's Ascendancy: Opportunity or Threat ? was published in November 2007 by International Publishing House for China's Culture. The second edition has received extensive and excellent reviews from world experts and came out in March 2008; it is marketed by the world's largest B&T book distributor and online bookstore Amazon.com.

She can be reached at Curra888@yahoo.com or at her biligual website, www.ChinaUSFriendship.com.

References

Chapter I

1. Samuel P. Huntington, *The Clash of Civilizations and the Remaking of World Order*, Simon & Schuster, paperback edition, 2003.
2. Zbigniew Brzezinski, *The Grand Chessboard*, Basic Books, 1997.
3. www.crystalinks.com/confucious.html
4. ibid.
5. www.bbsland.com, 08/13/2006
6. Joseph S. Nye, Jr., *Soft Power: The Means to Success in World Politics*, Public Affairs, New York, 2004.
7. www.crystalinks.com/confucious.html
8. ibid.
9. www.nytimes.com, 03/03/2007
10. "The Rise and Fall of the Roman Empire," by Danielle T, Mrs. Kling's Class, April 1997.
11. www.bbsland.com, Xi Long, "Why Can China Be United and Europe Divided," 03/03/2006
12. www.crystalinks.com/confucious.html
13. www.scmp.com, 05/22/2006
14. www.bbsland.com, 09/20/2006
15. www.creaders.net, 03/24/2006
16. Iris Chang, *The Rape of Nanking: The Forgotten Holocaust of World War II*, Basic Books, 1997.
17. www-chaos.umd.edu/history/prc.html/
18. ibid.
19. Robert Temple, *The Genius of China: 3,000 Years of Science, Discovery and Invention*, Prion Books Limited Imperial Works, London, 1998.
20. www.scmp.com, 03/22/2006
21. www.creader.org, 03/24/2006

Chapter II

1. http://homepage3.nifty.com/ubiquitous/text_db/US_1990s/01.htm
2. J. Ingrid Lesley, *A Storm of Shot and Shell: Weapons of the Civil War*, appeared as part of a Chicago Public Library Exhibition presented from July 26, 1996, through January 5, 1997.
3. U.S. Army Col. Ernest Dupuy, *The Nature of the Battle*, New York City: Hawthorn Books, Inc., 1961, 1956.
4. ibid.
5. Census Bureau, U.S. Department of Commerce. Current Population Reports, Population Projections of the United States by Age, Race, and Hispanic Origin: 1995–2050.
6. www.worldjournal.com, 03/08/2006
7. www.creaders.net, 03/29/2006)
8. www.worldjournal.com, 04/01/2006
9. www.creaders.net, 03/29/2006
10. Theodore W. Allen, "Race" and "Ethnicity:" History and the 2000 Census, 2000.
11. www.creaders.net, 03/28/2006
12. Samuel P. Huntington, Who *Are We? America's Great Debate*, Simon & Schuster UK Ltd, 2004.
13. www.gc.cuny.edu/faculty/research_briefs/aris/key_findings.htm
14. op. cit. Chapter 1, no. 2

Chapter III

1. www.China-Window.com
2. www.China.org.cn
3. www.cnn.com transcripts, 02/19/1997
4. Fareed Zakaria, "China's Century," *Newsweek*, March 9, 2005.
5. Xinhua English, 02/09/2006
6. ibid., 07/20/2006
7. ibid., 08/30/2006
8. www.wenxuecity.com, 07/21/2006
9. The Associated Press, 03/28/2006
10. *Shanghai Daily*, 07/25/2006
11. www.creaders.net, 11/01/2005
12. ibid., 02/21/2006
13. www.wenxuecity.com, 02/09/2006

14. *China Daily*, 02/21/2006
15. www.worldjournal.com, 02/25/2006
16. Xinhua English, 12/21/2005
17. ibid., 03/11/2006
18. www.scmp.com, 02/24/2006
19. *China Daily*, 02/20/2006
20. www.creaders.net, 11/01/2005
21. ibid., 02/23/2006
22. Xinhua English, 02/17/2006
23. The Associated Press, 10/27/2005
24. www.creaders.net, 02/23/2006
25. www.scmp.com, 04/20/2006
26. www.bbsland.com, 09/02/2006
27. www.singtao.com, 04/12/2006 and www.scmp.com, 04/09/2006
28. Xinhua English, 02/23/2006
29. www.people.com.cn, 10/14/2005
30. www.creaders.net, 02/26/2006
31. www.sina.com, 03/28/2007
32. www.infoworld.com, 03/13/2007
33. Xinhua English, 03/23/2006
34. www.wenxuecity.com, 01/16/2006
35. Xinhua English, 03/01/2006
36. ibid., 03/09/2006
37. ibid., 02/24/2006
38. www.nytimes.com, 07/02/2006
39. www.wenxuecity.com, 09/07/2006
40. The Associated Press, 11/02/2006
41. www.scmp.com, 07/27/2006
42. ibid., 08/02/2006
43. www.guardian.co.uk, 10/24/2005
44. Adapted from the *Observer*, 10/25/2005
45. www.worldjournal.com, 04/232006
46. ibid., 03/22/2006
47. Xinhua English, 03/07/2006
48. ibid., 02/24/2006
49. Reuters, 08/27/2006
50. www.creaders.net, 03/08/2006
51. Xinhua English, 02/24/2006
52. ibid., 09/21/2006

53. ibid., 02/24/2006
54. The Associated Press, 02/27/2006
55. Xinhua English, 02/25/2006
56. www.scmp.com, 03/05/2006
57. *Xinhua English*, 03/04/2006
58. www.worldjournal.com, 03/05/2006
59. www.reference.com
60. www.creaders.net, 03/21/2007
61. Xinhua English, 03/04/2006
62. www.chinatimes.com, 11/30/2005
63. Xinhua English, 03/23/2006
64. ibid., 12/20/2005
65. www.scmp.com, 03/24/2006
66. Xinhua English, 03/22/2006
67. ibid., 03/06/2006
68. ibid., 06/17/2006
69. www.wenxuecity.com, 08/09/2006
70. Xinhua English, 10/20/2005
71. ibid., 11/05/2005
72. ibid., 10/31/2005
73. www.scmp.com, 03/17/2006
74. ibid., 03/22/2006 and www.washingtonpost.com, 03/21/2006
75. www.singtao.com, 03/22/2006 and www.bbaland.com, 03/26/2007
76. Xinhua English, 03/17/2006
77. *Shanghai Daily*, 03/27/2007
78. www.bbaland.com, 03/26/2007
79. www.chinanews.com, 09/22/2004 and Xinhua English, 12/21/2005
80. www.singtao.com, 03/05/2006
81. Xinhua English, 05/24/2006
82. ibid., 02/19/2006
83. Neville Maxwell, "Sino-India Border Dispute Reconsidered," Economic and Political Weekly, Vol. 34, No. 15, April 10–16, 1999.
84. www.scmp.com, 03/15/2006
85. The Associated Press, 03/10/2006 and www.scmp.com, 03/15/2006
86. Xinhua English, 06/18/2006
87. Xinhua News Agency, 01/13.2006
88. Xinhua English, 11/10/2005
89. *Indian Economic Trade Review*, 2001
90. Xinhua English, 03/16/2006

91. www.people.com.cn, 11/11/2005

92. www.cnn.com, 07/29/2006

93. Gavin Rabinowitz, "India's New Missile Falls Short in Test," www.washing-tonpost.com, 07/10/2006

94. Xinhua English, 07/29/2006

95. www.chinatimes.com, 07/09/2006

96. www.wenxuecity.com, 07/12/2006

97. Xinhua English, 11/02/2005

98. www.creaders.net, 10/31/2005

99. www.nytimes.com, 02/11/2006

100. www.singtao.com, 09/11/2006

101. Esther Pan, "Council on Foreign Relations," 02/11/2006

102. David E. Sanger, "Bush's Shift: Being Patient with Foes," 07/10/2006

103. Online News Hour: "Thawing Relations," 10/11/2000

104. www.nytimes.com, 03/09/2006)

105. Molly Ivins, "Maybe If We Tried a Slingshot," www.truthdig.com, 06/28/2006

106. www.worldjournal.com, 09/20/2005

107. www.creaders.net, 07/04/2006

108. www.washingtonpost.com, 07/04/2006

109. *Newsweek*, 10/16/2006

110. www.scmp.com, 02/14/2007

111. www.bbsland.com, 09/05/2006

112. www.wenxuecity.com, 08/31/2006

113. www.cnn.com, 03/30/2007

114. www.nytimes.com, 01/18/2006

115. ibid., 01/16/2006

116. www.washingtonpost.com, 03/09/2006

117. www.cnn.com, 03/09/2006

118. ibid., 07/30/2006

119. The Associated Press, 07/04/2006

120. www.washingtompost.com, 07/11/2006

121. www.nytimes.com, 07/12/2006

122. www.cnn.com, 07/30/2006

123. www.washingtonpost.com, 08/03/2006

124. www.nytimes.com, 08/07/2006

125. Xinhua English, 08/14/2006

126. www.washingtonpost,com, 08/23/2006

127. www.wenxuecity.com, 08/31/2006

128. www.washingtonpost.com, 03/24/2007

129. www.bbsland.com, 03/27/2007
130. Xinhua English, 01/12/2006
131. ibid.
132. Reuters, Associated Press, and Agence, France-Presse in Beijing, 01/13/2006
133. Xinhua English, 01/26/2006
134. ibid., 11/12/2005
135. ibid., 12/20/2005
136. ibid., 01/20/2006
137. ibid., 02/23/2006
138. China/National, Xinhua updated, 10/24/2006
139. www.bbsland.com, 09/17/2006
140. www.cgdev.org, January 2007
141. www.creaders.com, 04/07/2007
142. Xinhua English, 03/01/2006
143. ibid., 12/12/2005
144. ibid., 12/22/2005
145. ibid., 01/23/2006
146. "Set American Free," 12/29/2006
147. Xinhua English, 09/08/2006
148. ibid., 10/13/2005
149. ibid., 11/07/2005
150. ibid., 02/28/2006
151. ibid., 11/30/2005
152. ibid., 03/09/2006
153. ibid., 11/04/2005
154. ibid., 11/10/2005
155. www.worldjournal.com, 11/10/2005
156. Xinhua English, 11/10/2005
157. www.scmp.com, 05/22/2006
158. www.people.com.cn, 11/14/2005
159. Xinhua English, 11/12/2005
160. Xinhua News Agency, 04/13/2006
161. Xinhua English, 01/20/2006
162. ibid., 03/09/2006
163. ibid., 12/10/2005
164. ibid., 03/17/2006
165. www.chinatimes.com, 03/09/2005
166. www.bbsland.com, 08/24/2006
167. www.wenxuecity.com, 08/25/2006

References

168. ibid., 08/25/2006 and www.zaobao.com, 03/25/2007
169. www.scmp.com, 08/25/2006
170. www.people.com.cn, 11/04/2005
171. "CRS Report for Congress," 04/20/2005
172. www.worldjournal.com, 12/07/2005
173. ibid., 03/23/2006
174. http://news.wenxuecity.com, 04/05/2006
175. Xinhua English, 04/03/2006
176. www.scmp.com, 04/04/2006
177. ibid., 04/06/2006
178. www.singtao.com, 04/08/2006
179. www.scmp.com, 04/08/2006
180. www.worldjournal.com, 05/06/2006
181. The Associated Press, 06/27/2006
182. Xinhua English, 03/02/2005
183. www.enerationaldynamics.com, 08/23/2004 and www.people.com.cn, 10/17/2005
184. www.washingtonpost.com, 12/14/2005
185. Xinhua English, 12/12/2005
186. ibid.
187. ibid.
188. www.chinatimes.com, 12/13/2005
189. www.worldjournal.com, 12/14/2005
190. ibid.
191. www.people.com.cn, 10/31/2005
192. Xinhua English, 03/15/2006
193. ibid., 09/04/2006
194. www.wenxuecity.com, 12/07/2005
195. The Center for Strategic and International Studies at the Institute for International Economics, "China: The Balance Sheet," Public Affairs, New York, 2006.
196. Reuters, 08/27/2006
197. China Institute, WPS Media Monitoring Agency, 02/09/2007
198. www.bbsland.com, 09/17/2006
199. www.cnn.com, 12/14/2005
200. www.worldjournal.com, 12/13/2005
201. The Associated Press, 12/14/2005
202. ibid.
203. www.creaders.net, 12/18/2005

204. www.cnn.com, 12/15/2005

205. www.chinatimes.com, 12/18/2005

206. www.washingtonpost.com, 07/25/2006 and www.worldjournal.com, 07/24/2006

207. www.scmp.com, 08/30.2006

208. The Associated Press, 08/29/2006

209. Xinhua English, 12/20/2005

210. ibid., 10/22/2005

Chapter IV

1. www.reference.com

2. http://usinfo.state.gov/usa/infousa/facts/funddocs/billeng.htm.

3. "The Presidency, War, and Foreign Affairs: Practice under the Framers" by Abraham D. Sofaer in *Law and Contemporary Problems*, Vol. 40, No. 2, *Presidential Power:* Part I (Spring, 1976), pp.12–38), http://links.jstor.org/

4. "The Iraq War of 2003 and the Politics of Denuclearization," by Bruce D. Larkin, 11/17/2003, http://www.gcdd.net/TX=2003/TX.028=2003.11.11.IraqWar.pdf

5. www.political.com

6. www.thisnation.com

7. www.worldjournal.com, 03/17/2007

8. ibid., 06/29/2006

9. www.bbsland.com, 03/17/2007

10. www.zaobao.com, 03/23/2007

11. Lee Kuan Yew, *From Third World to First: The Singapore Story: 1965–2000*, HarperCollins Publishers Inc., 2000.

12. http://economics.about.com/, U.S. Department of State

13. www.Reference.com

14. http://financenews.sina.com, 04/07/2006

15. www.cmilitary.com, 03/20/2007

16. www.worldjournal.com, 03/19/2007

17. www.creaders.net, 12/21/2005

18. http://news.sina.com, 03/10/2006

19. www.creaders.net, 12/21/2005

20. Zbigniew Brzezinski, *The Grand Chessboard*, Basic Books, 1997.

21. Fareed Zakaria, "How Long Will America Lead the World?" www.newsweek.com, 07/03/2006

22. www.chronicle.com, 02/17/2006

23. www.historylearningsite.co.uk, 2000–2007

24. Henry A. Kissinger, *Diplomacy*, Simon & Schuster, 1994.

25. www.archives.gov

26. www.state.gov

27. www.foreignaffairs.org

28. www.state.gov

29. Keir A. Lieber and Daryl G. Press, "The Rise of U.S. Nuclear Primacy," *Foreign Affairs*, March/April, 2006.

30. "Recovering History and Justice in Cambodia" by Ben Kiernan, http://www.yale.edu/cgp/KiernanComparativ2004.doc

31. Chi Hsing, *One Country, Two Systems in Taiwan,* new edition, English translation by Sheng-Wei Wang, International Publishing House for China's Culture, 2006.

32. www.atimes.com, 02/13/2001

33. www.worldjournal.com, 09/09/2006

34. www.washingtonpost.com, 02/24/2006

35. www.newsweek.com, 03/10/2006

36. www.worldjournal.com, 03/20/2007

37. http://news.sina.com, 03/17/2006

38. www.msnbc.msn.com, 04/03/2006

39. www.worldjournal.com, 03/20/2007

40. Reuters, 12/09/2005

41. www.taipeitimes.com, 03/19/2007

42. "Repeal the USA Patriot Act," by Jennifer Van Bergen, April 1–6, 2002, http://truthout.com/docs_02/04.02A.JVB.Patriot.htm

Chapter V

1. Gregory Clark, *Reviving the China Threat*, www.japanfocus.org, 01/15/2006

2. www.islamic-world.net, 12/23/2005

3. http://mdn.mainichi-msn.co.jp, 02/14/2006

4. www.asianresearch.org

5. www.firstworldwar.com, 09/29/2002

6. Caleb Wan, "Security Flashpoint: International Law and the Islands Dispute in the Far East," The *New Zealand Postgraduate Law E-Journal*, Issue 2, 2005.

7. www.chinareviewnews.com, 03/23/2007

8. KBS World Radio, 09/14/2006

9. Iris Chang, *The Rape of Nanking: The Forgotten Holocaust of World War II*, Basic Books, 1997.

10. Deutsche press - *Agentur*, 02/11/2007

11. www.scmp.com, 03/04/2007

12. *San Francisco Chronicle*, letters to the editors, 03/09/2007 and 03/17/2007

13. www.scmp.com, 03/18/2007

14. www.japantimes.co.jp, 11/06/2005

15. http://mdn.mainichi-msn.co.jp, 11/15/2005

16. www.chinanews.com, 05/16/2006

17. www.creaders.net, 11/17/2005

18. www.cnn.com, 03/22/2006 and www.worldjournal.com, 04/02/2007

19. http://news.wenxuecity.com, 01/03/2006

20. Yuan Hong, Institute of World Economics & Politics, Chinese Academy of Social Sciences, "The Implication of TMD System in Japan to China's Security," The Sixth ISODARCO Beijing Seminar on Arms Control, October 29–November 1, 1998, Shanghai, China.

21. http://people.com.cn, 02/12/2001

22. www.wenxuecity.com, 03/17/2006

23. *Daily News*, Japan, 05/18/1997

24. www.worldjournal.com, 04/09/2006

25. ibid., 04/18/2006

26. www.cmilitary.com, 02/11/2006

27. www.wenxuecity.com, 07/03/2006

28. www.taipeitimes.com, 01/21/2007

29. www.worldjournal.com, 12/22/2005

30. www.creaders.net, 12/01/2005

31. Xinhua News Agency, 03/13/2006

32. www.nytimes.com, 09/11/2005

33. www.wenxuecity.com, 04/04/2007

34. www.scmp.com, 04/19/2006

35. www.nytimes.com, 09/11/2005

36. www.singtao.com, 07/09/2006

37. www.wenxuecity.com, 08/07/2006

38. The Associated Press, 04/18/2006

39. University of Minnesota, Human Rights Library

40. UCLA Center for East Asian Studies Documents

41. ibid.

42. www.taipeitimes.com, 10/08/2003

43. www.bbsland.com, 10/27/2006

44. op. cit., no. 6

45. www.wenxuecity.com, 03/24/2006

46. *Japan Times*, 03/30/2006
47. The Associated Press, 08/26/2006
48. ibid., 08/25/2006
49. www.creaders.net, 05/11/2006
50. Posong Jin, "China Saved Japan," www.creaders.net, 05/11/2006
51. www.wenxuecity.com, 06/06/2006
52. "Chinese Food Security: Debate over Brown Highlights Anxieties," a report from U.S. Embassy Beijing, November 1996.
53. http://.people.com.cn, 01/04/2006
54. Xinhua English, 09/01/2006
55. www.scmp.com, 07/21/2006
56. www.bbsland.com, 09/18/2006
57. www.wenxuecity.com, 06/06/2006
58. *People's Daily* Online, 04/05/2006
59. www.wenxuecity.com, 07/13/2006
60. www.bbsland.com, 03/26/2007
61. www.chinadaily.com.cn, 11/13/2004
62. www.xinhuanet.com, 02/10/2004
63. www.bbsland.com, 07/17/2006
64. www.sina.com, 08/02/2006
65. ibid., 08/02/2006
66. www.wenxuecity.com, 08/12/2006
67. www.cmilitary.com, 04/09/2006
68. www.wenxuecity.com, 07/21/2006
69. The Associated Press, 12/20/2006
70. ibid., 12/31/2006
71. www.washingtonpost.com, 03/26/2007
72. www.zaobao.com, 03/22/2007
73. ibid., 03/28/2007
74. *Japan Times*, 03/21/2007
75. www.nytimes.com, 04/01/2007
76. ibid., 03/07/2007 and www.singtaousa.com, 03/26/2007
77. The Associated Press, 03/29/2007
78. www.msnbc.com, 03/05/2007
79. www.bloomberg.com, 03/28/2007
80. www.scmp.com, 11/19/2005
81. Samuel P. Huntington, *The Clash of Civilizations and the Remaking of World Order*, Simon & Schuster, paperback edition 2003.
82. The *Atlantic Monthly*, 06/25/05

83. Larry Lin, *China in America's Cross-Hairs: Robert D. Kaplan and Neo-conservative Hawks Clamor for New Cold War,* www.fromthewwilderness.com, 2005
84. Chester Holcombe, *The Real Chinaman*, Burr Printing House, New York, U.S.A.
85. www.bbsland.com, 08/22/2006
86. www.nytimes.com, 03/03/2007
87. Zbigniew Brzezinski, *The Grand Chessboard*, Basic Books, 1997
88. www.bbsland.com, 08/02/2006
89. ibid., 09/19/2006
90. www.wenxuecity.com, 08/31/2006 and 09/07/2006
91. ibid., 09/07/2006
92. Thomas P. M. Barnett, *Blueprint for Action,* the Penguin Group, 2005
93. Xinhua English, 06/28/2006
94. www.wenxuecity.com, 07/08/2006
95. ibid., 07/08/2006
96. www.scmp.com, 04/09/2006
97. www.wenxuecity.com, 04/22/2006
98. www.worldjournal.com, 07/21/2006
99. *World Policy Journal*, 03/17/2007
100. www.worldjournal.com, 03/23/2007 and www.cnn.com, 05/02/2007.
101. ibid.
102. www.foreignpolicy.com, March 2007 issue
103. Xinhua English, 03/21/2007
104. www.scmp.com, 08/01/2006
105. The Associated Press, 07/31/2006
106. ibid., 03/20/2007
107. www.bbsland.com, 03/23/2007
108. www.scmp.com, 03/19/2007
109. ibid., 03/19/2007
110. www.wenxuecity.com, 03/14/2007
111. "Human Rights Record of the United States in 2005"
112. ibid.
113. www.edotorandpublisher.com, 02/21/2007
114. www.worldjournal.com, 03/20/2007
115. www.taipeitimes.com, 03/20/2007
116. www.wenxuecity.com, 03/19/2007
117. Xinhua English, 10/19/2005
118. www.scmp.com, 03/09/2006
119. www.nytimes.com, 03/09/2006

120. "Country Reports on Human Rights – 2006, China (includes Tibet, Hong Kong, and Macau)"

121. "Country Reports on Human Rights Practices – 2005," released by the Bureau of Democracy, Human Rights, and Labor, 03/08/ 2006"

122. www.nytimes.com, 03/09/2006

123. www.scmp.com, 03/10/2006

124. www.washingtonpost.com,, 09/26/2005

125. ibid., 10/12/2005

126. U.S. Bureau of Justice, in www.ojb.usdoj.gov/bjs, 2005

127. www.nytimes.com, 12/20/2005

128. The Associated Press, 01/09/2006

129. www.washingtonpost.com, 10/24/2005

130. The *Baltimore Sun*, 10/21/2005

131. www.ojp.usdoj.gov/bjs

132. *Newsweek*, 09/19/2005

133. The *Wall Street Journal*, 05/25/2005

134. *USA Today*, 10/12/2005

135. www.washingtonpost.com, 10/28/2005

136. Reports from The *Washington Post*, the *New York Times*, the *Washington Weekly* and other news media

137. www.worldjournal.com, 09/07/2006

138. Xinhua English, 05/27/2006

139. www.bbsland.com, 08/14/2006

140. Xinhua English, 04/06/2007

141. www.sina.com, 08/04/2006

142. Eric Teo Chu Cheow, "Beijing versus Washington Consensus: A Potential Clash of Developmental Models and 'Soft Power' Influence?" Taiwan Perspective e-Paper, Institute for National Policy Research, 01/02/2006

143. op. cit., no. 35

144. "Neocon 101," www.csmonitor.com

145. www.israeli-weapons.com, 1948–2007

146. ibid., 1948–2007

147. www.wenxuecity.com, 07/23/2006

148. ibid., 07/23/2006

149. www.washingtonpost.com, 07/31/2006

150. www.worldjournal.com, 03/17/2007

151. www.washingtonpost.com, 08/03/2006

152. www.cmilitary.com, 03/20/2007

153. www.cnn.com, 07/24/2006

154. www.nytimes.com, 07/27/2006

155. www.singtao.com, 07/27/2006

156. www.wenxuecity.com, 07/25/2006

157. Xinhua English, 07/27/2006

158. www.scmp.com, 07/25/2006

159. www.worldjournal.com, 07/27/2006

160. www.nytimes.com, 07/30/2006

161. www.washington.com, 08/12/2006

162. Xinhua English, 09/18/2006

163. www.wenxuecity.com, 08/18/2006

164. www.sina.com, 08/05/2006

165. http://people.com.cn, 07/23/2006

166. Joshua Cooper Ramo, "The Beijing Consensus," The Foreign Policy Center, 05/11/2004

167. ibid.

168. www.creaders.net, 02/26/2006

169. Cheng Li, "Educational and Professional Backgrounds of Current Provincial Leaders," *Chinese Leadership Monitor*, No. 8, p. 3, 2003

170. The Center for Strategic and International Studies and the Institute for International Economics, "China: The Balance Sheet," Public Affairs, 2006

171. China's new Five-Year Plan, 10/11/2005

172. Xinhua English, 07/25/2006

173. *People's Daily* Online, 12/18/2006

174. www.scmp.com, 07/29/2006

175. www.creaders.net, 07/29/2006

176. Xinhua English, 08/02/2006

177. www.scmp.com, 07/31/2006

178. Xinhua English, 08/08/2006

179. ibid., 09/19/2006

180. news.yahoo.com, 01/26/2007

181. Xinhua English, 07/30/2006

182. www.worldjournal.com, 08/11/2006

183. www.wenxuecity.com, 08/07/2006

184. ibid..com, 08/07/2006

185. www.sina.com, 08/13/2006

186. www.bbsland.com, 08/17/2006

187. Xinhua English, 04/03/2006

188. Weekly Review, "Mutually Assured Dependence," *Guardian Weekly*, July 14–20, 2006)

189. www.bbsland.com, 08/12/2006

190. op. cit., no. 170

191. www.scmp.com, 01/10/2006

192. Xinhua English, 03/10/2006

193. William Blum, *Rogue State: A Guide to the World's Only Superpower*, Third Edition, Common Courage Press, 2005

194. Sun Tzu, *The Art of War*, Tuttle Publishing, 1996

195. www.asiamedia.ucla.edu, 07/20/2006

196. Xinhua English, 01/29/2006

197. op. cit., no. 166

198. Wang Jisi, "China's Search for Stability with America," www.foreignaffairs.org, September/October, 2005

199. op. cit., no. 166

200. ibid.

201. op. cit., no. 198

202. op. cit., no. 166

203. Xinhua English, 08/12/2006

204. www.wenxuecity.com, 02/01/2006

205. Robbie Robertson, "Globalization Is Not Made in the West," Yale Center for the Study of Globalization, 2005.

206.. www.cmilitary.com, 06/24/2006

207. www.bbsland.com, 04/02/2006

208. The Associated Press, 03/10/2006

209. www.scmp.com, 07/04/2006

210. op. cit., no. 43

211. Xinhua English, 10/02/2006 and www.worldjournal.com, 03/17/2007

212. www.chinadaily.com.cn, 01/10/2007

213. www.scmp.com, 03/27/2006

214. www.bbsland.com, 03/13/2006

215. Xinhua English, 09/01/2006

216. ibid.

217. www.people.com.cn, 11/07/2005

218. www.worldjournal.com, 11/10/2005

219. Xinhua English, 09/04/2006

220. ibid.

221. Xinhua English, 04/01/2006

222. ibid.

223. Xinhua English, 04/07/2006

224. www.worldjournal.com, 04/09/2006

225. Xinhua English, 04/21/2006

226. ibid.

227. www.scmp.com, 04/01/2006

228. *Shenzhen Daily*, 04/09/2006

229. Xinhua English, 04/02/2006

230. www.nytimes.com, 03/30/2007 and Xinhua English, 03/29/2007

231. www.wenxuecity.com, 04/01/2007

232. www.washingtonpost.com, 04/09/2007

233. www.scmp.com, 03/30/2007

234. George Wehrfritz, "China's Wealth Woes," *Newsweek*, 09/04/2006

235. "The Debate on China's Exchange Rate – Should or Will It Be Revaluated?" by Jialin Zhang, *Essays in Public Policy* No. 112, Hoover Institution Press, 2004.

236. www.scmp.com, 04/21/2006

237. www.worldjournal.com, 09/18/2006

238. ibid., 11/30/2005

239. www.bbsland.com, 04/22/2006

240. ibid., 08/06/2006

241. www.wenxuecity.com, 08/23/2006

242. www.worldjournal.com, 05/12/2006

243. www.sina.com, 05/11/2006

244. Xinhua English, 08/31/2006

245. www.scmp.com, 08/31/2006

246. ibid., 08/31/2006

247. www.wenxuecity.com, 11/03/2005

248. op. cit., no. 245

249. "Asset Price Bubble in Japan in the 1980s: Lessons for Financial and Macroeconomics Stability," by Shigenori Shiratsuka, Discussion Paper, No. 2003-E-15.

250. The Associated Press, 08/22/2006

251. www.wenxuecity.com, 08/19/2006

252. "Asian financial crisis of 1997: Causes and policy responses," *The Multinational Business Review* by Suk H. Kim and Mahfuzul Haque, Spring 2002.

253. www.pbs.org

254. www.monthlyreview.org/0402halevi.htm, Volume 53, Number 11, April 2002.

255. www.bbsland.com, 07/17/2006

256. www.scmp.com, 09/05/2006

257. Xinhua English, 09/04/2006

258. ibid., 09/09/2006

259. ibid., 09/06/2006

260. www.sina.com, 08/30/2006

261. www.scmp.com, 08/30/2006

262. www.bbsland.com, 09/18/2006 and www.washingtonpost.com, 09/19/2006

263. www.scmp.com, 09/20/2006

264. www.worldjournal.com, 09/22/2006

265. www.scmp.com, 09/22/2006

266. Xinhua English, 09/10/2006

267. www.bbsland.com, 09/08/2006

268. Xinhua English, 08/07/2006

269. www.sina.com, 03/29/2007

270. Xinhua English, 08/18/2006

271. The Associated Press, 03/27/2007

272. www.wenxuecity.com, 04/01/2007

273. Xinhua English, 08/18/2006

274. *Shanghai Daily*, 03/17/2007

275. www.scmp.com, 03/18/2007

276. www.worldjournal.com, 03/19/2007

277. The Associated Press, 03/27/2007

278. www.bbsland.com, 09/11/2006

279. www.wenxuecity.com, 09/11/2006

280. www.scmp.com, 03/28/2006

281. www.worldjournal.com, 02/16/2006

282. Xinhua English, 09/08/2006

283. ibid., 03/31/2006

284. ibid., 05/13/2006

285. ibid., 04/02/2007

286. www.scmp.com, 04/20/2006

287. Xinhua English, 04/22/2006

288. www.scmp.com, 04/12/2006

289. *Shanghai Daily*, 08/17/2006

290. Xinhua English, 08/24/2006

291. www.scmp.com, 05/17/2006

292. Pete Engardio, "'Substantial Benefits' from China Trade?" www.businessweek.com, 02/08/2006

293. ibid.

294. ibid.

295. Xinhua English, 03/28/2006

296. www.worldjournal,com, 08/26/2006

297. ibid., 08/26/2006

298. Fareed Zakaria, The Real Story of Pricy Oil," *Newsweek*, 05/15/2006

299. www.worldjournal.com, 08/25/2006
300. www.chinatimes.com, 03/27/2006
301. Xinhua English, 07/31/2006
302. ibid., 06/13/2006 and www.scmp.com, 06/22/2006
303. ibid., 09/12/2006
304. ibid., 09/01/2006
305. www.wenxuecity.com, 08/20/2006
306. Xinhua English, 09/11/2006
307. www.scmp.com, 01/16/2006
308. www.wenxuecity.com, 09/04/2006
309. www.scmp.com, 07/10/2006
310. www.wenxuecity.com, 09/04/2006
311. www.worldjournal.com
312. www.scmp.com, 08/07/2006
313. www.cnn.com, 03/13/2006
314. Xinhua English, 09/05/2006
315. www.wenxuecity.com, 08/15/2006
316. www.scmp.com, 09/04/2006
317. www.bbsland.com, 03/18/2006
318. Xinhua English, 03/18/2006
319. ibid., 09/10/2006
320. ibid., 03/09/2006
321. www.chinatimes.com, 04/09/2007
322. The Associated Press, 03/10/2006
323. www.bbsland.com, 08/23/2006
324. www.worldjournal.com, 08/07/2006
325. www.bbsland.com, 08/15/2006
326. Xinhua English, 09/05/2006
327. www.scmp.com, 08/04/2006
328. ibid., 08/16/2006
329. www.worldjournal.com
330. www.scmp.com, 08/04/2006
331. ibid., 08/02/2006
332. The Associated Press, 08/01/2006
333. Xinhua English, 08/24/2006
334. www.wenxuecity.com, 08/27/2006
335. www.scmp.com, 08/31/2006
336. The Associated Press, 04/05/2007
337. www.scmp.com, 09/08/2006

338. ibid., 08/27/2006
339. Xinhua English, 09/04/2006
340. www.bbsland.com, 11/19/2005
341. Xinhua English, 08/29/2006
342. ibid., 08/24/2006
343. www.wenxuecity.com, 08/19/2006
344. www.chinadaily.com.cn, 06/23/2006
345. Xinhua English, 08/22/2006
346. www.wenxuecity.com, 08/19/2006
347. www.worldjournal.com, 09/13/2006
348. www.miibeian.com.cn, 03/13/2007
349. www.wenxuecity.com, 08/19/2006
350. Xinhua English, 08/31/2006
351. The Associated Press, 02/07/2006
352. Fareed Zakaria, "The Year of Living Fearfully," *Newsweek*, 09/04/2006
353. The Associated Press, 02/07/2006
354. www.worldjournal.com, 02/09/2006
355. www.cnn.com, 03/12/2006
356. www.scmp.com, 03/06/2006
357. www.singtao.com, 03/05/2007
358. www.wenxuecity.com, 03/16/2007
359. "What An African Woman Thinks" on Al Jazeera English, 03/12/2007
360. Xinhua English, 05/12/2006
361. www.scmp.com, 07/18/2006
362. ibid., 09/07/2006
363. *The Shanghai Daily*, 09/07/2006
364. Xinhua English, 03/22/2007
365. www.nytimes.com, 03/24/2007
366. http://johnib.wordpress.com, 03/25/2007
367. www.bbsland.com, 08/07/2006
368. www.sina.com, 11/16/2005
369. www.worldjournal.com, 07/21/2006
370. www.people.com.cn, 11/04/2005
371. Xinhua English, 08/24/2006
372. www.singtao.com, 04/22/2006
373. www.cmilitary.com, 06/30/2006
374. www.bbsland.com, 07/04/2006
375. www.sina.com, 11/16/2005
376. www.creaders.net, 04/08/2007

377. www.taipeitimes.com, 03/11/2007

378. www.worldjournal.com, 03/12/2007 and www.taipeitimes.com, 03/11/2007

379. ibid., 03/12/2007 and ibid., 03/11/2007

380. www.worldjournal.com, 03/12/2007

381. www.nytimes.com, 03/18/2007

382. Xinhua English, 03/16/2007

383. www.worldjournal.com, 03/16/2007

384. www.scmp.com, 03/18/2007

385. ibid., 03/18/2007

386. ibid.

387. www.worldjournal.com, 03/16/2007 and *Backgrounder*, published by The Heritage Foundation, No. 1998, 01/19/2007.

388. Chi Hsing, *"One Country, Two Systems" in Taiwan*, new edition, English translation by Sheng-Wei Wang, International Publishing House for China's Culture, 2006.

389. www.sina.com, 03/26/2007

390. Robert B. Zoellick, "Whither China: From Membership to Responsibility?" http://www.state.gov/s/d/rem/53682.htm

391. Xinhua English, 03/20/2007

392. www.creaders.net, 03/27/2007

393. www.sina.com, 03/24/2007

394. op. cit., no. 388

395. www.washingtonpost.com, 03/29/2004

396. op. cit., no. 388

397. www.washingtonpost.com, 03/24/2005

398. www.bbsland.com, 03/27/2007

399. www.washingtonpost, 07/08/2007

400. www.worldjournal.com, 07/15/2007.

401. www.scmp.com, 09/02/2006

402. ibid., 09/02/2006

403. www.zaobao.com, 04/05/2007

404. www.spacewar.com, 03/10/2007

405. www.cmilitary.com, 06/30/2005

406. www.taipeitimes.com, 07/23/2005

407. www.cnn.com, 07/14/05

408. The Xinhua News Agency, 07/21/2005

409. www.taipeitimes.com, 07/23/2005

410. op. cit., no. 92

Chapter VI

1. www.wenxuecity.com, 09/05/2006
2. ibid., 08/27/2006
3. Robert B. Zoellick, "Whither China: From Membership to Responsibility?" http://www.state.gov/s/d/rem/53682.htm
4. The *Financial Times*, 09/19/2005
5. www.bbsland.com, 04/07/2007
6. *Newsweek*, 09/04/2006
7. www.wenxuecity.com, 09/10/2006
8. Xinhua English, 09/11/2006
9. www.washingtonpost.com, 07/14/2007.
10. www.scmp.com, 09/06/2006

Glossary

AFTA: ASEAN Free Trade Area

AIT: American Institute in Taiwan

APEC: Asia-Pacific Economic Cooperation

ASEAN: Association of Southeast Asian Nations

ASL: Anti-Secession Law

CIA: Central Intelligence Agency

CNOOC: China National Offshore Oil Company, Ltd.

CNPC: China National Petroleum Corporation

CPC: Communist Party of China

CPI: Consumer Price Index

CPPCC: Chinese People's Political Consultative Conference

CSEPA: Chinese State Environmental Protection Administration

CSIS: the Center for Strategic and International Studies

CVD: Countervailing Duty

DDQDR: Defense Department's Quarterly Defense Report

DMZ: demilitarized zone

DPP: Democratic Progressive Party

DPRK: Democratic People's Republic of Korea or North Korea

E.U.: European Union

FDI: Foreign Direct Investment

FTA: Free Trade Agreement

GDP: Gross Domestic Product

IAEA: International Atomic Energy Agent

ICJ: International Court of Justice

IMF: International Monetary Fund

IPR: intellectual property rights
KMT: Nationalist Party or Kuomintang
LDCs: less developed countries
LDP: Liberal Democratic Party
MAD: mutual assured destruction
NATO: North Atlantic Treaty Organization or the "Western Alliance"
NMD: National Missile Defense
NPC: National People's Congress
NPT: Nuclear Non-Proliferation Treaty
NUC: National Unification Council
NUG: National Unification Guidelines
OEF: Oxford Economic Forecasting
PBC: People's Bank of China
PRC: the People's Republic of China (in the mainland of China)
PVA: People's Volunteer Army
RMB: renminbi
ROC: the Republic of China (now in Taiwan)
ROK: Republic of Korea or South Korea
SCO: Shanghai Cooperation Organization
SDF: Self Defense Force
TMD: theater missile defense
U.N.: United Nations
UNSC: U.N. Security Council
U.S.: the United States
WFP: World Food Program
WTO: World Trade Organization